# Derrida

*and the time of the political*

# Derrida

## *and the time of the political*

Edited by Pheng Cheah and Suzanne Guerlac

DUKE UNIVERSITY PRESS

*Durham and London* 2009

© 2009 DUKE UNIVERSITY PRESS
All rights reserved
Printed in the United States
of America on acid-free paper ∞
Designed by Amy Ruth Buchanan
Typeset in Carter + Cone Galliard by
Keystone Typesetting, Inc.
Library of Congress Cataloging-in-
Publication Data appear on the last
printed page of this book.

Satoshi Ukai's piece was previously
published in French as "De beaux risques
ou l'esprit d'un pacifisme et son destin" in
*La democratie à venir*. © Editions Galilée,
2004. Reprinted with permission.

Rodolphe Gasché's piece previously
appeared in *Critical Inquiry* 33, no. 2
(2007): 291–311. © 2007 by the
University of Chicago. Reprinted
with permission.

# Contents

# Acknowledgments

We are very grateful for the broad interdisciplinary support we received from the Berkeley community for the conference "Derrida and the Time of the Political," February 10–11, 2006. Specifically we would like to thank the departments of Art History, Comparative Literature, English, French, German, Italian Studies, Philosophy, Political Science, and Rhetoric for contributions that made the conference possible. We would also like to thank the French Studies and Jurisprudence and Social Policy programs for their support, as well as the Dean of Letters and Sciences, the Maxine Elliot Funds, and the Townsend Center. Finally, we would like to express our appreciation to Elizabeth Waddell, Brooke Belisle, and Colin Dingler for their indispensable help with the conference and to Colin Dingler for his assistance in the preparation of the manuscript for this volume.

# Introduction:

# Derrida and the Time of the Political

PHENG CHEAH AND SUZANNE GUERLAC

The main purpose of this collection of essays is to offer a critical assessment of Derrida's later work on the political, with respect to its position within his entire corpus and to its contribution to the study of the political and politics. Skepticism concerning the importance of deconstruction for political thinking has been widespread among American critics, especially those curious about the relation between deconstruction, Marxism, and socialist politics. The impatient series of questions that the American Frankfurt School social theorist Nancy Fraser posed at the beginning of her 1984 polemic is representative: "Does deconstruction have any political implications? Does it have any political significance beyond the Byzantine and incestuous struggles it provoked in American academic lit crit departments? Is it possible — and desirable — to articulate a deconstructive politics? Why, despite the revolutionary rhetoric of his circa 1968 writings, and despite the widespread, often taken-for-granted assumption that he is 'of the left,' has Derrida so consistently, deliberately and dexterously avoided the subject of politics?"[1]

The essays in this volume engage with the multifarious ways in which deconstruction directly bears on the delimitation of the political sphere and the implications of Derrida's thought for urgent instances of concrete politics. Needless to say, considerable work has been done on the question of deconstruction and politics, and we can give only a very selective and brief indication of the existing secondary literature here. Partly in reaction to the overly literary focus of the now defunct Yale School, more politically minded literary theorists of a Leftist persuasion in the late 1970s and the 1980s, most notably Gayatri Spivak and Michael Ryan, sought to articulate deconstruction together with Marxism, either by arguing for the usefulness of deconstructive concepts such as *différance* and trace for Marxist ideology critique even as they tried to supplement deconstruction with critical social theory, or by reading Marx as a deconstructivist *avant la lettre* who demonstrated the "textual" character of value and the capitalist system.[2]

The implications of deconstruction for feminist theory and politics, especially the concept of sexual difference and its relation to "French feminist" thought was, of course, a topic of heated discussion from the 1980s onward and has led to much productive ferment.[3] Spivak used deconstruction to forge an innovative form of postcolonial Marxist feminist critique, and Derrida's accounts of iterability and performative language were creatively reformulated in Judith Butler's account of gender performativity.[4] The reception of Derrida's work in social and political theory was, however, more muted. In their theory of radical democracy, Ernesto Laclau and Chantal Mouffe pointed to the solidarity between their understanding of the social as a contingent discursive field that is riven by antagonisms and Derrida's early arguments about the dissolution of the transcendental signified by the infinite play of signification.[5] This motif of the differential play of signification was most alluring for sympathetic social and political theorists, who used it to envision radical forms of community and nonpositivistic, nonfoundationalist understandings of politics.[6] But most of these appropriations of Derrida were not based on a systematic study of his corpus and largely focused on his pre-1980 writings.

A more sustained engagement with Derrida's work took place after 1990, in the wake of his association with the Cardozo Law School, where deconstruction was endowed with an ethical significance by being read in relation to Levinas's ethical philosophy of alterity. Drucilla Cornell, a legal scholar then at Cardozo Law, positioned Derrida's work in relation to the ethical and political philosophy of Kant, Hegel, Adorno, and Levinas as well as Niklas Luhmann's systems theory. She characterized deconstruction as a philosophy of the limit, a utopian ethics that gestures toward the Other of any community or system, and explored its implications for legal and political transformation.[7] Simon Critchley's *Ethics of Deconstruction* likewise explored Derrida's indebtedness to, and departure from, Levinasian ethics. But unlike Cornell, Critchley concluded that Derrida's work leads to an impasse of the political because it fails to move from ethics to politics: "Deconstruction fails to thematize the question of politics . . . as a place of contestation, antagonism, struggle, conflict, and dissension on a factical or empirical terrain." Indeed, Critchley argued that because "the rigorous undecidablity of deconstructive reading fails to account for the activity of political judgment, political critique, and the political decision," he needed to articulate "a political supplement to deconstruction," a politics of ethical difference in which politics is persistently interrupted by ethics.[8]

In the meantime, the publication of Derrida's long-deferred study of

Marx led to reassessments of the relations between deconstruction, Marxist thought, and socialist politics from Leftist philosophers and intellectuals such as Laclau, Fredric Jameson, and Antonio Negri.[9] *Specters of Marx* and *Politics of Friendship*, a book on concepts of fraternity and its relation to democracy, fueled another body of commentary (written under the tutelage of Geoffrey Bennington, a translator and accomplished scholar of Derrida's work, and a contributor to this volume) that specifically considered how traditional understandings of the political and politics are overturned by Derrida's deconstruction of their underlying logics.[10] Richard Beardsworth's *Derrida and the Political* is a cogent reconstruction of Derrida's argument that the aporia of time always exceeds any form of political organization and points to a promise beyond any given or ideal community. Alex Thomson's recent book, *Deconstruction and Democracy*, offers a useful assessment of the differences between liberal and radical democracy and the deconstructive understanding of democracy.

But compared to the literature available in French, there has been little analysis in the Anglo-American context of Derrida's later work, which specifically took up political and ethical themes such as democracy, responsibility, fraternity, hospitality, forgiveness, and sovereignty. Even fewer authors critically consider this work in relation to Derrida's entire corpus in an attempt to determine the legacy of his contribution to our thinking about politics and the political.[11] This collection of essays attempts to do this in a user-friendly manner. It is intended not only for those who have been long influenced by Derrida's thought but also for newer and even uninitiated readers who are curious about how his later texts open up a different critical perspective on the political.

The choice of such a topic — the *later* writings of Derrida *on the political* (although the relation between the political and the ethical is very much at stake) — raises from the start the issue of the legitimacy of introducing any kind of periodic division in Derrida's writings, such as that between his early and late work, given that deconstruction's radical rethinking of time challenges models of linear development. Implicitly, it also raises the question of a political turn in Derrida's thinking. Derrida explicitly rejected any suggestions of such a turn. "There never was in the 1980s or 1990s . . . a political turn or ethical turn in 'deconstruction,'" he insisted, "at least not as I experience it. The thinking of the political has always been a thinking of *différance* and the thinking of *différance* always a thinking *of* the political, of the contour and limits of the political, especially around the enigma or the autoimmune double bind of the democratic."[12] Derrida saw his engagement with ethical and political issues as an elaboration of some of the practical implications and consequences of the aporias that had always concerned him.[13] Indeed, deconstruction was always "political" because it analyzed European ethnocentrism and phallogocentrism as defining characteristics of the inherited tradition of European thought. However, he added that this did not mean that nothing changed over the years, "that nothing new happens between, say, 1965 and 1990. But what happens remains without relation or resemblance to . . . the figure of a 'turn'" (R, 39).

Derrida rejects the figure of the turn not only because it implies a turn toward something that was not there before, but also because it implies the conceptual preexistence of something toward which one turns, and therefore a certain teleology. Indeed, instead of turning toward a field of political thought, Derrida's "political" writings investigate and challenge the borders between the political, the ethical, and "politics," or merely instrumental action. He insists that works such as *Specters of Marx* and *Politics of Friendship* neither constituted a political theory nor proposed a deconstructive politics. "I don't think that there is such a thing as a deconstructive politics," he remarks, "if by the name 'politics' we mean a program, an agenda, or even the name of a regime."[14] Derrida's writings, as we shall see, challenge and displace our understanding of the term.

In various interviews, Derrida has enriched this somewhat predictable response to the question of the political turn. He has characterized a shift that took place in his work as a "becoming more explicit" of the political force of his thinking, a shift that began with *Specters of Marx* and continued with *Politics of Friendship* and the seminars which surrounded the latter on questions of nationalism and cosmopolitanism, as well as subsequent works such as "Force of Law" and various engagements with legal theory undertaken in conjunction with the Cardozo Law School. Two conditions were necessary for this shift, he added. The first concerns the reception of his thought. Before turning to explicitly political or ethical questions, Derrida had to establish the specific force — even the necessity — of the work of deconstruction. The specificity of deconstructive operations, the thinking of différance, had to be assured philosophically, that is, in relation to Husserl and the critique of phenomenology, and to the thinking of Heidegger, Nietzsche, and Freud, before the Derridean treatment of political issues and themes could have any chance of being understood.

The second condition for this becoming more explicit of the political involved changes in the world historical context, changes that would exert pressure on the reception of any discourse. Specifically, Derrida explains, he could write on Marx only after the fall of communism if what he had to say was to be heard. It is as if Marxism had to die on the historical scene before it could be written in the spectral mode, as a haunting.

In an interview given in 2004 in *L'Humanité* Derrida characterized deconstruction as "a singular adventure whose gesture depends each time on the situation, the context, above all political, of the subject, on his or her rootedness in a place and a history."[15] Deconstruction happens not only in language and in texts but also in the world or in history. As Derrida put it, politics — the classical tradition of politics as a politics of sameness, of the nation-state — "is being deconstructed in the world," for example, through the undoing of the distinction between manual and intellectual labor in the late capitalist valorization of information technology, or the generation of virtual realities in science and technomediation that render untenable the classical philosophical opposition between act or actuality (*energeia*) and potentiality (*dynamis*). The deconstructive notion of absolute hospitality, for example, is called for by events of the world such as globalization and postnationalism. "These questions are not destabilizing as the effect of some theoretico-speculative subversion. They are not even, in the final analysis, questions but seismic events. *Practical* events, where thought *becomes act* [*se fait agir*], and body and manual experience (thought as *Handeln*, says Heidegger somewhere)."[16] It is in response to the deconstruction occurring in events of the world that philosophical deconstruction can become an activity that intervenes. The need for a deconstruction of concepts such as politics, democracy, friendship (or the friend/enemy opposition) occurs in relation to changing events in the world, changes associated with a certain "modernity," as Derrida puts it — or, as others might prefer, postmodernity.

In Derrida's explicitly political writings, différance sometimes goes by the name "mutation," especially when it comes to the historical scene. In *Politics of Friendship*, for example, Derrida writes that if deconstruction introduces a necessary mutation into the thinking of the political field, this is because "we *belong* . . . to the time of this mutation, which is precisely a terrible tremor [*secousse*] in the structure or the experience of the belonging [*l'appartenance*]."[17] Deconstruction happens in time, and yet Derrida's radical rethinking of time has led to critiques of historicism, models of linear progress, teleology, and eschatology that would prevent any easy division of his own oeuvre into phases of "early" and "late" on the basis of either a sharp break or a narrative development. We therefore adopt Derrida's figure of mutation to account for shifts in his work because it allows for a repartition of before and after without any historicist affirmation of continuous development and provides a way to speak of différance as diversification. "There is a history of 'deconstruction,' in France and abroad, during the last thirty years," Derrida has written, but he characterizes this history in terms of diversification, speaking of "the essential diversification" of deconstruction.[18]

We thus insist on a visible mutation in Derrida's writings since the late 1980s for at least three reasons. First, Derrida did not refrain from marking epochal shifts in philosophical discourse, as evidenced by his delineation of "the Age of Rousseau" and "the Age of Hegel."[19] Second, in 1980, at the first Cérisy conference on his work, where the politics of deconstruction was first broached in a concerted manner, Derrida himself pointed to a change in emphasis in his work beginning in the late 1970s, from that of an obligation to infinite questioning, the obligation of maintaining the question (*garder la question*), to that of attending to a call (*appel*), order, or demand of the other:[20] "Although I am always concerned with Lévinas' questions, I could not write it like that today. . . . Why wouldn't I write like I had in 1964? Basically it is the word *question* that I would have changed there. I would displace the accent of the question toward something that would be a call. Rather than it being necessary to maintain a question, it is necessary to have understood a call (or an order, desire or demand) [of the other]."[21]

This affirmation and response to the call of the other gave deconstruction an explicitly affirmative character.[22] Insofar as Derrida links the unconditionality of justice, ethical responsibility, and democracy to an affirmative experience of absolute alterity, his writings on ethical and political issues from the late 1980s until 2004 are part of the phase of affirmative deconstruction. This phase was signaled in 1978 in an engagement with Nietzsche on woman (the other in sexual difference) as an affirmative power that escapes the proper and the process of propriation; subsequent texts, such as Derrida's suggestive readings of Blanchot and Joyce, were concerned with double affirmation ("Yes, Yes").[23]

Finally, what distinguishes Derrida's writings since the late 1980s and indicates a distinct mutation *within* affirmative deconstruction is the inflection of the aporias of affirming and responding to the other in terms of a structure of urgency, decision, contamination, and negotiation that he located at the heart of any ethical responsibility and political imperative. At the 1980 Cérisy conference, Philippe Lacoue-Labarthe and the American theorist Christopher Fynsk noted that Derrida's work was marked by a certain reserve or remove (*retrait*) in relation to the political and to politics, as evidenced by his reticence to offer a theoretical elaboration of the conjunction between the Marxist text and deconstruction.[24] Subsequently, for a time, the *retrait du politique*, "an 'eclipse' [*se-retirer*] of the political (and . . . of politics and of the world henceforth determined, in quasi-exclusive fashion, as political)," emerged as the guiding thread of a deconstruction of the political.[25] This implied a sharp delimitation of politics (*la politique*), an empirical category that refers to events in the world and the taking of political positions and actions concerning these events, from the political (*le politique*) as an autonomous domain with its own essence and a field of philosophical inquiry. In this spirit, Lacoue-Labarthe and Jean-Luc Nancy warned against speaking of politics simplistically without a preliminary deconstruction of the political itself: "In speaking of *the political*, we fully intend not to designate *politics*. . . . What remains to be thought by us, in other words, is not a new institution (or instruction) of politics by thought, but the political institution of so-called Western thought."[26]

Derrida's later writings specifically diverge from Lacoue-Labarthe and Nancy's position concerning the need to quarantine the political from contamination by "mere politics." These writings embrace the contamination of politics as an exigency that follows directly from the very aporias of deconstruction. Hence, although Derrida also deconstructs the classical philosopheme of the political in the name of something unconditional and ultrapolitical, "something in politics, or in friendship, in hospitality which cannot, for structural reasons, become the object of knowledge, of a theory, of a theoreme," he argues that the unconditional gives rise to a structure of urgency and precipitation, an exigency that forces the reasoning subject to respond in a decision in which what is unconditional and incalculable is necessarily contaminated by the calculations and negotiations we associate with politics.[27] As we shall see in more detail further on, Derrida's late writings specifically perform this "contamination" or interaction between politics and the ultrapolitical, the conditioned and the unconditioned.

Furthermore, deconstruction can itself be considered an event and an activity insofar as it brings about a confrontation between philosophemes and categories of knowledge and decisive mutations in the world, causing an interruption of the former by the latter in order to force a mutation in thought so that it can be adequate to the task of thinking these important shifts, instead of being outstripped and rendered irrelevant or *effete* by them.

Only in this way can thought live on instead of being imprisoned within a past present. Deconstruction intervenes by tracking the points of instability within political institutions and systems articulated around presence with the aim of intensifying these instabilities in the interests of emancipatory transformation. In *Philosophy in the Time of Terror*, Derrida characterizes the philosopher as someone who, "in the future, . . . [would] demand account-ability from those in charge of public discourse, those responsible for the language and institutions of international law. A 'philosopher' . . . would be someone who analyzes and then draws practical and effective consequences from the relationship between our philosophical heritage and the structure of the still dominant juridico-political system that is so clearly undergoing mutation. A 'philosopher' would be one who seeks a new criteriology to distinguish between 'comprehending' and 'justifying.'" [28] And the task is urgent. Concerning the political violence of the present day Derrida has written, "If intellectuals, writers, scholars, professors, artists . . . do not . . . stand up together against such violence, their abdication will be at once irresponsible and suicidal. . . . Our acts of resistance must be, I believe, at once intellectual and political. We must join forces to exert pressures and organize ripostes and we must do so on an international scale . . . always by analyzing and discussing the very foundations of our responsibility, its dis-courses, its heritage and its axioms" (A, 125–26).

This political commitment of thought might be called a nonsubjective, nonegological or impersonal engagement. It implies an imperative to com-mit and engage that comes to thought not from within the proper subject of thought but from an outside that constitutes thought as a nonsubjective or impersonal activity. This impersonal engagement, however, can also be con-crete, marked by a signature. "The question of biography does not bother me at all. . . . It is necessary to restage [*remettre en scène*] the biography of philosophers and the engagements they underwrite, especially political en-gagements, in their proper name."[29] The engagements signed "Jacques Der-rida" were numerous, varied, and significant. He intervened and directly addressed pressing concrete ethical and political issues of his (and our) time such as feminism, racism, the future of Marxism, the vicissitudes of neo-liberal global capitalism, the situation in Algeria, cosmopolitanism and hu-man rights, the place of Europe in the contemporary world, the destabiliza-tion and reinvention of sovereignty, hospitality to migrants and refugees, forgiveness in historical situations of war crimes and crimes against human-ity, and the death penalty. Specifically, he intervened in favor of striking workers in 1995; took positions in support of dissident intellectuals from Eastern Europe, founding, with Jean-Pierre Vernant, the Fondation Hus in 1981; took positions against racial violence, the Iraq war, the expulsion of the *sans papiers*, the death penalty, and in support of the rights of the Palestinian people and of reconciliation in the Israeli-Palestinian conflict, Mumia Abu-Jamal, Algerian intellectuals, and Nelson Mandela. "I venture to think that these forms of engagement [*engagement*], and the discourses that supported them, were in themselves in accord . . . with the ongoing work of deconstruction. . . . I don't feel my writing and my actions [*engagements*] were at odds with one another, [there have been] just differences of rhythm, of modalities of discourse, of context, etc."[30] Indeed, Derrida's writing has always been "political" in that it has always been strategic, interested in shifts in tone, in various ways of saying things, and in addressing different interlocutors differently, whether in terms of location — France or the United States, for example — or of medium: the seminar, the book (according to different venues), the interview.

### The Other Friend: Toward Another Politics

Although there are many paths into the more explicitly political writings of Derrida, the work that announces the problem of the political as such, even in its title, is *Politics of Friendship*. If, as we have already noted, the shift to affirmative deconstruction implies responding to the call of the other, Derrida elaborates this stance through an exploration of the figure of the friend. *Politics of Friendship* examines a traditional notion of friendship, one that poses the friend as brother in a tradition that runs from Aristotle through Cicero to Montaigne, among others, and that Carl Schmitt takes up again in modern political theory with his friend/enemy opposition. It explores the alliance or complicity between this conception of the friend as an idealized version of the self and a traditional political conception of democracy. As Derrida subsequently puts it in *Rogues*, the politics of fraternity "privilege[s] . . . the masculine authority of the brother, . . . genealogy, family, birth, autochthony, and the nation" (*R*, 58). This politics, which is structured around concepts such as the nation and national citizenship, he argues, is in the process of being left behind in today's world of transnational institutions, globalization, and "rogue" nations. It is a politics we must seek to displace in our thinking, for as a politics of exclusion based on race, class, and gender, it leads to war, often in the especially virulent forms of civil war and genocide.

"I tried in *Politics of Friendship*," Derrida writes, "to deconstruct . . . the Greek, Abrahamic, Jewish, but especially Christian and Islamic privileging of the figure of the brother in ethics, law, and politics, and particularly in a certain democratic model" (*R*, 57–58). He deconstructs this figure of the friend, finding in the classical tradition that promoted it the outlines of another friend. In Aristotle, we find "friendship, knowledge and death, but also survival [*la survie*] inscribed in one and the *same* configuration" (*PF*, 7). Cicero, writing in the tradition of Aristotle, proposes the notion of the *true friend* that is such only in relation to death. This other friendship implies the strange temporality of a relation in which one "feels oneself . . . engaged to love the other beyond death" (*PF*, 12). Here, friendship implies the temporality of survival and mourning, a friendship that Derrida reconstructs in reference to another notion of "friend," already elaborated by Maurice Blanchot, where the friend is radically other, absolutely singular, unknowable, and never present as such. This friend cannot be reduced to a version of oneself.

Blanchot had initially approached the question of friendship in relation to the act of writing, with the friend as other figuring the position of the reader. Increasingly, however, the figure of the friend as radical other becomes an ethical term for Blanchot, one linked to a notion of radical hospitality and of absolute responsibility (specifically after his encounter with Robert Antelme, author of a powerful account of experiences in German camps during the war).[31] For Blanchot the friend is someone we must "welcome in a relation to the unknown [*accueillir dans le rapport avec l'inconnu*]" and whom we encounter — if this can indeed be called an encounter — in a mode of infinite distance, through a "fundamental separation, on the basis of which what separates establishes a relation."[32] The friend as radical other is associated with a refusal of all hope in the kind of mass political movements that resulted in the disasters of the Holocaust. Hence, Blanchot's elaboration of this figure of friendship calls into question the very possibility of political association and even of the social bond.[33]

Blanchot elaborated the paradoxical relation to the friend as other in a particularly enigmatic fashion in the narrative text *Celui qui ne m'accompagnait pas* (1953). In his lengthy commentary on this text, Derrida reads Blanchot through Nietzsche and analyzes the figure of the friend in terms of an experience of radical alterity and singularity that remains irrecuperably other, as opposed to the Levinasian conception of the ethical relation as an immediate encounter with the other.[34] In *Politics of Friendship* (based on seminars dating from 1988) Derrida takes the risk of exploring what the political implications might be of the Blanchotian figure of the friend as radical other. Having deconstructed the classical notion of the friend, revealed its complicities with a certain politics, and displaced the figure of the friend onto the heteronomous, even transcendent figure of the absolutely other, he goes on to ask what kind of politics this notion of the friend might imply: "Let us dream of a friendship that goes beyond this proximity of the congeneric double . . . [and] let us ask what the politics would be of such a 'beyond the principle of fraternity'" (*PF*, viii). What might this politics be? If democracy is a politics of friendship, where friendship is constructed on the basis of resemblance or identification, the notion of friend as other will be associated with another conception of democracy: democracy to come.

The friend, as written by Blanchot and rewritten in another register by Derrida, implies a temporality of that which cannot be fixed or even figured in the present. For Blanchot, the friend is not someone or something one can even talk about. One can only speak *to* the friend, and, since the friend is never fully present (at best, the friend survives), one can only speak to the friend through the trope of apostrophe, addressing the other in his or her absence in a gesture toward the future. It is in this sense that Derrida reads the celebrated statement of Aristotle, repeated by Montaigne in the *Essais*: "O my friends, there is no friend." There is no friend because the friend, as other, is never fully present and cannot be fixed or thematized in a third-person statement; a friend can only be addressed — "O my friends" — spoken to even in absence ("there is no friend") or in the survival associated with the act of mourning.

We do not pose this other friend as a reflection of ourselves. It comes to us. Its encounter is an event that comes to us from the otherness of an unknown future. The question of the other, then, carries with it the question of the otherness of time considered as the giving, or coming, of time from the unconditionally other, from we cannot know where, bringing we cannot know what. The friend as other thus implies an engagement with the very happening, and contingency, of time as it is experienced through the coming of events in their surprise. We can compare this to the time of becoming that Bergson elaborated in terms of "qualitative multiplicity" and radical heterogeneity. Time is here understood as force, with respect to which, as Bergson put it, "the same does not remain the same."[35] This force of time, which is a force of invention, implies radical singularity such that we never feel the same thing twice. This experience of time cannot be spatialized, mapped out, represented, anticipated, or mastered. Similarly, Derrida speaks of the "*passage* of time *through* time [*le passage du temps à travers le temps*]" (*PF*, 16) to characterize time as an opening onto the unknown and the unknowable. Friendship, in the way Derrida rewrites it after Blanchot, opens time. The friend as other implies contingency and singularity, and the politics of *this* friendship implies a notion of democracy that is to be thought within the flow of time — time as the coming of what comes. The friend as radical other therefore announces the temporality of democracy to come.

Democracy, Derrida suggests, has always been "to come" in the sense that the concept has always remained plastic; there has always been a whole spectrum of democracies — from constitutional monarchy to the plebiscite — and to this extent democracy has always been open to transformation. It is "the only name of a . . . quasi regime open to its own historical transformation, to taking up . . . its interminable self-criticizability [*auto-criticité*], one might even say its interminable analysis" (R, 25). In the Enlightenment tradition of Rousseau and Kant, this openness is called "perfectibility."

Democracy, therefore, has always been open to self-difference. "Democracy is what it is only in the différance by which it defers itself and differs from itself . . . at the same time behind and ahead of itself," Derrida writes in *Rogues* (38). Even as a concept, democracy is always already deconstructive; it "sends us or refers us back [*renvoie*] . . . to différance . . . as reference or referral [*renvoi*] to the other, . . . as the undeniable experience . . . of the alterity of the other, of heterogeneity, of the singular, the non-same, the different, the dissymmetric, the heteronomous" (R, 38). It is in this sense that democracy is never simply present; it is always in a mode of survival and promise: a democracy to come.

Through the notion of autoimmunity, Derrida intensifies the deconstruction of a stable idea of democracy by pushing the notion of perfectibility, rephrased as "interminable self-criticizability," in the other direction of self-undoing. Democracy's openness to alterity also implies a certain alterity to itself that is not simply conceptual but operational or pragmatic, including on the scene of events. The logic of modern representative parliamentary democracy is autoimmune, Derrida notes, because democratic processes are structurally vulnerable to undemocratic forces, which can be democratically elected to power: "The *alternative to* democracy can always be *represented* as a democratic *alternation* [*alternance*]" (R, 31). We see this in the case of Algeria, where an Islamist regime with the intention of abolishing democratic processes was likely to gain power democratically. Democracy is always to come, then, also because it is always undoing itself and is never fully present.

In *Philosophy in the Time of Terror*, Derrida analyzes the world political situation in terms of autoimmunity, demonstrating concretely that "repression in both its psychoanalytical sense and its political sense — whether it be through the police, the military, or the economy — ends up producing, reproducing and regenerating the very thing it seeks to disarm" (A, 99). As he reminds us, the attacks of 9/11 were planned in the United States and carried out with pilots trained here, using American planes. Efforts to "attenuate or neutralize the effect of the traumatism [of 9/11] (to deny, repress, or forget it, to get over it) are but so many desperate attempts. And so many autoimmunitary movements . . . which produce, invent and feed the very monstrosity they claim to overcome" (A, 99). The war in Iraq is one of the most obvious and irremediably tragic cases in point at the present time.

If, for Derrida, democracy is intrinsically (as a concept) and historically (in its operations) aporetic or "autoimmune," how are we to understand the notion of democracy to come? Certainly not, Derrida insists repeatedly, as the anticipation of an ideal democracy, one that would eventually overcome the aporias of historical democracies as we have known them. If anything, Derrida's elaboration of democracy to come renders explicit and even affirms its aporetic structure.

## Time of the Political: Teleology and Sovereign Ipseity

To arrive at a deeper understanding of the aporetic structure of democracy to come and its main implications for rethinking the political, we need to grasp why it is that for Derrida our experience of time as such is necessarily aporetic. Democracy to come is certainly a privileged syntagm and the guiding thread in Derrida's final writings on the political. But as a structure or movement of interminable opening that refers to an unconditional other, its aporias are figures of the aporia of time that deconstruction has been concerned with from the start. Simply put, Derrida's argument is that under conditions of radical finitude, time can be thought only as coming from an absolute other beyond presence. But because the relation to alterity also constitutes the order of presence and experience in general — since presence or experience presupposes persistence in time — any presence is subject to a strict law of contamination by an other that destabilizes, disrupts, and makes presence impossible even as it maintains, renews, and makes presence possible by giving it a to-come.

The central premise behind Derrida's challenge to the political field is that all canonical understandings of the political and politics presuppose concepts of time that deconstruction radically puts into question. For instance, fundamental concepts pertaining to the political sphere such as force, violence, power, and freedom; a state of nature versus a state of civility or society; the various forms of human power and their institutions, such as the law, sovereignty, economic exchange, economic exploitation through the extraction of surplus value computed in terms of labor-time (Marx), and political domination, are all underwritten by pre-deconstructive understandings of time—what Derrida called the metaphysics of presence, and Bergson, spatialized time. Normative categories of political thought, such as legitimation and justification (Kant), teleology (Hegel and Marx), and the public sphere (Habermas), also presuppose such dogmatic notions of time. Hence, a radical reposing of the question of time, one that does not take time for granted as a given but that attends to the aporetic giving of time, will necessarily shake up canonical political concepts and categories. Indeed, there is an immediate political import to this questioning: ontologies of presence, as they have informed political philosophies, institutions, and practices, necessarily lead to reactionary and repressive forms of politics. "Nondemocratic systems," Derrida suggests, "are above all systems that *close* and *close themselves off* from this coming of the other. They are systems of homogenization and of integral calculability. In the end and beyond all the classical critique of fascist, Nazi, and totalitarian violence in general, one can say that these are systems that close the 'to come' and that close themselves into the presentation of the presentable."[36] Accordingly, Derrida has repeatedly indicated that the *à-venir* (to-come) is the condition of "another concept of the political," a rethinking of the political and of politics beyond all current concepts.[37]

The à-venir, first discussed at length by Derrida in *Specters of Marx*, is the thought of an opening onto a future that is not a future present.[38] It is an advent or coming that is structurally imminent to every present reality insofar as it is the pure event that interrupts present reality but without which reality could not maintain or renew itself as a presence. This imminence is not something that can be predicted or anticipated precisely because the coming is that of the other. Indeed, the other *is* this coming and should therefore not be regarded as another subject, substance, or presence. Instead of the Heideggerian understanding of thinking as an openness to the advent of Being, as letting Being be, deconstruction is the opening of a space that lets the other that disrupts and renews presence come.

The main elements of Derrida's thinking of the aporetic time of the political are a deconstruction of temporal concepts such as teleology, eschatology, and messianism that underwrite most political movements (progressive and conservative); a deconstruction of the ontotheological concept of sovereignty; a new understanding of fraternity and democracy based on an openness to the other; and a rethinking of responsibility and of the relation between the ethical and the political.

Teleology and eschatology are modes of thinking that inform philosophical accounts of moral progress and historical and political transformation such as those of Kant, Hegel, and Marx, as well as the neoliberal U.S.-centric vision of globalization popularized by Francis Fukuyama that Derrida severely critiques in *Specters of Marx*. Crudely put, teleological and eschatological modes of thought understand history as the fulfillment of a telos that one can rationally anticipate in advance in the form of an idea that we can hope to approximate (Kantian teleology), work toward actualizing (as in Hegelian-Marxist teleology), or anticipate as a coming to an end (*eskhaton*) that is revealed through philosophical thought, divine revelation, or faith (philosophical and Christian eschatology).

Derrida rejects teleology and eschatology on two philosophical grounds. The invention of time — time as the giving of the new — is the time of the coming of, or as, an event. In the first place, since the end (telos or eskhaton) is an ideal presence that is grasped in advance, it effaces the coming of time in, and as, singular event and neutralizes or cancels historicity by reducing it to a program or plan that we pursue through rational calculation. Second, such an ideal end opens up a horizon that can be infinitely deferred and contrasted to the finite and profane present. While this can provide a basis for a critique of the present, it can also lead to quietism and inaction, to a patient waiting for the promised end.

In the place of eschatoteleology, Derrida offers an understanding of historicity based on the concept of a "messianism without content," which carries a force of emancipatory promise thanks to the very openness of the future which leaves open the eventuality, the perhaps or maybe (*peut-être*), of what is hoped. Thus, while challenging both teleology and eschatology, the à-venir is also "the messianic without messianism": an open-ended because absolutely undetermined "messianic hope" that is marked by an urgent injunction to act in the present (*SM*, 65). Derrida thus inherits from Marx the injunction for radical action which, when coupled with a critique of Marx's "ontology of presence as actual reality and as objectivity," becomes a generalized messianicity (*SM*, 170). At the same time, we can understand this contentless messianicity by analogy with the unconditionality of the

Kantian moral law. On the one hand, it is a purely formal principle, without content. On the other hand, it carries an injunction to act, according to the celebrated formula: You can, therefore you must.

The structure of autoimmunity (a figure that evokes the AIDS virus and that Derrida locates both in the historical scene of democracy and as an aporia of democracy to come) leads to the most radical challenge Derrida poses to traditional political thinking: the deconstruction of sovereignty. Because autoimmunity implies a contamination of the self in its very constitution, it undermines what he refers to as the ipseity of the subject. Ipseity is the philosopheme at the heart of any positive form of sovereignty (that of the state, a people, an individual, etc.), the "I can" or power of a self to constitute itself by gathering itself unto itself and mastering itself. Sovereign ipseity and eschatoteleology are different aspects of the power of reason. The realm of ipseity is precisely the realm of the possible and the potential, what "I am able to do," just as the regulative idea as telos and eskhaton is the intelligible figure of an end that is possible as long as I can think it in advance. What ipseity and teleology have in common is that they neutralize the alterity and singularity of the event that characterizes the à-venir's movement of opening up by reducing the event to something within the domain of the sovereign rational subject.

From Derrida's viewpoint, since the ipseity of a finite being is always compromised because it cannot give itself time, sovereignty is necessarily ruptured in its constitution by an exposure to the other from which time comes. Sovereignty is autoimmune. The critique of ipseity thus reinscribes fundamental features of the critique of the subject that have belonged to deconstruction all along and that are informed to an important extent by psychoanalytic reflection. For the structure of autoimmunity "tak[es] into account within politics what psychoanalysis once called the unconscious" (*R*, 110). The other exists not only outside the self (as friend) but also within it, as the other that is marked off by repression but that is always active. It not only operates on the level of the individual (or the sovereign) but pertains also to the demos itself, which is divided from itself, and hence to its very power, or *kratos*. "How many votes [*voix*] for an unconscious?" Derrida asks in *Rogues*. "Who votes . . . in the psychic and political system? . . . The superego? The ego? The subconscious? The ideal ego [*le moi idéal*]? . . . The primary process, or its representatives? How are the votes to be counted?" (*R*, 54–55). The radical nature of Derrida's reflections on the political derives in part from the fact that he does not steer clear of the wrench psychoanalytic reflection throws into the political field but incorporates it into his deconstruction of that field.

From a geopolitical perspective, the deconstruction of sovereignty in the name of democracy to come is a response to the undermining of national state sovereignty by various modalities of globalization, including the proliferation of alternative nonstate forms of sovereignty such as that of international human rights regimes. As Derrida puts it, "Such a questioning of sovereignty . . . is at work today; it is what's *coming*, what's *happening*. It *is* and it *makes* history through the anxiety-provoking turmoil we are currently undergoing" (*R*, 157). We see here that the crucial point of the à-venir is not the infinitely deferred point of arrival—the telos or eskhaton that never arrives—but the process of an "it happens" (*ça arrive*) that is not subject to the rational subject's power or control because it comes from the other, from the future, a happening with which it is nevertheless urgent to engage.

## *The Im-possible Political: The Passive Decision and Unconditionality*

Three fundamental consequences follow from the deconstruction of sovereignty. First, Derrida fractures the apparently indivisible unity of sovereignty and unconditionality. According to Schmitt's definition, the sovereign's ability to make the exceptional decision, that is, to decide on the exception and to suspend the law, means that sovereignty is indivisible. This indivisibility follows directly from the fact that reason of state—reason as the state, the power of reason concentrated in the indivisible unity of the legitimate state—is unconditional. The sovereign is absolute and lies beyond all conditions and relativism. When the legitimacy of the state is called into question, whether by the popular nation (revolutionary nationalism), the public political culture of a democratic society (Rawls), the critical public sphere of civil society as this is legally institutionalized in procedures of democratic public discussion (Habermas rewriting Kant's "public use of reason"), or simply by individual human beings asserting prepolitical rights, what is disputed is the embodiment of sovereign reason in the state. According to these conventional analyses of sovereignty, sovereign reason itself remains absolute and unconditional; it is simply relocated in the nation or the people, democratic political culture, the public sphere, the individual.

According to Derrida's view, however, the sovereign's unconditionality is only *apparent*. As an instance of ipseity, sovereignty is necessarily autoimmune. Hence, as we have seen, it opens itself up to the unconditionality of the coming of the other, to the event, and to time. We could say that only the à-venir is unconditional, and that this unconditionality is without sovereignty because it does not presuppose ipseity, that is, self-mastery and power. Derrida calls it a weak force, a force without power, a force that is vulnerable precisely because it opens up unconditionally, without alibi or defense, to the coming of the other. Indeed, Derrida suggests that the very fact that national state sovereignty can be contested or challenged by the doctrine of human rights, which presupposes the sovereignty of human beings, indicates the divisibility, shareability, and therefore autoimmunity of sovereignty.

Second, the deconstruction of ipseity, and therefore of sovereign reason, leads to a radical rethinking of freedom. "Freedom," Derrida argues, "is the faculty or power to do as one pleases, to decide, to choose to determine *oneself*, to have self-determination, to be master, and first of all master of oneself (*autos, ipse*). A simple analysis of the 'I can,' of the 'it is possible for me,' of the 'I have the force to' (*krateo*), reveals the predicate of freedom, the 'I am free to,' 'I can decide.' There is no freedom without ipseity and, vice versa, no ipseity without freedom — and, thus, without a certain sovereignty" (*R*, 22–23). The critique of ipseity, however, implies that freedom must now be thought beyond its canonical definition as autonomy and self-determination that informs almost all accounts of political freedom today, from liberalism to communitarianism. In Derrida's words, "What must be thought here . . . is this inconceivable and unknowable thing, a freedom that would no longer be the power of a subject, a freedom without autonomy, a heteronomy without servitude" (*R*, 152).

This perspective is clearly at odds with the entire Frankfurt School tradition. Insofar as deconstruction involves a questioning of calculative reason (although one that arises from Heidegger's critique of calculative thinking (*das rechnende Denken*), it is partly in solidarity with the Frankfurt School's critique of instrumental and technical reason. But Derrida's dissociation of the unconditional from sovereign reason and his characterization of unconditionality in terms of an opening toward the absolutely other problematizes, and even undoes, the critical reason celebrated by the Frankfurt School. Whereas critical reason is still a figure of ipseity and so remains imprisoned within the closure or circle of presence, deconstruction points to an outside that is prior to reason and that leaves its trace within reason.

Freedom, in Derrida's understanding, is not, in the first instance, reason's capacity for autonomy. It comes from the other, and to this extent, autonomy, quite paradoxically, arises only in response to this other. Speaking of the experience of friendship and justice as examples of this freedom, Derrida observes that "responsibility assigns freedom to us *without leaving it with us*, as it were—we see it coming from the other. It is assigned to us by the other, from the place of the other, well before any hope of reappropriation allows us the assumption of this responsibility—allowing us . . . to assume responsibility . . . in the space of *autonomy*" (*PF*, 231–32). The deconstructive openness to the event thus implies a hyperbolical sense of responsibility insofar as this becomes situated in the call of, and response to, the other who escapes rational calculation. The event as other therefore imposes an infinite responsibility that cannot be discharged precisely because it cannot be assumed or appropriated by the rational subject who can then clear its conscience. Responsibility in this sense cannot be reduced to freedom of conscience. It should not lead, as Derrida puts it, to "a community of complacent deconstructionists, reassured and reconciled with the world in ethical certainty, good conscience, satisfaction of service rendered, and the consciousness of duty accomplished (or, more heroically still, yet to be accomplished)."[39]

Third, the thought of this constitutive opening to the other leads to the difficult and enigmatic concept of a passive decision, as distinct both from the sovereign decision of exception (Schmitt) and the deliberation of public reason (Habermas). For if the freedom of the rational subject comes in or is its response to the other, then decision is prompted by, and also comes from, the other. It is therefore in the original instance passive and unconscious, not active and conscious (*PF*, 68–69).

This notion poses a clear challenge to all theories of the sociodiscursive construction of identity, including that of Habermas. Such theories are invariably based on the philosopheme of recognition. In the Habermasian discourse ethics version, the intersubjective formation of ethical agents occurs through rational-discursive deliberation over the shared norms, values, and traditions of concrete communities. Ideally, such discursive deliberation should lead in multicultural societies to a moral universalism that is sensitive to difference, where respect is shown to all the members of a community through a nonappropriating inclusion of the other.[40] But however much it may attempt to include the other in its otherness, from the perspective of deconstruction the dyadic structure of self-constitution in recognition will always efface the absolute other because recognition, staged by Hegel in the master/slave dialectic (and restaged, prominently, by Sartre), remains within the domain of intersubjectivity. Regardless of how different the other may be, it is always another *human subject* that is recognized in and through discursive deliberation. Recognition itself thereby becomes a mode of appropriation of the other into (dialectical) sameness. Accordingly, the public space of political morality or right (*Recht*) and ethics (*Sittlichkeit*) opened up through recognition is always blind to the event and forecloses the passive decision.

In contradistinction, Derrida's account of friendship as a relation to alterity focuses, as we have seen, on the structure of address, apostrophe, and appeal that radically opens up the rational subject to an indeterminable other instead of seeking to include the other within the domain of the self as an "other self" through the structure of recognition. What Derrida calls "pure ethics" would imply an economy that exceeds the structure of recognition (a "general economy," as he put it in his early essay on Bataille): "Pure ethics, if there is any, begins with the respectable dignity of the other as absolute *unlike* [*l'absolu dissemblable*], recognized as nonrecognizable [*reconnu comme non reconnaissable*], indeed as unrecognizable [*méconnaissable*], beyond all knowledge, all cognition and all recognition" (*R*, 60). And, Derrida adds (implicitly contra Habermas), "far from being the beginning of pure ethics, the neighbor as like [*le prochain comme semblable*] or as resembling, as looking like, spells the end or the ruin of such an ethics, if there is any" (*R*, 60).

This is perhaps why literary discourse is crucial to Derrida's deconstruction of the political in its most affirmative aspect. For this language (as Paul Valéry put it in his definition of poetry) cannot ever be paraphrased, just as the friend cannot be spoken of in the third person. It is in this spirit that Derrida calls our attention to the irony that operates at the grammatical crux of the expression "démocratie à venir": "the *to* [*à*] of the 'to come' [*à venir*] wavers between imperative injunction (call or performative) and the patient *perhaps* [*peut-être*] of messianicity (nonperformative exposure [*exposition*] to what comes . . . )" (*R*, 91). This hesitation between "the two *to*'s" implies "the secret of irony" and connects the publicity of public space not to the certitude of critical deliberative reason but to the right to fiction, the secret, and literature *(R*, 91–92). It is in this context that the politics of democracy to come, as hyperethics or hyperpolitics, requires "the poetic invention of an idiom whose singularity would not yield to any nationalism" (*R*, 158).

Derrida's affirmation of nonperformative exposure clearly indicates (perhaps surprisingly for some) that the concept of the passive decision involves a radical questioning of the idea of performativity that deconstruction is conventionally associated with. In his view, performativity remains tainted with ipseity, the power or mastery of an "I can" that effaces the event. In the ethical, juridical, and political domains, performatives are modalities of language that produce events. However, insofar as a successful performative presupposes a set of norms or conventions that are the defining conditions of this ability to produce an event, and because it then produces an already codified "event," it also immediately neutralizes, through calculation, the eventness of the event associated with the temporality of the to-come (*R*, 152). Performativity is therefore inherently conservative in its creativeness. A performative presupposes an authority or rightful condition, and it in turn establishes a range of possibilities for the subject that secures its power to act. In Derrida's words:

> Performativity for me is . . . that which neutralizes the event, that is to say, what happens (*ce qui arrive*). . . . The academic investment in the Western universities . . . in this theory of performativity, the investment in political theory (because the juridical is at work in the performative) has fertile, liberating effects, but also protectionist effects. . . . In a certain way, theories of the performative are always at the service of powers of legitimation, of legitimized or legitimizing powers. And consequently, in my view, the ethical must be exposed to a place where constative language as well as performative language is in the service of another language.[41]

The effacing power of performativity that Derrida points to here must be rigorously distinguished from arguments about political violence in contemporary political theory. Two examples stand out: first, the ontological paradox that the foundation of a new political order always involves violence because it requires the destruction of the previous order and the imposition, on human beings by human beings, of a new legitimate authority that vainly aspires to approximate the absoluteness of divine authority, and second, the historical-relativist argument that the legitimacy of any given political foundation is always contestable because of its historical link to violence (for instance, the Marxist concepts of primitive accumulation or class struggle).[42] These arguments about the violence of founding are now commonplace topoi in political theory and have sometimes made use of Derrida's writings, especially "Force of Law" and his reflections on the American Declaration of Independence.[43] In contradistinction, the neutralization of the event by the performative that concerns Derrida here refers to a more fundamental, quasi-transcendental violence in which any kind of rational calculation necessarily effaces the eventness of the event.

Derrida's point about the conservative nature of the performative would also apply to accounts of performative subversion in which an oppressive social norm that serves to exclude or marginalize a stigmatized group can be contested and subverted by its performative repetition.[44] For while the performance of a norm can lead to its destabilization, the subversive power generated is conservative in two senses. First, it conserves a counterpower, another ipseity. More important, the subversion actually issues from the norm itself since it is the norm's negation. The subversion is calculable and foreseeable precisely because it is measured in terms of the norm that it destabilizes. Hence, performative subversion also forecloses the event.

Indeed, what is common to uses of the performative in contemporary political theory is a certain relativism whereby instituting acts, whether acts of political foundation or of the constitution of hegemonic subjects, are exposed as contingent performatives by virtue of their connection to concrete scenarios of historical, social, and political forms of violence and exclusion. From a Derridean perspective, the blind spot of these critical analyses of sociopolitical performativity is that they are necessarily conditioned by their location and are, therefore, conditional. They cannot appeal to an unconditional force because they regard any claim to unconditionality as a ruse of hegemonic power and authority. They thus inevitably end up in a historicist or cultural relativism.

Derrida's idea of the originary violence in the effacement of the event also leads to an accounting of the violence in the founding and maintenance of the political domain or of the relational constitution of a hegemonic subject or order. These are seen as determined cases of originary violence. However, because deconstruction severs the link between unconditionality and absolute power, mastery, or sovereignty and defines the former in terms of the pure event, it simultaneously leads to a radical questioning of any state of power or hegemony and enables a move beyond relativism. For unconditionality is now rethought in terms of the sheer exposure and destabilizing interruption of any present state of power to and by the weak messianicity of the pure event.

The passive decision that accompanies the coming of the event therefore implies a radical rethinking of power as such, or more precisely, the concept of the possible that underwrites all conventional accounts of power, capacity, or ability deriving from the concept of *dynamis* or *potentia*. Derrida sometimes characterizes this exposure to the event as "a force without power" or "an unconditionality without power."[45] Even more to the point, it is also the force of the im-possible that paradoxically makes the possible possible even as it subjects it to contamination:

> When the impossible *makes itself* possible, the event takes place (possibility *of* the impossible). . . . For an event to take place, for it to be possible, it has to be, as event, as invention, the coming of the impossible. . . . The issue is thus nothing less than the powerful concept of the *possible* that runs through Western thought, from Aristotle to Kant and Husserl (then differently to Heidegger), with all its meanings, virtual or potential: being-in-potential, in fact; *dynamis*, virtuality . . . , but also power, capacity, everything that renders skilled, or able, or that formally enables and so on. . . . What renders possible renders impossible the very thing that it renders possible, and introduces; but as its chance, a chance that is not negative, a principle of ruin in the very thing that it is promising or promoting. . . . The *im-* of the im-possible is surely radical, implacable, undeniable. But it is not only negative or simply dialectical: it *introduces* into the possible, it is *its usher today*: it gets it to come, it gets it to move according to an anachronic temporality.[46]

The im-possible is therefore not a counterpower that can be deployed against a given state of power. It is not the dispersal of power into a mobile field of relations between micro-powers (Foucault). It is instead the constitutive exposure of power as such (which has been conventionally thought in terms of the circular economy of appropriation or the return-to-self of self-mastery) to what makes it vulnerable and defenseless.

In insisting that the im-possible does not have a negative relation to the possible, Derrida also emphasizes that the im-possible is not utopian, or that which can never be real. As we have already seen, the à-venir is precisely not merely ideal. Similarly, the im-possible is the very structure of reality, the force of a propulsion or precipitation that, in giving time, opens up the real, renews it, and gives it a to-come. As Derrida puts it, "*Utopia* . . . can too easily be associated with dreams, or demobilization, or an impossible that is more of an urge to give up than an urge to action. The 'impossible' I often speak of is not the utopian. Rather, it gives their very movement to desire, action, and decision: it is the very figure of the real. It has its hardness, closeness, and urgency."[47] For Derrida, this force is the origin of imperativity and responsibility, whether moral, juridical, or political. It is the structural condition of transforming reality both in the sense that it generates the imperative to act in the practical subject and also because it renders present reality amenable to transformation. This urgent propulsion of the impossible into the realm of the possible is precisely the structure in which the unconditional or incalculable other demands that we as rational subjects respond and be responsible by calculating and inscribing the unconditional within present conditions even as this is a violation of the other's alterity. It is a question precisely of an "impossible transaction between the conditional and the unconditional, the calculable and the incalculable," "a transaction without any rule given in advance . . . between these two apparently irreconcilable exigencies of reason, . . . calculation and the incalculable" (R, 150–51).

We witness such transactions at work in concrete settings in Derrida's figures for unconditionality, such as hospitality, the gift, forgiveness, justice, and democracy. For example, when Derrida characterizes democracy as impossible and always still to come in a deliberately paradoxical formulation, he points to its inherently aporetic nature. First, democracy and sovereignty are both indissociable and in mutual contradiction (R, 100). Second, democracy is impossible because it yokes together, again in aporetic fashion, "freedom and equality — that constitutive and diabolical couple" (R, 48). For "equality tends to introduce measure and calculation (and thus conditionality) whereas freedom is by essence unconditional, indivisible, heterogeneous to calculation and to measure" (R, 48). Finally, democracy is impossible because although it should in principle be universal and imply absolute hospitality as an unconditional welcoming of the absolutely other (that is, a figure of unconditionality without sovereignty), it "still remains a model of intranational and intrastate political organization within the city" (R, 80). Absolute hospitality is impossible in the sense that it could never be politically or juridically instituted. And yet, for Derrida, it remains to be thought as a condition of possibility of hospitality in the more limited sense of the right to asylum, the right to immigration and citizenship rights, and even cosmopolitan right in the Kantian sense: "Only an unconditional hospitality can give meaning and practical rationality to a concept of hospitality. Unconditional hospitality exceeds juridical, political, or economic calculation. But no thing and no one happens or arrives without it" (R, 149).

If it were a question of only the unconditional term, we could say, as is sometimes charged, that Derrida's deconstruction of the political field has led to a kind of hyperethics. This can be debated, as Derrida himself acknowledges, and it is debated by the essays in this volume. But since Derrida insists that "*both* calculation *and* the incalculable *are necessary*," it is precisely the force of the political that is retained and, indeed, intensified by the aporetic tension of democracy to come (R, 150).

*Transactions, Legacies*

Derrida's deconstruction of the political field raises a number of difficult questions. One important question concerns the place of committed action. As we have seen, Derrida suggests that the deconstruction of the political field occurs in the becoming of the world, and committed thought is the thinking of the unfolding of the to-come and the changes that occur beyond the limits of our acquired categories of thought. But what is the role of committed action in this picture? How can we even think political action given Derrida's notion of the passive decision and his radical critique of ipseity and teleology, central concepts conventionally associated with political action? Indeed, if the to-come is an imminent coming that always haunts and destabilizes presence as its condition of (im)possibility, is the possibility of action not always predetermined by this coming and, therefore, in a sense, "fated," unfree? What can Derrida's notion of "a freedom without autonomy, a heteronomy without servitude" mean in concrete settings?

Derrida's critique of ipseity and teleology stems from the privilege he gives the unconditional other. This raises the important question of how deconstruction envisions the relation between the ethical and the political. Does the paramount place of unconditionality in Derrida's thought indicate a subordination or even reduction of the political to the ethical? Does the insistence on the unconditional function as an appeal to what he called "pure ethics" at the expense of politics and political engagements, which require negotiating with the calculable and the empirical? Conversely, if one points to the remainder of sovereignty within democracy as an instance of the inevitability of calculation, does Derrida's attempt to allow for the contamination of the political (the political as contamination) end up contaminating deconstruction itself with an ontotheological concept? Does it imply a conservative politics? And how can one concretely imagine the transactions in which the relation to the unconditional is played out or experienced in ethicopolitical relations? What does the formulation of calculating with the incalculable enable us to think when it comes to concrete problems such as the rearticulating of citizenship and rights in an era of the decline of state sovereignty, the reconfiguration of national culture, the critique of ethnonationalism in multicultural Europe, and the hospitality that should be shown to migrant workers without citizenship in an age of global migration?

Finally, from what geopolitical site is the discourse of unconditional hospitality articulated? Does Derrida's deconstruction of a Western or European political field not follow its contours, with the result that the deconstructive discourse of the transaction between the conditional and the unconditional, restated in terms of an affirmation of aporetic features, nevertheless remains, at some level, a Western or European perspective? Does the paradoxical notion of a universalization of the singular to which Derrida appeals not remain a universalization of features of Western thought that might itself limit an encounter with the otherness of non-Western practices or modes of thinking the political field?

The contributors to this volume engage with a number of these questions and assess Derrida's deconstruction of the political and its contribution to our understanding of the urgent political issues of our time from a number of different perspectives. Some contributors examine the political and ethical aporias that deconstruction tracks and consider how they shape Derrida's conceptualization of fundamental political concepts. Balibar, Cheah, Bennington, and Brown analyze specific concepts, focusing on Derrida's critiques of teleology and sovereignty in order to draw conclusions concerning the politics of his deconstruction of the political. Rancière questions the boundary between politics and ethics in Derrida and concludes that he sacrifices politics to ethics. To gain critical purchase on the nuanced elaborations of deconstruction, a number of contributors assess how Derrida's understanding of the political and his positions on various political issues differ from those of other figures in the history of Western philosophy, contemporary philosophers, and progressive intellectuals. So, placed in dialogue with Derrida, we hear the voices of Althusser (Balibar), Habermas (Cheah), Patočka (Gasché), Ricoeur (Guerlac), Arendt (Jay), Mauss (Hénaff), Levinas (Ukai), and Lyotard (Rancière). Bennington returns to Rousseau, Hobbes, and Spinoza, and Cheah looks back at Kant in order to explicate Derrida's deconstruction of sovereignty and teleology.

Whereas Ukai demonstrates the concrete usefulness of Derrida's account of the promise for understanding current debates on pacifism and sovereignty in postwar Japan, Hénaff challenges the European standard that informs Derrida's notion of pure giving. Brown and Norton argue that Derrida's understanding of the place of Islamic societies in relation to democracy to come is neo-Orientalist and Eurocentric. Tlatli takes an altogether different approach to the question of the European limits of deconstruction and argues for the pertinence of Derrida's Algerian background to his analysis of the archive and its relevance to a critique of postcolonial Algerian nationalism.

The first section of the book considers Derrida's deconstruction of two important political concepts: teleology and sovereignty. Étienne Balibar's essay addresses the implications of Derrida's thought for understanding history and historical change. He argues that Derrida points to Louis Althusser's failure to distinguish between teleology and eschatology and offers a nonmetaphysical reformulation of eschatology as the "messianic without messianism." By reading Derrida's elaboration of messianicity alongside Althusser's nonteleological history based on an aleatory materialism of the encounter, Balibar arrives at an instructive contrast between Althusser's understanding of the event as a revolutionary action that opens up the historical process and the deconstructive understanding of the event as the interruption of time. Focusing on *Rogues*, Pheng Cheah, on the other hand, argues in his chapter that Derrida yoked eschatology together with teleology, considering both to be modes of thought that reduce the other to ideality. He elaborates on Derrida's attempt to distinguish the à-venir from the Kantian regulative idea that governs the unfinished project of modernity taken up by the heirs of the Frankfurt School such as Habermas. Cheah also considers Derrida's deconstruction of sovereignty, offering a critical assessment of Derrida's account of the autoimmune character of democracy within the framework of contemporary globalization by comparing it to Habermas's project of global democracy. He evaluates the cosmopolitan vocation of democracy to come and questions Derrida's critique of nationalism in light of the promise of revolutionary postcolonial nationalism as a form of resistance to neoliberal global capitalism.

Bennington and Brown also address Derrida's thinking on sovereignty and democracy. Geoffrey Bennington argues that unlike political philosophy, which attempts to reduce the "politics" of politics by turning politics into an object of theory, deconstruction foregrounds this and affirms the impossibility of rendering politics purely theoretical. In the case of sovereignty, this impossibility is elaborated in terms of autoimmunity. Bennington's essay places Derrida's seemingly "eccentric" conception of autoimmunity in a genealogy of canonical political thinkers by tracing similar paradoxes in the political philosophy of Rousseau, Hobbes, and Spinoza. "This non–self-coincidence of any sovereignty and any demos," Bennington argues, "allows Derrida to open up the dimension of the *à-venir* . . . that consistently marks his [understanding of] democracy" as an interminable movement of pluralization, division, and dispersal of sovereignty. Bennington continues the deconstructive project by embedding it deeper into the field of political theory.

Wendy Brown's provocative essay argues that in spite of his deconstruction of sovereignty through the critique of ipseity, Derrida actually reconstitutes a notion of absolute sovereignty in relation to democracy to come. In contrast to Bennington and Cheah, she argues that Derrida's refusal to abandon the political-theological concept of sovereignty is the consequence of his liberal understanding of freedom as the ability of the individual to do whatever he or she pleases. Hence, she argues, democracy to come is a fundamentally liberal conception that does not take into account more contestatory forms of democratic freedom where the emphasis falls on the power of the demos to rule itself: "ruling together or taking responsibility for the whole," "governance in common," and "participation in power that is greater than *one*self." Brown's argument resonates with Rancière's conclusion that Derrida's destabilization of the notion of the demos according to the aporias of autoimmunity and his retention of the figure of the absolute other indicate that he sacrifices the political as force of the demos to the ethical and even religious register.

The second section of this volume focuses on the geopolitical setting of deconstructive responsibility and hospitality and deconstruction's relation to non-European others. It explores in greater detail a theme that Cheah broached concerning postcolonial nationalism and that Brown raised in her polemical claim that the equation of democracy with freedom that Derrida shares with other post-Marxist Left European thinkers is symptomatic of a neo-Orientalism that conserves the democratic West by differentiating it from a theocratic non-West. Rodolphe Gasché's essay examines the genealogical roots of Derrida's concept of responsibility, asking whether or not it is specifically European. In a careful reading of Derrida's *The Gift of Death* in comparison with the work of Jan Patočka, Gasché reminds us that there are two fundamentally distinct and incompatible European traditions concerning responsibility: the Platonic model that requires knowledge and transparency (a democratic model of responsibility) and a Christian model, which requires interiority, secrecy, and the possibility of heretical acts. For Derrida, he argues, to be responsible includes a responsibility to cultural inheritance, which in this case entails an aporetic responsibility to both traditions of responsibility. This radical concept of hyperbolical responsibility, Gasché suggests, implies a novel conception of Europe that demands an unconditional receptiveness to the traditions of the non-European other.

Anne Norton offers a quite different analysis of *The Gift of Death* that is in stark counterpoint to Gasché's. Norton reinscribes the difference between

Athens and Jerusalem, ancient Greece and Judeo-Christianity as the two traditions inherited by Europe, as the difference between Arab and Jew. She suggests that Derrida's reading of Abraham's sacrifice of Isaac is a response to Carl Schmitt's account of the sovereign exception and the autonomy of the political. Schmitt's account, she argues, is based on a Christian theology of incarnation, and it implies the exclusion of Jews and is connected with the Holocaust. Although Derrida takes issue with Schmitt's account of the exception in his reading of Abraham's sacrifice, Norton argues that Derrida performs another exclusion: that of the Muslim. He throws into the shadows the figure of Ishmael, which Norton identifies with the Marrano and the Arab. This exclusion becomes the guiding thread for a symptomatic reading of various texts in Derrida's corpus. Where are the Muslims hidden? and Why is Arabic not heard in Derrida's texts? Norton asks. The shift to posing the question of the constitution of Europe as a political and ethical tradition in terms of "the Arab and the Jew" requires us to think not only the basis of the political in the theological but how the very concept of political theology leads to a conception of political community that can include the Christian and the Jew, but nevertheless excludes Muslims.

Soraya Tlatli's chapter provides an indirect answer to Norton's questions by showing that Derrida lived the memory of Algeria and that it left traces in his thinking on the archive and his critique of nationalism. Returning to Derrida's critique of national belonging that was broached by Cheah, she explores how the notion of a personal trauma — the trauma of lost identity — structures Derrida's treatment of the question of historical memory in *Archive Fever*. Because the construction of an archive always involves political control of memory and history and, therefore, violence, "the institutionalization of the archive," Tlatli points out, "is politics itself revealed in its historical essence." Insofar as archives are the basis of national identity, Derrida's conception of the archive, she suggests, leads to a politics of critical refusal of the nation-state and community membership as forms of selfhood that deny internal otherness and self-division. This denial is the basis of violence toward external others. Tlatli argues that Derrida's archival politics has an important bearing on the contemporary Algerian situation: it enables a critique of the reactive, vengeful, and homogenizing nationalism found in Algeria today.

Like Tlatli, Satoshi Ukai maintains that Derrida's thought is important for understanding concrete non-European political situations. His contribution brings Derrida's examination of the structure of the promise and its "performative contradictions" to bear on postwar constitutional pacifism in Japan. He harnesses the insights of deconstruction in an analysis of the translation effects that went into the production of the modern Japanese Constitution and the problematic nature of Japan's national sovereignty that results from its pledge to renounce war as a sovereign right. To whom is this promise of peace made? How is this promise necessarily compromised by the fact that the sovereign power capable of promising is itself compromised by the historical situation of defeat in an atomic war indexed by the names of Nagasaki and Hiroshima? How is this promise compromised from within as a result of the exclusionary definition of "the people" in the Constitution? How is the spirit of pacifism repeatedly betrayed by external circumstances, such as the refusal of the Japanese government to take full responsibility for its war crimes, and the need for Japanese rearmament in various geopolitical scenarios (the Korean War and the rise of China)? Ukai's analysis of the failures of constitutional pacifism in Japan affirm Derrida's argument contra Levinas that peace does not lie beyond the political realm.

The chapters in the volume's third section address the relation between ethics and politics and explore some of the affirmative aporias of cultural performance to which Derrida devoted a number of seminars and a significant portion of his writing from the 1980s on. Giving, pardoning, lying: these are ethical performances that have taken on political value in the contemporary world, and Derrida regards them as examples of the inseparability of ethics and politics. The first three essays in this section analyze Derrida's treatment of these performances in which the apparently ethical gesture, aligned with the unconditional, is yoked to the political, which is to say, to technics and calculative reason. The section ends with Jacques Rancière's forceful challenge to Derrida's thinking of the political as being fundamentally ethical at the expense of the political.

Marcel Hénaff's essay challenges Derrida's conception of the aporia of the gift. He argues that Derrida's conception derives from a misunderstanding of the nature of ceremonial gift exchange and a fundamental misreading of Marcel Mauss's celebrated essay, *The Gift*. According to Hénaff, Derrida assumes that Mauss (and other anthropologists) reduced all empirical forms of giving to the structure of exchange and economy, according to which reciprocity necessarily implies a return to the self and self-interest. Derrida then contrasts this with an absolute or pure giving, found only in the giving of time, which escapes the circularity of exchange. Hénaff suggests that this notion of pure giving derives from a distinctly Western (and theological) understanding of pure giving as grace that is suspicious of all forms of reciprocity. He argues that ceremonial gift-giving implies a completely different framework of reciprocity, one that is not economic but instead implies a collective logic of generous reply that is essential to the forming of alliances between groups. Unlike the selfish structure of indebtedness and restitution characterizing exchange, this mode of reciprocity operates according to the alternating principle of a game structure that imposes an obligation to respond. What is at stake in Hénaff's challenge to Derrida is whether or not there can be a mode of recognition that accommodates absolute otherness, and whether or not the deconstructive attempt to protect radical otherness does not, in spite of itself, impose a certain universalization of Western standards, here a standard of pure generosity as nonreciprocal giving associated with Christian grace. Such an ethicotheological standard, Hénaff argues, misses the specifically political dynamic of the formation of group alliances in ceremonial gift-giving.

Suzanne Guerlac's essay examines the way Derrida constructs the ethical principle of the pardon in terms of what he elsewhere calls the "impossible transaction between the conditional and the unconditional, the calculable and the incalculable," (R, 150–51). She reads the pardon as a figure for the political force of deconstruction itself, for the inscription of deconstruction within history. The pardon becomes a political matter specifically in the case of South Africa, with which Derrida was personally engaged. In a reading of Derrida's "The Admiration of Nelson Mandela," Guerlac demonstrates that this inscription of deconstruction within history is far from neutral but rather implies a powerful denunciation of racism. Finally, Guerlac contrasts Derrida's theorization of the pardon as im-possible, a formulation intended to maintain its unconditional edge, with that of Ricoeur. She demonstrates that the fundamental difference between the two thinkers results from Ricoeur's shift to a Bergsonian framework concerning time, recognition, and memory as forgetting. This enables Ricoeur to affirm the possibility of the pardon in the political context without endorsing amnesty. Ricoeur's elaboration of the pardon, finally, suggests that although Derrida theorizes the pardon in a manner quite distinct from Ricoeur, he writes the figure of Mandela precisely as a figure of what Ricoeur would call the capable man.

Derrida's treatment of the pardon was closely related to his seminars on the question of perjury, which also address the political implications of the ethical prohibition of lying. Martin Jay's contribution is a critique of Derrida's reading of Hannah Arendt's essays on truth and lying in politics. Jay notes that although Derrida and Arendt are both "Heidegger's children," and although Derrida appreciatively engages with Arendt's writings on lying and values her analysis of the absolute lie of the modern age, where reality is not hidden but actually destroyed by the lie (a phenomenon that Arendt links to totalitarian politics), he distinguishes his position from hers on various grounds. These have to do with Arendt's preservation of the primacy of truth and a self-knowing subject that is always transparent to itself and therefore always intends to lie and knows that it is lying. Such a subject, Derrida argues, cannot lie to or deceive itself. The possibility of radical self-deception that is at work in the technoperformativity of contemporary mass media points instead to a conception of a radically divided self that is better elucidated through psychoanalysis, Heidegger's existential analytic, and Marx's theory of ideology. Here, Derrida extends his critique of ipseity to analyze the radical nature of deception in political life. Jay argues, however, that Derrida's critique of Arendt is a simplification that fails to take into account the full complexity of her understanding of political mendacity. He points out that although Arendt stubbornly holds on to a residue of truth in the political realm, her notion of truth involves an ongoing struggle among competing opinions and values, the very lifeblood of politics. For Jay, this battle of opinions and even the ability to lie itself are signs of the inextinguishability of human freedom, our rational ability to resist the domination of sacred imperatives.

In his essay Jacques Rancière also wonders whether the deconstructive understanding of the political subordinates it to a heretical form of theology. Rancière distinguishes his understanding of democracy from Derrida's by asking What is the supplement to democracy carried by the phrase "democracy to come"? "Is it a supplement *of* politics or a supplement *to* politics?" For Rancière, the democratic supplement already occurs within democracy: it is the demos and its kratos. He suggests that the anarchic principle of the "democratic supplement," which includes a principle of substitutability, "makes politics exist as such." In contradistinction, the Derridean supplement of a "democracy to come" is an ethical supplement to a conception of politics that turns on a notion of sovereignty and its problematization. Rancière argues that Derrida's suspicions about reciprocity (something Hénaff also discusses) and his focus on the asymmetrical relation to the other preclude democratic reciprocity or substitutability. Hence, "democracy to come" is a democracy without a specifically political capacity. It "means a democracy without a demos, with no possibility that a subject perform the *kratos* of the *demos*." In place of political thought, he argues, Derrida offers the ethical thinking of hospitality: "The *hospes* is the subject that comes in the place of the demos." Democracy to come, finally, means a substitution of *aporia* for political *dissensus*. This, Rancière suggests, makes politics dependent on a theology of the unconditionality of the Other that Derrida inherits from Levinas.

To inherit, Derrida has written, includes an active work of selective and critical retrieval from writings we receive from the past, even a reinvention of them in terms of what speaks meaningfully at a given time. The volume we present performs this work in light of the present moment and of uncertainties to come.

Friendship, as we have seen, was an important intellectual terrain for Derrida's reflection on the political and the ethical. It was also, as Michel Deguy put it after Derrida's death, "a daily act of courage [*une prouesse quotidienne*]" for Jacques Derrida.[48] It is fitting that the critical and analytical essays in this volume be introduced by Hélène Cixous, who lived a singular friendship with Derrida, one that spanned over forty years, crossing the divide of gender but also the radical otherness (and the proximity) of literature to philosophy and, finally, today, of life and death. Her essay is unlike any other in this volume. It speaks to, with, and across the language of Jacques Derrida, performing, in its address, the strange temporality of friendship that is also, in a slightly different way, the temporality of the "hyperethical" and the "hyperpolitical" as Derrida elaborated these terms with an eye to the future and memories of the past. We are grateful to her for opening this volume of essays and to Judith Butler for closing the frame of this volume with incisive critical remarks that open out onto future thought on the political.

*Derrida and the Time of the Political* is not meant to be a commemorative volume. It performs a work of critical inheritance that addresses most specifically readers of Derrida to come. The framework of friendship, performed textually here by Cixous, does not imply uniformity of thinking. It establishes instead a framework of respect for radical otherness and for the singularity of diverse critical voices outside any notion of a community of friends that would impose sameness. Derrida's logic of friendship calls for this. Inheriting his thought implies the act of carefully explicating it as well as contesting it. This is the only legacy that could be meaningful, the only act of inheriting that might open onto the future and open up to readers to come.

*Notes*

1   Fraser, "The French Derrideans," 127. See also Said, "The Problem of Textuality"; Sprinker, "Textual Politics"; and Foley, "The Politics of Deconstruction."

2   See Ryan, *Marxism and Deconstruction*; Parker, " 'Taking Sides' "; and Spivak, "Scattered Speculations," and "Speculations on Reading Marx."

3   See, for instance, Cornell, *Beyond Accommodation;* Holland, *Feminist Interpretations of Derrida*; and most recently, the special issue of *differences: A Journal of Feminist Cultural Studies*, entitled *Derrida's Gifts* and edited by Weed and Rooney.

4   Spivak, "Feminism and Deconstruction," and "Can the Subaltern Speak?"; Butler, *Gender Trouble*.

5   Laclau and Mouffe, *Hegemony and Socialist Strategy*, 111–12.

6   See Corlett, *Community without Unity*, and Martin, *Matrix and Line*.

7   Cornell, *The Philosophy of the Limit*.

8   Critchley, *The Ethics of Deconstruction*, 190. The previous quote is from 189. As we will see, Critchley's judgment is mistaken given the importance of the interruptive decision in Derrida's work.

9   See Laclau, " 'The time is out of joint' "; and Sprinker, *Ghostly Demarcations*.

10  See Bennington, *Legislations* and *Interrupting Derrida*, especially chapter 2, "Derrida and Politics."

11  The bearing of deconstruction on the political has been repeatedly addressed in the volumes from the four Cérisy colloquia on Derrida's work. The memorial volume, *Jacques Derrida*, edited by Mallet and Michaud, has a section on politics with contributions by Étienne Balibar, Egidius Berns, and Paola Marrati. See also Zarka, *Derrida politique*. In contrast, Beardsworth's study was published too early to take into account Derrida's writings of his last decade on themes such as democracy, sovereignty, and cosmopolitanism. He has discussed this later work in "In Memoriam Jacques Derrida: The Power of Reason." Thomson's book was written before the publication of *Voyous* and focuses on *Politics of Friendship*. But see his essay, "What's to Become of 'Democracy to Come.'" Martin, in *Humanism and Its Aftermath*, discusses Derrida's ideas about justice and responsibility to 1991.

　　Although Spivak does not offer a systematic commentary on Derrida's writings, her persistent engagement with the political implications of deconstruction is exceptional. "The Setting to Work of Deconstruction," the appendix to *A Critique of Postcolonial Reason*, 423–31, offers a succinct and astute mapping of the trajectory of Derrida's work in relation to the political that is generally consonant with the one we elaborate below.

12  Derrida, *Rogues*, 39. Hereafter *R*.

13  See Derrida, "As If It Were Possible," 89.

14  "Politics and Friendship: A Discussion with Jacques Derrida."

15  "Jacques Derrida, penseur de l'évènement," interview in *L'Humanité*, January 28, 2004, www.humanite.fr.

16  Derrida, *Specters of Marx*, 170. Hereafter *SM*.

17  Derrida, *Politics of Friendship*, 80. Hereafter *PF*, translation modified where appropriate.

18  Derrida, "Autrui est secret parce qu'il est autrui."

19  An Age refers to a specific problematical configuration within philosophical discourse that arises from a weave of political, economic, and social forces. It is indexed by an exemplary proper name that gives it the most thorough systematization, but it exceeds the historical moment of its genesis. The Age of Rousseau refers to the determination of presence as self-presence within consciousness and feeling and includes Lévi-Strauss's structuralist anthropology. See Derrida, *Of Grammatology*, 97–100. The Age of Hegel refers to the entrusting of the teaching of philosophy to state structures and civil servants at a time when the state seeks to ground itself in philosophical reason. Derrida, "The Age of Hegel," 137.

20  Derrida's remarks were a response to Jean-Luc Nancy's discussion of a passage from Derrida's essay on Levinas, "Violence et Métaphysique," in which Derrida defined philosophers as constituting "a community of the question about the possibility of the question." Nancy had suggested that for Derrida, the fundamental injunction is "one of maintaining the question, as a question." Nancy, "La voix libre de l'homme," 170; "The Free Voice of Man," 39.

21  Derrida's response is transcribed in Nancy, "La voix libre de l'homme," 184, and is translated in "The Free Voice of Man," 54.

22  Subsequent comments sharpened the distinction between "maintaining the question" and affirmative deconstruction. See, for instance, Derrida, "On Reading Heidegger," 171: "My own gesture is to sketch a movement of thinking, tracing, writing, that begins in affirmation. . . . In addition to what Heidegger calls *das Gefragte, Befragte*, and *das Erfragte*, there must be someone or something else involved in questioning: there is a call of the other [*l'appel de l'autre*] that precedes, must precede, philosophy and the path of thinking." Compare "As If It Were Possible," 86: "Everything begins not with the question but with the response, with a 'yes, yes,' that is in origin a response to the other."

23  See Derrida, *Spurs*, 97, 121. On Blanchot and Joyce, see Derrida, "The Law of Genre," and *Ulysse gramophone*.

24  See Fynsk, "Intervention," "Séminaire 'politique,'" 488, "Contribution I," "'Political' Seminar," 88, and Lacoue-Labarthe, "Intervention," "Séminaire 'politique,'" 494, "Contribution II," "'Political' Seminar," 95.

25  Lacoue-Labarthe, "Intervention," "Séminaire 'politique,'" 494, "Contribution II," "'Political' Seminar," 95 (translation modified). The Center for Philosophical Research on the Political, with its premise "the essential co-belonging of the philosophical and the political," opened in November 1980 at the École Normale Supérieure. Lacoue-Labarthe and Nancy asserted that the deconstruction of philosophy also meant the deconstruction of the philosophical determination of the political that would extend to a radical "questioning of the philosophical *as* the political"

("Opening Address to the Centre for Philosophical Research on the Political," 109–10). They defined the project of retreating the political by means of three negative principles. First, the critique of a philosophy of the political would undermine any "pretension to political theory, and . . . to anything that could evoke a 'political science' or a 'politology'" since that would involve a philosophical appropriation of the political ("Opening Address," 108). Second, a philosophical concept of political practice as the completion of the philosophical through its practical realization or actualization (*Verwirklichung*) must also be renounced (Lacoue-Labarthe, "Intervention," "Séminaire 'politique,'" 495, "Contribution II," "'Political' Seminar," 96). Third, they sounded a warning about lapsing into a simplistic politics that is suspect for two reasons: because politics is deemed obvious and everywhere and, therefore, something to which we must submit, and because political phenomena and activity are taken as simple positive facts of social-anthropological existence (Lacoue-Labarthe, "Intervention," "Séminaire 'politique,'" 495, "Contribution II," "'Political' Seminar," 97; Lacoue-Labarthe and Nancy, "Opening Address," 109).

26 Lacoue-Labarthe and Nancy, "Opening Address," 110.
27 "Politics and Friendship: A Discussion with Jacques Derrida."
28 Derrida, "Autoimmunity," 106. Hereafter A.
29 Derrida, "Autrui est secret parce qu'il est autrui." See also Derrida, "Otobiographies," 9.
30 Derrida, "Autrui est secret parce qu'il est autrui."
31 Antelme, *L'Espèce Humaine*, translated by Haight and Mawler as *The Human Race*.
32 Blanchot, *L'Amitié*, 329.
33 As Blanchot puts it, the Second World War "put an end to all faith in groups [*a mit fin à l'espérance des groupes*]" (*La Communauté Inavouable*, 38). Blanchot's essay was written in dialogue with Jean Luc Nancy's *La Communauté désoeuvrée*.
34 Derrida's essay "Pas," on Blanchot's *Celui qui ne m'accompagnait pas*, was first published in the review *Gramma*. It was subsequently republished in a collection of essays on Blanchot, *Parages*.
35 Bergson, *Les Données immédiates de la conscience*, 39, 115; in English, *Time and Free Will*, 53, 153.
36 Derrida, "Politics and Friendship," 182.
37 See Derrida, *SM*, 75; and "Politics and Friendship," 177–78.
38 The à-venir was already announced in 1980 in Derrida's reading of the Apocalypse of St. John: "The event of this 'Come' [*Viens*] precedes and calls the event. It would be that starting from which there is any event, the coming [*le venir*], the to-come [*l'à-venir*] of the event that cannot be thought under the given category of the event" ("D'un ton apocalyptique adopté naguère en philosophie," 476; "Of an Apocalyptic Tone Recently Adopted in Philosophy," 33).
39 Derrida, "Passions," 17.
40 See Habermas, *The Inclusion of the Other*.
41 Derrida, "Performative Powerlessness," 467.

42 On the violence of political founding, see Arendt, *On Revolution*, especially her gloss on Machiavelli on 28–34.

43 See, for instance, Honig, "Declarations of Independence"; and McCormick, "Derrida on Law."

44 The idea of subversive performativity is most clearly articulated in Butler, *Gender Trouble*.

45 The latter phrase is from Derrida, "Performative Powerlessness," 468.

46 Derrida, "As If It Were Possible," 90–91.

47 Derrida, "Not Utopia, the Im-possible," 131.

48 Michel Deguy, "Il faisait de l'amitié une prouesse quotidienne," *Libération*, October 11, 2004, www.derrida.ws.

# PART I

Openings

# Jacques Derrida: Co-Responding Voix You

HÉLÈNE CIXOUS · *Translated by Peggy Kamuf*

*(Exergue)*

His thoughtful, insistent worry in the face of every scene of political con-vocation, several times a year — and each time unique naturally — could be translated more or less exactly in these terms: "If I knew what I must do, then I would know how to do it. But how to speak of the GATT? So compli-cated. How *to find the schema*, as Kant would say, between philosophical thought and the scene of ordinary decision? Very difficult."

In other words, "How not to respond?" to a situation that is apparently novel? What good way of disappointing expectations can I invent? [*Quel bon faux bond inventer?*]

## The Time of the Political

1. Before I begin, allow me to confide that I am not sure I understand this title, or know where it is leading us.

Am I supposed to understand that the Time of the Political is "now"?

Or *to come*? Or else is it the call to a phenomenology of Time qualified as political? Is it an allusion to *Politics of Friendship* and to the undecidable leitmotiv of the *Time is out of joint*? Is not Time more or less always out of joint? Like you and me moreover . . .

I will go on endlessly turning around this phrase and its reasons . . .

2. That said, allow me to declare that everything Jacques Derrida will have given to be thought, in the movement of the deconstructions whose stakes he will have constantly raised, is directly political in its cause or its effect, including the apparently autobiographical texts or those that intersect with psychoanalysis or literature.

## Voix You

Several *parerga*, outworks, dedicated to the *voyou* that he is, and that I am, to the rogue-that-I-am / follow, the *voyou-que-je-suis* as he would say by antonomasis, cautiously and slyly, drawing right away from two French words—*je suis*—a philosophy of the equivocal.

Parerga of the twenty-six parerga that "precede" (but can one say "precede"?) the premises (but can one say "premises"?) of those reflections inventoried under the subtitle *Crypts*, encrypted under the Post-Scriptum, followed by a post-cryptum and that in fifty-two points enumerated February 28, 1994, by Jacques Derrida will have made the philosophical light required to think what comes.

To accomplish here my role as Prologue, it would suffice that I read you the powerful pages from "Faith and Knowledge" where Jacques Derrida will have assembled everything needed to think "Jacques Derrida and Politics or the Political": everything—and the rest, naturally.

If I choose "Faith and Knowledge" today, it is (1) by chance, (2) by economic calculation, (3) while resuscitating one of our conversations, which dates from January 1993 (1994) 1995—whose echo I will let you hear in a moment.

Let's say that it is apropos "Religion," Faith, and Knowledge that one time, on an island, site of the philosophical dream par excellence, Jacques Derrida will have, one time among countless others, given the political to be thought, what there will be to think for still longer than more than one century, by linking right away, on this occasion "the question of religion to that of the evil of abstraction" and

> to radical abstraction. Not to the abstract figure of death, of evil or of the sickness of death, but to the forms of evil that are traditionally tied to *radical extirpation* and therefore to the deracination of abstraction, passing by way—but only much later—of those sites *of abstraction* that are the machine, technics, technoscience, and above all the transcendence of tele-technology. "Religion and mechanē," religion and cyberspace," "religion and the numeric," "religion and the digital," "religion and virtual space-time": in order to take the measure of these themes in a short treatise, within the limits assigned to us, to conceive a small discursive machine that, however, finite and perfectible, would not be too powerless.[1]

Please pardon the Prologue that I am for "adding" to this and even piling it on.

—If I do so it is because one must always repeat the message, relaunch the thinking, since mortals have a short memory.

So as to rule out from the start the sort of discourse I hear circulating here and there, and that claims — whether out of naïveté, bad faith, or dimness — that Jacques Derrida is not, has not always been, would not have always been "political," whereas from the first trace of his thinking, just as from the first trace on his body, which will have made him the poison-gift of the inevitability of the poison-gift, of the wound, the traumatism, as what presides over cultural, political destiny . . . etc. of every being. Thus, with the first trace of the thinking of the trace in *Of Grammatology*, the whole machine that tends to replace the word "writing" in the ordinary sense by "trace" or the word "speech" by trace, had as its final purpose that writing, speech, trace are *not the proper characteristic of the human*. There is animal trace, animals write. From the beginning, the deconstruction of the *properly human*, and thus of its empire, its rights, is in place. Jacques Derrida has always resisted the opposition between the human and the animal, just as he does the opposition and thus the hierarchization between man and woman; this is the absolutely permanent, archoriginary trait of his political trajectory.

---

Jacques Derrida will have always been *archi*political, *acted* and *acting*, and therefore *acting reflexively* and, with time, more and more broadly, forcefully, insisting, testifying, warning, even while thematizing and ramifying the networks of everything there is to think otherwise about the coming times.

If one had to say "two words," as he would say, on the subject of the Politics of Deconstruction, of Deconstruction as Politics, it would of course be *à venir*, to come. This à venir to which he will have joined, in an unforgettable way, the word, the idea, the dream of democracy. From now on it will no longer be possible to think Democracy otherwise than through this phrase: Democracy *to come*. And not Democracy *coming*. It is not, as he takes care to repeat, a matter of messianic anticipation, not of messianism but of messianicity, of a promise, of a horizon that regulates law. It is necessary that Democracy *remain to come*. It is necessary to think it and to think of it with a thought that will *always and still* remain beyond what is realizable. Beyond the possible, that is to say, beyond that for which I am prepared, beyond what I can claim, beyond what I, myself, a finite and delimited being, can do. Responsibility, in its secret splendor, consists in going further than one's own power. And this is to be lived, with difficulty, as he lived it, in the daily renewal of effort, fatigue, in a courageous insistence at the heart and core of discouragement.

I could recount here a hundred concrete acts of "engagement" in which I participated or that I witnessed during the more than forty years of friendship in activity where we crossed (conjugated) our presence, speech, acts, but I don't have the time to establish the archive of an entire life inspired by the tireless, exhausting sense of *responsibility*. I would need a book to cite all the causes to which he devoted himself—and I emphasize here, that he always did so generously, that is, as modestly as possible, without seeking to capitalize through the media, without *selling* the cause for his image.

I will cite among the examples of institutions that we have at the same time instituted or co-initiated and then left in a big hurry once these brand new machines that we were fabricating like dreaming children and that we assumed to be more or less *pure*, yes, pure (for the philosophy of contamination arises from a desiring reference to *incorruptible purity*), were being changed and corrupted in a nonnegotiable manner, I will cite Paris 8 for both of us—and for him the GREPH and the Estates General of Philosophy, the mock-heroic episode of the new CNL, where we lived like the kings in Rimbaud "a whole morning," the Collège International de Philosophie, then the International Parliament of Writers. But there would also be all the causes from apartheid up to the latest commitments for the new Russell Tribunal against Bush's engagement in Iraq or else the animal cause (President of the Association for the Abolition of Bull-Fighting in 2004).

One can designate the principles of all these philosophical actions that come in such heterogeneous guises: each time it was a matter of giving refuge, thus of saving life, thus of forcing the retreat of all the death penalties beginning with the *Death Penalty* properly speaking. Practically, this means:

1. Finding oneself on the side of those who are the current victims, in a precise *historical* moment, of violence and the denial of justice, but without ever letting oneself be *appropriated* by a cause or *a party*, or another community, serving solely and rigorously *the idea of justice*.

   Thus no blank check, no identification, no idealization . . .

2. Without illusion, without ever giving the opposition good/evil a chance to seduce, knowing full well that there is always more contamination in store, feeling full well that there are *plural* incalculable resources *in* compassion.

In reality, in practice, in his life, in his relation to the world, to others, and first of all to himself, always vigilant, careful, and at the same time letting himself give in at moments to the temptation to *believe*, at least briefly, in his life as in the different scenes of his creation—always at work to think politically otherwise, as never yet. That he loathed demonstrations did not prevent him from letting himself at times be dragged by friendship into the streets, his loathing of spectacular action making his surrender out of solidarity all the more worthy of affection.

Between action and thought, there is always reflexive exchange, circularity. Thus it is with his great unleashed and unleashing seminars that reweave all philosophies and their specters around some event, be it secret or worldwide. I will cite for example the great years devoted to philosophical Nationality and nationalism, to (Politics of) friendship, to Eating the other, to the Secret, to Testimony, to the Lie, to Hostility/hospitality, to Perjury and pardon, to the Death Penalty, to the Beast and to the Sovereign.

An immense living pedagogical work, vibrating with an address to that vast public, which took the place not of a party but of the people who are heir, he says in *Voyous*, to that mysterious thing never yet seen, Democracy. Responsibility is his mission and his torment: no one will ever measure how far he went putting himself under *obligation* to *answer* for the world to the world, from day to day, welcoming into his thought surprise-scenes. (Example: September 11 he was in Shanghai. From one moment to the next, overwhelmed, he *set himself* to thinking the unthinkable, *applying himself*, plying himself to analyzing and deconstructing what he will have called "the event" as yet unnamed, this eruption, this seism in political time that leaves creatures mute and defenseless.) I cannot recall a single moment, a single episode arising on the French or worldwide stage to which he remained indifferent, from war, beginning with all the wars of decolonization, up to what is no longer recognizable as "war" (see the concept of September 11), up to scenes of another species of cruelty, like that of bullfighting, which he became involved in combating in 2004. To each minimal or cosmic cause he applied his heart and the forces of his thought. And at home, constantly appealed to, the telephone like a divine or prophetic switchboard: what to think, how to think?

He sleeps little. He is like that lone man awake and standing under the starry sky at the edge of the encampment where humanity sleeps that Kafka talks about: "There has to be one who keeps watch." The responder, or answering machine, that he is, however, is not reassuring. His Message is disturbing because not trenchant, not deciding but deferring, complicating, indicating in every case a supplementary fold, a step beyond. Not comfortable, not exalting. Similar to one of those prophets or poets who do not command, do not direct, but spread over the gaping anxieties sentences that welcome the unnameable (see *Psychoanalysis Searches the States of Its Soul*). Yes, he says, we are suffering, and we do not exactly know who *we* is, or what suffering is, or what is suffering in us, but there is some friendship in thinking how-to-suffer.

---

So I chose to call my Prologue "Voyous / Voix You" while obeying the *dictation* that decides in me in my place, as it always decided in him. I find in this more than one pleasure and more than one emotion.

1. As you know, he unites under this word (Is it *one* word? Is it not more than one word?) and this name two great political texts engendered in 2002, which contain all imaginable problematics for the mortal human beings that we are, poor passers-by, or criminals, subject to an autoimmunitary fatality.

2. As you know, this text is *roué* in all senses of this French word, beginning with that of cunning, but above all that of cruelly tormented, drawn and quartered. And the first to be tortured on the wheel, *la roue*, is he. As he admits at the outset after having cited with urgency *On Democracy in America* (I must recall that here) (*Voyous*, 34–35) in order to *link up with*, or to *unleash*, as the Proteus-Prometheus that he is, the theological and the political

> God, circle, volt, revolution, torture: I should perhaps confess that what tortures me, the question that has been putting me to the question, might just be related to what structures a particular axiomatics of a certain sphere, and thus the ipseity of the One, the *autos* of autonomy, symmetry, homogeneity, the same, the like, the semblable or the similar, and even, finally, God, in other words everything that remains incompatible with, even clashes with, another truth of the democratic, namely, the truth of the other, heterogeneity, the heteronomic and the dissymmetric, disseminal multiplicity, the anonymous "anyone," the "no matter who," the indeterminate "each one."[2]

3. You know that he put (himself) America to the question by tormenting himself etc. I thus note here, leaving it pending, that the first of the four algebraico-comical pseudo-definitions of Deconstruction that it amuses him to wave about is (1) Deconstruction is America. It amused him to say that in 1984 by way of "boutade" as one says in French,[3] a little like saying it's a dream, it's the jackpot, it's Eldorado, it's the end of the world. It's not by chance if this very religious, hegemonic, but fragile country offers Deconstruction a scene, if not a battlefield or a field of privileged confrontation. *But*

Deconstruction happens everywhere naturally; it has no frontiers. Why not say: Deconstruction is Europe? Precisely, he is concerned with it more and more, observing the aporias of the Europe to come ever since "Europe" has forced itself into a dislocated assembly. How to inherit from this thing called the European "spirit," phantasm and memory, without Eurocentrism? Another turn of the wheel.

Torment and chance, travail and uncertainty: he will have wished for and analyzed, without concession, all these elements that make up the contrary forces of Deconstruction, whether this putting to the question applies to Israel and Palestine, to North Africa or South Africa, or yet again to misogyny and phallocratism, which are not always the simple prerogative of men, as one may sometimes forget.

4. I persist in saying *Voyou* and not *Rogue*. (1) First of all this word has its references in Jacques Derrida's childhood (and mine as well, in Algeria). "Petit voyou," scolding adults used to say to rascals in Jackie's mold. But also to little Arabs, with another intonation. *"Le voyou" que je suis*, as he says boasting now, is this delinquent, the *shamarab*, the Frenjew, the philosofrenjew, the kid from El Biar, the saint mock turtle, etc.

Being and thought without pause, without full stop, without external borders, without homogeneity, and without *homo* sexuality either, the divided itself. The self, the same divided, clawed from himself and grafted from himself. Himself grappling with himself, neither victor nor vanquished, rolling in the dust beyond the beyonds, in permanent revolution. The *voyou* of philosophy, "belonging" as Frenjew to a culture, a political field, as philosofrenjew belonging to a philosophical history whose first concepts were produced in the Greek language, speaking Greek in French. It's complicated because at work inside these national roots is the universalizing vocation and thus the work of *uprooting accompanies constantly the inheritance of the language* and of belonging.

That is why I call him Voyou — but not just in French. Voyou as in Voix you, ou Voie you or Vois you, Voyou, as *term with more than one tongue*.

Voyou says more than one tongue to the voyaging ear.

*Voix-you*

(2) *Plus d'une langue* (more than one/no more of one language) is the second of the "four" serious, amusingly and awfully serious definitions of Deconstruction (obviously he could give four more or forty more), but let us play dice — let us be played by Jacques Derrida — by taking the smallest common denominator, four definitions: *four*, for, a deconstruction in four

directions, four-forked, "on all fours" as you say (his manner of sprinkling English on everything he says as if to say *"monolingual, my eye,"* four, for. *For*: *Pour*.

I said *let's play*, for he will have reminded us that everything is destined to *playing*, there is *some play*, it plays, like the earth on its axis, it is not frozen, fixed, stuck, it slides and this is right away already of the order of the political it reminds us that one cannot *bank on*, *fix*, posit, stabilize, pose a thesis without a perhaps, an if, an as-if, and then a *but-if/but-yes*, a *mais-si* — that is, a messiah, right away getting mixed up in it. The political and comical, humorous dimension of Derridean derision shows itself as each page turns: we believe we hold, or hold ourselves, straight, upright, firm, and all we do is totter, move from one hesitation to the next, blind, followed by *après-coups*, escorted by verbal skids, and it is this gait of the wobbly being that makes us laugh, that is the tragic itself. "Nous nous croyons," as one used to say in Algeria: we believe ourselves, we believe ourselves to be . . .

As for him, he never overlooks the unconscious. This is ruination for all those who fail to recognize the incalculable spectral role of the unconscious in everything that seems to us decided or decidable.

*Nota bene* right away: Warning. This vision of "we humans" as players played in no way lessens the measure of responsibility. It makes it more difficult to exercise responsibility, but it also makes it more desirable.

We are not simply played, playthings, or playboys, roués. We are disputed. I is not simply an other, for Jacques Derrida, it's more complicated. There is in me an other that I am (following), at the same time. I am/follow the one that I am/follow. (*Je suis celui que je suis*: All of this can be felt only in French.)

In the third definition (3) *Deconstruction is the impossible*. For the fourth definition (4) Deconstruction is *what* happens, or *who* happens, arrives, it is the arrivant. Note that, of course, the arrivant is not the arrived, but the movement toward the shore, *la rive*, at which arrivance arrives without ever arriving. Arrives, like an event: unforeseen, unforeseeable, impossible.

It's like this word *voyou* that just goes on arriving at, happening to Jacques Derrida and consequently to us, and this all of a sudden, and yet for centuries. And which or who, speaking to us in more than one language, of more than one language, goes about denominating, denaming, overnaming, nicknaming the States that conduct themselves like outlaws, that is to say, almost all States.

I note that what arrives is that for which one was not prepared and which arrives as impossible. For something or someone to *arrive*, he says, *it, he, or she must arrive as impossible*. My emphasis.

For example: the end of the world, love, death. These are lightning bolts that only arrive as impossible, but arrive as impossible. *As* impossible. I don't mean that one does not expect death, or love. But it is in vain that one prepares for it as Montaigne does, death, like love, happens to us unawares: one cannot appropriate them. My death remains impossible like your death. Your death happens to me — arrives at me — and does not happen to me. "Je m'attends à la mort." "I am expecting death, I am waiting for myself at death." "Je t'attends à la mort." "I am waiting for you at death." "On en reparlera à la maison." "We'll talk about it again back home." All of this happens, arrives in French.

--------

Thus I come back to *plus d'une langue:*

Deconstruction is more than one / no more of one language, a language that is more than one language. *Plus d'une langue*: here several books ought to take off, all those of Jacques Derrida, all those to come

all those among those of Jacques Derrida that set about listening to great examples of *plus d'une langue: Glas, Pas, Shibboleth, Ulysses Gramophone, Fichus* (or if I may *HC*)

putting to work in an incandescent manner (the scene, the stage) the theater of events in language, which makes for poetry (Poetry is more than one language): an alliance of improvisations and in such a way as to master what happens to the pen while you are speaking.

1. To be sure a language always speaks more than one language (the "myth" of monolingualism), but for there to be deconstruction there must be simultaneous efforts to hear what befalls us and to put it back to work.

2. I speak more than one language — I do not know what *I* say. I say something other than what I believe, think, want, say.

3. Let's talk about the discourse of politics as that discourse is administered by States and Parties: there all utterances are subject to critical deconstruction, to pastiche, to parody. It seems that the expression *langue de bois* (wooden tongue) was introduced only recently in French, the metaphor would have first appeared in Russian in the context of political propaganda. (I would like to know how people said "langue de bois" in the past.)

4. The Derridean makes French speak more than one French, more than one French speaker in French. And never will French have been more powerful, more poetic, more thoughtful than when (Jacques Derrida) the ingenious *voyou* disturbs it, causes the other to come into its mouth.

The voyou-that-I-am (following) is full of voices, like Prospero's island. *This isle is full of voices*, this I is full of you's.

If I had the time I would begin here an immense chapter, in dialogue naturally, that would evoke the different states of the questions, places, voices of polysexuality, that put in question all the received ideas concerning sexual difference, at the same time as they blur the signature, and put in question what is monological in traditional philosophic discourse. This was one of the themes of our conversation in May 2004, as yet unpublished. I cite a few moments from the answer he gave me:

Even there where there are dialogues, in Plato . . . these dialogues remain in the service of the monologic thesis. In my case — and I'm not going to compare myself with Plato! — monologism, univocity, a single voice — is impossible, and plurivocity is a non-fictional necessity, a necessity that I put to work in a fictional fashion of course but that is not feigned. . . .

It happens, it has often happened to me that I begin to write a text in a normal monologic mode, and then I notice along the way that I would not be able to pull it off, that I had to change voices, that I had to make several persons speak; this has happened to me more than once.

Something is always dictated. Next I am able to take some initiative with this dictation, I can calculate — naturally I calculate a good deal how to put the dictation into a work. But the essential thing comes from another voice in some manner, from another voice in me, which is probably not always the same, which is the same and not the same. This is the sexual question as well, it's the same it's not the same, one is the same and not the same. And when I go back to texts that are explicitly entrusted to several voices — I'm thinking of *Pas*, that was in '73 or '74, it was a feminine voice, I'm thinking of *The Truth in Pointing*, on Heidegger and Van Gogh, there too there are feminine voices, I'm thinking of a certain text on Levinas ("At this very moment . . .") it is a woman's voice who protests constantly against Levinas. But there are others. . . .

These are texts where not only the multiplicity of voices is dictated to me, but I orient it willfully, deliberately, toward a political critique, a politico-philosophical protest against misogyny, machismo, or phallocentrism, which I've been trying to theorize since forever long before this. And then even before these voices sexualize themselves in some way, before they take the mark of this or that sex, of *he* or *she*, or sometimes remain indeterminate, sometimes one cannot tell if it is *he* or *she*, one doesn't really know if it is *he* or *she*, who is *he* who is *she* [But even before this multiplicity of voices is sexualized, I have also undergone the necessity of writing several texts at once, with several hands at once, to set on the page several discourses at once in the same space. And there it was not a matter of sexual difference, but only of difference of voices, difference of discourses that are simultaneous, set on the page, responding to each other without responding to each other, but that are there, to be read together].....

About myself, I would say, going now really simply, directly to the simplest, that the places and voices of woman, and the cause of women, in my texts and in my life, stem first of all from the fact that a certain masculinity, a certain heterosexuality, which is dominant in me, has always taken the form—which is not as common as people believe—of the love of women, the love of woman....

And that this love of women or of woman, with me, which has always been there, I would say even before puberty, has always the sense or the impulse to want the best for them and to want to be just with them, or to repair an injustice or to be just, which supposes on the one hand revolt against injustice, but which also supposes, despite everything, a certain compassion, and thus identification with woman. Compassion for woman, identification with woman, which means despite everything that I take the woman inside me, or that I take myself for a woman in a certain way, even though I am, in a massive sense, a heterosexual man, I say to myself that in this movement of identification with woman, of compassion for woman, the concern to do woman justice, to put myself in her place in some way, there must be a femininity. (*Conversations HC-JD*, Ris-Orangis, May 26, 2004)

His women's voices are not just any ones. I will talk about that in another scene.

———————

A few words here to evoke the chameleon character of Jacques Derrida, the one he will have designated with the antonomasis *the animal-that-therefore-*

*I-am* (*following*). An expression that carries from the distance set in the scenes of man's naming of the animals, under the watchful eye of God in Genesis. An old story that had to wait a long time for Jacques Derrida to deconstruct it. Everything is hidden in this animal. By turns cat, hedgehog, silkworm, ram, who is he, in which language does he express himself? Through which voices? In whom, in what way, how is he therefore that?

But what I would like to underscore here is that writing is itself, for him, an animal ruse, a ruse of *protection* (in the etymological sense of this word). To write in order to protect oneself, so as to put pursuers off the scent. The proteiform is also the chameleon that takes on this or that color so as not to be killed. The hedgehog, the ram, all his animal avatars are threatened. He senses writing to be an animal strategy to defend his life. That is why he is interested in the Greek word *problemata*: this word says the shield, what one places in front of oneself to prevent the enemy from advancing, to *anticipate the danger. The problematization* to which he devotes himself all the time — and deconstruction is a manner of problematizing everything — also has this dimension of animal protection, of ruse in order to construct a shelter, bury a secret, hollow out a nest, a burrow, a work, a nest within which one takes shelter, and from which one can exit, where one can welcome but also let oneself be besieged.

In a double movement of his whole being: at the same time as if he were the ram of Abraham and Isaac, the one, the only, who is sacrificed, the one who gives his life for the other; and as if he were Ulysses's ram, the protector, beneath whose shielding belly the sheltered hero escapes execution. A complicated ram presides over his reflection on the two hospitalities, the unconditional and the conditional. Of this ferrying ram, promised and promiser of life and of death, there remains, once the end is passed, supernaturally, a *horn*. This ram's horn comes to life as a bugle, a horn, a shofar. Human animal throat from which is exhaled the endless, ageless cry of the being who remembers and who calls, interrupting with the power of a breath the essential solitude of being.

———————

As for his voices: as if he "gave" the most profound hospitality, not only, perhaps as if these were tutelary presences and they (inaugurated) presided over his so very urgent reflection on the two hospitalities (the unconditional and the conditional).

Today when the question of the welcome given the stranger, the foreigner has become the most *burning*, without metaphor, of all ethical and political questions, when everywhere countries are prey to excluding convulsions, when in Australia so many young Aussies dress up as Nazis, when brother strikes brother, and neighbor neighbor, when not a country in the world, in the East or the West, can believe it is safe from racisms, when globalization is accompanied by an exacerbation of nationalisms, ethnicisms, communitarianisms, fundamentalisms, there is an absolute need to reread and hear again the voice full of all the voices of Jacques Derrida.

---

I cannot "finish" speaking of the speech of Jacques Derrida, of giving speech back to him, my speech, his, of giving him, the time, the duration,

since everything he recalls for us is to be thought as to come, I can therefore only pass on to him, as always, the turn of Jacques Derrida of everything that is to say and to come. Yes, there is, there will always be (Jacques Derrida), something to be thought. There will thus always be Jacques Derrida recalling himself to us, recalling us to the difficult path of the *least:* destroy the least possible, destroy oneself the least possible.

*Notes*

1 Derrida, *Foi et savoir*, 10; "Faith and Knowledge: The Two Sources of 'Religion' at the Limits of Reason Alone," 43.
2 Derrida, *Voyous*, 35; *Rogues*, 14–15.
3 From *bouter*, "to push," thus "to push a point."

# PART II

The *à-venir*: Undoing Sovereignty and Teleology

# Eschatology versus Teleology:
# The Suspended Dialogue between
# Derrida and Althusser

ÉTIENNE BALIBAR

A great philosophy (and Derrida's philosophy is undoubtedly a great one by any standards of depth, originality, complexity, influence, and provocation) can be properly understood and discussed only in terms of its confrontation and interaction with others, more or less "equal," or which at some point allow it to better understand which *choices* it has made. What is at stake here is not just a background or a time, an *esprit du temps*, but it is a little more complicated and compelling than that.

To be sure, this background matters considerably. The terms "French theory" and "structuralism and poststructuralism" refer to its specificity only in a very superficial manner. I prefer to speak of the great debate on *humanism* (humanism as philosophy, humanism as politics) and its relationship with the more technical question of the transformations of anthropology, its temporary or tentative elevation by many contemporaries to the status of foundational discipline. Seen at a distance, it might seem that Althusser and Derrida intersected at least inasmuch as they both took part in the critique of philosophical humanism and related categories, albeit not exactly from the same point of view, since a critique of bourgeois juridical ideology is not the same as a deconstruction of metaphysics, even if their adversaries, or "victims," if you prefer, tended to feel that they were converging. A rereading of certain decisive texts immediately shows that things were probably more complicated and less harmonious than that. For instance, it is difficult (at least for me) to read again "Les fins de l'homme" (written and first published by Derrida in 1968, the same year as Althusser's intervention on *Lénine et la philosophie*) without perceiving that some fairly rude but also allusive criticism directed against those who would have a tendency to easily and hastily depict Hegel, Husserl, and Heidegger as "humanists" could very well refer to Althusser or his followers. But the text also refers to so-called anthropologism as a common implicit assumption of dominant Marxist, social democratic, and Christian democratic political discourses, and to the anthropological reading of Hegel by Kojève, in terms fully compatible with Althusser's own critique of these discourses and readings. In our memory (I say "our" in a generational or quasi-generational sense) there remains the impression that certain deconstructionist arguments concerning in particular the self-negating character of every philosophical use of the category of the *origin* (for example, in Rousseau and his uninterrupted legacy until the present) were fully endorsed and borrowed by the Althusserian critique of philosophy, whereas the general orientation of an anti-Hegelian reading of Marx, or use of Marx to rethink the political, was at least tacitly assumed by Derrida on the other side.

But a more precise examination, in retrospect and perhaps also with a programmatic intention, is needed in order to pass from global classifications, in the style of the "history of ideas," to the understanding of the exact nature of the *points of heresy* articulating discourses, underlying concepts, and opposing trajectories (I am borrowing a Pascalian and Foucauldian terminology here). In this respect, the confrontation of Althusser and Derrida, which has been rarely if at all attempted, is probably as important as the Derrida-Foucault or the Althusser-Foucault or the Derrida-Lacan or the Althusser-Lacan confrontations, but it is also more elusive. I speak of a *suspended dialogue* not only in the sense of a dialogue interrupted by the vicissitudes of life and death, but in the sense of a dialogue that remained virtual, that *should have taken place* but remained blocked and in a sense impossible, for reasons personal (the closer you are in institutional space and the friendlier in sentiments — which also often cover more ambivalent attitudes and feelings — the more difficult it seems to really *discuss*) but also political and conjunctural, and ultimately intrinsic and philosophical. It is our task therefore to construct in retrospect what has remained virtual, and in fact to *create* a philosophical framework within which it becomes possible to have these two voices speak to one another about their philosophical concerns and see if the conversation still means something for our own conjuncture today.

To begin this construction, we apparently have very few elements. We have the implicit references to which I alluded a moment ago in the context of the "humanism-antihumanism" debate. We have scattered references to Derrida (among others) in Althusser's posthumously published drafts and correspondences, sometimes very emphatic and always very general, around the issues of "contingency" and "encounter" (the so-called *matérialisme de la rencontre* or *matérialisme aléatoire* of the "late Althusser"), which seem to suggest that Althusser, while working on, or dreaming of, a radical reformulation of his philosophy in terms of a final "settlement of accounts" with the idea of dialectics (choosing the *materialist* against the *dialectical* side of Marxism, as it were), was trying to draw inspiration from the way Derrida associated his own presentation of the primacy of the future, or better perhaps, the anticipated repetition (iteration) of the "past" in undecidable and unrecognizable forms, with an idea of the essential indetermination of time. The key formula of the "late" (in fact posthumous) Althusser on "le matérialisme aléatoire de la rencontre" (aleatory materialism of the encounter) was a quasi-literal, albeit unacknowledged quotation from Derrida's "La loi du genre" (on Maurice Blanchot), later reprinted in *Parages*.[1] This is tiny, and it is enormous, at least for anyone who is interested in the "Althusser case" in philosophy, not as a sealed story but as an open problem. On his side Derrida seldom referred to Althusser explicitly and from a theoretical point of view, the major exception being a phrase in the middle of *Spectres de Marx*, not surprisingly, we may think. I will in a moment organize my discussion around this phrase, which I will then have to quote at length. But let me add some additional preparatory remarks.

First, *Specters of Marx*, deriving from a paper presented at a conference in Riverside the same year,[2] was published in 1993. This is three years after the death of Althusser, which roughly coincided with the collapse of the Soviet system in Eastern Europe and the proclamation of the End of History by some U.S. ideologues who had taken the Kojevian reading of Hegel without the slightest touch of irony and believed (once again) that they had witnessed its empirical verification. It is therefore not impossible to read in this book, and particularly in the phrase on Althusser, something like an *after-effect* (*ein Nachträgliches*), which is at the same time an *afterthought* and an *after-affect*, combining the labor of mourning with a reflection on the vicissitudes of Marxism and its internal critiques, dissidences, and reconstructions in the postwar period (and more generally in the twentieth century).[3] Althusser and Soviet communism "died" practically in the same year (1989–90), but in both cases (the individual philosopher and the political system) it is possible to assert that the real death had long anticipated the official date. The man who had most eloquently declared that a certain communism and Marxism was in fact a dead corpse, where no theoretical or thinking activity was perceptible (but only to suggest that Marxism could become resurrected in a new theoretical presentation), this man was himself reduced to silence (or had reduced himself to silence) long before he actually died. How could this strange repetition be interpreted? Would it mean that a certain "internal" critique of Marxism was not radical enough, not critical enough? Or would it mean that, in a sense, *politically*, *practically* (to use a more general term), the important aspect of Marxism should not reside in its "truth," therefore also not in what within Marxism would become the focus of much theoretical dispute and epistemological rectification, but in a different element, more immediate and less discursive, the *indeconstructible claim of justice* to which—by chance perhaps, and in any case by historical contingency—according to Derrida it gave its "theoretical" and "practical" form over a century? That was not what Althusser and his followers would have admitted, at least not initially.

But we are tempted to add a supplementary twist to this parallel consideration of the silence or death of Marxism and the silence or death of its internal critics, the "critical Marxists" of various orientations, of whose common inefficacy Althusser could be considered an emblem. It could be added that Derrida thought and claimed that *he had been silenced himself*, that is, that he had accepted (however reluctantly) being silenced himself. He said it in a kind of postscript to *Specters of Marx*: the conversation with Michael Sprinker at the end of the symposium volume *Ghostly Demarcations* (with the title "Marx & Sons"), where he was also asked about his relation to Althusser and the Althusserians in the 1960s.[4] I quote from memory: There was a sort of intellectual *terrorism*, he said, there were things that could not be said, or if said they would not have been heard, or if heard they would have been understood in a wrong way (for example, as a critique of Marxism *from outside*, as there were so many critiques at the time, associating it purely and simply with totalitarianism).

But what does it mean that they could, or could not, have been said? *Who says* this was the case? That is Derrida in 1993, mourning his friend and intimate adversary, not to say rival, *regretting* that for a number of personal and general reasons a conversation, a controversy perhaps, did not take place twenty or twenty-five years before, when the status of Marxism was totally different. And what should have been the content, the *object* of that discussion? Presumably what was *now* being said, in 1993: that the important element of Marxism with respect to politics was not its scientific or theoretical element, not its ideological element either (for example, its religious, or secular-religious side), but rather its "spectral" element, or the spectral element that it more or less willingly and consciously transmitted or reiterated, which is located beyond the distinction of the scientific and the ideological, in a quasi-transcendental manner. This was said in 1993, twenty-five years after 1968, *as if* it could have been said at the time of the intellectual domination of Marxism in the form of various critical Marxisms.[5] But the fact is that we return to this question again later, in a new situation where it is not the death of Marxism but the crisis of capitalism that is trumpeted by many. And, again, our retrospective readings change their conditions.

From all this I draw two conclusions. The first is that the virtual controversy between Althusser and Derrida *is not and still is* about "Marxism." It is not about Marxism, but about much more general issues: science, ideology, metaphysics, politics, teleology, therefore historical time and the ends of history. But it is about Marxism because *the fact is* that Marxism concentrates and perhaps keeps concentrating these issues in a manner that crosses politics with philosophy without equivalents. This was true yesterday and is true today. Hence my second conclusion: there have been successive conjunctures. In 1965–68, Althusser was criticizing Marxism *from the inside* of a "Marxist" organization in order to amend it or reformulate it. Derrida was or had been pushed aside, therefore could not speak about it. In 1993 it was Althusser who was eliminated and Derrida who somehow managed to make Marx and Marxism speak — one effect of this being the necessity to criticize Althusser's critique (or indicate the necessity of such a critique). And in 2006 neither of them is here. On the other hand, we witness what we believe we are able to describe at the same time as an unchallenged expansion of capitalism, involving millions of new humans in its "industrial revolution," *and* a deep crisis of its capacity to regulate contemporary societies. One of the consequences — already to be observed — might be, will be, sooner or later, *the return of Marxism*. But in which form? That is the entire question. What Derrida described as a specter could materialize again, with or without an organized support (party, forum, network, etc.). It would also, for that reason, lose its quasi-transcendental function and become again a science or an ideology (perhaps a religion, or an antireligion). Is this a good thing? Well, it cannot be entirely bad, the dismissal of Marxism having deprived us and our contemporaries of a much needed critical instrument. But I suspect that it is also the right time to try to crystallize the dialogue which has remained suspended, because the virtual interlocutors were never in a position to speak to each other, in the same time or context. This is what I have in mind while summoning these specters.

And now I will start again, in a second wave. To the texts! Let us first read again what Derrida writes about Althusser in *Specters*:

> To critique, to call for interminable self-critique is still to distinguish between everything and almost everything. Now, if there is a spirit of Marxism which I will never be ready to renounce, it is not only the critical idea or the questioning stance. . . . It is even more a certain emancipatory and *messianic* affirmation, a certain experience of the promise that one can try to liberate from any dogmatics and even from any metaphysical-religious determination, from any *messianism*. And a promise must promise to be kept, that is, not to remain "spiritual" or "abstract," but to produce events, new effective forms of action, practice, organization, and so forth. To break with the "party-form" or with some form of the State or the International does not mean to give up every form of practical or effective organization. It is exactly the contrary that matters to us here. In saying that, one is in opposition to two dominant tendencies: *on the one hand*, the most vigilant and most modern reinterpretations of Marxism by certain Marxists (notably French Marxists and those around Althusser)[6] who believed that they must instead try to dissociate Marxism from any teleology or from any messianic eschatology (but my concern is precisely to distinguish the latter from the former); *on the other hand*, anti-Marxist interpretations that determine their own emancipatory eschatology by giving it a metaphysical or onto-theological content that is always deconstructible. A deconstructive thinking, the one that matters to me here, has always pointed out the irreducibility of affirmation and therefore of the promise, as well as the undeconstructibility of a certain idea of justice. . . . This critique belongs to the movement of an experience open to the absolute future of what is coming, that is to say, a necessarily indeterminate, abstract, desert-like experience that is confided, exposed, given up to its waiting for the other and for the event.[7]

When you reread this passage carefully (I had to omit the broader environment) you realize that nearly every important theme of the book is concentrated here, around one target which concerns Althusser's (and "his followers'") incapacity to make a *conceptual* distinction between "teleology" and "eschatology" (or "messianic eschatology"), his (their) incapacity to really understand that these are two different concepts and problems. Among the consequences are his (their) wrong tendency to concentrate the critique on "teleology" (or *finalism*); his (their) insistence on opposing "science" (which is not or should not be teleological) and "ideology" (which is both "teleological" and "eschatological"), on stripping Marxism of its "ideological" (or its *imaginary*) elements, in order to isolate and liberate the theoretical or "scientific" elements; his (their) recurring to Spinoza and Freud to ground this radical dichotomy of the ideological-imaginary and the scientific-conceptual in a formal epistemology and a substantial ontology. *But perhaps more than all that:* his (their) incapacity to locate the main problem on the side of "eschatology."

And this, again, possibly, on two accounts. *First*, it would be the incapacity (or refusal) to concentrate the critical and self-critical deconstructive work on the eschatological element of Marxism, with its ambivalent characteristics which directly lead to the riddle of the messianic (or *messianicity*) *with and without* messianism. Does the revolutionary (emancipatory) *injunction*, the calling, awaiting, promising of the *other* of capitalism, which testifies *from the inside* for its impossibility, or its impossible realization, necessarily involve the "ontotheological" messianism of the proletariat as collective (hardly) secularized Redeemer of Mankind, whose "necessary" advent and victory would have been prepared by the whole history of technologies, economies, and societies? This is, as we know, the crucial question ceaselessly asked by Derrida. But also, *second*, this strange philosophical confusion of teleology and eschatology would perhaps prevent Althusser from noticing and discussing *his own eschatological problem*, almost certainly concentrated in his understanding of the *present time*, the "conjuncture," the current situation, which he saw characterized by an impossible tension between the *irreversible* union or fusion of Marxist theory with the labor movement, therefore the imminence of revolution, and a tragic *scission* of the revolutionary movement itself, separated from itself as it were on the side of theory as on the side of practice, which made this imminent achievement impossible. In reality, we "Althusserians" should have been aware that this was a repetition of the form in which, particularly in the *18th Brumaire*, Marx himself had tried to account for the paradoxical coexistence of imminent revolution and triumphant counterrevolution in the same conjuncture. What would Derrida have said if he knew some of the "private" correspondences of Althusser in which, prompted by the emergence of liberation theology, he advocated the reunification of the two great messianic organizations, the Communist Party and the Catholic Church, to make possible the triumph of communism, already there in the "loopholes" of capitalist society?[8] But in fact he may have known them, or heard of them.

But all this prejudges the issue. Are *teleology* (or the doctrine of the historical and intellectual process as *realization of an already given end or telos*, a
process with a conscious or unconscious *purpose*) and *eschatology* (or the
speculation on *ta eskhata*: the "extreme" or "ultimate" moments and events
which immediately precede or accompany the end of history, its reversal into
eternity) radically distinct? And what is the point in opposing them, not only
as concepts, but as *problems*? Everybody understands that this is a complicated problem, which has deep roots in the history of philosophy and its
relationship to theology, and which particularly concerns the modalities of
displaying a philosophical *discourse on the essence of time* before and after Hegel
(therefore also a philosophical discourse on *praxis, violence, community*). This
is not the moment to fully develop such a discussion; there is no room for
that, and I will have to do it in greater detail some coming day. For the time
being, I will limit myself to summarizing what I think should be said in this
respect and indicate schematically which conclusions it could lead to.

Let me then enunciate three points and indicate why they seem significant, before I give more precise details on each and conclude (without
concluding, in the absolute sense).

The first point I want to insist on is the fact that Derrida himself was not
always a defender of a rigorous distinction between the problems of teleology and eschatology, that is, the problem of the orientation and meaning of
*history* and the problem of the *event* which interrupts history, or "comes after
its end" and therefore manifests its limits in the very moment in which they
are exceeded or transcended.

The second point concerns the fact that Althusser renounced teleology
rather rapidly to formulate his critique of Marxist evolutionism and historicism in terms of a rejection of teleology, in particular because he defended the idea that there was a crucial aspect of the Hegelian legacy in
philosophy (including Marxism) which went *beyond teleology*: what he called
the "process without a subject or an end," which in fact followed closely the
way Hegel himself had *overcome* (or *aufgehoben*) the problem of teleology in
the *Logic* and the *Encyclopaedia*.

The third point concerns the fact that the dilemma of a political philosophy of time oriented toward the analysis of the *tendencies and the results* of
historical becoming, thus "teleology," and a political philosophy of time
oriented toward the *radical uncertainty* of the meaning and the outcome of a
situation deemed "extreme" or "apocalyptic," where the forces of exploitation and the forces of emancipation are neutralizing each other, is not a

dilemma that is projected on Marx from outside, by philosophical or theological readings of his work. It is a dilemma that crosses and divides his entire conception of capitalist development and anticapitalist revolution.

The consequence of all this could be that Derrida was entirely right to draw our attention to the importance of such a distinction, but may have been a little quick in attributing the blockage of Marxism and internal critiques of Marxism along Althusserian lines to a simple neglect of taking into account the eschatological element. And it could even lead us to suggest, in a sort of epistemological *chiasm*, that if Derrida had some excellent reasons to suggest that Althusser, because he was *still* a prisoner of the metaphysical, anti-eschatological element in Hegel (and in Marx),[9] remained unable to specify a content for what he was constantly requesting, namely, a *political future for communism*, beyond the logic of capitalist historical tendencies, on his side Althusser might have had some good reasons to resist such a conclusion by in fact denouncing in the motive of eschatology — even and above all a *negative* eschatology — a restoration of the Kantian moment of a teleology "without a (given or determinable) telos," a *zwecklose Zweckmässigkeit*. This would not be a deconstruction of the metaphysics of becoming, or the actualization of the virtual, which every modern philosophy ultimately inherited from Aristotle, but in fact a return to its *subjective form* (associated with the phenomenological experiences of waiting, hoping, imagining, or postponing the "end"). Not by chance it would coincide with what Derrida suddenly (and particularly in *Specters of Marx*) declared to be the *indeconstructible aspect of deconstruction* (identified with Justice, or Justice to come beyond every Law), therefore an *absolute*, at least in its formulation, which religion and philosophy always associated with the element of Faith. The consequence would be something like a philosophical neutralization, a reciprocal "grip" or critical control of each of the interlocutors over his adversary. But it is such a purely static or destructive conclusion that I want precisely to qualify, and in fact to avoid drawing.

---

On the first point, it will suffice, I believe, to recall a famous passage in "Les fins de l'homme" ("The Ends of Man") in which Derrida discusses the anthropological character of the Hegelian phenomenology or, rather, of the "subject" of phenomenology, called here "consciousness" and presented as the unity of the finite and the infinite, the human and the divine, the singular and the collective, therefore the resolution of the metaphysical antinomies.

Such a unity — speculative indeed — has to be considered at the same time a *destination* and a sublimated *death*, and for that reason it is not only associated with the perfection of metaphysics but with its (onto)theological determination, with the theological dimension of the reference to an end or a destination of the human, which is present in every humanism (including Marxism):

> All the structures described by the phenomenology of spirit . . . are the structures of that which has *relevé* man. In them, man remains in relief. His essence rests in *Phenomenology*. This equivocal relationship of *relief* doubtless marks the end of man, man past, but by the same token it also marks the achievement of man, the appropriation of his essence. *It is the end of finite man* [*C'est la fin de l'homme fini*]. The end of the finitude of man, the unity of the finite and the infinite, the finite as the surpassing of the self — these essential themes of Hegel's are to be recognized at the end of the Anthropology when consciousness is finally designated as the "infinite relationship to self." The *relève* or *relevance* of man is his *telos* or *eskhaton*. The unity of these two *ends* of man, the unity of his death, his completion, his accomplishment, is enveloped in the Greek thinking of *telos*, in the discourse on *telos*, which is also a discourse on *eidos*, on *ousia*, and on *alētheia*. Such a discourse, in Hegel as in the entirety of metaphysics, indissociably coordinates teleology with an eschatology, a theology, and an ontology. . . . What is difficult to think today is an end of man which would not be organized by a dialectics of truth and negativity, an end of man which would not be a teleology in the first person plural. . . . The *we* is the unity of absolute knowledge and anthropology, of God and man, of onto-theo-teleology and humanism. '*Being*' and language — the group of languages — that the *we* governs or opens: such is the name of that which assures the transition between metaphysics and humanism via the *we*. . . . The teleology which governs Husserl's transcendental phenomenology can be read in the same opening. Despite the critique of anthropologism, "humanity," here, is still the name of the being to which the transcendental *telos* — determined as Idea (in the Kantian sense) or even as Reason — is announced. . . . Man is that which is in relation to his end, in the fundamentally equivocal sense of the word. Since always. The transcendental end can appear to itself and be unfolded only on the condition of mortality, of a relation to finitude as the origin of ideality. The name of man has always been inscribed in metaphysics between these two ends. It has meaning only in this eschato-teleological situation.[10]

The text continues, insisting on the fact that such an eschatological-teleological representation of the "Human" can be deconstructed only from the inside (this is a very significant thematic occurrence of the term "deconstruction," which had been used before mostly for its etymology). Derrida performs this deconstruction by developing a reading of Heidegger's *Dasein* in which he emphasizes the ambiguous relationship of this ontological-existential category with the anthropological essence, the idea of the Human as such in every human being, namely, its proximity with being, which at the same time erases the reference to a natural "human species" *and* absolutizes the relationship with the Non-Human, or the in-human (for example, animality). The same discussion is carried on in every other discussion of Heidegger, particularly in "*Geschlecht* II: Heidegger's Hand," and *Apories* (*Mourir — s'attendre aux limits de la vérité*), where Derrida proposes a criterion for the reversal or displacement toward a *different*, *nonmetaphysical* consideration of eschatology and ta eschata (the extremes and extremities), namely, *the substitution of the Other's death*, or the acceptance of the death of the Other (hence the labor of mourning) for Heideggerian authenticity, which is only the appropriation of *one's own death*, as the only indisputable *proper* (*das eigene*), the "possibility of the impossible."

Now this puts us on the track of where Derrida might have acknowledged, in the form of a reading, that *there is an eschatological discourse which is irreducible to metaphysics*, ontotheology, and therefore teleology as well. It is not in Heidegger, in spite of his having himself insisted on the difference of the two notions, particularly in his essay on Anaximander ("Der Spruch des Anaximander"), once again emphasizing the purity and unique character of the Greek origin. As many readers have suggested, it is rather in Levinas, who associated the imperative of responsibility to any Other who is completely other with a notion of the *infinity of time*, implying that it is as such "without an end."[11]

But it is above all in Benjamin where the messianic dimension is explicit. I completely endorse the idea that the critical dialogue with Benjamin (whose reading by Derrida — in which year? — should mark something like a break) forms the deepest motive of Derrida's retrieval — dare we say also *relève* or *Aufhebung* — of the eschatological perspective, therefore immediately confers upon its invocation of a "we," a community involving the living and the dead, a theologico-political character. But this is also where, perhaps, Derrida should admit that the Aufhebung, as always, must remain ambiguous in its own terms. After all, just as the Heideggerian *Dasein* proves to become even more essentially human when it is dissociated from the name "Man," the *Other* and the *Dead* and finally the *Specter* (as the *Angel*) can appear as even more fully theological entities in the moment in which they are deprived of the substantial, redemptory, all-powerful aspects of historically religious divinities. In short, "messianic without messianism," the formula coined by Derrida after a model borrowed from Blanchot, which marks the distance with Benjamin and the whole Jewish-utopian-socialist-Marxist tradition,[12] is a *question* much more than an answer. It should be permanently qualified by adding the phrase Derrida uses whenever he refers to the eschatological categories (Gift, Pardon, Justice, Event, and the Incalculable): *if it exists, if there is such a thing*. And perhaps even: if it has meaning, if it can be thought.

Let us turn to Althusser now, in an equally telegraphic and abstract manner. I am particularly thinking of the developments in *Reading Capital* on "historical time" and "absolute historicism." It is striking that Althusser here no longer explicitly uses the category "teleology," as he did, for example, in *Pour Marx* when criticizing readings of philosophical texts which located their truth-content in the *final* problematic into which their analytical elements should become integrated, from an evolutionist point of view (as in the famous case of the "young Marx" and the "mature Marx"). But, by way of a summary of the Hegelian Idea that had been transferred into a certain Marxism, a certain Marx, and even to a large extent into Marx's own perception of his "dialectical" transformation of the economy, Althusser provides what is perhaps one of the clearest definitions of teleology (and the metaphysics of telos) ever written. See, for example, this passage:

> Il suffit de franchir encore un pas dans la logique du savoir absolu, de penser le développement de l'histoire qui culmine et s'accomplit dans le présent d'une science identique à la conscience, et de réfléchir ce résultat dans une rétrospection fondée, pour concevoir toute l'histoire économique (ou autre) comme le développement, au sens hégélien, d'une forme simple, primitive, originaire, par exemple la valeur, immédiatement présente dans la marchandise, et pour lire *Le Capital* comme une *déduction logico-historique* de toutes les catégories économiques à partir d'une catégorie originaire, la catégorie de valeur ou encore la catégorie de *travail*. Sous cette condition la méthode d'exposition du *Capital* se confond avec la genèse spéculative du concept. Bien plus, cette genèse spéculative du concept est identique avec la genèse du concret réel lui-même, c'est-à-dire avec le processus de l'histoire empirique.[13]

On the other hand, if you read the passages in Althusser concerning the question of the *historical present* while considering Derrida's question about the "metaphysics of presence," you realize that Althusser has adopted the deconstructive criterion of the *irreducible absence within presence* itself, what he also calls "non-contemporaneity," "inequality," and "over- and under-determination," as the ultimate instrument of his criticism against the "empirical-speculative concept of time." But this is not all: he also completely organizes his discourse around the possibility of distinguishing, essentially separating two regimes of presence, therefore of actuality and activity: the "presence" of *consciousness*, of *representation* (which is presence *for itself*, since every consciousness must be grounded in self-consciousness), and the presence of *conjuncture*, of "situations" and "events," by their very nature unpredictable and irreducible to the accomplishment of a preexisting law:

> Cela revient à dire que si nous ne pouvons pas effectuer dans l'histoire de "coupe d'essence," c'est dans l'unité spécifique de la structure complexe du tout que nous devons penser ces soi-disant retards, avances, survivances, inégalités de développement, qui *co-existent* dans la structure du présent historique réel: le présent de la *conjoncture*. Parler de types d'historicités différentielles n'a donc aucun sens en référence à un temps de base, où pourraient être mesurés ces retards et ces avances. . . . Parler de temporalité historique différentielle . . . c'est s'obliger à définir ce qui a été appelé sa *surdétermination* ou sa *sous-détermination*, en fonction de la structure de détermination du tout. . . . Et cela n'est rien d'autre que la théorie de la conjoncture indispensable à la théorie de l'histoire.[14]

Indeed, from a Derridean point of view such distinctions ultimately remain metaphysical, since they are based on concepts of "totality" and "causality" (or, as Althusser prefers to say in *Reading Capital*, "efficacy" and "efficiency," implicitly referring to the ancient notion of *causa efficiens*). They are also based on the insistence on the primacies of the invisible over the visible, the conceptual over the metaphoric, the eternal "in [a] spinozistic sense" over the temporal or the lived experience. This is fully consistent with Althusser's later proclamation that there is an element in Hegel which "escapes ideology," namely, the *positive* (or "scientific," *wissenschaftlich*) idea of the *absolute method*, as it is presented in the final section of the *Logic*, as "infinite process" or "transition" (*Fortgang, Progress*), which Althusser would retranslate as "process without a subject or an end," a process coming from nowhere and leading to nowhere. In Hegel this category is presented as the logical overcoming (Aufhebung) of "teleology" as such, that is, of the transcendental discussion concerning the point whether the ends, or goals, of a process such as knowledge, history, or life are *objective* real tendencies or *subjective* representations. But the teleological question is abolished if there are no ends or goals, because there is no end or final result, in short no telos from the point of view of the "absolute." Now in my opinion this does not show that Althusser "in the end" remained or became again a *Hegelian.* (Although I must say that the publishing of his early thesis, "L'idée de contenu dans la philosophie de Hegel,"[15] has forced me to think again about that. In any case, Althusser was always consistently Hegelian when it was a question of not being Kantian, as perhaps Derrida was always consistently Heideggerian when it was a question of not being Hegelian.) But in fact there is *no end* here either; this is not a *final stage*, it is only a moment that does not pass immediately, a question that remains open. I would tend to say that the Hegelian "process without a subject" is not Althusser's final word, but only the *site* where he himself desperately struggles toward an alternative to teleology, an alternative that would not be eschatological, messianic even "without messianism," that is, that would be radically *secular* or, his preferred word, "materialist."

I said "desperately" struggles. This is not completely accurate, and there is a text that could testify to the opening of the alternative. This is the manuscript *Machiavelli and Us*, practically finished in the early 1970s (the manuscript shows only minor corrections later than 1972) but published only posthumously, and after Derrida published *Specters of Marx*. I don't know if Derrida ever read it; in any case I know of no explicit oral or written reference to it. But if *we* compare this text with Derrida's deconstruction of eschatology and (anti-)eschatological wording of deconstruction, his attempt to in fact *liberate messianicity* (or the irreducible promise of emancipation) *from its association with eschatological messianism* (the awaiting of a Redeemer or redeeming force), without annihilating the idea of the *coming event* (or the event "to come"), we may have the feeling that we have actually reached the *point of heresy* around which the two discourses are antithetically disposed, or that we have arrived as close as possible to this point (an "absent" point, needless to say). This is where the enigmatic *repetition* of Derrida's phrase on "l'expérience aléatoire de la rencontre" as "le matérialisme aléatoire de la rencontre" — perhaps itself an unintentional "encounter," who knows? — which Althusser referred to as the Machiavellian interplay of *virtù* and *fortuna* (or "agency" and "chance"), becomes crucial. This is indeed where *two concepts of the event* and the relationship between the idea of the event and the idea of action, or transformation, or bifurcation within time, violently clash, because they are as close as possible to one another but ultimately incompatible, almost like reverse images. One concept sets the event, in fact the revolutionary event, as the *beginning*, contingent but without any predictable end, which occurs within the sudden *void*, or *opening* of the historical process, perhaps the void (this is the Machiavellian model) which has been created by *acting* itself, preceding or crystallizing its own conditions of possibility. The other concept sets the event as an interruption of time (this is Derrida's Benjaminian legacy), or manifestation of the heterogeneity, the "Out-of-Joint-ness" of time, where the possibility of the impossible becomes thinkable, therefore also imaginable, or imaginable without images, without an *incarnation*, in the form of "hopeless actions," always placed under the possibility, and in fact the inevitability, that the coming of justice will also be the repetition of death or the return of absolute violence.

To conclude, I will refer again to Marx himself. As I said a moment ago, without demonstration admittedly, the two kinds of philosophical problems which we try to associate with a critique of teleology as an ideology of the meaning of history, and with an eschatological (or anti-eschatological) question concerning the radical uncertainty of "revolutionary" situations, are both present, in fact they are decisive in Marx himself as a *text*, or a *texture*, a clearing of traces rather than a system or a doctrine. Marx was permanently obsessed with the possibility, more and more revealed by his "critique of political economy" and his observation of contemporary developments in the organization of firms and markets, that the immanent tendencies of capitalism, its so-called historical laws, would lead not to the simple *necessity of communism*, the "expropriation of expropriators" (a biblical messianic formula), but to a *multiplicity of possible outcomes*, contradictory with one another, including the possibility of a "simulacrum" of socialism within the limits of capitalism itself—not only a "capitalist socialization of labor" but a *capitalist socialism*. And he was haunted, particularly in the periods of bloody and failed revolutions (in 1848, in 1871), by the question of the *imminent reversal* or the *reversal to come* of catastrophic nihilistic conjunctures of bourgeois history (the general economic crises and the "global" wars at the scale of his time), into a communist breakthrough, where the proletariat would suddenly pass from the status of a crushed multitude to the condition of a "universal class," leading humankind as such to emancipation, particularly through its association with internationalism. It seems to me that, without each of them being restricted to one single side of this problematic divide, it could be said nevertheless that the ways Althusser and Derrida are *questioning Marx*, therefore *transforming Marx*, somehow mirror this symmetry. While reflecting on Marx's relation to philosophy, theology, and politics, they would have dug their holes beneath the Marxian surface on each side of the divide, the "teleological" and the "eschatological," producing something like an *antiteleology* and an *anti-eschatology*. Hence the importance of distinguishing both terms, as Derrida insists, but also of understanding why they constantly intersect around the political debate on *the future* (and the *future of the future*),[16] which is always also religious (perhaps the single definition of "religion" that we could give is: it is the concern for the future) and philosophical (since there is no question more fundamental, and more divisive to philosophy, than to elaborate a "critical concept of time"). And to the extent that today we are likely to witness a renewed interest in Marx, therefore a reactivation of his typical dilemmas, beyond or beneath the ready-made formulas, laws, and prophecies of "Marxism," the suspended dialogue of Althusser and Derrida seems to me of extraordinary relevance.[17]

## Notes

1 Cf. Althusser, *Écrits philosophiques et politiques*, vol. 1. Althusser's text (extracted from a larger manuscript, until now unpublished) contains several references to Derrida (539, 551, 561–63). Derrida's original formulation is to be found in his essay on Blanchot, "La loi du genre," 278–79: "Ce sont 'presque toujours' des femmes qui dissent *oui, oui*. A la vie à la mort. Ce 'presque toujours' évite de traiter le féminin comme une puissance générale et générique, il fait sa part à l'événement, à la performance, à l'aléa, à la rencontre. Et c'est bien depuis l'expérience aléatoire de la rencontre que 'je' parle ici." Since Derrida's essay was originally read as a paper for an international literary conference in July 1979, then published in French in 1980 and in English in 1981, that is, exactly the moment in which Althusser mentally collapsed (and killed his wife, then was hospitalized), it seems to me extremely unlikely that Althusser knew this passage when he wrote his own notes, allegedly in 1982 (therefore, in the hospital). Unless Derrida, who regularly visited him, had brought a copy of his talk or told Althusser what it was about. In any case, it would be another example of "encounter."

2 An international, multidisciplinary conference, "Whither Marxism? Global Crises in International Perspective," held April 22–24, 1993, at the University of California, Riverside, Center for Ideas and Society.

3 Derrida himself addressed the issue of the relationship between the writing and the themes of *Specters of Marx* and his ambivalent relationship to Althusser in a long

passage of his conversations with Elisabeth Roudinesco: *De quoi demain* (*For What Tomorrow*, 78–80).

4  Sprinker, *Ghostly Demarcations*.

5  To complicate (perhaps blur) this pattern of retroactive construction of the scene of the dialogue, Derrida in *Specters* takes his departure, in particular, from an essay by Maurice Blanchot, "Les trois paroles de Marx," which was initially published in 1968 with the title "Lire Marx" (echoing the Althusserian *Lire le Capital*), before being reprinted in 1971 in *L'amitié*.

6  The French text has "notamment français, et autour d'Althusser."

7  Derrida, *Specters of Marx*, 89–90; *Spectres de Marx*, 146–48.

8  I am referring to unpublished letters and an essay with the title "Thèses de juin" (around 1985), which can be consulted in the Althusser Archive at the Institut Mémoires de l'Edition Contemporaine, Caen.

9  Hegel rejects the eschatological question particularly in the *Phenomenology of Spirit*, at the end of chapter 7, when he gives his interpretation of the Christian idea of the "Death of God."

10 Derrida, "The Ends of Man," 121–23; "Les fins de l'homme," 143–47.

11 Levinas, *Totalité et infini*.

12 See the remarkable book by Löwy, *Rédemption et utopie*.

13 Althusser, *Lire le Capital*, 319. I quote from the new French edition, Presses Universitaires de France, collection Quadrige.

14 Ibid., 293.

15 Now translated by Goshgarian as *The Specter of Hegel: Hey! Hey!*

16 Derrida implicitly refers to the analyses of Koselleck and others on *Erwartungshorizonte* and the representations of the future which themselves have a history, a past, and a future.

17 When finishing this paper I found a recent book by a leading contemporary Marxist, Samir Amin, which interestingly is called *Spectres of Capitalism: A Critique of Current Intellectual Fashions*. There are a few pages on Althusser and on Derrida, but neither of the philosophical questions posed here is addressed. Both Althusser and Derrida are considered, to some degree, as ignoring the positivity of Marx's economic, sociological, and political analyses and forecasts.

# The Untimely Secret of Democracy

PHENG CHEAH

Reproaches about the apolitical nature of deconstruction are widespread in contemporary criticism. In many respects, they recall the questions Jean Beaufret posed to Heidegger in 1946 concerning the implications of his thought for political action and ethics, which led to the writing of the "Letter on Humanism." At stake is the bearing of a fundamental delimitation of metaphysics or ontology on the political sphere. It is, however, the very form of the question—that it is a matter of the relation of deconstruction to politics, of deconstruction's consequences for politics—that Derrida puts into question. He explicitly rejects the suggestion that deconstruction did not initially have a political dimension, that deconstruction and the political occupied distinct spheres, and that in response to critics, there was an ethico-political turn that sought to bring about a rapprochement.[1] Yet Derrida has also insisted that his engagement with the political did not constitute a political theory, and that justice and democracy are not only political concepts.

The aims of this chapter are threefold. First, I connect the early Derrida's deconstruction of Western metaphysics to his later interventions concerning the political in order to arrive at a more precise understanding of the cobelonging of *différance* and the political by showing how the question of the gift of time always already involves a delimitation of the political ontology of sovereignty. I then discuss how such a delimitation leads to a paleonymy of democracy in Derrida's thought of "democracy to come" (*démocratie à venir*), a democracy that cannot be reduced to positive historical forms of democracy even though it has a necessary relationship to them. Finally, I offer a critical assessment of democracy to come within the framework of contemporary globalization.

*Différance and Political Metaphysics:*
*Sovereignty, Ipseity, and Autoimmunity*

Throughout his corpus, Derrida was obsessed with the question of how it is that there is time. What is it that gives time? How do we and other beings in the world continue to be, to endure and survive beyond this or that moment? Derrida's formulation of the aporia of time radicalizes the problem of finitude in a manner that undermines any recourse to an infinite being capable of origination and, indeed, any desire for presence. Such a desire, he argued, still marked Heidegger's understanding of the original finitude of temporality. For Derrida, time is without being and is never simply present. It is neither an object nor a given. Yet we can apprehend time only through what it is not, namely, the objects that fill its form. Indeed, because time is not a thing, it is not part of temporality. Hence, even our experience of time as a succession of temporal presents is already an annulment of time in which it becomes "an instant already caught up in the temporalizing synthesis."[2]

Derrida argues that the thinking of time without presence necessarily leads to the gift and the pure event because they are also characterized by nonphenomenality. A genuine gift can appear only in its effacement and violation, for once it enters into the circuit of reciprocity, restitution, and exchange it is annulled. If it is not to be annulled, a gift cannot be apparent because its mere recognition by the donor or the donee will lead to indebtedness and the expectation of repayment, or at least self-gratification, praise, or self-congratulation for having been generous. Hence, the very preservation of the gift requires that it *not be recognized at all and not be identified as such* (*GT*, 13–14). The gift is aporetic because it can appear, preserve, and be present to itself only by being destroyed. In Derrida's words, the giving of time is "a giving that gives without giving anything and without anyone giving anything" (*GT*, 20). The gift is thus an apposite figure for the "experience" of time under conditions of radical finitude. First, this giving cannot be referred back to an infinite being that lies outside time, a donor who gives time, as it were. Such a donor would merely be a transcendent exteriority, either a divine presence or an absent cause or ground qua occulted presence. But by the same token, the gift of time also cannot be understood in terms of Heidegger's opposition between an original temporality and a vulgar, derived temporality. Temporalization is an annulment of time in the same way that any identification destroys the gift because temporalization involves "anticipatory expectation or apprehension that grasps or comprehends in advance" (*GT*, 14). But this annulment is not a fall into inauthenticity because time is not a pure presence but can be presented only by being destroyed. Better yet, time is the very process of presentation through annulment, the movement of self-contamination.

The same aporetic structure characterizes the pure event. Just as a gift cannot be recognized, an event cannot be one if it is anticipated in advance, if we can tell when and from where it is or will be coming. The event is that which is or comes from the entirely other. Hence, it can be experienced only as an unexpected eruption, an absolute surprise: "[A] gift or an event that would be foreseeable, necessary, conditioned, programmed, expected, counted on would not be lived as either a gift or as an event. . . . This is why the condition common to the gift and the event is a certain unconditionality (*Unbedingtheit*). . . . The event and the gift, the event as gift, the gift as event must be irruptive, unmotivated. . . . [The event and the gift] obey nothing, except perhaps principles of disorder" (*GT*, 122–23). The deconstructive thinking of the event as something that comes from beyond the order of presence thus breaks with Heidegger's understanding of *Ereignis* as the movement of propriation and coming into presence. Instead of being a form of presence, the true event is that which is always still to come.

This appeal to an unconditionality beyond presence indicates that there is something structurally untimely about our experience of time. First, temporalization as the conservation and maintenance of the present is a violation of the gift of time. But second, our being in time presupposes an otherness that tears or rends the flow of temporality. This alterity puts time out of joint. But since it gives time and is the coming of the event, it also makes possible and renews the flow of temporal presents. These two senses of the untimely—the conservative and the radically disruptive—correspond to the two senses of différance laid out in Derrida's 1968 essay: différance as the restricted economy of the play of differences and deferment in the constitution of any present being in its sameness, and différance as the relation to the entirely other that interrupts and disrupts every economy. The movement of deconstruction *takes place in* and *is* the transaction between absolute alterity and the order of presence. The unconditional other is non-deconstructible. But as it is inscribed within and gives rise to presence, as it is *experienced* within presence as the latter's condition of possibility and impossibility, it renders presence deconstructible. This quasi-transcendental operation is always already at play whenever any being, substance, or subject is in time, that is, constitutes and maintains itself as present.

The deconstruction of the political is grounded in the aporia of time. In 1968, Derrida had already linked différance to the political by observing that différance cannot be derived, "mastered and governed on the basis of the point of a present being, which itself could be some thing, a form, a state, a power in the world."[3] The political is always already metaphysical because it is a form of presence, whether this is understood as the calculative reason of a collective subject, a faculty, a capacity, or a force. Positive historical cases of political power and their institutional forms enact and put into practice a political ontology of presence. Hence, Derrida's writings after the alleged ethicopolitical turn merely elaborate the aporias of the political qua presence through an open-ended series of terms that arise from a specific situation, site of analysis, or context of intervention, where the order of presence is opened up to the inscription of the unconditional, for instance, the interruptive renewal of the circle of political economy by the chance of the gift, or the suspension of the calculations of law by an incalculable justice.

The metaphysical concept at the heart of democracy is sovereignty. In *Rogues*, Derrida suggests that sovereignty is reducible to ipseity, the power of a finite self that is not yet a subject, intentional consciousness, or person to constitute itself by giving itself its own law through the circular motion of relating or returning to itself as its own end. This power is an a priori sovereignty necessarily precomprehended by any positive case of political sovereignty. "Before any sovereignty of the state, of the nation-state, of the monarch, or in democracy, of the people, ipseity names a principle of legitimate sovereignty, the accredited or recognized supremacy of a power or a force, a *kratos* or a *cracy*" (R, 12/31). The political form the Greeks call democracy is the power that inheres in a people's ipseity. "Democracy would be precisely this, a force (*kratos*), a force in the form of a sovereign authority (sovereign, that is, *kurios* or *kuros*, having the power to decide, to be decisive, to prevail, to have reason over or win out over [*avoir raison de*] and to give the force of law, *kuroo*), and thus the power and ipseity of the people (*demos*)" (R, 13/33).

This power is coextensive with freedom understood as "the faculty . . . to do as one pleases, to decide, to choose to determine *oneself*, to have self-determination, to be master, and first of all master of oneself (*autos, ipse*)" (R, 22–23/45). The problem, however, is that a finite being's ipseity is always problematic. Because it cannot give itself time, it is always self-divided in the very constitution of its self through the iterability that allows it to relate to the same as itself. Its sovereignty thus always involves the returning detour of a circle, and this opens up sovereignty and freedom, sovereignty as freedom, to various turns and suspensions of freedom. We can schematize the correspondence between the aporias of time and sovereignty as follows: just as time as presence and a temporalized series of stigmatic points of the "now" is constituted and maintained through a restricted economy of difference and deferment that intimates a structural exposure to the radical alterity that gives time, so too the stigmatic indivisibility of sovereignty is constituted by various turnings that structurally open up sovereign ipseity to contamination by something unconditional.

In the aporia of time, the contamination moves in two directions. First, the gift's impossible phenomenality means that time necessarily gives itself to be violated by being arrested as duration and presence. Second, since the gift constitutes and renews time as presence and the temporal flow of "now"s, an alterity also divides the present and tears the flow of time. In *Rogues*, these two forms of contamination are concretely inflected in "specific" aporias of the democratic form of sovereignty. In his reading of Aristotle's *Politics*, Derrida points to a primary suspension of freedom within the very concept of democracy. Democracy pursues two fundamental goals: freedom and equality. But because equality is determined according to numbers and not worth, the decision of the majority constitutes justice. This means that democracy's two goals can be achieved only circuitously. A member of a democracy governs because he is free. But he is governed in turn because equality according to numbers means that he is governed by the majority. As part of a possible majority, he can also govern in turn. The people will always be self-determining and come back to itself after these various turns (*R*, 24/46–47). But in these turns, freedom always risks being suspended and even destroyed. For example, undemocratic forms of government such as fascist and Nazi totalitarianisms can come into power through normal and democratic electoral processes. Conversely, the democratic process can be abrogated in the name of democracy, as in the case of the 1992 suspension of elections in Algeria by the ruling party because the electoral process would have led to a nondemocratic Islamist regime (*R*, 33–34/57–58).

These paradoxes of democracy arise, Derrida suggests, because democracy is a political case of "the absolute freedom of a finite being," whose very power cannot be indivisibly present because it is constituted through exposure to alterity, which is also a radical contamination and compromise of the self's ipseity (*R*, 24/47). "Autoimmunity" is the name Derrida gives to this radical contamination. In the process of immunity, a body protects itself by producing antibodies to combat foreign antigens. In autoimmunization, however, this process is perverted: the organism protects "itself against its self-protection by destroying its own immune system."[4] It is therefore a form of suicide in which the organism immunizes itself against its own immunity.[5] Indeed, autoimmunization is a hyperbolical suicide because in compromising the very idea of selfhood, it renders suicide meaningless since suicide presupposes a self that decides to end its own life. As Derrida puts it, "The autoimmune . . . consists not only in compromising oneself [*s'auto-entamer*] but in compromising the self, the *autos* — and thus ipseity. It consists not only in committing suicide but in compromising *sui-* or *self*-referentiality, the *self* or *sui-* of suicide itself. . . . It threatens always to rob suicide itself of its meaning and supposed integrity" (*R*, 45/71).

## Paleonymy of Democracy

As a structural form of suicide, autoimmunization is literally the taking away of the time and life of the self. But although it leads to murder and death, the eruption of the untimely within democracy actually involves a radically affirmative view of surviving (*survie*) that cannot be derived from either life or death as life's simple negation. As Derrida puts it in his final interview:

> The meaning of survival is not added to living and dying. It is originary: life *is* survival [*la vie est survie*]. . . . [Survival] . . . is derived neither from life nor from death. . . . Survival is an original concept that constitutes the very structure that we call existence, Da-sein, if you will. We are structurally survivors, marked by this structure of the trace, the testament. But having said that, I would not like to give free rein to the interpretation that suggests that survival is more on the side of death, the past, than that of life and the future. No, deconstruction is always on the side of the *yes*, the affirmation of life.[6]

The affirmative dimension of the untimely corresponds to the second meaning of différance as the constitutive exposure to the wholly other. As the structural relation to alterity that renews temporality and enables a life to live on, the untimely is also the eruption of a to-come (*à-venir*). It is "a weak force," a "vulnerable force," or "force without power [that] opens unconditionally to what or who *comes* and comes to affect it" that accompanies the genesis of any form of actuality or concrete existence and can be thought only from within actuality as the latter's condition of (im)possibility (*R*, xiv/13). This weak force that is prior to the more powerful force of sovereignty is the basis of what I call Derrida's paleonymy of democracy.[7] Derrida suggests that the very compromises, suspensions, and destructions of democratic freedom indicate a democracy to come because they derive from democracy's structural noncoincidence or inadequation to itself. In other words, democracy's very lack of properness, which leads to its compromise, also gives it an essential historicity. It gives it a to-come, sends it into a future to-come beyond any positive forms of democracy. This is democracy's untimely secret.

The paleonymy of democracy has at least three fundamental features. First, Derrida distinguishes between positive forms of democracy and the thought of an unpresentable democracy, not unlike his earlier distinction between writing in the narrow and general senses. Such a thought of democracy would no longer belong to the order of the political or even to the order of presence insofar as it is linked to a justice that always exceeds law and its calculations (R, 39/63).

Second, although the untimely is the structural condition of ipseity, Derrida also argues that there is a special affinity between the à-venir and the political regime of democracy. Democracy's untimeliness can be seen in the fact that it is the only inherently plastic political paradigm, the only regime that is open to and welcomes the possibility of contestation and self-contestation. This openness stems from democracy's radically improper character, its lack of self-identity: "What is lacking in democracy is proper meaning, the very meaning of the selfsame [*le sens même du même*] (*ipse*, *metipse, metipsissimus, meisme*), the it-self [*soi-même*], the selfsame, the properly selfsame of the it-self. Democracy is defined, as is the very ideal of democracy, by this lack of the proper and the selfsame. And so it is defined only by turns, by tropes and tropisms" (R, 37/61). This is undoubtedly why Derrida repeatedly points to democracy's fabulous nature and its intrinsic link to literature. This freedom from being tied down to a proper ideality means that democracy is structurally incomplete. Its interminable adjournment enables a hyperbolical questioning of the idea of democracy, all actually existing political forms that take that name, and the contours and content of the determinate rights associated with it, even when such criticism can appear undemocratic. This right to public critique and radical self-critique in the interests of perfectibility indicates that democracy is the only constitutional paradigm that objectively expresses the autoimmune character of ipseity. It is the only political regime that is responsive to the à-venir and "the only paradigm that is universalizable, whence its chance and its fragility" (R, 87/127).

Although Derrida suggests that autoimmunity finds an optimal expression in the right to public critique found in *modern* democratic institutions of the European Enlightenment, this openness should be rigorously distinguished from the Habermasian understanding of *Öffentlichkeit* as the legitimation of political sovereignty through the public use of reason. Although publicness may be a product-effect of autoimmunity, it is primarily identified with the power of universal human reason to transcend particularistic interests through the work of idealization. In contradistinction, for Derrida, the right to public critique comes from the absolute historicity of finite existence. Its "futurity," if we can call it that, does not issue from the power of reason to project an ideal horizon for itself. Similarly, for Derrida, the democratic constitutional paradigm is universalizable not just because democracy is a form of political government that should include all human beings because they possess reason, or because it best expresses universal human interests and enables the realization of human reason's capacity for universal freedom, but because democracy embodies a finite being's structural exposure to the other.

This leads me to the third and most difficult feature of democracy to come. By linking democracy's open-ended nature to the perfectibility of public space and juridico-political institutions found in "that strange 'Europe' of the more or less incomplete Enlightenment," does not Derrida recall the operation of the Kantian idea (*Idee*) that organizes the unfinished project of modernity assumed by the Frankfurt School's contemporary heirs (A, 117)? What is at issue here is not merely whether democracy to come resembles Kant's idea of a perfect political constitution that will allow the greatest possible human freedom in accordance with laws that ensure that the freedom of each can coexist with the freedom of all others.[8] Kant regarded democracy as a form of despotism, and his ideal constitution is a republican monarchy.[9] The resemblance to Kant is deeper and concerns the relation between the deconstruction of metaphysics and the entire apparatus of transcendental philosophy. For instance, does not the relation of the gift to the economy of presence replicate the Kantian distinctions between noumena and phenomena, the intelligible and the sensible? Because the gift can be thought but not known, does it not resemble the noumenon in the negative sense, a transcendent exteriority that is the presupposed ground of appearance but cannot itself be known because it is unconditioned and cannot appear? Derrida repeatedly reminds us of such analogies: "The regulative Idea remains, for lack of anything better . . . a last resort. Although such a last resort or final recourse risks becoming an alibi, it retains a certain dignity. I cannot swear that I will not one day give in to it" (R, 83 / 122). "I know and recognize quite well what this thought no doubt owes . . . to the Kantian antinomies, but it seems to me always to mark them with a wholly other wrinkle [*pli*]."[10]

What motivates Derrida's distancing of the à-venir from the Kantian idea is the thinking of unconditionality beyond presence. The idea ultimately refers to the finitude of our cognitive faculties (*Erkenntnisvermögen*). According to Kant, we employ various principles as guidelines to follow in our theoretical and practical relations to the world. In our pursuit of theoretical knowledge, we either use a principle *constitutively*, if we can find an object that confirms or proves the principle, that is, if the principle's satisfaction can be exhibited directly in intuition, or merely *regulatively*, if satisfaction through direct exhibition in intuition is impossible. Ideas are principles of reason that do not have a corresponding object that can be exhibited in (pure or sensible) intuition. Hence, ideas such as the soul, the cosmos, and God, or universal progress in history, or nature as a teleological system cannot be used constitutively in our pursuit of theoretical knowledge because their reality can never be proven through experience. But they can be used regulatively as *foci imaginarius* to direct our understanding to certain goals and maximally extend our rational comprehension of the world, where constitutive principles alone are insufficient.[11] For example, we cannot have objective knowledge that nature is a system of ends, but the regulative use of the idea of nature's purposiveness can enable us to understand the functioning of organized life forms. Moreover, ideas such as the cosmopolitan federation that will bring about perpetual peace or the perfect constitution can be used by practical reason as archetypes (*Urbild*) or projected goals to guide our conduct as historical actors even if they may never be realized in experience because of our deficient character as sensuous creatures afflicted by passions.[12]

In Kant's view, our use of ideas is necessitated by our inability as finite beings with limited, deficient cognitive powers to intuit or create (or both) certain things that we can think. We proceed *as if* (*als ob*) these ideas were actual in order to extend our theoretical comprehension, or as if they are actualizable in order to facilitate the endeavors of practical reason. With regard to their practical use, regulative ideas outline an ideal horizon that is infinitely deferred precisely because they are not actualizable but can only be asymptotically approximated by our rational endeavors.[13] The "regulative idea" therefore has three characteristics. First, because it derives from an opposition between our finite reason and that of an infinite being, the temporality it generates is teleological. Its futurity and historicity come from a beyond that is nevertheless in accord with our reason, namely, a providential or intelligent nature. It opens up an ideal horizon in which humanity can develop capacities that are present in latency and rationally progress in an upward movement toward an infinite telos. For instance, the idea that history is governed by providential design can serve as a guiding thread (*Leitfaden*) "that opens up the comforting prospect of the future . . . in which we are shown [*vorgestellt*] from afar how the human species eventually works its way upward to a situation in which all the germs implanted by nature can be developed fully, and in which man's destiny can be fulfilled here on earth."[14]

Second, the idea is already fully present in the element of thought. It is defined in advance through rational calculation. Our practical endeavor consists of the programmatic approaching or pursuit of this telos, the following of its rule by the calculation of appropriate means. Third, the idea is a crucial component in Kant's canonical understanding of unconditionality as the power of self-present reason. The unconditionality (*Unbedingtheit*) of the moral law comes from its power to elevate us into a supersensible kingdom of ends in which we, as self-legislating moral actors, are free because we are unconditioned (*unbedingt*) by the mechanical causality that governs the world of appearances. The practical idea is a connecting device reason uses to make a passage (*Übergang*) between the realms of freedom and nature. By pointing to a teleological nature that is conducive to moral ends, it projects a horizon that gives us hope that the unconditioned world of moral freedom can be empirically realized.

Hence, the idea (and any telos in general) enhances the power of finite reason. It extends reason's limits by delineating through a figure that which is possible for us to strive toward. Reason achieves greater presence by projecting an ideal horizon in which we are able to transcend externally imposed conditions, that is, conditions we have not rationally set for ourselves. Reason's unconditionality is thus inseparable from its power of anticipating the future through an ideal end, which in turn becomes joined to the power of calculating how to achieve this ideal future.

Derrida's liberation of the historicity of the à-venir "not only from the Idea in the Kantian sense but from all teleology, all onto-theo-teleology," is a necessary corollary of the deconstruction of ipseity (*R*, 87 / 127). He suggests that what is truly unconditional is the constitutive exposure or vulnerability of any presence to the otherness of the event and the gift of time. This unconditionality is precisely what the idea neutralizes and annuls by anticipating it in a present(able) form. For Derrida, the unconditional can only be thought beyond the mastery and freedom of a self-present rational subject.

If an event worthy of this name is to arrive or happen, it must, beyond all mastery, affect a passivity. It must touch an exposed vulnerability, one without absolute immunity, without indemnity; it must touch this vulnerability in its finitude and in a non-horizontal fashion, there where it is not yet or is already no longer possible to face or face up to the unforeseeability of the other. In this regard, autoimmunity is not an absolute ill or evil. It enables an exposure to the other, to *what* and to *who* comes — which means that it must remain incalculable. Without autoimmunity, with absolute immunity, nothing would ever happen or arrive; we would no longer wait, await, or expect, no longer expect one another, or expect any event.

What must be thought here, then, is this inconceivable and unknowable thing, a freedom that would no longer be the power of a subject, a freedom without autonomy, a heteronomy without servitude, in short, something like a passive decision. (*R*, 152/210)

The à-venir is distinguished from the Kantian idea in at least three ways. First, it signifies an unconditional openness and responsiveness to the interruption of temporality and reason by the coming of an other that is completely unforeseeable and incalculably singular. The unconditional is therefore situated in a ground prior to practical reason's transcendence, namely, finite reason's autoimmunity or constitutive exposure to the other from which the event comes. Second, although the unconditional other is, strictly speaking, impossible because it exceeds the order of presence and the possible, it is not an inaccessible exteriority. As the condition of possibility of experience, the other is interminably endured as an *experience* of the impossible, which has a nonnegative relation to the order of presence and the possible. Third, because the unconditional is not coextensive with and exhausted by the freedom of practical reason, it is not an ideal whose actualization through action occurs within an infinitely deferred horizon. Instead of either paralyzing us into inaction or leading to quietism, the unconditional is characterized by a structure of urgent precipitation. In Derrida's words, "[The im-possible] announces itself; it precedes me, swoops down upon and seizes me *here and now* in a nonvirtualizable way, in actuality and not potentiality. . . . Such an urgency cannot be *idealized* any more than the other as other can. This im-possible is thus not a (regulative) *idea* or *ideal*. It is what is most undeniably *real*. And sensible. Like the other. Like the irreducible and nonappropriable différance of the other" (*R*, 84/123).

In Derrida's view, this structure of precipitation, which inscribes the unconditional within empirical conditions, is the origin of imperativity, responsibility, and ethics. It gives rise to the interruptive decision and, subsequently, to practical reason as the responsible accounting for any decision. Although this decision is not intentionally made but is passively endured, it is not irrational because it arises from the excess of reason itself (double genitive), the rational subject's structural or constitutive exposure to an other that intimately inhabits it. It leads to a hyperbolical responsibility. Because responsibility is assigned by the other, it cannot be satisfied by the calculations of reason, which must respond interminably. And although our response is a violation of the other, the unconditional demands that we be responsible in the present. As Derrida puts it, "Otherwise, it [the unconditional] gives nothing. What remains unconditional or absolute (*unbedingt*, if you will) risks being nothing at all if conditions (*Bedingungen*) do not make of it some thing (*Ding*). Political, juridical, and ethical responsibilities have their place, if they take place, only in this transaction . . . between the unconditional and the conditional" (A, 130).

## Another World to Come

The aporetic transaction between the unconditional and the conditional, the incalculable and calculation, is the leitmotif of Derrida's deconstruction of the political. This fundamental aporia takes the shape of specific aporias, such as that of justice and law, justice and politics, and, most important, democracy and sovereignty. For example, in "Force of Law" Derrida argues that although justice is incalculable and unpresentable and cannot be reduced to the law's calculative reason, justice demands that we calculate, even as the transformation of the law necessitates an appeal to a justice that always exceeds it. One way to evaluate the legacy of Derrida's final writings is to assess what the aporias he tracks contribute to an analysis and elucidation of contemporary political situations. I end with such a test of democracy to come by inscribing it within contemporary globalization.

We can better situate democracy to come by contrasting it with two other understandings of the time of democracy. In the first view, democracy is a universal political culture that has already been achieved. It is identified with institutions such as a republican constitution, elections, individual civil liberties, and the right to political participation and other public rights associated with the West or the North. Here, democracy is regarded as an actuality whose intensive universality needs to be spread extensively throughout the globe by transporting these prototypical institutions. The time of democracy is one of linear historical progress that is succinctly captured under the sign of "development," whether this is political, social, or economic. This conception of democracy is brutally performed by the U.S. invasion of Iraq in the second Gulf War, where the Tocquevillean argument about American exceptionalism was deformed to justify a preemptive imperialist war against global terrorism.[15]

The second understanding of the time of democracy is the contemporary revival of Kantian cosmopolitanism as a project of cosmopolitan democracy. Habermas's work is the most sophisticated example of this. He envisages a teleological time of democracy that hybridizes Kant and Hegel. We glimpse its Kantianism in Habermas's proceduralist reconceptualization of democracy as a process of will- and opinion-formation (*Willens- und Meinungs-bildung*) through institutions of the political public sphere that optimize the rational potentialities intrinsic in "quasi-transcendental" communicative practices.[16] Its Hegelian spirit rises in the argument that the complete self-actualization of the democratic process requires that it be liberated from the limitations that fetter its cosmopolitan vocation. Hence, the erosion of the territorial nation-state by globalization is salutary to the teleological time of democracy.[17]

Nothing needs to be said about why the first understanding of democracy's time is dangerous. It freezes democracy into a static reality embodied in various institutional fetishes that are to be dogmatically and mechanically transplanted to the rest of the world without considering the violence of this transplantation and the particularistic realpolitical interests that it serves, especially how this violates the spirit of democracy. With regard to Habermas's vision of global democracy, I have argued elsewhere that his projection of the autonomy of the political (Derrida would say ipseity) onto a global terrain ignores the unequal and uneven nature of capitalist globalization and how the international division of labor obstructs the formation of any genuine cosmopolitan democratic will at the level of an emergent transnational politics.[18] Ultimately, Habermas's project partakes of the Kantian idea's utopian metaphysics of presence. It holds on to the admirable belief that the universal rational validity of publicness and the democratic process constitutes a quasi-transcendent state of human reason that is somehow quarantined from the vicissitudes of the world of instrumental relations. Such ideas serve as a guiding thread for rational practice precisely because they cannot be contaminated. Whatever happens to them as positive historical forms is merely a contingency or accident, something that comes from outside their rational nucleus.

What is sorely lacking in both these accounts is the thought of the constitutive contamination, compromise, and interruption of the time of democracy by the forces of capitalist globalization. It is this structural contamination and compromise of democracy in the current global conjuncture that Derrida's views about the untimeliness of democracy — its autoimmunity, but also its à-venir — helps me to think. For reasons of economy, I outline four themes concerning the autoimmune character of democracy in telegraphic form.

First, Derrida argues that democracy and sovereignty are mutually inseparable and incompatible. They are inseparable because both appear unconditional insofar as they escape relativism. They are unconditional because of democracy's universal character and the value it accords equality, and because sovereignty is "the concentration, into a single point of indivisible singularity (God, the monarch, the people, the state or the nation-state), of absolute force and the absolute exception" (*R*, 154/211). Indeed, demo*cracy* is also a form of sovereignty. To be an effective form of governing, it requires a sovereign monopoly of power. In Derrida's view, however, the similarity is misleading. As I noted in my earlier discussion of the distinction between the à-venir and the Kantian idea, for Derrida, what is genuinely unconditional is not the transcendence of finitude but the structural exposure to the other that gives time. Democracy is marked by this unconditional exposure because its tendency toward universality and equality implies shareability and, therefore, temporality and duration. In contradistinction, the stigmatic indivisibility of the sovereign is characterized by atemporality. Sovereignty is not untimely but time*less*. It "neither gives nor gives itself the time; it does not take time" (*R*, 109/154). The exceptional decision is a withdrawal from and contraction of temporal traces into a timeless instant or indivisible presence. This is why democracy and sovereignty are fundamentally incompatible.

Moreover, sovereignty is always exercised over a closed totality. Hence, democratic equality has always been conditional when it is tied to sovereignty. It has been historically limited to those who are alike, principally citizens enclosed within the territorial borders of a nation-state, instead of being extended "to the whole world of singularities, to the whole world of humans assumed to be like me, my compeers [*mes semblables*] — or else, even further, to all nonhuman living beings, or again, even beyond that, to all the nonliving" (*R*, 53/81). Sovereign calculations of the exception and what are alike thus condition and limit democracy. Put more strongly, sovereignty compromises and violates democracy's incalculable and unconditional nature. Indeed, Derrida suggests that the theological idea of sovereignty is synonymous with forms of violence such as cruelty and the death penalty, and must be dissociated from democracy and unconditionality.[19]

The contamination of democracy by sovereignty is, however, part of democracy's autoimmunity. Just as the gift gives itself to be violated in the present, democracy gives itself to be violated by sovereignty in order to be effective. But this also means that democracy is never fully present in and reducible to sovereignty. Just as presence can renew itself only by being ruptured by the gift, democracy always exceeds and can destabilize sovereignty. Whenever political regimes need justification and legitimation, heteronomy, time, and the other disrupt sovereign indivisibility. Democracy is the structural deconstructibility of sovereignty.

This aporetic embrace between democracy and sovereignty leads to three specific themes concerning the current global conjuncture. Addressing the U.S. war against terrorism in the aftermath of September 11 and its diplomatic strategy of denouncing foreign regimes as rogue states that should be excluded from the international fraternity of nation-states because they have violated international laws for peace and security, Derrida argues that the aporia of democracy and sovereignty implies that all sovereign states are rogues. Sovereign indivisibility involves withdrawal from the other. The sovereign does not need to justify, explain, or give reasons for its actions, or it compromises itself and is no longer sovereign. Hence, "the abuse of power is constitutive of sovereignty itself": "as soon as there is sovereignty, there is abuse of power and a rogue state" (R, 102/145). Sovereignty thus betrays the universality of democracy. This gives rise to an imperative for the interminable circumscription of international politics at every level. States that denounce other states are themselves the original rogue states because in any given state of geopolitical hegemony, the sovereignty that enables such self-righteous denunciation always already implies force and abuse of power. Similarly, because of its corrupt structure and the abuse of power of its permanent members, the U.N. Security Council qua transnational executive power needs to be persistently interrogated.

Second, the deconstruction of sovereignty is not merely a speculation of political philosophy. It is happening in the world, as exemplified by the challenging of the state's sovereign immunity by universal human rights. Human rights discourse extends "the democratic beyond nation-state sovereignty, beyond citizenship," and is an important case of the invention of "new distributions and forms of sharing [*partages*], new divisions of sovereignty" (*R*, 87/127). At the same time, Derrida cautions us from too hastily declaring the end of sovereignty. Human rights express the sovereignty of the human being. But more important, nation-state sovereignty, especially in view of the globalization of neoliberal market structures, is *pharmakon*-like. Although it monopolizes violence and can exclude and repress noncitizens, the state and democratic citizenship can play a positive role in guarding against international violence and economic exploitation:

> One cannot combat, *head-on*, *all* sovereignty *in general*, without threatening at the same time, beyond the nation-state figure of sovereignty, the classical principles of freedom and self-determination. . . . These classical principles remain inseparable from a sovereignty at once indivisible and yet able to be shared. Nation-state sovereignty can even itself, in certain conditions, become an indispensable bulwark against certain international powers, certain ideological, religious, or capitalist, indeed linguistic, hegemonies that, under the cover of liberalism or universalism, would still represent, in a world that would be little more than a marketplace, a rationalization in the service of particular interests. (*R*, 158/216)

This persistence of sovereignty is not the consequence of a liberal-individualist understanding of freedom. It stems instead from an acknowledgment of the aporetic character of democracy as an incalculable movement of sharing or dividing that must give in to ipseity and calculation if it is to be effective.

Third, as the movement of sharing that breaks apart sovereign limitations and conditions, democracy entails in its negative aspect a questioning of the nation form and all other closed forms of community, and in its affirmative aspect an unconditional hospitality as the basis of worldhood. Derrida regards the nation form as an ontopology (an ontology of present place) and nationalism as an irrational relativistic regime of thought that suppresses democracy's openness to alterity by limiting it to members of a nation.[20] Nationalism, he argues, is a deadly form of thought that can "have no future" and can "promise nothing."[21] This rejection of nationalism is part of a larger questioning of fraternity as the basis of politics because it leads to a familial, androcentric, and fraternalist configuration of politics that closes off the political community from the other's coming by reducing the friend to a brother and determining the demos as a fraternal community.[22]

To the conditional hospitality of these closed communities of presence,

Derrida counterposes an unconditional receptivity to an "anyone" who "comes before any other metaphysical determination as subject, human person, or consciousness, before any juridical determination as compeer, compatriot, kin, brother, neighbor, fellow religious follower, or fellow citizen" (*R*, 86/126). Following his arguments about cosmopolitanism and a New International that extends beyond nation-states and citizenship, he argues that such unconditional hospitality is exemplified by an other worldwide-ization (*altermondialisation*), the world as a universal community that is distinct from the integrating processes of capitalist globalization (*Globalisierung*). He pointedly uses this term to refer to antiglobalization movements, new social movements such as those participating in the World Social Forum that are not against worldwide and world-forming intercourse per se, but against neoliberal capitalist globalization.[23] Derrida's concept of the world is not merely descriptive. Alluding to Heidegger's distinction between world and earth, he draws a philosophical distinction between the world (*monde, mundus, Welt*) and the earth, the terrestrial globe, and the pre-Christian cosmos. In its original conception in the Abrahamic tradition, *world* designates a dynamic process of humanization, "a particular space-time, a certain oriented history of human brotherhood, of what in a Pauline language . . . one calls *citizens of the world*, . . . brothers, fellow men, neighbors, insofar as they are creatures and sons of God."[24] Notwithstanding its predominantly Christian provenance, the concept carries a "universalizing exigency," a deterritorializing, expropriating, or uprooting force that underwrites human rights discourse.[25]

The worldwide-ization of the world thus refers to "a becoming-world of the world," an opening up that is not merely the mechanical integration of the globe through capitalist economic structures and teletechnological communications.[26] Indeed, globalization is antiworld. It effaces the world as opening by reducing it to a global marketplace. By exacerbating the economic inequality between North and South, it impoverishes the world. The globalization of free-market structures and capitalist production also consolidates ontotheological concepts of sovereignty because it requires bureaucratic-administrative and legal calculation to enforce contractual promises and regulate production. Globalization thus deprives us of the world as support and ground and makes us worldless (*weltlos; R*, 155/213). In contradistinction, the worldwide transmission of discourses and institutions of human rights, new instruments of international law, the concept of crimes against humanity, and the establishment of an international criminal court are instances of world-opening (A, 123, 132). In particular, the "new *altermondialist* gatherings" that oppose global political and economic hegemony such as the G8, the World Bank, the International Monetary Fund, and the World Trade Organization "represent . . . the only reliable force worthy of the future [*l'avenir*]."[27]

In my view, the aporetic embrace between democracy and sovereignty—their intrication, constriction, and cancellation of each other—offers an analytical schema of great elasticity for tracking the contamination of ideals and institutions such as progress, democracy, and human rights in contemporary globalization. For example, Derrida's argument that the abuse of power is constitutive of sovereignty can be extended to the compromised nature of all international negotiations, even those involving looser international arrangements and networks such as the transnational public sphere of intergovernmental organizations and nongovernmental organizations, including participants of the World Social Forum. At the same time, the idea that presence is structurally exposed to the other also opens up a to-come for these ideals and institutions that we cannot not want.

What puzzles me is Derrida's unconditional dismissal of nationalism in this picture of the world to come. We know that his emphasis on the hyperbolic unconditionality of the event is accompanied by an insistence on the necessity and urgency of a negotiation or transaction that inscribes the unconditional within concrete conditions so that it can be effective. This is the place of politics as calculation. Yet in all his negotiations concerning the current global conjuncture, Derrida never calculates with nationalism. He never gives the nation form a chance because he dismisses it as an irrationalism that is necessarily blind to the coming of the event. This suspiciousness can be explained in two ways. First, the perspective from which Derrida negotiates with the unconditional is that of a certain non-Eurocentric Europe. This Europe, he suggests, has a privileged, "irreplaceable" task in the worldwide extension of democracy to come after September 11 because of the Enlightenment's indispensable experience of the need to be cautious of the power of religious doctrine in the political realm:

> In the long and patient deconstruction required for the transformation to-come, the experience Europe inaugurated at the time of the Enlightenment (*Lumières, Aufklärung, Illuminismo*) in the relationship between the political and the theological or, rather, the religious, though still uneven, unfulfilled, relative, and complex, will have left in European political space absolutely original marks with regard to . . . the authority

of religious doctrine over the political. Such marks can be found neither in the Arab world nor in the Muslim world, nor in the Far East, nor even . . . in American democracy, in what *in fact* governs not the principles but the predominant reality of American political culture. (A, 116–17)

Europe thus "serves as an example of what a politics, a reflection, and an ethics might be, ones that have inherited from a past Enlightenment and that bear an Enlightenment to come, a Europe capable of non-binary forms of discernment."[28] It would be able to criticize both the anti-Islamist politics of the Israeli state as well as the anti-Semitic propaganda found in the Arab world and Palestinian suicide attacks, even as it supports the Palestinian right to self-determination.

Given that the European experience includes the history of National Socialist totalitarianism, racism, genocide, and European colonialism, Derrida is right to be suspicious of *European* nationalisms and contemporary xenophobic neonationalism in the European Union. Such suspicions connect with his argument that the national community cannot be open to the à-venir because as a form of fraternity formed by a symbolic projection of natural fraternity, it is fundamentally mystifying and violent. A genealogical tie is always an effect of discourse, Derrida argues, because we cannot intuit a blood or natural brother. Hence, the other's appearance as a brother occurs through a legal fiction, a filial schema of recognition that effaces the other's singularity. Nationalism is a second-degree mystification. In the contemporary world, it is always an instrument of the state. "Everything in political discourse that appeals to birth, to nature or to the nation — indeed, to nations or to the universal nation of human brotherhood — this entire familialism consists in a renaturalization of this 'fiction.'"[29] "Nationalism, today, is always *state*-nationalism, a zealous, that is, a *jealous* and vindictive vindication of a nation constituted as a sovereign state. . . . I am not certain that some kind of nationalism is not already at work, however discreetly, as soon as one has entered into even the most sympathetic national consciousness, the most innocent affirmation of belonging to a particular national, cultural, or linguistic community."[30]

But is nationalism always that of the blood and soil? Is the nation always the ideological naturalization of a fiction, as opposed to a universalizing form of solidarity that questions its own self-instituting or self-positing? In dismissing nationalism as irrational, Derrida does not discriminate between different kinds of nationalism: popular and statist, radical and conservative, religious, ethnic, and secular. He also seems to set aside a tradition of nationalism based on spiritual or material activity that includes Lenin's defense of the democratic content of nationalism as the political self-determination of a colonized people, or revolutionary anticolonial and radical postcolonial nationalism in the Third World. Such nationalisms are not regressive mystifications or aggressive cultural chauvinisms. Nor do they necessarily lead to the formation of xenophobic closed communities because they are in principle components of socialist internationalism.

A brief reference to Frantz Fanon suffices to make my point. The grandeur of the initial spontaneous revolt against the colonial oppressor is a militant example of ontotheological sovereignty.

> Every colonized subject in arms represents a piece of the nation on the move. . . . These revolts are governed by a simple doctrine: The nation must be made to exist. . . . In the valleys and in the forests, in the jungle and in the villages, everywhere, one encounters a national authority. The action of each and everyone substantiates the nation and undertakes to ensure its triumph locally. . . . On their continuing road to self-discovery the people legislate and claim their sovereignty. . . . The villages witness a permanent display of spectacular generosity and disarming kindness, and an unquestioned determination to die for the "cause." All of this is reminiscent of a religious brotherhood, a church, or a mystical doctrine.[31]

But Fanon reminds us that revolutionary leaders know that self-conscious enlightenment and organization are crucial to transform a peasant revolt into a revolutionary war and an ongoing struggle against neocolonial forces and tribal division after independence. Of course, Fanon's nation remains a community of presence and the telos of a dialectical process. But as an example of sovereign ipseity rather than an irrationalism, it can be interrupted by and can have an à-venir.

Significantly, Derrida has not engaged with Frantz Fanon's writings. In an autobiographical recounting of his childhood journeys with his father, a traveling salesman, to different Algerian towns, he alludes to Fanon: "I was especially determined to help my father, to demonstrate a sort of 'political solidarity' with him, to show my concern for this 'wretched of the earth.' . . . In my childhood I looked upon him as a sacrificial victim of modern times, and his 'voyages' as an intolerable ordeal. My first political experience linked the unjust suffering of two unfortunates: the 'Arab,' and my father, the 'traveler.'"[32] But this solidarity with the colonized Arab is not an identification. Derrida's "painful love for Algeria," he emphasizes elsewhere, is "not the love of a citizen, precisely, and thus the patriotic attachment to a nation-state."[33] The openness to the à-venir that drives Derrida's final writings can include Europe's hospitality to the Third World, but it is resolutely a *European* hospitality. My point here is that by inscribing democracy to come within Europe and by downplaying revolutionary nationalism, Derrida ends up practicing a limited hospitality that obscures other inscriptions of the unconditional in the postcolonial South that can give rise to nationalist exigencies and responsibilities.

Indeed, the new social movements Derrida regards as bearers of *altermondialisation* are not clearly antinational. Although transnational advocacy networks at the grassroots level may be unconnected to traditional political parties within the national system of electoral democracy, although they are animated by globally oriented principles and voice their interests in global fora, it is questionable whether the members of such movements no longer harbor feelings of national solidarity or the desire to make their respective nation-states take better care of their people. For example, the concept of food sovereignty — the idea that "every people, no matter how small, has the right to produce their own food" — articulated by the Sem Terra Movement of landless agrarian workers in Brazil indicates that the movement's global goals begin from the principle of a people's integrity.[34] Moreover, these social movements have to connect with the nation-state because it is the primary site for the effective implementation of equitable objectives for redistribution on a large scale. Here, Derrida's insistence on the need to negotiate with nation-state sovereignty as a protective barrier against neoliberalism can be useful for tracking the modulation between the liberating and oppressive dimensions of the nation-state for peoples in the postcolonial South as they engage in remaking the world against globalization.[35] But this would take us to another scene of responsibility beyond Europe.

## Notes

1 See Derrida, *Rogues*, 39; *Voyous*, 64. Hereafter *R*, cited parenthetically in the text with page references from the translation followed by those of the French text.

2 Derrida, *Given Time*, 14. Hereafter *GT*.

3 Derrida, "Différance," 15.

4 Derrida, "Faith and Knowledge: The Two Sources of 'Religion' at the Limits of Reason Alone," 73 n. 27.

5 Derrida, "Autoimmunity," 94. Hereafter A.

6 Jacques Derrida, "Je suis en guerre contre moi-même," *Le Monde*, August 18, 2004. I am grateful to Jonathan Culler for helping me with the translation.

7  For the practice of paleonymy or the strategic keeping of an old name onto which is grafted a new concept, see Derrida, *Positions*, 71.

8  See Kant, *Critique of Pure Reason*, B 373, 397; *Kritik der reinen Vernunft*, 324. Hereafter *CPR*, with page references from the translation followed by those of the German text.

9  Kant, *Toward Perpetual Peace*, 324; *Zum ewigen Frieden*, 206.

10 *R*, 174 n.14/207n. On the gift as a "sort of transcendental illusion" that "should not be a simple reproduction of Kant's critical machinery," see *GT* 29–30.

11 See *CPR* A 644, 591/565.

12 On the unrealizable nature of the perfect civil constitution, see *CPR* B 373–74, 397/324. Cf. Kant, "Idea of a Universal History with a Cosmopolitan Purpose," 46; *Idee zu einer allgemeinen Geschichte in weltbürgerlicher Absicht*, 41. Hereafter IUH, with page references from the translation followed by those of the German text. It is debatable whether such practical ideas can strictly be considered "regulative" in Kant's terms since the regulative/constitutive distinction applies only to theoretical principles. "Regulative" would have only the less robust meaning of "regulating conduct." I have benefited from discussing Kant's use of the terms "regulative" and "idea" with Allen Wood and György Markus.

13 For arguments that Kant's views changed after the Second Critique and that he subsequently regarded regulative practical ideas such as perpetual peace and the highest good as realizable or, at least, as ends we should rationally pursue as long as they have not been proven to be impossible, see, respectively, Markus, "The Hope to Be Free," 79–106, and Guyer, "Nature, Morality, and the Possibility of Peace," 425–34. If the practical idea is realizable, the term "regulative" would undergo a drastic change of meaning.

14 IUH 52/49, translation modified.

15 For a topical reflection on the significance of the invasion of Iraq as America's attempt to implant democracy, see Michael Ignatieff, "Who Are Americans to Think That Freedom Is Theirs to Spread?," *New York Times*, June 26, 2005.

16 Habermas, "The Postnational Constellation and the Future of Democracy," 110–11; "Die postnationale Konstellation und die Zukunft der Demokratie," 165–66.

17 Habermas, "The Postnational Constellation and the Future of Democracy," 102–3; "Die postnationale Konstellation und die Zukunft der Demokratie," 154–55.

18 See Cheah, "Postnational Light," 45–79.

19 On the violent character of sovereignty, see Derrida, "Psychoanalysis Searches the States of Its Soul," 271–76; Derrida and Roudinesco, *For What Tomorrow*, 144–48. On the dissociation of sovereignty and unconditionality, see Derrida, "The University without Condition," 206–7, 232.

20 On ontopology, see Derrida, *Specters of Marx*, 82–83. On irratio-nation-state-ism, see *R*, 149/204.

21 Derrida, *Specters of Marx*, 169.

22 See Derrida, *Politics of Friendship*, especially the reading of Michelet on 237–38.

23 Derrida, "Une Europe de l'espoir." A partial translation is available in English with

the title "Enlightenment Past and to Come." For an interesting reading of this essay, see Naas, "A Last Call for 'Europe.'" Quotations are from Naas's translation of selected passages. On transnational movements against neoliberal globalization, see Mertes, *A Movement of Movements*.

24 Derrida, "Globalization, Peace, and Cosmopolitanism," 375.

25 Ibid.

26 Derrida, "The University without Condition," 203, 223–25.

27 Derrida. "Une Europe de l'espoir," translated in Naas, "A Last Call for 'Europe.'"

28 Ibid.

29 Derrida, *Politics of Friendship*, 93.

30 Derrida and Roudinesco, *For What Tomorrow*, 93–94.

31 Fanon, *The Wretched of the Earth*, 82–84.

32 Malabou and Derrida, *Counterpath*, 32.

33 Derrida, "Taking Sides for Algeria," 119.

34 Stedile, "Brazil's Landless Battalions," 43.

35 For an analysis of the autoimmune nature of the postcolonial nation-state, see Cheah, *Spectral Nationality*, 381–95.

# Sovereign Stupidity and Autoimmunity

## GEOFFREY BENNINGTON

The context for this very preliminary paper is a larger project tentatively called "The Politics of Politics." Its guiding thought is that any relatively complex organization (including conceptual organizations) involves something that can reasonably be called politics, and that the organization we habitually and apparently most properly call "politics" (i.e., the constitution, organization, and administration of the polis itself) is no different from this. Politics has its politics like other organizations, and *that* politics (the politics of politics, a kind of *doubling up* of politics) is, to put it a little dramatically, both its chance and its ruin. That conjunction of chance and ruin implies that the politics of politics is something that can be neither simply celebrated nor simply deplored. The narrower (?) question I am attempting to address in this project is the status of the word and concept "democracy" in the ensuing situation, and Jacques Derrida's reflections on political questions are my principal guides in this endeavor.

Most political philosophy (or at least political philosophy insofar as it is under the sway of theory, of *theorein*) attempts to reduce the politics out of politics, and does this almost inevitably by trying to treat politics as the object of a theory (rather than the object of a politics). The failure of this attempt to be purely theoretical would mark political philosophy as political. I draw some support for this argument from a passing comment of Derrida's in one of the sessions from his seminar on "La bête et le souverain," remarking on the insertion of political theories (such as Hobbes's) into contemporary political events.[1] Although I am sure that this is not a historicizing comment in any normal sense of that term, it does bespeak an *exposure* of political philosophy to politics (I'm tempted to say it's a kind of *transcendental* exposure) that my "politics of politics" doublet is attempting to capture, and which will resonate in due course with what Derrida calls "autoimmunity."

One salient way in which what I'm calling the politics of politics shows up is around the issue of sovereignty and its inherent aporias, much discussed by Derrida in his late work. I want to say that these aporias, however apparently different, are importantly *the same* across a very wide range of authors (such as Bodin, Hobbes, Spinoza, Rousseau, Kant, Schmitt, and Bataille) — without wanting to make this a historical issue (of, say, "modernity"), if only because something of the "same" aporias show up in ancient thinkers too, if we are to believe Derrida himself, or indeed Agamben, whatever the latter's ambiguous attachment to a concept of "modernity." At least in the case of sovereignty, the transcendental exposure I've mentioned has to do with a kind of stupidity (or *bêtise*, precisely, as in "La bête et le souverain"), I think, in ways I shall try to specify, and which have perhaps to do with Derrida's twice explicitly remarking, in the seminar I have mentioned, on the possibility that the sovereign be stupid (and not merely animalistic, wolfish, say) without that stupidity compromising its sovereignty — and we might suspect that the predicate "necessarily-possibly-stupid" will, in standard Derridean logic, entail "always (in some sense) stupid."[2] *Le souverain est une bête, et le souverain est bête.*

One of the most salient problems or aporias of sovereignty shows up in the question of the relationship between the sovereign (as legislative power) and the government (as executive power). I think that this diremption affects concepts of sovereignty (in Bodin, say) before clear distinctions between legislative and executive become standard, but it's easier to draw out the consequences when these distinctions are made, and so I'd like to spend a little time illustrating this rather topical (in the United States, at least) issue from the political thought of Jean-Jacques Rousseau.

In the *Contrat social*, Rousseau memorably and persuasively argues that even the best constituted state will decline, according to the operation of a kind of death drive at work in the body politic. In book III, chapter 11, for example ("De la mort du corps politique"), he writes, "The body politic, just like the body of man, begins to die from the moment of its birth and bears within itself the causes of its destruction."[3] This "death" is caused in the first instance by the fact that sovereign authority cannot fail to be usurped by the executive (the government), and this usurpation is itself the product of the founding tension in all Rousseau's political thought, between particularity and generality of the will. The opening of the immediately preceding chapter ("De l'abus du gouvernement, et de sa pente à dégénérer"), goes as follows:

> Just as the particular will ceaselessly acts against the general will, so the government makes a continual effort against sovereignty. The more this effort increases, the more the constitution becomes corrupt, and as there

is here no other collective will balancing that of the Prince by resisting it, it must happen sooner or later that the Prince end up by oppressing the sovereign and breaking the social treaty. That is the inherent and inevitable vice that, from the birth of the body politic tends relentlessly to destroy it, just as old age and death destroy the body of man. (421)

This inevitable tendency does not *supervene on* the body politic but is a constitutive and originary factor of it, an always-already, as an earlier Derrida might have said, a factor of autoimmunity in his later terms.

This is as much as to say that sovereignty is from the start on the way to being usurped, and that this becoming-usurped is therefore part of what sovereignty essentially is in its efforts to be itself. As Rousseau makes eloquently clear in several places in his work, government (as executive) *as such* is usurpatory with respect to sovereignty (which is in principle legislative and only legislative) *as such*.[4] Execution is already a usurpation of legislation. (Execution of the law, we might say, is *execution* of the law — and thereby of the sovereign — or as Derrida puts it in *Etats d'âme de la psychanalyse*, is regicide, paregicide, and even, we might add, paregisuicide.)[5] This originary usurpation is possible only because sovereignty is from the start a little less than sovereign, is *willing*, by definition, but is thereby also *wanting* or failing,[6] just because it needs an executive in the first place to supplement itself and secure itself as sovereign. A sovereign that remained merely itself, purely sovereign, in its defining self-sufficiency, indivisibility,[7] inalienability, and perfection, in the bubble or burrow of its eternally instantaneous temporal self-coincidence,[8] would not *even be* sovereign, insofar as its will would find no possibility of execution, and it would therefore do nothing and be nothing, certainly not sovereign. A truly or simply sovereign sovereign would not even be sovereign.[9]

In order to "be" sovereign at all, then, the sovereign has to descend a little from the sovereign heights, from the summit of its most-highness (as Bataille or Nancy might say),[10] and give itself an executive, an *arm* or *branch*. (Earlier, because it is *dumb*, it had to give itself a *voice* in the figure of the legislator or lawgiver, another story I've told elsewhere:[11] giving itself the means to give itself the law, the sovereign necessarily first sees, or rather hears, the law come from another and cannot ever really know that it is in fact the law. The sovereign is stupidly at the mercy of the foreign legislator who always might be a charlatan.)[12]

So the sovereign, in order to be sovereign, has to give itself a primary supplement in the form of a government, and that government cannot fail to undo the sovereign in the very fact of making it sovereign, or to undermine it in the very act of supporting it. Here then is a case of autoimmunity: the very attempt the sovereign makes to establish itself as self-same and thereby immune from the other entails opening itself up to usurpation and eventual destruction. But how is the sovereign even to give itself an executive (a government) and yet itself hope to remain sovereign? The sovereign is sovereign only insofar as it expresses the *general* will in the form of law. The sovereign cannot simply and self-identically *be* the executive, because that would be the end of politics (and *ex hypothesi* politics [and even the politics of politics] is Rousseau's subject in the *Contrat social*):

> Once the Legislative power has been firmly established, we come to do the same for the executive power; for this latter, which operates only by particular acts, not being of the essence of the other, is naturally separate from it. If it were possible that the Sovereign, considered as such, should have the executive power, right and fact would be so confused that one would no longer know what is law and what is not, and the body politic thus denatured would soon fall prey to the violence against which it was instituted. (432; that violence being of course the "state of nature" from which politics supposedly emerges)

The government deals with particularities, the sovereign with generalities (and essentially only the all-important and self-important generality of itself in its his-majesty-the-baby-like narcissism). But the government not only deals with particularities, it *is* a particularity: so *that there be* a government can be a law, but the actual constitution or naming of the government is no longer a general but a particular act. As Rousseau puts it in this surprisingly late chapter of book III of the *Contrat social*, "The difficulty is that of understanding how one can have an act of Government before the Government exists, and how the People, which is only Sovereign or subject, can become Prince or Magistrate in certain circumstances" (433). The answer to this problem is curious and almost magical—I'm going to say it's *fabulous*: "Here again we discover one of those astonishing properties of the body politic, whereby it reconciles apparently contradictory operations. For this one is done by a sudden conversion of sovereignty into democracy, so that, with no sensible change, and merely a new relation of all to all, the citizens become magistrates move from general acts to particular acts, and from law to execution" (433). This apparently gives democracy a certain priority (or at least a certain distinction) with respect to other possible forms of government. Just because democracy is the rule of all, it can be produced from sovereignty by a kind of enharmonic change, a change without change, and this would seem to give it an unassailable "advantage" (as Rousseau says) insofar as this is the only legitimate way a government of whatever form can be instituted. Whatever government is permanently (or semipermanently) instituted, it will always (if it is to be legitimate) have its roots in this radically "democratic" moment. So even though, for reasons to which I shall return, Rousseau does not really think that democratic government is feasible, democracy is in at the beginning of politics, at the precise point, in fact, at which the political emerges from the natural and in so doing begins its inevitable decline back to the natural.

Let me break off from Rousseau for a moment to pursue a little further this "natural" moment. Like most post-Hobbesian theorists, Rousseau (just like Kant too, for example) needs a notion such as that of the contract to mark a clear-cut distinction between a state of nature and a state of politics. (Derrida makes this point forcefully apropos of Hobbes in his seminars.)[13] It is interesting, then, to see how Spinoza, in chapter 16 of the *Tractatus Theologico-Politicus*, derives a theory of sovereignty directly from nature and in continuation with nature.[14]

Spinoza says that natural right is coextensive with the power of nature, which is the same as the power of God, and that "it is the sovereign law and right of nature that each individual should endeavour to preserve itself as it is, without regard to anything but itself; therefore this sovereign law [*lex summa*] and right belongs to every individual, namely, to exist and act according to its natural conditions" (200–201).

Sovereignty is importantly the same for humans and animals, for the rational and the irrational, the sane and the insane:

> We do not here acknowledge any difference between mankind and other individual natural entities, nor between men endowed with reason and those to whom reason is unknown; nor between fools, madmen, and sane men. Whatsoever an individual does by the laws of its nature it has a sovereign right to do, inasmuch as it acts as it was conditioned by nature, and cannot act otherwise. Wherefore among men, so long as they are considered as living under the sway of nature, he who does not yet know reason, or who has not yet acquired the habit of virtue, acts solely according to the laws of his desire with as sovereign a right as he who orders his life entirely by the laws of reason.
>
> That is, as the wise man has sovereign right to do all that reason dictates, or to live according to the laws of reason, so also the ignorant

and foolish man has sovereign right to do all that desire dictates, or to live according to the laws of desire. This is identical with the teaching of Paul, who acknowledges that previous to the law — that is, so long as men are considered of as living under the sway of nature, there is no sin. (201)

The natural law of desire and force is as sovereign as the law of reason. And there is even reason to think that it is in some important sense *more sovereign*, more originally sovereign, than the laws of reason, for as Spinoza goes on to say, reason appears only very late in the story he is telling, and nothing like so naturally as the nature that gives desire and force:

> The natural right of the individual man is thus determined, not by sound reason, but by desire and power. All are not naturally conditioned so as to act according to the laws and rules of reason; nay, on the contrary, all men are born ignorant, and before they can learn the right way of life and acquire the habit of virtue, the greater part of their life, even if they have been well brought up, has passed away. Nevertheless, they are in the meanwhile bound to live and preserve themselves as far as they can by the unaided impulses of desire. Nature has given them no other guide, and has denied them the present power of living according to sound reason; so that they are no more bound to live by the dictates of an enlightened mind, than a cat is bound to live by the laws of the nature of a lion. (201)[15]

This nonrational natural situation will nonetheless give rise, still naturally, to a political organization. The argument goes as follows: nature (wherein man "is but a speck" [*particula*: Elwes translates the same word as "atom" in the corresponding passage of the *Tractatus Politicus*])[16] may well be beyond the grasp of the laws of reason, and therefore our perception of certain elements of nature as "ridiculous, absurd or evil" is merely to do with the narrow limits of our rationality; *nevertheless*, it is better for us to live according to the laws of reason (however limited they may be in the general context of nature). This is so, first, because reason has the good for its object, but also (rather more convincingly in this context, perhaps) because otherwise men (asserting their natural sovereign right to whatever they desire and can obtain by force) will necessarily, in Hobbesian fashion, live in fear of each other, and so the best way of securing something of their sovereign right is to collaborate and form a collective sovereign. Whence a "compact," motivated, still entirely naturally, by fear: only fear will really, and naturally, maintain the good faith of those who form a society:

As we have shown that the natural right of the individual is only limited by his power, it is clear that by transferring, either willingly or under compulsion, this power into the hands of another, he in so doing necessarily cedes also a part of his right; and further, that the Sovereign right over all men belongs to him who has sovereign power, wherewith he can compel men by force, or restrain them by threats of the universally feared punishment of death; such sovereign right he will retain only so long as he can maintain his power of enforcing his will; otherwise he will totter on his throne, and no one who is stronger than he will be bound unwillingly to obey him.

In this manner a society can be formed without any violation of natural right, and the covenant can always be strictly kept — that is, if each individual hands over the whole of his power to the body politic, the latter will then possess sovereign natural right over all things; that is, it will have sole and unquestioned dominion, and everyone will be bound to obey, under pain of the severest punishment. (205)

As in Rousseau (and indeed Hobbes), this situation is explicitly described as one of *democracy*, just because it "wields all its power as a whole," as Spinoza puts it, and sovereignty is here already *exceptional* and *absolute:* "The sovereign power is not restrained by any laws, but everyone is bound to obey it in all things" (205). Some strange consequences flow from this; for example, just by ceding all rights to the whole (which they must, on pain of "dividing and consequently ruining the state"), "and, therefore, having acted (as we have shown) as reason and necessity demanded, they are obliged to fulfill the commands of the sovereign power, however absurd these may be, else they will be public enemies, and will act against reason, which urges the preservation of the state as a primary duty. For reason bids us choose the least of two evils" (205). So, once the sovereign is constituted politically, it inherits, as it were, the intrinsic potential irrationality or absurdity that characterizes sovereignty as naturally given. But at this level of the description, it would be irrational to oppose that sovereignty (however absurd or irrational it in fact be). The always potential irrationality of the State rationally trumps the possible rationality of the individual. And just this is democracy insofar as it is natural: "I think I have now shown sufficiently clearly the basis of a democracy: I have especially desired to do so, for I believe it to be of all forms of government the most natural, and the most consonant with individual liberty. In it no one transfers his natural right so absolutely that he has no further voice in affairs, he only hands it over to the majority of a society, whereof he is a unit. Thus all men remain as they were in the state of nature, equals" (207). Democracy is, then, a kind of degree zero of politics, on the very edge of the state of nature, the state-of-nature-of-politics, the nature that remains to haunt politics even as politics is supposed to be the emergence from nature.[17]

It is true, says Spinoza, that this potential irrationality of the sovereign tends to be limited: first by the fact that the sovereign is sovereign only to the extent that it has the power to enforce its will (and it would tend to lose that power by too often imposing irrational commands), and second by the fact that, as democratic, it is still less likely to be irrational or capricious, just because, as Spinoza sees it, "it is almost impossible that the majority of a people, especially if it be a large one, should agree in an irrational design" (206). And this is why Spinoza will go on to say that democracy is "of all forms of government the most natural, and the most consonant with individual liberty" (207).

This primacy of democracy is also the case in Hobbes, though perhaps less obviously in *Leviathan* than in *Elements of Law* and *De Cive*. In chapter 21 of *Elements*, for example ("Of the Three Sorts of Commonwealth"), Hobbes writes:

> Having spoken in general concerning instituted policy in the former chapter, I come in this to speak of the sorts thereof in special, how every one of them is instituted. The first in order of time of these three sorts is democracy, and it must be so of necessity, because an aristocracy and a monarchy, require nomination of persons agreed upon; which agreement in a great multitude of men must consist in the consent of the major part; and where the votes of the major part involve the votes of the rest, there is actually a democracy.
>
> In the making of a democracy, there passeth no covenant, between the sovereign and any subject. For while the democracy is a making, there is no sovereign with whom to contract. For it cannot be imagined, that the multitude should contract with itself, or with any one man, or number of men, parcel of itself, to make itself sovereign; nor that a multitude, considered as one aggregate, can give itself anything which before it had not. Seeing then that sovereignty democratical is not conferred by the covenant of any multitude (which supposeth union and sovereignty already made), it resteth, that the same be conferred by the particular covenants of every several man; that is to say, every man with every man, for and in consideration of the benefit of his own peace and defence, covenanteth to

stand to and obey, whatsoever the major part of their whole number, or the major part of such a number of them, as shall be pleased to assemble at a certain time and place, shall determine and command. And this is that which giveth being to a democracy; wherein the sovereign assembly was called of the Greeks by the name of *Demus* (*id est*, the people), from whence cometh democracy. So that where, to the supreme and independent court, every man may come that will and give his vote, there the sovereign is called the people.[18]

This primacy of democracy is short-lived in Hobbes: *Elements of Law* continues to describe democracy famously and strikingly as really only "an aristocracy of orators."[19] But this democratic moment cannot fail to continue to haunt the discussion of the other forms (aristocracy and monarchy), just because they can come into being (even if they supposedly do so inevitably) only through this primal moment of democracy.

Unlike in Hobbes, however, Spinoza, having laid out this kind of formal account of the possibility of a state naturally grounded in a contract, draws some less than absolutist consequences about sovereignty. For it seems to flow from the nature of the naturality in the argument here (the same nature that means that a cat cannot be made to live as a lion, but also that humans are always still less than rational and still somewhat animal) that the transition from natural right into politics is *essentially* limited. Spinoza says at the beginning of the following chapter that this means that the theory "must . . . always remain in many respects purely ideal" (chapter 17). This ideality leaves an *essential* (and not merely contingent) role to the less-than-ideal (what I earlier referred to as a kind of "transcendental exposure"). Spinoza puts it like this: "No one can ever so utterly transfer to another his power and, consequently, his rights, as to cease to be a man; nor can there ever be a power so sovereign that it can carry out every possible wish" (214).[20] So it would seem that, as we saw in a different way in Rousseau, the sovereign is never quite or entirely sovereign.

This kind of configuration, with all the important differences one might bring out between Rousseau and Hobbes and Spinoza, seems at the very least to *double democracy up*. On the one hand it gives it this primary position, as a kind of originary (and quasi-natural) state of the State. In Hobbes, the other forms can come into being only on the basis of this primary democracy; in Spinoza, democracy is explicitly the most *natural* form; in Rousseau, as we have seen, it is as it were the *obvious* (if impractical) form of government for the Sovereign to adopt, or at least the only legitimate way that any form of government can be instituted. On the other hand, as it were *after* this archidemocratic moment, democracy is just one form of government or regime among others. I want to argue that *all* forms of government (monarchy, aristocracy, and democracy, in whatever form) remain haunted by this primary moment, which is constitutive of sovereignty itself, and importantly a moment of *nature*. As is perhaps clearest in Spinoza, democracy has a *natural* quality to it, and this quality brings with it something less than, or other than, rationality. Via a rather different route, this might bring us back to Derrida's reasons for associating sovereignty and animality and provide some basis for his contestation of the usual assumption that politics is specifically human.

I want to suggest that this archidemocratic moment (which you will have understood, I hope, that I am not invoking in any pious attempt to feel good about democracy because of this supposed natural priority; there might be some reasons to feel good about democracy, though probably even better reasons to think of democracy as an antidote to certain kinds of feeling good, although in principle, as Derrida says, it has always been difficult rigorously to separate good and evil when it comes to democracy, whence indeed "autoimmunity")[21] says something important about the political as such, insofar as it implies a plurality or multiplicity that will always work against the unitary aspirations of sovereignty, but also that its somewhat *fabulous* quality is problematic, marking any particular empirical instantiation of democracy as rather less than fabulous, or as intrinsically wanting. We're always dissatisfied with our democracy, which seems by definition never quite democratic enough. But you will perhaps not be surprised that I want to argue that this quality of being wanting is also democracy's best (indeed only) *chance*.

Rousseau famously says (as Derrida recalls in *Voyous*), that "a people of gods would govern itself democratically." This is in fact part of a general configuration in Rousseau's thought, which we have already begun to see, whereby the very condition of possibility of politics itself is its necessary imperfection or failure. For example, in making his famous distinction between the "volonté générale" and the "volonté de tous," Rousseau adds this note: "If there were no different interests, one would scarcely fell the common interest which would never encounter any obstacle: everything would proceed automatically, and politics would cease to be an art" (371n); and, discussing the law, "All justice comes from God, He alone is its source; but if we knew how to receive it from so high we should need neither government

nor laws" (371). Democracy in Rousseau's thought occupies the same position as an oppositionless general will or the pure justice of God in the
sentences I have just quoted. He writes, for example in the chapter of book
III on democracy:

> He who makes the law knows better than anyone how it should be
> executed and interpreted. So it seems that one could have no better
> constitution than one in which the executive power is joined to the legis-
> lative: but that is the very thing that makes this government insufficient in
> certain ways, because the things that ought to be distinguished are not
> distinguished, and because the Prince and the Sovereign are the same
> person, they form, so to speak, only a government without government.
> (404; this is Rousseau, not Blanchot . . . )

And, just a little later, "A people that would never misuse government would
not misuse independence either; a people that always governed well would
have no need to be governed" (404). Democracy is a kind of limit case of
government — whence its fabulous character.

This curious status of democracy (which is presumably what justifies
Derrida's repeated observation in his political writings that democracy has
never been simply one regime name among others [e.g., *V*, 49], or, as he says
several times in *Voyous*, that democracy has no essence nor even a clear idea or
ideal [62], no real self or propriety [61], an "opening of indeterminacy or
undecidability" in its very concept [47], and to that extent no simple ipseity)
could be verified in political philosophy more generally. What interests me
here, however, is a curious consequence of this positioning of democracy,
whereby it seems as though it should be the best (the *most* sovereign) form
of sovereignty (or at least, as in Rousseau, the only properly sovereign way
that a sovereign can establish and maintain itself as sovereign by governing),
but constantly shows up as the *least* sovereign form. Democracy *would be* the
best form, says Rousseau, as Derrida recalls, for a "people of gods," for which
read, for a people *without* politics, for a nonpolitical polis. Democracy is
fabulous just because it is the form politics would take if it were not political.
The "politics of politics," however, means that politics *is* political, and therefore that democracy is struck by a kind of impossibility.[22] Rousseau himself
says, "If we take the term rigorously, no true democracy has ever existed, and
never will" (404), and a little later points out, "There is no government so
subject to civil wars and internal agitations as the democratic or popular,
because there is none that tends so strongly and continually to change its

form, nor one that demands more vigilance and courage to maintain it in its own form" (405). This quality of democracy (to be compared with Hobbes's "aristocracy of orators" remark) is also what motivated a much more ancient perception, in Plato among many others, also picked up on by Derrida (*V*, 100), of the tendency of democracy to degenerate into, or to become indiscernible from, demagogy, for the popular to be difficult to separate from the populist.[23]

This perception, the force of which I think only a misplaced (though unfortunately widespread) piety could prevent one from registering, flows directly from the nature of sovereignty itself. The matrix for the errors and stupidity of the tradition of thinking about sovereignty is the tendency to assume, along with the sovereign, already siding with the sovereign, that the sovereign is *one*, which tendency (even in Carl Schmitt) leads to all the features analyzed by Derrida in his rapprochement in *Voyous* of sovereignty and subjectivity, or more generally what he calls *ipseity*, as self-identical and self-authorizing, "the sovereign and reappropriating gathering of self" (*V*, 30). One of the many virtues of Rousseau's political thought is the clear (if nonetheless troubled) perception that by definition the sovereign is *not one*, and that politics would simply end if it were.[24] The politics of politics is that the sovereign is plural, divided, and dispersed, and just this is why "democracy" is not a bad name for thinking the political as such,[25] and why there is, as Derrida often claims, an affinity between democracy and deconstruction. The principle of *différance* that deconstructs also democratizes. But just as the thought of différance escapes the Hegelian construal of Absolute Difference by a kind of internal or intrinsic inhibition, restraint or falling short (by a kind of conceptual modesty or *pudeur*, in fact), holding itself short of itself in order to be, if not ever quite itself, then at least something *like* itself, so with democracy, which is and remains political only to the extent that it never is quite itself, and the demos, thank goodness, somewhat in spite of itself, never quite becomes a people of gods.

This non–self-coincidence of any sovereignty and any demos is what allows Derrida to open up the dimension of the *à-venir*, the to-come, that consistently marks his thinking about democracy, the opening to the unforeseeable event as such, the other, the *arrivant*, the "messianic" opening through which, a priori, no Messiah will ever enter. And just this dimension is what enables him, in his late work, to play the unconditional against the sovereign. But the unconditional in this sense is not so much just *opposed* to sovereignty (in spite of some appearances, perhaps) as at work already *in* sovereignty as the inevitable motivation for its ambitions, and as its principle of ruin or dispersion. Indeed, that opening is none other than the possibility of the very "exception" that defines sovereignty itself in Schmitt's famous definition (and in truth has defined sovereignty since Bodin, as Schmitt himself would certainly not deny). For in spite of the slightly lurid appeal of Schmitt's famous definition, and the no less lurid satisfactions that can be had from literalizing, historicizing, and denouncing the so-called state of exception, that "exception," as Schmitt makes very clear, inhabits the most everyday structure of decision, cutting into the supposed flow of time with the repeated *kairos* of the event. This event can only be that of the "arrival" or advent, perhaps even terrifyingly (*V*, 39) of that other that cannot be the Messiah, but without which there would be no time or politics at all. As we could also try to show by reading Bataille, this opening constitutively compromises the supposed sovereignty of the sovereign, the being-sovereign of the sovereign, by compromising the ipseity of the *ipse* (as formulated in "L'expérience intérieure," for example), which is, in Bataille's usage,[26] *anything but* the autonomy or self-presence of the so-called sovereign subject, but which is also difficult to reduce to some concept of "bare life."[27]

As Rousseau shows more lucidly than most, the plurality that intrigues Derrida in the "peuple de dieux" that would govern itself democratically, the sovereign cannot *be* sovereign unless it involves this opening, this opening that it may seem bound to want to close (that it *contains*, then). This opening is clearly as good as it is bad, like the autoimmunity that becomes Derrida's favorite figure in his later work, for the structure I have been trying to bring out (the sovereign's very efforts toward immunity perversely also produce it as autoimmune, to some extent self-destructive or suicidal, *and this cannot simply be bad*).[28]

If I am not mistaken, just this is what "democracy to come" is attempting to capture, and why it relates to an unconditionality other than sovereignty. "Democracy" in this formulation bespeaks just what is befalling sovereignty (even democratic sovereignty) as it is falling and failing, as its autoimmunity itself, as what brings politics to politics — and "sovereignty" the endless, unavoidable, and natural stupidity of thinking itself immune from that coming.

*Notes*

1  Derrida, "La bête et le souverain," 467–68.
2  Ibid., 446 ("Un souverain dont on sait d'ailleurs qu'il peut être très bête"), and 473 ("Comme Dieu, le souverain est au-dessus de la loi et de l'humanité, au-dessus de tout, et il a l'air un peu bête").

3  Rousseau, *Du contrat social*, in *Œuvres complètes*, 3: 424. Subsequent page references to this edition will be given in the text. All translations are my own.

4  See too the longer narrative account in the *Lettres écrites de la montagne*, in *Œuvres complètes*, 3: 815:

> The Sovereign People wills by itself, and by itself it does what it wants. Soon the inconvenience of this concourse of all in everything forces the Sovereign People to charge some of its members with the execution of its wishes. After having fulfilled their charge and reported on it, these Officers return to the common equality. Soon these charges become frequent, and eventually permanent. Insensibly a body is formed that acts always. A body that acts always cannot report on every act: it only reports on the principal ones; soon it gets to the point of reporting on none. The more active the acting principle, the more it enervates the willing principle. Yesterday's will is assumed to be today's; whereas yesterday's act does not dispense one from acting today. Finally the inaction of the willing power subjects it to the executive power; the latter gradually renders its actions independent, and soon its will: instead of acting for the power that wills, it acts on it. There then remains in the State only an acting power, the executive. The executive power is mere force, and where mere force reigns the State is dissolved.

5  Derrida, *Etats d'âme de la psychanalyse;* see my paper "Superanus," originally presented in French to the Journées Philosophie-Psychanalyse de Castries in 2001.

6  Cf. my paper "La souveraineté défaillante," 131–43, translated as "The Fall of Sovereignty," 395–406.

7  As Derrida has it in the seminar sessions, first glossing the traditional concept, "Indivisibility is an analytical part of the concept of sovereignty: a divisible or shareable sovereignty is not a sovereignty" ("La bête et le souverain," 465), but then adding, "Sovereignty . . . is posited as immortal and indivisible precisely because it is mortal, and divisible" (463).

8  Rousseau himself relates sovereignty to an *absolute* present which, or so it would seem, has the same formal properties as those posited by Bataille, for example, in the so-called Geneva manuscript, where he says, "The general will which must direct the State is not that of a past time, but that of the present moment, and the true character of sovereignty is that there is always agreement of time, place and effect between the direction of general will and the use of public force" (3: 296), or again, in a fragment, "Each act of sovereignty, and each instant of its duration is absolute, independent of the preceding instant, and the sovereign never acts because it has willed, but because it wills (now)" (3: 485).

9  This pure instantaneous nothingness of sovereignty is what suggests that Bataille and Rousseau (for example) are still speaking the same language. Whence too, no doubt, the topos of the helpless sovereign (cf. Derrida, *Etats d'âme de la psychanalyse*, 52), and, in Bataille, the sovereign destined to be sacrificed.

10  For a discussion of the disconcerting logic of the summit as Bataille develops it, see

my "Lecture: De Georges Bataille," 119–47. See too Nancy's text "*Ex nihilo summum* (de la souveraineté)," 145–72. Although I am very close to many of Nancy's formulations, I take issue with his alignment of sovereignty and "la révolte du peuple" in "La souveraineté défaillante."

11 See my *Sententiousness and the Novel*, chapter 4; and especially my *Dudding: Des noms de Rousseau*.

12 This would be the principle of heteronomy that Derrida suggests must in fact provide the basis for any "autonomy" in *Etats d'âme* (58–59). This originary heteronomy, which flows directly from Derrida's earliest insights about *différance*, situates his thought as far as can be from any subject-based philosophy (see, for example, the early "Cogito et l'histoire de la folie," in *L'Ecriture et la différence*, or the very trenchant remarks in *Politiques de l'amitié*, 86–88), and thereby, in the political sphere, from any kind of liberalism.

13 Derrida, "La bête et le souverain," 463.

14 When asked by a correspondent about his difference from Hobbes, Spinoza replied tersely, "As regards political theories, the difference which you inquire about between Hobbes and myself, consists in this, that I always preserve natural right intact, and only allot to the chief magistrates in every state a right over their subjects commensurate with the excess of their power over the power of the subjects. This is what always takes place in the state of nature" (Letter L). I do not believe that Derrida discusses Spinoza in the unpublished parts of his sovereignty seminars. He is, of course, a hero in Hardt and Negri's *Empire* and *Multitude* and in the work of other recent theorists, but is not at all the object of what could be called *reading*. Although it is out of the question to attempt to demonstrate this here, I believe that reading is a crucial component of "the politics of politics," and therefore that the absence of reading in, say, Negri and Hardt leaves their claims and positions vulnerable to various kinds of naïveté and piety. I discuss in some detail the recent reception of Spinoza in the forthcoming project of which this is a part. I quote Spinoza's *Theologico-Political Treatise* from the translation by Elwes and cite page references in the text.

15 Curious example, but the mythologically "sovereign" nature of the lion cannot be an accidental feature here.

16 I pursue the possibilities of an "atomistic" reading of democracy in "La démocritie à venir," 599–613, and in "The Matter with Democracy."

17 I explore at length this never-quite-left-behindness of nature in the context of Kant's political thought in *Frontières kantiennes*.

18 Hobbes, *The Elements of Law, Natural and Politic*, 118–19.

19 Ibid., 120:

> In all democracies, though the right of sovereignty be in the assembly, which is virtually the whole body; yet the use thereof is always in one, or a few particular men. For in such great assemblies as those must be, whereinto every man may enter at his pleasure, there is no means any ways to deliberate and give counsel

what to do, but by long and set orations; whereby to every man there is more or less hope given, to incline and sway the assembly to their own ends. In a multitude of speakers therefore, where always, either one is eminent alone, or a few being equal amongst themselves, are eminent above the rest, that one or few must of necessity sway the whole; insomuch, that a democracy, in effect, is no more than an aristocracy of orators, interrupted sometimes with the temporary monarchy of one orator.

20  "If it were really the case, that men could be deprived of their natural rights so utterly as never to have any further influence on affairs, except with the permission of the holders of sovereign right, it would then be possible to maintain with impunity the most violent tyranny, which, I suppose, no one would for an instant admit" (214–15). Given the persistence of "nature" in Spinoza's account, we can see that what keeps humans human, and so holds them short of a complete or thoroughgoing politicization, is also their residual animality.

21  Derrida, *Voyous*, 43; subsequent references are cited parenthetically in the text as *V*.

22  In earlier work, I often used the formula "the end of politics is the end of politics" to suggest that politics and political theory tend to work teleologically toward their own demise in an achieved nonpolitical state. See especially my *Frontiers*. I now want to say that the politics of politics is just what prevents politics achieving this end, and therefore keeps it political.

23  See the famous descriptions of the *kyklos* of political forms in *Republic*, books 8 and 9. I discuss this, and its complex Aristotelian counterpart, in "Demo."

24  This is also a crucial point in Aristotle's critique of Plato's political theory, as, for example, in the *Politics:*

> Yet it is clear that if the process of unification proceeds with too much rigour, there will be no *polis* left: for the *polis* is by nature a plurality [*plethos*], and if its unification is pushed too far, the *polis* will become a family, and the family an individual: for we can affirm that the family is more unified than the *polis*, and the individual more unified than the family. Consequently, even supposing that one were in a position to operate this unification, one should refrain from doing so, because it would lead the *polis* to its ruin. The *polis* is composed not only of a plurality of individuals [*pleionon anthropon*], but also of specifically distinct elements . . . even in *poleis* founded on the liberty and equality of the citizens [i.e., democracies], this differentiation must exist. (1261a 17–33; cf. 1277a 5–10)

In *Voyous*, Derrida tends to assimilate Plato and Aristotle in their "political salute to the One God" (110–11). I try to reopen some space between them on this point in "For Better and Worse."

25  This is one of several points where what I am advancing here converges with the thought of Jacques Rancière. I attempt both to register those convergences and to bring out some important differences in forthcoming work.

26 "Because the *ipse* must communicate — with others like it — it resorts to degrading sentences. It would fall into the insignificance of the 'I' (equivocation) if it did not insist on communicating. . . . Now I cannot myself be *ipse* without having thrown this cry towards them [i.e., readers]. By this cry alone I have the power to destroy in me the 'I' as they will destroy it in themselves if they hear me" (Bataille, "L'expérience intérieure," 135–36). Derrida invokes Bataille only very briefly in *Voyous* (100), seeming to assimilate him to the idea of a "criminal and transgressive counter-sovereignty."

27 By the time Agamben has worked through his thinking in *Homo Sacer* and *State of Exception* I would be close to agreeing with him, when he states, for example, "Bare life is a product of the machine and not something that precedes it" (*State of Exception*, 87–88). But how much unhelpful pathos along the way! See too Derrida's brief comment in *Voyous* (46) contesting Agamben's opening distinction between *bios* and *zoe*, the trenchant nature of which does indeed seem untenable.

28 Derrida, *Voyous*, 210:

> If an event worthy of the name is to happen, it must, beyond all mastery, affect a passivity. It must touch a vulnerability that is exposed, without absolute immunity, without indemnity, in its finitude and in a non-horizontal way, where it is not yet or already no longer possible to face, to face up to, the unforeseeability of the other. *In this respect, auto-immunity is not an absolute evil* [my emphasis]. It allows exposure to the other, to *what* comes and to *who* comes — and must therefore remain incalculable. Without auto-immunity, with absolute immunity, nothing would ever happen. One would no longer wait, no longer expect, no longer expect each other, nor any event.

> Not an absolute evil for reasons already given at the end of §37 of *Foi et savoir*, 71: "There is nothing *common*, nothing immune, safe and sound, *heilig* and holy, nothing intact in the most autonomous living present without a risk of auto-immunity. As always, the risk is doubly charged — the same finite risk. Twice rather than once: with a threat and a chance. Briefly, it has to take on board, to en-gage, the *possibility* of that **radical evil** without which one could not do good."

# Sovereign Hesitations

WENDY BROWN

This essay works critically with *Rogues*, Derrida's text on sovereignty and democracy, with the aim of tracing some of its limiting liberal political attachments and consecrations. This aim in turn is born of a desire, shared with Derrida, to theoretically limn the possibilities of a future brighter for justice than the present. Thus, my critique of this inordinately rich text has nothing to do with merely outing its flaws or failures. Rather, as I suggest near the end of the essay, Derrida's problem is our problem, which is why I want to tarry with it at length.

---

In Plato, Hobbes, Bodin, and Schmitt, the figure of sovereign power stands for everything deconstruction unsettles: unity, identity, oneness, self-sufficiency, autarky, indivisibility, pure will, decisiveness, primacy without dependence, domination without predicate, enduring sameness over time. Deconstruction unsettles the intended *effects* of sovereignty as well: the drawing and policing of definite boundaries, the production of determinate identity, the establishment of clear lines between insiders and outsiders, life and death, friend and enemy, familiar and foreigner. From Schmitt's tracing of all political concepts to theological origins to the grandly staged rivalry between God and man with which Hobbes opens *Leviathan*, political sovereignty appears as precisely the human appropriation of a divine form of power that deconstruction has taken as its task to disrobe.

What we would expect from the encounter of deconstruction with sovereignty, then: deconstruction would trouble sovereign claims in every venue or seat of power—language, reason, subject, state, king, and God. Deconstruction would be compelled to undo sovereignty—to reveal it as predicated, dependent, internally divided, vulnerable, and hence not sovereign at all—and by this undoing would vanquish sovereignty, not because deconstruction aims to vanquish its objects but because sovereignty simply cannot survive being undone. Yet curiously, in *Rogues*, Derrida does not approach sovereignty this way. Rather, as he probes the complex relation of sovereignty and democracy in Western thought, he recuperates a conditional and conditioned sovereignty from its absolutist and unconditional heritage, and he identifies this transformed notion of sovereignty with the possibility of a democracy to come.[1] As he attempts to wrest the unconditional from sovereignty, he relays the unconditional to freedom and refounds sovereignty as conditioned, divisible, and shared. At the same time, he attempts to detach freedom from the premise of an autonomous subject and to detach reason and faith from absolutism.

Why? Why these arduous endeavors of recuperation and rescue, protection and relocation, in lieu of a more radical challenge to sovereignty? Why not join Agamben, Hardt, Negri, and other contemporaries in identifying sovereign power as what must be challenged on behalf of global justice, as what must be left behind in the democracy to come? Or why not join Foucault, Deleuze, or Connolly in an *exposé* of sovereignty's conceits as philosophically untenable, historically outmoded, empirically false? Derrida's answer: "It would be imprudent and hasty, in truth hardly *reasonable*, to oppose unconditionally, that is, head-on, a sovereignty that is itself unconditional and indivisible. One cannot combat, *head-on*, *all* sovereignty, sovereignty *in general* without threatening at the same time, beyond the nation-state figure of sovereignty, the classical principles of freedom and self-determination" (158). In short, sovereignty underwrites the individual freedom that Derrida takes to be at democracy's heart. Thus, even as he argues that "it is no doubt necessary, in the name of reason, to call into question and to limit a logic of nation-state sovereignty . . . to erode not only its principle of indivisibility but its right to the exception," and argues too that "such a questioning of sovereignty is not simply some formal or academic necessity [but] . . . is already under way . . . is what's *coming*, what's *happening*" (157), he also regards democracy as requiring sovereignty. Moreover, if the erosion of sovereignty under way in thought and in politics opens certain possibilities of a democracy to come, for Derrida it opens as well possibilities of a barbarism to come: a barbarism of terror, of world war, of all rogue states (and so no rogue states), of global capitalism, of theocracy, of anti- rather than post-Enlightenment—above all, a barbarism of unfreedom and lack of self-determination. Sovereignty, then, harbors the premise and promise of freedom as self-determination and secures the rule of reason, law, and rights. One could say here, and I in fact conclude with this thesis, that for Derrida sovereignty promises to secure civilization against its barbarous opposite. (Even if, as Derrida says, sovereign states are always already rogue states, even if sovereignty has brought us to the current pass in which all sovereign states act out their rogue nature, Derrida does not pursue this dissolution of Westphalian sovereignty into its opposite and seeks instead to recover something of sovereignty's original promise.)

My concern in this paper is with *the politics* of holding out for a liberal democratic form of sovereignty (located in parliaments, the rule of reason, rights, and recourse to courts of law as decisive, even if these are all internationalized, beyond the nation-state) in the name of a democracy to come. I want to examine the formulation of democracy from which Derrida's attachment to sovereignty emerges and which it in turn secures. To this end, I consider, first, Derrida's account of the relationship between democracy and sovereignty; second, his ambivalent formulation of democracy as both empty of fixed meaning and suffused with a distinctly liberal meaning; and third, how this formulation divides individual freedom from political sovereignty in such a way as to subvert popular sovereignty with statism. Finally, I take brief leave from Derrida's text to speculate about the preoccupation with democracy on the part of the contemporary post-Marxist European Left, a preoccupation Derrida shares with Rancière, Balibar, Habermas, Laclau, Mouffe, Agamben, even Negri. How has the overtaking of Western political life by neoliberal rationality and by a figuring of Islam as theocratic produced a circling of the diverse wagons of this Left around an articulation of democracy that shores up the identification of the Euro-Atlantic world with civilization signified by individual freedom? And how does this articulation itself insulate us from a reckoning with the Euro-Atlantic world's own capacities for barbarism, on one hand, and subjection by global powers that mock the potency of the political, on the other?

*Democracy and Sovereignty*

The relationship between democracy and sovereignty is posed as a question today consequent to the partial, uneven deconstitution of the sovereign nation-state in late modernity, a deconstitution effected by unprecedented flows of economic, moral, political, and theological power across national boundaries. It is a question posed as well by the overtly imperial conduct of the world's "oldest" continuous democracy, the putative aim of which is a universal instantiation of democracy, an aim that paradoxically entails domestic subversions of democracy and disregard for other nation-state sovereignties. It is posed, too, by the occupation of Iraq, in which the twin policy aims of installing managed (market) democracy and producing Iraqi sovereignty appear only vaguely linked and are both seriously stalled. And it is a question posed by the evolution of the European Union, as postnational political forms intersect with transnational economic powers to foment anxiety about the means by which democracy can be secured and practiced.

But even prior to the emergence of this set of conundrums, the relationship between sovereignty and democracy was a puzzle. If "popular sovereignty" has tripped off the tongues of Westerners for three centuries, it remains one of the more strikingly catachrestic terms to enter ordinary discourse in the era of nation-states. It is nearly impossible to reconcile the classical features of sovereignty — power that is not only foundational and unimpeachable, enduring and indivisible, but above all decisive and supralegal — with the requisites of rule by the demos. And the very fact that the people are declared sovereign in the United States while we give the appellation of sovereign power to autocratic state action and especially to action that violates or suspends democratic principles suggests that we have known all along that popular sovereignty was, if not a fiction, at least an abstraction with a tenuous bearing on political reality. What, otherwise, does it mean to identify as sovereign those state acts that suspend or abridge the rule of law that signifies democracy, or to speak, as we often do today, of expanded executive or state powers in terms of resurging or expanding sovereign power?

Here is another way in: popular sovereignty in liberal democracy works in a double register, one of routine legitimacy, law, and elections and another of state action or decisionism. What we call the state in liberal democracies comprises both, which is why Locke subdivided the powers of the state yet formulated federative or prerogative power (state sovereignty) as precisely that which can suspend or set aside legislative power (popular sovereignty).[2] Insofar as the people authorize the suspension of their own legislative power, they suspend their sovereignty in the name of their own protection or need. But a sovereign that suspends its sovereignty is no sovereign.

More generally, the problem with formulating sovereignty as divided, separated, or circulating is its incompatibility with the most basic qualities of sovereignty — not its unconditioned, a priori, or unitary aspect (all of which Derrida challenges), but its finality and decisiveness.[3] It is these last qualities that make sovereignty something that either is or isn't: as the current predicament of Iraq attests, the idea of "partial," provisional, or shared sovereignty is not just unstable but incoherent. Nor can there be multiple sovereigns or sites of sovereignty in a single jurisdiction or entity; sovereignty pertains in part to delimiting jurisdiction and political identity. Indeed, it is precisely over such contesting sovereign claims that wars are fought, lawsuits filed, religions clash (with each other or with states), and human beings psychologically disintegrate. If, as Schmitt suggests, political sovereignty borrows its shape from God, it does more than episodically trump and more than stand as symbolic origin of power or authority. It is final and absolute, hence indivisible and nontransferable; it cannot circulate, cede, transmogrify, delegate, or self-suspend any more than divine power does. If the people are sovereign, if this is the meaning of *cracy* by the *demos*, then their shared power must be decisive, in which case a sovereign state cannot suspend this power. Conversely, where sovereignty rests with the state or an executive, democracy does not actually prevail; the "rule of the people" is at best a discontinuous, episodic, and subordinate *practice* rather than sovereign power. Or, if sovereignty is separated from rule, if the people are only episodically decisive (every four years), then rule is not a form of self-determination and sovereignty is not a form of rule.

The incoherent splitting of sovereignty in liberal democracy is the contradiction at its heart seized upon by Rousseau and also pursued relentlessly by Marx in "On the Jewish Question." The very existence of the state as that which overcomes our particularity and, in Hegel's words, realizes our freedom, is evidence for Marx that we do not actually rule ourselves or live freely. If we did, the state would not be required for these functions. Yet — and here is where we no sooner pick up Marx than leave him again — it would also seem there can be no political life without sovereignty, that is, not simply without decisiveness and finality but without a power that gathers, mobilizes, and, above all, deploys the collective force of an entity on behalf of and against itself, as its means of governing and ordering itself. Sovereignty gives and represents political form. This is the paradox to which I will repeatedly return in this paper: sovereignty is inherently antidemocratic insofar as it must overcome the dispersed quality of power in democracy, but democracy, to be politically viable, to be a (political) contender, appears to require the supplement of sovereignty. Derrida seems to affirm this paradox in his passing remark, "It is not certain that 'democracy' is a political concept through and through" (39).

Derrida, however, does not tarry with the catachrestic quality of popular sovereignty. Rather, he sets it aside with the remark that "democracy and sovereignty are at the same time in contradiction and inseparable from each other" (100) and moves instead to rework the complex mutual dependence of sovereignty and democracy on *ipseity*: "selfhood" or "being properly one-self." He seeks to loosen democracy from an ipseity that makes the subject or the polity stand strictly for itself through sovereignty, and an ipseity that makes the individual the source of his or her own governance and will. In its stead, Derrida articulates a conditioned, decentered, incomplete, nonidentical ipseity, a standing for oneself that can remain at the heart of the freedom he identifies with democracy but that doffs many of the classical features of sovereignty. Put slightly differently, if democracy appears to require sovereignty, sovereignty undercuts a democracy that features openness, difference, impropriety, and hospitality to what is outside — all the qualities Derrida wants to cultivate. So he has to go after the indivisibility and absolutism, the unconditioned and the forceful quality of sovereignty. He has to unsettle the unified and unconditioned quality of sovereign decision, to "divide it, subject it to partitioning, to participation, to being shared" (101), and he does so by reformulating the ipseity at its heart.

But even as he challenges and radically reworks the concept, ipseity remains the critical link between sovereignty and democracy. Why ipseity? Ipseity signifies the "power that gives itself its own law, its force of law, its self-representation, the sovereign and reappropriating gathering of self in the simultaneity of an assemblage" (10–11). Thus, ipseity represents a certain truth of democracy (in the soul or in the city) apart from its formal constitution: ipseity orders the diverse parts of the self to bring forth the self that would be free, gathers a self out of internal dispersion or collision, and distinguishes self-rule of an assemblage from autocracy on one side and anarchy on the other. As a certain faculty of self-possession, ipseity carries the connection between a sovereign self and a sovereign people; both are produced by a force of their own that gathers and rules them, however incompletely. In Derrida's words, "Before any sovereignty of the state, of the nation-state, of the monarch, or in democracy, of the people, ipseity names a principle of legitimate sovereignty, the accredited or recognized supremacy of a power or a force, a *kratos* or a *cracy*" (13).

A principle of legitimate sovereignty *before* any actual sovereignty: this would be the sovereignty of every "I" or "we" that aspires to rule or govern itself, every entity that can act on its own behalf. The structure of sovereignty prior to its formal constitution is the bringing forth of a self through self-rule, thus, paradoxically, its inherently democratic moment.

What Derrida achieves conceptually in his reworking of ipseity and linking of it to sovereignty is this: instead of being opposed or in tension, democracy becomes one with sovereignty insofar as sovereignty signifies the capacity to rule what it possesses, what is its own, the capacity of an entity to be in possession of itself. The opposite of ipseity is occupation, foreign domination: any power of rule imposed from outside, any self denied its self-possession. If democracy is a form of collective self-possession, it must remain a certain practice of ipseity, selfhood, hence sovereignty: a people in possession of itself. Nor does ipseity conjoin only democracy with sovereignty; it also conjoins sovereign power with freedom: ipseity remains at the heart of freedom understood as self-governance.

Near the end of the text, Derrida also calls for imagining freedom not *wholly* bound to ipseity, "a freedom that would no longer be the power of a subject, a freedom without autonomy, a heteronomy without servitude" (152). He joins Jean-Luc Nancy in trying to "open the way back to a freedom 'that cannot be presented as the autonomy of a subjectivity in charge of itself and of its decisions'" (42). The effort here, of course, is to replace the unconditionality of *ipseity* with an affirmation of its historical, social, and cosmological conditioning, an affirmation that does not reject but reconstructs ipseity as the conceptual architecture for both democracy and sovereignty, and the link between them.

But here's the rub. Even as Derrida has reworked it, ipseity emphasizes the dimension of force and gathering critical to sovereignty, a force and unification that is ultimately undemocratic insofar as it violates precisely the dispersal of power that shared rule requires. Absolute, unifying, subordinating, violating and violent, producing a unified self and will, ipseity signifies the force, authority, and identity that make self-representation possible. Just as this absolutism, unification, subordination, and violence makes the "I" possible, ipseity makes democracy possible in Derrida's account: it *constitutes* the *state* that we know as constitutional democracy. For a person to stand for himself or herself, for a people to stand for themselves, would seem to require the establishment of a "state" above the parts of the self or the people, a state that unifies, gathers, and represents self-possession, a state that possesses the self and puts an end to dispersion.

The reworking of *ipseity* through which Derrida relates sovereignty and democracy thus returns us to the paradox we greeted earlier but now approach from another direction: democracy requires sovereignty, but sovereignty undercuts democracy. Self-possession requires a certain self-subordination; democracy produces itself through certain antidemocratic supplements. Derrida tries to loosen this paradox but not fully escape it. I return later to the question of whether he is right to posit it as inherent. For the moment, note how the current impasse in U.S. ambitions for Iraq can be seen to take shape here. As the United States struggles to establish managed market democracy in Iraq, this struggle is confounded by the radical absence of ipseity in the nation called Iraq, a lack figured not just by a disunified people but by the literal absence of anything resembling a state. Without a state, there is no lodging for the sovereignty that parliamentary democracy requires and no way of producing or representing the democracy that sovereignty would secure. Neither elections (taken to be a sign of democracy) nor the Iraqization of the military and the police (taken to be a sign of sovereignty) can compensate for this absence. The United States cannot "transfer sovereignty" to what cannot receive it (Bodin also reminds us that sovereignty cannot be conferred without negating itself) and cannot implement democracy without sovereignty to secure and represent it. Without ipseity, liberal democracy and sovereignty cannot secure each other. Nothing more profoundly emblematized this bind than images of Iraqi soldiers guarding election booths in January 2006, assuming poses of armed readiness, complete with trigger fingers in position, but humiliatingly absent the guns their American occupiers did not yet trust them to wield. Pretend soldiers guarding pretend sovereignty and overseeing pretend democracy in a land without ipseity.

## Democracy?

For some time, Derrida had been saying that democracy, an old word, is yet unfilled, unknown, and unrealized (5). He remarks in *Rogues* that his decade-long use of the syntagma "democracy to come," which emptied the concept of its historical or local contents, would permit "a meaning in waiting, still empty or vacant of the word or the concept of democracy . . . a word whose heritage is undeniable even if its meaning is still obscured, obfuscated, reserved" (9). This formulation of democracy as open and unsatisfied yet also urgent and insistent has unquestionable appeal for the Left. It saves democracy from all that has been made of it, especially lately, while holding out for the value of self-governance. It saves us from having to limit our political ambitions according to the failures and disappointments of "actually existing democracy." We've been here before, with communism, with revolution, with people power of every sort.

(In fact, in *Rogues*, the figure of democracy appears as a specter haunting European post-Marxists, replacing communism so precisely as to reveal their continued ghosting by communism's now dead promise. Consider: "democracy to come," democracy as it has long been dreamed but never been realized, has all the attributes of post–nation-state, worldwide, universalizing-without-colonizing redress and redemption of most of the wrongs of history and the present once held out by communism. Democracy, as Derrida renders it, is also the only political form commensurate with the epistemological and ontological principles of deconstruction, as communism was commensurate with principles of Enlightenment rationality, especially those of transparency and noncontradiction. Democracy, as communism once was, is harbored in the forces of the present, comes on the heels of the nation-state, and promises to finish off the nation-state as the scene of sovereignty and the political. Democracy is cosmopolitical and postnational, the sole political suitor of [what Derrida calls] "mondialization" borne forth by the World Court, international law, and international human rights. Democracy transforms the sovereign state and the sovereign individual, the ipseity of both. It comes after the decidability, unity, fixity, and proper meaning they presuppose. Democracy is what cannot be prefigured in its precise meaning and organization but carries the dream of freedom and equality dreamed since the beginning of time.)

But Derrida is not merely striving to keep open the signification of a venerable political term. He is also participating in a long-standing political theoretical recognition that democracy is peculiarly contentless or empty compared with other political forms. He calls this the "vacancy or disengagement, the free wheel or semantic indecision at the center of *demokratia*" (40). Spinoza identifies it as democracy's lack of a binding and animating principle. Plato, describing democracy as a "many-colored quilt," says democracy has no *eidos* of its own, and even denies it the status of a distinct regime or a constitution (26). Sheldon Wolin draws on Aristotle for a convergent claim, insisting that democracy cannot be constitutionalized without compromising it, and hence is inherently episodic or fugitive, "an ephemeral phenomenon rather than a settled system" or political form.[4]

"What is lacking in democracy," Derrida writes, "is proper meaning. . . . Democracy is defined, as is the very ideal of democracy, by this lack of the proper and selfsame. And so it is defined only by turns, by tropes, by tropism" (37). He will make literal this turning, this dynamic and indefinable quality, both by affirming Aristotle's account of democracy as ruling and being ruled in turn, and through a formulation of democracy as *rotating* or oscillating between freedom and equality, mastery and measure, heterogeneity and sameness, incalculability and calculability (48). Democracy does not settle, indeed cannot settle among its contrary terms, each of them necessary, each of them in danger of being canceled by its opposite unless democracy remains unfixed and on the move.

For Derrida, the lack of proper meaning in democracy, its unpresentability, constitutes both its promise, its exceeding of its present form (74), and its terrible vulnerability, the ease with which it can be distorted, hijacked, turned against itself. This lack of proper meaning also constitutes both the inherently free and the inherently suicidal nature of democracy. There is "a freedom of play, an opening of indetermination and undecidability in the very concept of democracy, in the interpretation of the democratic" (25), which means that to fix or even stabilize its meaning, to give it content, is to de-democratize, or to kill it:[5] "Democracy could not gather itself around the presence of an axial and univocal meaning that does not destroy itself and get carried away with itself" (40). Derrida goes quite far with the suicidal tendency of democracy: "Democracy has always been suicidal," he writes, not only because of its impossible semiotic condition (an emptiness that cannot stay empty) but because of the tendency of the majority to kill it by having their way with it. To have one's way with and in democracy is to destroy democracy by giving specific content to this fragile, contentless creature. To have one's way in democracy, which is the very meaning of majority rule, is thus to risk killing democracy. And what democracies have not committed suicide, often even electing to kill themselves? Athens during the Peloponnesian Wars is the original suicide, but there is also the ancient Roman republic (and thereby a cautionary tale about democracy-destroying empires emerging from robust and self-congratulatory democracies). There are also the suicides that have come to be codified in single names or phrases: the Terror, Stalinism, late Weimar, and, in the United States today, de-democratization at the convergence of neoliberalism, neoconservatism, and empire.

But before exploring how democracy's relation to suicide and availability for hijacking is related to the supplement of sovereignty already discussed, I want to consider the disjunction between Derrida's casting of democracy as an open signifier and all that he insists democracy consists in and comprises. I begin with the odd way Derrida parses "democracy," a term we know issues from the Greek *demos* and *cracy*: the people rule. Yet repeatedly in *Rogues*, Derrida substitutes the cognate term *kratos* (strength, force) for *cracy*; at one point he actually translates *cracy* as "force" (75). Democracy, he writes, is "a force (*kratos*) . . . in the form of a sovereign authority . . . and thus the power and ipseity of the people (*demos*)" (13). Elsewhere he starts a sentence by saying that democracy features "two guiding concepts . . . the people and power," and then moves in the same sentence to *kratos* and *kraitein*, which he identifies with "prevailing, bringing off, being the strongest" (22).

The effects of transposing cracy and kratos, rule and force, are several: foregrounding the power-political dimension of sovereignty and the force entailed in its expression, it obscures to the point of erasing the shared governance that democracy promises. Indeed, it replaces this governance with an abstract force; it stresses an episodic expression of popular sovereignty over the continuous action of rule or governance. Thus Derrida's translation occludes the most difficult feature of democracy: the regular practice of sharing power, of self-governance. Shared rule, shared power, cherished by radical and republican modes of democracy and nearly extinguished by representative modes, is very different from the collective *force* of the people *on* something or *against* something, the Lockean moment of the people's rebellion against a state carried away with itself. Derrida's transposition of force and rule diminishes the difficulty of democracy as a practice of governance even as it underlines sovereign force.

Apart from construing the demos as a force *behind* democracy rather than its governing power — apart from colluding with liberalism's ruse regarding popular sovereignty as that force is rendered abstract or episodic, separate from the matter of rule — Derrida adds more liberal content to democracy as he locates freedom, defined as personal or individual liberty, at democracy's heart: "It is on the basis of freedom that we will have conceived the concept of democracy. This will be true throughout the entire history of this concept, from Plato's Greece onward" (22). If this claim were stretched to comprise freedom as it takes shape in republican, socialist, or participatory democracy, this would be a less contentious move. But Derrida does not make this stretch. "Freedom," he writes, "is essentially the faculty or power to do as one pleases, to decide, to choose, to determine oneself, to have self-determination, to be master, and first of all master of oneself (*autos, ipse*)" (22–23). Now, whatever the *reputation* of democracy with regard to freedom (and Derrida himself notes the oddity of Plato's and Aristotle's discussions of democracy in terms of "what is said" about it [23]), neither the inherent connection of democracy and personal freedom nor the stability of this meaning of freedom is obvious. To the contrary, as Rousseau made clear, maximized personal liberty is not necessary to practice collective self-governance, any more than governing ourselves, being democrats, is a guarantee that liberty will be enshrined as a value or institutionally protected. Moreover, within liberal democracy, the articulation and protection of most civil liberties and the securing of legitimate representative government through universal suffrage and fair elections occupy two distinct institutional and practical fields; they neither directly entail nor require each other.

Derrida's location of democracy's soul in individual liberty produces a fundamental conundrum in this text on sovereignty and democracy. If, as he says, democracy secures the freedom to do as one pleases, then it secures our freedom *from* one another, including our freedom from ruling together or taking responsibility for the whole. This construes democracy as standing for a libertarian freedom *from* the difficulty of sharing power and governing ourselves in common, hence a freedom *from participating in rule by the demos*. The identification of democracy with individual liberty disarticulates it from governance in common, from shared political power. At the same time, this identification separates freedom from rule and requires that we be ruled by something external to us. In short, it requires the supplement of the state. If the guarantee of personal liberty recuses the individual from the burden and power of collective life, it requires that this burden and power constellate elsewhere. In sum, if individual freedom rather than shared power is located at and as the heart of democracy, then the demos will not rule.

## Democracy and Statism

Derrida's unwillingness to conceive democracy as shared rule, his account of democracy as composed of the "force" of the people on the one hand and their individual freedom on the other—his substitution of a homological association of freedom and political sovereignty through ipseity for a political logic that would link them through power—returns us to the oscillation between the sovereignty of demos and of state in the notion of popular sovereignty with which I began. The force of the people appears ghostly, spectral in all senses of the word (including unreal and unrealizable), while actual political sovereignty, deposited in the state as law and decisionism, extends right up to the point where it meets individual *ipse*, the individual sovereignty of the subject. This distinctively liberal form of democracy entails a sharp distinction between personal liberty and political rule, precisely the distinction liberalism savors. When the freedom to do as one pleases is situated at the heart of democracy, state sovereignty — not the sovereignty of the people — simultaneously secures the right of individuals to be free of one another and the freedom of the state to rule. It reconciles individual ipseity with political ipseity by dividing their realms or jurisdictions. State sovereignty sacrifices the political sovereignty of the people as it secures personal liberty for the individual.

We need to linger a moment longer with this problem. Derrida formulates democratic freedom as the "power, faculty or ability to act . . . in short, to do as one pleases, the energy of an intentional and deciding will" (44). He makes freedom in the individual and the state distinct yet homologous; both express sovereignty insofar as they are unconditioned, unconstrained, willful. This formulation cannot feature *shared* power, shared governance, or participation in power that is greater than *one*self. It centers on doing *as one pleases*; it reiterates and requires the unity, autarky, and indivisibility of classical sovereignty — precisely the unity, autarky, and indivisibility that democracy must reject in order to realize itself. But democracy cannot be about doing *as one pleases* and doing *as the many agree to do* unless these are sorted into two distinct realms, individual and political, where the individual establishes the sovereign limit on the political in ordinary times and the political is the sovereign limit on the individual in the time of the exception.

Does this mean that radical democracy cannot prioritize individual freedom without sacrificing shared governance as a process of deliberation concluded by binding decision? Does it mean that liberal democracy cannot prioritize shared political rule without sacrificing individual freedom? Is the choice between the freedom of the isolated individual and the freedom of the people to self-govern, between Locke or Mill on one side and Rousseau or Marx on the other, between license that cancels shared rule and shared rule that cancels license? If we return again to the paradox of democracy's apparent requirement of an antidemocratic sovereign supplement, we can now grasp this paradox as one particular to, or at least particularly strong within, a liberal formulation of democracy. In liberal democracy, even as sovereignty circulates between its abstract and ghostly popular instantiation and its often unavowed state version, it remains unconditioned, absolute, indivisible, decisive, the source of law and above the law, the element of force and the legitimation of force, constant and unchanging. By contrast, the democratic principle of sharing power transforms the meaning of sovereignty insofar as it is necessarily conditioned, partial, divisible, deliberative, contingent, episodic, and protean. But in his fidelity to individual liberty and the liberal democratic tradition that enshrines it, Derrida backs into a fidelity to classical sovereignty as well, one derived from God and the absolutist state made in God's image. He affirms the circuit between state sovereignty and individual sovereignty required by the liberal formulation of freedom.

One can feel Derrida's uneasiness about having landed here. And so he strives to enlarge the reach of the liberal conception of freedom to encompass the inanimate and nonhuman world, and to render it a civic atmosphere and ethos rather than an individually held or wielded property. Thus while he affirms the freedom to "think, speak, criticize, or reject (even democracy)" and to act, do, or not do as one pleases,[6] he also seeks to loosen freedom from the "I-can of a free will" and from "the attribute of a subject, of a mastery or a measure." He seeks to extend freedom "to everything that appears in the open . . . including whatever comes in the free form of nonhuman living being and of the 'thing' in general, whether living or not." Freedom extends beyond the human and the agentic to become a general *scene* of openness and unfixity but also, borrowing from Nancy, a "force" rather than an individually held and exercised property, detached from unconditional ipseity (54).

Derrida also seeks to "extend . . . the democratic beyond nation-state sovereignty" and into what he calls an international juridico-political space which invents new "divisions of sovereignty" and imposes limits on state sovereignty (87–88). But to enlarge the domain and conceptual coordinates of individual freedom, to stretch it from a property to a force, from an attribute to an ethos, and beyond the nation-state, is not yet to articulate freedom in terms of political power or as a practice of governance or rule. And it does not recognize the sharing of political power as both condition and expression of democratic (as opposed to liberal) freedom. Put the other way around, the eschewal of the project of democratizing power in Derrida's treatment of freedom reveals the hold of liberalism on his formulation of democracy. As he builds on Nancy's philosophical effort to detach freedom from the conceit of the unconditioned and autonomous subject, freedom is rendered as an ethos of the public sphere and becomes a force bearing on the entire cosmos, not just humans or citizens. Well and good. But this cosmological leap overflies the most critical site of democratic freedom: the power of the demos to rule itself. As freedom is detached from concrete subjects, it is also detached from power and the political, thereby reiterating the depoliticized status of freedom assigned to it by liberalism three centuries ago, in which, rather than embodying the rule of the people, freedom becomes the vehicle for its opposite: the means by which individuals are left alone and left out of political power. This, of course, is our predicament today as we confront a coherent discourse by an imperial sovereign power that, *in the name of democracy*, claims to secure our freedom on the one side and bring freedom to the tyrannized on the other.

## Power and Freedom

Tellingly, Derrida's brief for freedom is more often posed against belonging — to place, family, language, culture, nation, class, party, identity of any sort — than to the more conventional Left foils of oppression, subordination, or repression. In *A Taste for the Secret*, he formulates freedom as "the condition not only for being singular and other, but also for entering into relation with the singularity and alterity of others."[7] Freedom is identified with a separation from a coercive solidarity and carries the promise of emancipation from such power, especially the power of the collective, the ensemble, the brotherhood, the nation, the natal family, religion, or ethnicity.

It is complicated here. While Derrida claims to love the word "sharing" and needs the notion for his elaboration of hospitality as a political orientation, he makes no secret of his aversion to notions and practices of community, solidarity, fraternity, and comradeship.[8] His critique of political fraternity in *Politics of Friendship* and *Rogues* is relentless: fraternity is always familial, always about sharing the remains of the father, always about the exclusions of brotherhood, always about the right of citizenship by birth and blood, hence at once masculinist, racist, nationalist, nativist (59–66). Equality, he insists against Nancy, does not require the "sharing of the incommensurable" (56), and political fraternity not only compromises individual singularity, it undermines the inclusiveness, the hospitality, the opening up to the excluded that democracy promises.

However, the democratic project of sharing power does not require community or fraternity; it need not hue to the republican political tradition and, given the masculinist citizen-warrior element of that tradition, would be better off if it did not.[9] Sharing power does not require that we adhere to a common position, take a loyalty oath, subordinate ourselves to the party, love or even like one another. It requires only that we agree to be democrats, that we agree to share the power that governs us, and that we commit ourselves to democratizing the powers that would otherwise rule us. I think Derrida conflates such sharing with fraternity, with subordination to the law of the father, with the brotherhood that ensues from the patricide. In this conflation he resurrects a liberal shibboleth about the spirit of communist principles: that they inherently oppose freedom rather than aim at its radical realization. He spurns the Marxist insight into the reconciliation of collective and individual freedom *through* shared power, a reconciliation that would also overturn what he designates as the inherent oscillation between freedom and equality in democracy. This conflation and this spurning require splitting off individual freedom from political sovereignty and force the latter to take shape as an antidemocratic supplement to democracy. Hence Derrida's telling question in *Rogues:* "Is democracy that which assures the right to think and thus to act without it or against it?" (41). In this question democracy slides from signifying individual liberty to signifying the sovereign regime against which individual liberty acts. Democracy is divided and dividing here: it divides freedom from power, freedom from governance, the individual from the regime.

This is precisely the division and divisiveness that empire makers capitalize on today as they render as despotism nonliberal experiments in shared power — from Latin America to Palestine — and as they de-democratize at home under the sign of democracy. If we raise our objection to this de-democratization primarily by championing civil liberties — individual freedom — rather than a share in power, we will not reclaim democracy from a sovereign power antagonistic to it but will have only upturned this sovereign power's other face. And beyond this sovereign power, at the scene of its erosion in late modernity, a global "democracy to come" that heralds individual liberty while abandoning the project of shared rule in turn abandons putatively free individuals to the unprecedented and freshly decontained powers of global capital on one side and the violence of theological-civilizational politics on the other.

## A Postscript on Democracy

Why the absorption with democracy in post-Marxist Left European thought today? And why the tendency to equate democracy and the political? (As Derrida puts it, "the political . . . in the free play and extension of its meaning, in the opening up of its meaning . . . the democratic" [29]). And to equate democracy with freedom? A speculative answer: equating the political with democracy and democracy with freedom recenters the West as a beacon of civilization at precisely the moment it is (a) being decentered and (b) looking episodically barbaric.

On the one hand, as Amer Mohsen reminded my 2006 graduate seminar on "The Autonomy of the Political?," democracy has been a colonial discourse in the West since its emergence in ancient Greece. Democracy as concept and practice has always been limned by a nondemocratic periphery and contains an undemocratic substrate that at once materially sustains the democracy and is what democracy defines itself against. That is, there is an excluded inside in all democracies, whether slaves, natives, women, the poor, subordinated races or religions, or (today) illegals and aliens, *sans papiers*. And there is also always a constitutive outside: the "barbarians" first so named by the ancient Greeks and reiterated ever after. Yet even as we know this history, intellectuals, from Left to Right, proceed today as if it were incidental. They formulate democracy as universal (for Derrida, "the only paradigm that is universalizable" [28]); they cast its exclusions and subordinations as deformations or incomplete realizations; they render its imperial dimension as distortions, even suicide; they treat conquest and subjection in its name as misbegotten instrumentalization of the form.

Moreover, Mohsen further reminded us, for Left theorists and state imperialists alike today, democracy is a category that nation-states are either in or out of. In *Rogues*, Derrida literally divides the globe this way, arguing that most of the world identifies itself with democracy today with the single exception of "those with a theocratic Muslim government" (28). Of course, if a nation is designated as outside of the category "democracy," imperial or colonial military conquest can bring it in, at which point a new process, democratization, is set in motion and assisted by corporate capital, nongovernmental organizations, the International Monetary Fund, the World Bank, and other "democratizing" transnational institutions.

So the Third World, and especially the Islamic world today, is categorized in one of two categories of *lack* vis-à-vis democracy: either undemocratic or democratizing. Third World nations, leaders, and cultures are either the radical Other of democracy or in a temporal lag vis-à-vis democracy. Of course, this is the way the non-Euro-Atlantic world has been positioned in relation to civilization, development, modernity, and Europe throughout modernity, as either their Other or their primitive precursor. This construction in turn establishes First World countries as always already democratic, not democratizing, but fully Arrived.

In this context, it would seem that the current valorization of democracy on the part of post-Marxist intellectuals reveals us as being in the grip of an old Orientalist reflex. We in the West affirm ourselves as free, agentic, progressive, and at the frontiers of history by means of a constitutive outside figured as unfree, captured, mired, and at the rear of history. Moreover, as

Mi Lee, another member of that graduate seminar, helped me understand, the equation of the political with the democratic, and the construction of both as relatively autonomous of the theological, cultural, and economic, resurrects the free collective and individual subject in the face of the transnational forces of capital, culture, religion, and governance that are eroding it. This is the subject Derrida does such handstands to recuperate in *Rogues*, and that so many other European post-Marxists, from Habermas and Balibar to the late Foucault, have resuscitated as well. For none of them, of course, is this subject wholly unified or continuous in time; for none of them is this an unreconstructed Kantian subject. But so long as this subject appears even episodically, we may conceive of ourselves as free.

My tendentious though tentative thesis, then, is that we're seeing an unwitting neo-Orientalism on the European Left, one that figures anxiety about (a) identification with the putatively fundamentalist, theocratic, ideological, unfree Other; (b) the many sources and sites of unfreedom in constitutional democracies in the age of globalization; and (c) the barbarism inside Euro-Atlantic democracy and the barbarism wreaked by democracy. The equation of the political with democracy, and the equation of democracy with individual freedom rather than rule by the demos, are equations that establish an opposition between the "democratic West" and the "theocratic East." In the latter there is imagined to be no autonomous sphere of political life (theocracy is defined in part by the lack of such a sphere) and hence no freedom. But the theoretical persistence of the conceit of the autonomy of the political in democracy is ironic at a moment when such a conceit is so sharply undermined by the effects of global capital. Indeed, the saturation of political life by neoliberal rationality in late modernity promises to eliminate the line not only between economic and political activity and domains, but between economic and political forms of *reasoning*. In these conditions, the prospect of rule by the demos has never seemed more remote, even in the theoretical imagination. But if not democracy distinguishing Us from Them, then what?

*Notes*

1  Derrida, *Rogues*, 141–43. Subsequent references are cited parenthetically in the text.
2  Agamben has famously formulated this first type of sovereignty in terms of a permanent state of exception today. See *Homo Sacer*.
3  Connolly, *Pluralism*, chapter 5.
4  S. S. Wolin, *Politics and Vision*, 601–6; quote is from 602.

5 Wolin says something parallel: "When democracy is settled into a stable form, such as prescribed by a written constitution, it is also settled down and rendered predictable. Then it becomes the stuff of manipulation" (ibid, 602).

6 One senses here that Derrida was affected by the inflection acquired by democracy and freedom and their equation in the immediate aftermath of 1989, and the festival of openness and license that seized the former socialist bloc. I recall a 1991 cab ride in Prague, where the driver gleefully zipped the wrong way down a one-way street, yelling, "Who is going to stop me? We have freedom now!"

7 Derrida and Ferraris, *A Taste for the Secret*, 27.

8 In a recent essay for *Critical Inquiry*, Vincent Leitch gathers these elements from *Politics of Friendship*, *A Taste for the Secret*, *Negotiations*, and "Marx and Sons." "Late Derrida: The Politics of Sovereignty," 229–47.

9 Derrida here follows the lead of Nancy, who, drawing from Heidegger, makes the problem of "sharing" one of being rather than one of "power." In so doing, Derrida depoliticizes the specifically democratic *project* of sharing and asserts for it a general ontological character inappropriate to the specificity of the political. Nancy, *The Experience of Freedom*.

# PART III

Responsibilities within and without Europe

# European Memories:
# Jan Patočka and Jacques Derrida
# on Responsibility

RODOLPHE GASCHÉ

Having evoked various reflections and presentations of Europe, ranging from Hegel to Paul Valéry and from Husserl to Heidegger, Jacques Derrida remarks in *The Other Heading* that these European discourses on Europe are dated. Although they are modern discourses and even "the most current, [and, indeed,] nothing is more current," they also are somehow dated.[1] They are always already traditional discourses in the sense that they speak of Europe from the perspective of its end, as an end (in the sense of telos) about to be realized or something that is no longer—something that has come to an end. As the heirs of these discourses, Europeans, like all inheritors, are in mourning. But, according to Derrida, Europe must also assume these traditional discourses, particularly those aspects that are of acute concern today. The Europeans' capital, their first and most current duty is to take responsibility for that heritage of discourses on what Europe is. Derrida writes, "We bear the responsibility for this heritage, right along with the capitalizing memory that we have of it. We did not choose this responsibility; it imposes itself upon us."[2] This responsibility is ours insofar as, qua Europeans, we are heirs to the discourses in question.

In the brief remarks in *Specters of Marx* devoted to the concept of inheritance in general, Derrida points out that *to be* means to inherit. One is an heir even before one explicitly assumes or rejects a particular inheritance. "That we *are* heirs does not mean that we *have* or that we *receive* this or that, some inheritance that enriches us one day with this or that, but that the *being* of what we are *is* first of all inheritance, whether we like it or know it or not." Indeed, Derrida continues, "inheritance is never a *given*, it is always a task"; it is something still before us, to which we have to bear witness as that which "we *are* insofar as we *inherit*."[3] For Europeans, this task consists above all in *being* such that they assume the memory of Europe. To be by taking responsibility for their inheritance in no way reveals nostalgia or traditionalist fervor. On the contrary, understood as a task, the affirmation of this inheritance does not exclude — indeed, it may even call for a radical transformation of what has been handed down. The prime duty of the European is to take responsibility for this heritage, that is, the modern tradition of reflecting on European identity.[4] This is so not only because these discourses concern being European but also because such identity is always established in relation to alterity, to the other, to the non-European. Responsibility to this heritage is thus also responsibility to the other. It consists in the double injunction of being faithful to "an idea of Europe, [to] a difference of Europe, but [to] a Europe that consists precisely in not closing itself off in its own identity."[5] In other words, the responsibility that Europeans bear for all of the traditional discourses on European identity, of which "old Europe seems to have exhausted all the possibilities," is thus a responsibility to responsibility, indeed, to the concept of responsibility itself.[6]

At this point, however, I would like only to highlight the fact that for Derrida the prime responsibility of the European is to the tradition of the discourses and counterdiscourses concerning his or her own identification. This point is made even more explicitly, though in more general terms, in *For What Tomorrow . . . A Dialogue*, where Derrida remarks that "the concept of responsibility has no sense at all outside of an experience of inheritance."[7] We should remind ourselves of this as we turn to Derrida's discussion of a discourse on Europe that he characterizes as heretical "with respect to all the important [or grand] European discourses."[8] All the possibilities of the grand discourses of Europe have apparently been exhausted. And yet Jan Patočka's views on Europe and European responsibility, which have the capacity to produce explosive implications if extended radically, sound a heretical note within the traditional discourses of the modern Western world, not the least because they also seek to break the ties to a certain memory and to a certain tradition.

In the first two chapters of *The Gift of Death*, Derrida engages Patočka's genealogy of European responsibility as it is presented in *Heretical Essays*. To my knowledge, this is the only occasion on which Derrida has broached the work of the Czech phenomenologist. Although his discussion is limited to the *Heretical Essays* and, moreover, largely to one of its essays ("Is Technological Civilization Decadent, and Why?"), it provides an exemplary reading of Patočka's conception of Europe and responsibility, of its intricacies and ambiguities, as well as of the major tenets of Derrida's own conception.[9] Needless to say, *The Gift of Death* is not limited to a discussion of Patočka's views on Europe and responsibility. In this work, Derrida also engages the thought of Heidegger, Levinas, and, in particular, Kierkegaard. Although I will briefly, and very schematically, sketch out Derrida's main concerns within the essay as a whole, no comprehensive reading can be attempted here. In any event, I must elaborate in some detail on Derrida's assessment in *The Gift of Death* of Patočka's fundamental and original thesis of the *Heretical Essays* and *Plato and Europe*, namely, that the Platonic motif of the care of the soul (*epimeleia tes psyches*) is the embryo of European life and the starting point of the genealogy of responsibility in the history of Europe.[10] Without doing so, I would not be able to illuminate Derrida's own understanding of responsibility, hence of what Europe is.

So, before turning to Derrida's reading of Patočka, let me first explain, however briefly, what this Platonic motif is. The notion of the care of the soul is a fundamental and elementary notion in Plato's earliest dialogues, around which all of Socrates's concerns are gathered. Although this theme is to be found primarily in the *Apology*, the *Phaedo*, and *Alcibiades I*, it is, according to Patočka, the central issue not only of all Plato's thought but of Greek philosophy as a whole. Recall that for the Greeks, the soul — that is, the mover and user of the body — is the human being's true self. As Socrates argues in *Alcibiades I*, "There is nothing which may be called more properly ourselves than the soul."[11] For the Greek philosopher, the body is only an instrument, or a tool, for a good life. But the prerequisite for a good life is that the soul be in command of the body. The philosopher's first duty, or responsibility, is, therefore, to get to know himself in order to be able to look to that which is most properly himself, rather than tending to what does not expressly belong to himself: money, reputation, honor, as well as anything bodily. The soul achieves not only self-control (*sophron*) but also purity and transparency within itself by shunning everything corporeal. It is guided in this by the knowledge of what is and emulates the eternal, the unchangeable order of the cosmos, the Divine, or the Good. As is made clear in the *Phaedo*, such severing of all ties to the body culminates in the care of death, which, as this dialogue shows, is an intrinsic part of the care of the soul. By caring for death — that is, by learning how to face death easily — the soul, having freed itself from any contamination with the body, becomes able "to collect and concentrate itself by itself, trusting nothing but its judgment."[12] Thus, within his lifetime, the philosopher's soul will achieve a state that resembles the one that only the gods should enjoy and will thus also secure its full release from the body upon death.

What sets Patočka's discourse unmistakably apart from the traditional discourses on Europe—particularly those of Husserl and Heidegger—is what Derrida calls Patočka's "essential Christianity" (*GD*, 22). Undoubtedly, Derrida makes this point first of all in order to distinguish Patočka's interpretation of the theme of the care of the soul from Heidegger's analysis of care (*Sorge*) in *Being and Time* as a fundamental existential structure of *Dasein*. Heidegger constantly sought to separate his thought from Christianity, while at the same time ontologically recovering—and de-Christianizing—Christian themes and texts by inquiring into their originary possibility. Patočka, on the other hand, "makes an inverse yet symmetrical gesture. . . . He reontologizes the historic themes of Christianity and attributes to revelation or to the *mysterium tremendum* the ontological content that Heidegger attempts to remove from it" (*GD*, 23). But this reference to an essential Christianity also acknowledges that the emergence of responsibility in the face of everydayness and the sacred is, for Patočka, intimately connected to the history of religion. Patočka is intent on overcoming both the inauthenticity of everydayness and the demonic and the orgiastic that are escapes from it. *Plato and Europe* establishes Plato as the Greek philosopher who brought the motif of the care of the soul into being and also as the thinker who transformed myth into religion, the one who "recommends faith." All differences considered, "faith, as the Greek philosophers saw it, is the foundation of what we call faith in the Christian tradition"; nevertheless, only Christianity is religion in an eminent sense.[13] Indeed, as Derrida remarks, Patočka's thought is remarkably consistent in taking "into account the event of Christian mystery as an absolute singularity, a religion par excellence and an irreducible condition for a joint history of the subject, responsibility, and Europe. That is so even if, here and there, the expression 'history of religions' appears in the plural, and even if one can only infer from this plural a reference to Judaic, Islamic, and Christian religions alone, those known as religions of the Book" (*GD*, 2). If the genealogy of responsibility developed by Patočka "follows the traces of a genius of Christianity that is the history of Europe" (*GD*, 3), it is precisely because it is only in, or as, Christian Europe that the motif of the care of the soul—the central theme of what is European—is transformed (or, as we will see, *could* be transformed) into a true principle of responsibility. Christianity is the only religion that can secure the possibility of a responsibility that is truly European and at the same time really realize the concept of responsibility. What thus sets Patočka's reflections on Europe apart from those of Husserl and Heidegger is precisely the significance of religion—particularly of the religion par excellence that is Christianity.

The Christianity of Patočka's texts on the care of the soul and European responsibility is not just any Christianity. It is not only an essential but also a heretical conception of Christianity. According to Patočka's highly stratified genealogy of responsibility, the history of the responsible self is built upon the heritage of the Platonic conception of the care of the soul through a series of ruptures and repressions "that assure the very tradition they punctuate with their interruptions" (*GD*, 7). Although the novel twist to which Christianity subjects the theme of the care of the soul consists, according to Patočka, in an "about-face" by means of which Christianity seeks to extricate itself from its Platonic inheritance, Christianity has proved unable to think through and draw the radical implications of its mutation of the theme in question precisely because its overcoming of Platonism is not complete.[14] As Derrida points out, if European Christianity is at its heart still haunted by the persistent presence of a type of Platonism—and of a type of Platonic politics—it is, according to Patočka, because it "has not sufficiently repressed Platonism in the course of its reversal, and it still mouths its words" (*GD*, 23). Now, the specificity of the reversal that the motif of the care of the soul undergoes in Christianity consists in this: the responsibility of the self or the soul does not derive from knowledge of the Divine, the cosmos, or the Good, but from the soul's exposure to the gaze of an other, ultimately the gaze of God as a Person, a gaze that constitutes the soul as a person and, for that, as a responsible self. Indeed, the Christian version of the care of the soul is unable to come into its own because it continues to subordinate responsibility (and decision making) to knowledge, the knowledge of the Good, just as is the case with the Platonic model. Patočka inscribes his discourse on Europe, responsibility, and politics "within the perspective of a Christian eschatology," that is, within a happening in which Christianity and, by extension, the only true conception of responsibility are still hampered by the remnants of the Platonic heritage. He is thus forced to acknowledge that something "remains 'unthought' in Christianity. Whether ethical or political, the Christian consciousness of responsibility is incapable of reflecting on the Platonic thinking that it represses, and at the same time it is incapable of reflecting on the orgiastic mystery that Platonic thinking incorporates" (*GD*, 24). Christianity's inability to determine the notion and status of "the place and subject of all responsibility, namely, the *person*," is indicative of what remains unthought (*GD*, 24), for, in the Christian mystery, the person is not in a relation to an objectively knowable transcendent object such as the Platonic Good but to God as a Person, to He who transfixes the self by His gaze without being seen Himself.[15] What follows from this inability and neglect of what Patočka judges to be an inadequate thematization is that Christianity remains only "on the threshold of responsibility. It doesn't thematize what a responsible person *is*, that is, what he *must be*, namely this exposing of the soul to the gaze of another person, of a person as transcendent other, as an other who looks at me, but who looks without the subject-who-says-I being able to reach that other, see her, hold her within the reach of my gaze" (*GD*, 25). Furthermore, as Derrida concludes, "an inadequate thematization of what responsibility is or *must be* is also an *irresponsible* thematization; not knowing, having neither a sufficient knowledge or consciousness of what being *responsible* means, is of itself a lack of responsibility" (*GD*, 25). In sum, the Christian version of the care of the soul is, in spite of all its radicality, "limited by the weight of what remains unthought, in particular its incorrigible Platonism" (*GD*, 28), an unacknowledged debt, which also explains the inadequate thematization of what makes the soul a truly responsible self.

Christianity is also infused with a certain irresponsibility as far as its conception of responsibility is concerned. Patočka's essential Christianity is a heretical conception of Christianity in that, "according to the logic of a messianic eschatology," he advocates a more "thorough thematization" of what sets the Christian notion of the care of the soul apart from the Platonic (and Roman) model, which bears not only on its understanding of responsibility but also on its political realization. Derrida writes:

> Something has not yet arrived, neither at Christianity nor by means of Christianity. What has not yet come about is the fulfillment, within history and in political history, and first and foremost in European politics, of the new responsibility announced by the *mysterium tremendum*. There has not yet been an authentically Christian politics because there remains this residue of the Platonic *polis*. Christian politics must break more definitely and more radically with Greco-Roman Platonic politics in order to finally fulfill the *mysterium tremendum*. Only on this condition will Europe have a future. (*GD*, 28–29)

The realization of a European politics based on a Christian version of the care of the soul hinges on drawing upon the full philosophical, religious, and political consequences of what is promised with the emergence of Christian

Europe. This, however, is possible only on the condition of a radical rupture with the Platonic heritage, that is, precisely with a model of the care of the soul that is predicated on knowledge, in particular, the knowledge of the Good. Undoubtedly, "heretical" in the title of Patočka's *Heretical Essays* refers, at first, to the vulgar Marxist conceptions of the philosophy of history. But its heresy, which also marks a rupture with Husserl's and Heidegger's views on history, as Ricoeur has noted, derives, as Derrida implicitly suggests, from Patočka's hyperbolic conception of Christianity.[16] "Taken to its extreme," Patočka's text is heretical with respect to the grand discourses on Europe by Husserl and Heidegger because it "seems to suggest on the one hand that Europe will not be what it must be until it becomes fully Christian, until the *mysterium tremendum* is adequately thematized. On the other hand it also suggests that the Europe to come will no longer be Greek, Greco-Roman, or even Roman. The most radical insistence of the *mysterium tremendum* would be upon a Europe so new (or so old) that it would be freed from the Greek or Roman memory that is so commonly invoked in speaking of it; freed to the extent of breaking all ties with this memory, becoming heterogeneous to it" (*GD*, 29). Patočka's conception of Europe, even though it is a version of the care of the soul, is heretical with respect to all the traditional discourses on Europe because of its attempt to emancipate Europe from the memory of both Athens and Rome — that is to say, from a memory of responsibility that rests on knowledge of the Good or of the universal state. Built exclusively on the "mysterium tremendum" — in other words, on the unseen gaze of an absolutely self-less Goodness, who shakes the soul (the self or person) because it is unable to adequately respond to this gift of love — Europe is to become something entirely new, something, in other words, that is no longer responsible to the memory of Athens and Rome.[17] Yet before we can provide a hint of what the implications of this radical break of European responsibility with its Platonic and Roman heritage would be, it is first necessary to briefly highlight the major aspects of the essential Christian conception of responsibility that orthodox Christianity has failed to make good on.

The Platonic responsible self or soul cares for itself and achieves in this manner a resemblance, however temporary, to the gods by measuring itself against the Good. The Christian self's responsibility rests on its relation to an other. It is neither a relation of the self to itself, nor a relation that the self can freely choose to take upon itself, nor a relation that it can ignore. Rather, "the Christian 'reversal' that converts the Platonic conversion *in turn*, involves the entrance upon the scene of a gift" (*GD*, 40). Patočka argues that, in Christianity, "the responsible life is itself presented as a gift from something which ultimately, though it has the character of the Good, has also the traits of the inaccessible and forever superior to humans—the traits of the *mysterium* that always has the final word."[18] Understanding responsibility as a gift makes all the difference. Such an understanding makes responsibility into a function of an event, the singular event of a gift by another, which, furthermore, is addressed to the human as a singular human being. In fact, the gift, insofar as it is always directed specifically at *this* human being, is constitutive of his or her singularity and irreplaceability. But, according to Christianity, responsibility is also a gift that comes from an absolute Other, that is, a self-effacing Goodness that gives this gift in selfless love and to which the donee is thus constitutively unable to respond in kind. As a consequence, "there is a structural disproportion or dissymmetry between the finite and responsible mortal on the one hand and the goodness of the infinite gift on the other hand. . . . It inevitably transforms the experience of responsibility into one of guilt: I have never been and never will be up to the level of this infinite goodness nor up to the immensity of the gift, the frameless immensity that must in general define (*in*-define) a gift as such" (*GD*, 51). Addressed to finite beings, the selfless gift is constitutive of their singularity; it also condemns such singular beings to guilt inasmuch as they are responsible. Furthermore, the gift of responsibility that occurs in the mysterium tremendum is a gift by a self-denying and self-effacing Goodness, which also remains inaccessible because of its very withdrawal. To be responsible is, in Patočka's words, to stand in an inscrutable relation to "a Person who sees into the soul without being itself accessible to view" and "in whose hands we are not externally, but internally."[19] That which makes me responsible is something that remains impenetrable to me—in other words, secret. It is also something that shatters me because I cannot adequately respond to such a self-denying gift. Thus, Platonic responsibility is a function of what Patočka terms looking-in, or looking-into-what-is (*nahlednuti*)—namely, into eternal being—which, like the Platonic Good, can effectively be known. Christian responsibility, however, is not in the power of the subject, who is overpowered, crushed by it precisely because its source—self-renouncing and self-withdrawing Goodness—remains unfathomable.[20] Finally, as Derrida puts it, the gift of responsibility is a gift by "a goodness whose inaccessibility acts as a command to the donee. It subjects its receivers, giving themselves to them as goodness itself but also as law" (*GD*, 41), that is, as a universality to which the donee is subject as a singular and irreplaceable being. As the result of this gift, Christian responsibility takes into account the uniqueness and irreplaceability of the singular individual precisely by subjecting him or her to a universal Law.

Patočka holds that it is only in Christianity that the most powerful plumbing of the depths of responsibility has occurred, in other words, that only here is it conceived in a truly fundamental manner. He can do so because this conception of responsibility articulates, as it were, the only conditions under which responsibility is possible. In Christianity alone it becomes clear that "responsibility demands irreplaceable singularity" (*GD*, 51). Christian responsibility is also, therefore, tied to a gift of death, of "*another death*" (*GD*, 40), which is not the one to be found in the Platonic version of the care of the soul. As Derrida reminds us, when Patočka argues that "the *mysterium tremendum* announces, in a manner of speaking, *another death* . . . another way of giving death or of granting death," "the word 'gift' is uttered" (*GD*, 40). This gift of death is a gift in an eminent sense. It is the gift by the Other, on which the gift of responsibility itself rests or with which responsibility coincides. Only through this gift of death does access to genuine responsibility become possible, because "only death or rather the apprehension of death can give this irreplaceability [without which there can be no true responsibility], for it is only on the basis of it that one can speak of a responsible subject, of the soul as conscience of self, of myself, etc." (*GD*, 51; translation modified). This gift is another way of giving oneself death, first and foremost, in the sense of apprehending death. In the originary Platonic version of the care of the soul, the philosopher, by giving herself death as that which will affect her only as a bodily being, frees herself from death; she collects and gathers herself within herself. Derrida writes that the (philosopher's) self "comes into being as such at the moment when the soul is not only gathering itself in the preparation for death but when it is ready to receive death, giving it to itself even, in an acceptation that delivers it from the body, and at the same time delivers it from the demonic and the orgiastic. By means of the passage to death [*passage de la mort*] the soul attains its own freedom" (*GD*, 40). By contrast, in the Christian paradigm death is apprehended neither as something from which the soul can distance itself through care nor as something from which it can sever itself, thus collecting itself within itself. Christian death is experienced as intrinsically linked to my selfhood, as precisely something that is exclusively mine, that no one can take from me or assume for me, which constitutes my irreplaceability as a singular self. Remember that for Patočka the Christian way in which I give myself death rests on "the gift made to me by God as he holds me in his gaze and in his hands while remaining inaccessible to me, the terribly dissymmetrical gift of the *mysterium tremendum*" (*GD*, 33). The human being to whom this gift is made is no match for the gift of death that accompanies the responsibility to which God's self-less gift calls me. It is a gift that makes the finite subject tremble in terror because he or she is unable to adequately respond to it: the gift of an awareness of death as eternal death. Derrida writes, "For what is given in this trembling, in the actual trembling of terror, is nothing other than death itself, a new significance for death, a new apprehension of death, a new way in which to give oneself death or to put oneself to death. The difference between Platonism and Christianity would be above all 'a reversal in the face of death and of eternal death'" (*GD*, 31). Radically guilty in the face of a gift that is addressed to him in his very singularity, the human confronts his death — that which is irreducibly his own and on which his uniqueness hinges — as the complete extinction of himself, unless he is redeemed by the grace of God. This gift of death is also the gift of a new way of putting oneself to death in the face of the prospect of eternal death, since in order to merit the grace of God the trembling creature must offer its "whole being in the sacrifice of repentance."[21] What Christianity brings to light is not only the fact that without the singularity, or the irreplaceability of the individual, there cannot be any responsible self, but also that if singularity is to be the condition of the possibility of responsibility it cannot be a given, but must be constantly in danger of extinction.

The Christian version of the care of the soul plumbs the soul deeper than Platonism because this responsibility, which originates in the gaze of an unfathomable Other, precedes the relation between subject and object that informs the classical version of the responsible self. Derrida writes, "The dissymmetry of the gaze, this disproportion that relates me, and whatever concerns me, to a gaze that I don't see and that remains secret from me although it commands me, is, according to Patočka, what promises itself [*s'annonce*] in Christian mystery as the frightening, terrifying mystery, the *mysterium tremendum*. Such a terror has no place in the transcendent experience that relates Platonic responsibility to the *agathon*. Nor does it have any place in the politics that is so instituted. But the terror of this secret exceeds and precedes the complacent relation of a subject to an object" (*GD*, 27–28; translation modified). Yet such a radical way of conceiving responsibility is only announced or is only promised by Christianity. Christianity as a whole cannot be identified with this understanding of responsibility because its persistent Platonism has prevented it from thinking through this deepened conception. What is thus announced by Christianity is perhaps no longer anything Christian, unless it is Christian in a hyperbolic sense.[22] In any case, Christianity remains the privileged locus in which the depths of responsibility can best be plumbed.

At this juncture let me return to the Platonic motif of the care of the soul and the first awakening of responsibility that is the core idea of European life, but with which the Christian understanding of the responsible self must also, according to Patočka, make a clear break. Knowledge of what is eternal — justice, beauty, the Good — is the basis of Greek responsible life. Responsibility itself is something public because it is based upon knowledge, of a kind to which everyone has access in principle. It is possible to account for the concept of responsibility and to universally establish what responsibility and being responsible consist of, but such an understanding of responsibility also implies that the responsible self must be able to give reasons for any of his or her actions and beliefs, publicly whenever possible. According to this Platonic conception of responsibility, "not knowing, having neither a sufficient knowledge or consciousness of what being *responsible* means, is of itself a lack of responsibility. In order to be responsible it is necessary to respond to or answer to what being responsible means" (*GD*, 25). To the extent that the Platonic conception of the care of the soul is the first awakening of and to responsibility and hence that this understanding of responsibility is the first moment in the genealogy of responsibility in (or as) Europe, this demand that knowledge be involved in responsible decision making is at the heart of the history of the concept. It dominates the thought on responsibility in Europe from Plato's to Husserl's reflections on an absolutely self-responsible universal science. Derrida refers to this Greek moment and endorses it, thus highlighting a certain continuity between his own thought and that of Husserl on this issue when he writes that responsibility consists, "according to the most convincing and most convinced *doxa*, in *responding*, hence in answering to the other, before the other and before the law, and if possible publicly, answering for itself, its intentions, its aims, and for the name of the agent deemed responsible" (*GD*, 26–27). The Greek understanding of responsibility that constitutes the first moment in Patočka's genealogy of responsibility excludes any secrecy. Although the Platonic moment incorporates demonic mystery, there is no place for secrecy and mystery in the philosophy and politics of the Platonic tradition. Everything is in the open, in the light of day, for all to judge. Like Greek political life, Greek civic responsibility "openly declares that secrecy will not be allowed." It "presents itself as a moment without mystery" (*GD*, 33). The Platonic model of responsibility and politics is, consequently, one of democracy.

Yet since the Christian model of responsibility rests on a deepened interiority and is the gift of a self-less Other who remains inscrutable, this new model has a definite place for secrecy, for the mysterium, for the mystical, unlike the Greco-Roman version, which supersedes so radically as to break entirely with its memory. Christian responsibility has its origin in a gift, in a "gift that is not a present," and it is from the outset tied with secrecy for essential reasons. Indeed, as Derrida points out, "a gift that could be recognized as such in the light of day, a gift destined for recognition, would immediately annul itself. The gift is the secret itself. . . . Secrecy is the last word of the gift which is the last word of the secret" (*GD*, 29–30). Originating in the elusive event of such a gift, even the transition from Platonism and Neoplatonism to Christianity remains obscure; it cannot be accounted for simply in positive terms. But since the gift of responsibility is a gift from a self-effacing Goodness (which holds the human being in its hands from within) to the individual in all his or her creatural singularity, it is "the gift of something that remains inaccessible, unpresentable, and as a consequence secret" (*GD*, 29). The donee is exclusively responsible to the donator, and hence, as Derrida's discussion of the Abrahamic story of the sacrifice of Isaac in the second half of *The Gift of Death* demonstrates, the donee is relieved of the necessity of explaining his or her deeds to others. Indeed, being the unique addressee of the gift, the responsible individual must, at the limit, relate to others in an irresponsible fashion. How the donee responds to the divine Law remains secret — that is, unaccounted for — and ultimately secret to himself or herself as well, for such responsible decision making must, in principle, be unaccountable.

How does Derrida respond to this conception of responsibility, a conception that is entirely heterogeneous to the Greek conception and to the tradition to which it gave rise, one that he has characterized as "the most convincing and convinced *doxa*"? In seeking to answer this question, let us bear in mind that the Platonic idea of responsibility is the beginning of the genealogy of responsibility in Europe, of the European tradition of thinking about responsibility, although, according to Patočka, it is to be entirely replaced by the Christian model. But the Christian version of responsibility is also part of European memory, which thus consists of at least two different memories regarding what constitutes responsibility, despite Patočka's description of Christian responsibility as thoroughly heterogeneous to its Greek antecedent. Further, since the lingering presence of Platonism in Christianity has prevented a full rupture with the Greek model of responsibility that Christianity is to accomplish, the break with this tradition must be completed if the very essence or future of Europe is ever to be realized. Yet, as we saw at the beginning of this essay, for Derrida the concept of responsibility makes no sense whatsoever without an experience of inheritance. Consequently, responsibility is first and foremost a responsibility for and to the specific traditions of responsibility that have been bequeathed to us. It is, first and foremost, a responsibility before any particular responsibilities to oneself, the other, God, the animal, the world, and so forth. Such responsibility to the various conceptions of responsibility that have been handed down to us, or to the grand discourses on Europe in which they are laid out, does not exclude selection and critique. But would not any attempt to ignore, reject, or break with one of those legacies be tantamount to irresponsibility? Indeed, if responsibility is first of all a responsibility for and to an inheritance, to abandon or to deliberately renounce a part of the tradition in its entirety would be the gravest irresponsibility, all the more so in the case of a part of the tradition that concerns the concept of responsibility itself. Among the several things that Derrida seeks to achieve in *The Gift of Death*, the attempt to do justice to the conflicting models of responsibility within the European tradition — that is, also of thinking about Europe itself — prevails. The most insistent concern in *The Gift of Death* is that of assuming the heritage of responsibility in all its forms, particularly, the most "living" part of it, that which is most current because it continues to put limits on any traditional view of responsibility that would impose itself at the exclusion of all others. All of the other concerns in *The Gift of Death* presuppose this equitable treatment of the contradictory views of responsibility to be found in the traditional discourses of the modern Western world. But far from amounting to a wholesale underwriting of all the major positions on responsibility, such responsible treatment does not exclude critique, radical transformation, or the opening to other possible models of understanding responsibility. In fact, as we will see, Derrida's attempt in *The Gift of Death* to respond responsibly to the various facets of the European heritage of responsibility represents a novel concept of responsibility — that is, a novel conception of Europe.

Before I elaborate further on Derrida's response to Patočka in *The Gift of*

*Death*, a brief and very sketchy outline of what this text seeks to achieve is warranted. We should keep in mind Derrida's observation in the first chapter, "Secrets of European Responsibility," that what separates Patočka's interpretation of the motif of the care of the soul from Heidegger's influence is its essential Christianity. Whereas Heidegger constantly seeks to separate himself from Christianity, "repeating on an ontological level Christian themes and texts that have been 'de-Christianized,'" "Patočka makes an inverse yet symmetrical gesture" by ontologizing "the historic themes of Christianity and attribut[ing] to revelation or to the *mysterium tremendum* the ontological content that Heidegger attempts to remove from it." Thus, Derrida holds that Patočka's gesture "amounts to the same thing" as Heidegger's because it is symmetrical and merely the inverse. He adds that Patočka's "own heresy [regarding Christianity] intersects with what one might call, a little provocatively, that other heresy, namely, the twisting or diverting by which the Heideggerian repetition, in its own way, affects Christianity" (*GD*, 23). *The Gift of Death* is, of course, not limited to the mapping of the similarities and differences between Patočka and Heidegger; it also includes an analysis of Levinas and, above all, of Kierkegaard's Protestant interpretation of the Abrahamic story of the sacrifice of Isaac. It is in *The Gift of Death* that Derrida seeks to establish the matrix, if I may call it that, that at once makes these four undeniably distinct positions on responsibility possible but also limits their range, distinctiveness, radicality, and even their originality. Indeed, by inquiring into the various modalities of giving (oneself) death and of taking death (upon oneself), Derrida develops an economic model that accounts for the different positions on responsibility, their mutual contamination and passage into one another—in particular, as regards their overdetermination by themes of Christianity, Platonism, and deliberate de-Christianization, as well as of Judaism. This concern with the intersections between distinct positions also frames Derrida's discussion of Patočka's dismissal of the Platonic conception of responsibility on the basis of a decided predisposition to Christianity's potential to conceive responsibility, which is not yet adequately thematized, hence, outstanding.

As we have seen, to conform to the most convincing and convinced doxa, that is, the Platonic tradition, the responsible party must know what responsibility means. The responsible self must be able to account for what he or she believes and does, and such rendering of accounts should, whenever possible, be public, taking place in a way that is intelligible to everyone. According to what Derrida describes as "the most reliable continuity," the concept of responsibility requires "a decision or responsible action to answer for itself *consciously*, that is, with knowledge of a thematics of what is done, of what action signifies, its causes, ends, etc." (*GD*, 25). Where this element of knowledge and justification is lacking, decision making is irresponsible. As Derrida emphasizes, "We must continually remind ourselves that some part of irresponsibility insinuates itself wherever one demands responsibility without sufficiently conceptualizing and thematizing what 'responsibility' means" (*GD*, 25–26). Yet although Derrida subscribes to this demand of knowledge and that of giving reasons for all decisions, demands that are constitutive of the conception of responsibility from Plato to Husserl, he also agrees with Patočka that to subordinate responsibility to objective knowledge—to established theorems and time-honored norms—amounts to merely executing a program fixed in advance and thus to annulling responsibility. Therefore, he can also write:

> Saying that a responsible decision must be taken on the basis of knowledge seems to define the condition of possibility of responsibility (one can't make a responsible decision without science or conscience, without knowing what one is doing, for what reasons, in view of what and under what conditions), at the same time as it defines the condition of impossibility of this same responsibility (if decision-making is relegated to a knowledge that it is content to follow or to develop, then it is no more a responsible decision, it is the technical deployment of a theorem). (*GD*, 24)

In addition to acknowledging with Plato and Husserl that the possibility of responsibility is based on knowledge and on rendering accounts, Derrida thus recognizes another equally compelling demand without which responsibility is not possible. The Christian paradigm exemplifies this further condition of possibility of responsibility. According to this new conception, responsibility requires a break with established or sanctified dogmas (including the most convincing and convinced doxa). Rather than seeking conformity, one may have to set oneself apart from what is publicly or commonly accepted. In other words, responsibility is tied here to heresy in all the senses of the term, particularly, as is the case with Patočka, to a "departure from a doctrine, difference within and difference from the officially and publicly stated doctrine and the institutional community that is governed by it" (*GD*, 26). Heresy is not only "an essential condition of responsibility," it "also destines responsibility to the resistance or dissidence of a type of secrecy. It keeps responsibility apart . . . and in secret. And responsibility *depends on* [*tient à*] what is apart and secret" (*GD*, 26; translation modified). Indeed, if knowledge remains only on the threshold of a responsible decision, if a decision is a decision on the condition that it exceeds simple consciousness and simple theoretical determination, the responsible self must, in principle, be unable — that is, run the risk of not being able — to fully account for the singular act constitutive of a responsible decision. It follows from this that responsibility is necessarily linked to the secret — not, of course, in the form of withholding knowledge regarding a specific decision, but in the form of an essential inability to ultimately make the reasons for one's actions fully transparent. According to this essential Christian conception of responsibility (which is also, for essential reasons, heretical), decision making without secrecy remains ultimately irresponsible. But while a decision that is based merely on knowledge annuls responsibility, a decision that foregoes knowledge and defies the demand to give reasons is not without problems that threaten responsibility as well.

As we have seen, there is no place for secrecy or mystery in the Platonic paradigm of responsibility. The Platonic model is a democratic model based on responsibility as universally accessible knowledge and on a demand of transparency. Returning to the memory of Europe, Derrida remarks that as long as Europe pays homage to its Platonic heritage and keeps that memory alive, it "either neglects, represses, or excludes from itself every essential possibility of secrecy and every link between responsibility and the keeping of a secret; everything that allows responsibility to be dedicated to secrecy" (*GD*, 34). But apart from seeking to secure the democratic demand of full transparency and generalized accountability, the fact that this heritage seeks to achieve this demand by neglecting, repressing, or excluding the possibility of secrecy clearly suggests some kind of irresponsibility that is inseparable from the demand in question. As Patočka's analyses of the decadence of modern Europe resulting from technological civilization seek to show, it takes very little for such a democratic model of responsibility and of rendering reason to become totalitarian. Indeed, the legitimate demand intrinsic to the concept of responsibility to publicly account for oneself and one's deeds can easily turn into a means of oppression — as has been amply demonstrated under Stalinism and Zhdanovism in the former Soviet Union, but examples of which can also be found in the United States, with its obsession with public confession — and thus this conception of responsibility based on the demand for knowledge must also "call for respecting whatever refuses a certain responsibility, for example, the responsibility to respond before any and every instituted tribunal."[23] This right not to respond and to keep a secret is the necessary antidote to a conception of responsibility that, based on knowledge, can always become a tool for the benefit of the worst. But the Christian paradigm of responsibility, which rests on the mysterium tremendum, by which the unique and singular self is called to responsibility by God's gift alone, harbors a similar, or rather, inverse risk. Christian responsibility requires of the self a complete departure from everything established by doxa and tradition, from all rules and doctrines—in particular, from the necessity to give an account to others—so that one's actions will have been exclusively one's own. As such, it is also fraught with the danger of the worst possible irresponsibility. That Christian responsibility could become tied to the worst repression is a possibility as well. Furthermore, to demand of Europe that it abandon all memory of Platonism and become exclusively Christian—by making secrecy and mystery into the sole condition of European politics and responsibility—is tantamount to calling for a reign of arbitrariness and terror.

Against Patočka's attempt to free Christianity from its Platonic foundation and to conceive of a Europe emancipated from both Athens and Rome, Derrida stresses the need to remain faithful to both aspects of European memory. As the inheritors of both conceptions of responsibility, Europeans are what they are thanks to these conceptions and the demands that they articulate; hence, they are responsible for and to them. But this double heritage of the meaning of responsibility is not a simple given and does not entail traditionalist submission. Responsibility for and to both traditions demands first of all acknowledging that any one of these conceptions of responsibility is necessarily fraught with risks and dangers. But such responsibility calls not only for the affirmation of what has been inherited but also for the radical transformation of the heritage. In other words, responsibility for and to the tradition is inevitably heretical.

In response to Patočka's claim that Christianity has failed to adequately thematize what a Person is—that is, the Person that penetrates the soul with its glance without in turn being seen and that constitutes the soul as a responsible self—Derrida writes that such a reference to "inadequate thematization . . . seems to appeal to some ultimate adequacy of thematization that could be accomplished" (*GD*, 27). In the tradition of responsibility, its Greek moment may come closest to the ideal of full thematization because it demands knowledge of the reasons, the aim, the meaning of what is done and of the circumstances of one's decisions or actions. Although Derrida emphasizes that we must be continually aware of the fact that whenever we do not sufficiently thematize what *responsibility* means some irresponsibility insinuates itself into our actions, he also remarks that this is always and everywhere the case. No action, if it is to be a responsible action, is ever consciously or cognitively sufficiently determined. Derrida adds, "One can say *everywhere* apriori and nonempirically" (*GD*, 25–26). If this is so, it is because an action must transcend knowledge to be responsible as well as to include knowledge of what responsibility means. Unless it is the execution of a preestablished theorem or norm, an action merits the title "responsible" only if it is also effectuated without full theoretical determination. It follows from this that the thematization of responsibility is, for structural reasons, always lacking, even in the case of the Platonic notion of responsibility rejected by Patočka on the basis that it makes responsibility a function of the knowledge of the good. This is even more the case for the heretically Christian conception of responsibility. Derrida observes that thematization "is, if not denied, at least strictly limited in its pertinence by that other more radical form of responsibility that exposes me dissymmetrically to the gaze of the other. . . . The concept of responsibility is one of those strange concepts that give food for thought without giving themselves over to thematization. It presents itself neither as a theme nor as a thesis, it gives without being seen [*sans se donner à voir*], without presenting itself in person by means of a 'fact of being seen' that can be phenomenologically intuited" (*GD*, 27). In a move that proves Derrida even more heretical than Patočka, he shows that the concept of responsibility resists all final thematization. It is a "paradoxical concept" in that, in addition to seeking to cognitively unify what responsibility means in one intuition, it also defies such an effort insofar as "it has the structure of a type of secret—what is called, in the code of certain religious practices, mystery. The exercise of responsibility seems to leave no choice but this one, however uncomfortable it may be, of paradox, heresy, and secrecy. More serious still, it must always run the risk of conversion and apostasy: there is no responsibility without a dissident and inventive rupture with respect to tradition, authority, orthodoxy, rule, or doctrine" (*GD*, 27). With this we have already begun to broach Derrida's own—radically heretical—take on responsibility.

Derrida upholds both injunctions of the tradition in question rather than solely privileging the structurally necessary element of secrecy, which Patočka associates with heretical Christianity, to the detriment of the cognitive element in responsibility advanced by Platonism. Yet his innovative interpretation of the heritage of responsibility consists neither in attempting to mediate between both demands nor in establishing their golden mean. Instead, what distinguishes Derrida's interpretation of the Platonic and Christian heritages is, first of all, the recognition that "the relation between the Platonic and Christian paradigms throughout the history of morality and politics" is defined by the "aporia of responsibility" (GD, 24). Responsibility to this inheritance is itself aporetic; it excludes the choice of one of the inherited conceptions of responsibility at the expense of the other—that is, it requires that both traditions be simultaneously honored without any mitigation of the radicality of their demands. The injunctions—on the one hand, of full knowledge of one's actions; on the other, of secrecy—are mutually exclusive; moreover, we are unable to account for either of them. Thus, no program exists that can prescribe a way out of this dilemma.

Responsibility for and to this double heritage requires the invention, each time anew, of a rule according to which both contradictory demands can be met simultaneously or of an action from which such a rule can, after the fact, be construed. Such a rule, which at the same time does justice to the conflicting imperatives, cannot be a rule of their dialectical sublation and reconciliation. It must necessarily be a rule that maintains the aporicity of the demands in the action that responds simultaneously to both imperatives. In this sense the singular and innovative response to the challenge posed by the aporia of responsibility can at the same time also be a principle for any response worth the name. In short, responsibility to the two paradigms of the tradition requires a response to their conflicting injunctions which must contain within itself the unique rule (principle, or *arche*) from which it is derived. More precisely, it must be a response that is coeval with this rule in that in its very singularity it can, at the same time, serve also as a universal or absolute law for any response in a singularly determined context to the aporetic demands in question. In Patočka's parlance, such responsibility to the memory of Europe is inevitably heretical. Indeed, the relation to this memory is a responsible one only if the contradictory injunctions are met in a way that amounts to a transformation of the tradition that is new each time, one that is singular. Needless to say, what we have seen in regard to the relation to the memory of Europe is valid as well for all other responsible decision making insofar as it takes place against the backdrop of an experience of tradition. Any responsible decision making must face the demand to give reasons without at the same time being reduced to knowledge that would merely be put into effect.

What, then, is for Derrida European responsibility, or responsibility as something specifically European? The conflicting exigencies formulated in the foregoing discussion of the concept of responsibility require the invention of a new way to renew, revive, or replay the figure, concept, or idea of Europe. European responsibility is, first of all, this openness to *both* traditions of responsibility that characterize its history, namely, Platonism and Christianity. It consists in exposure to the radically conflicting demands that these two traditions make upon their heirs as responsible selves. European responsibility is above all the uncompromising willingness to assume the challenge posed by the aporetic nature of inheritance itself, that is, by the constitutive lack of handed-down rules or norms to negotiate contradiction. Consequently, Europe is the name for a responsibility that also goes hand in hand with the necessity of having to invent, each time anew, new ways of meeting mutually exclusive demands. As a simultaneous responsibility to, at first, two opposite traditions, European responsibility consists in not letting one of the traditions overturn, outplay, or outdo the other. By doing justice to its double heritage and not shunning the necessity of negotiating conflicting demands in the absence of pregiven norms or rules, such responsibility not only entails a radical refusal of traditionalism, for structural reasons, but is distinguished by openness to other traditions and demands. Indeed, from the moment Europe is understood as a responsibility to more than one tradition or set of injunctions, its responsiveness and responsibility extend to all other traditions. Apart from being hospitable to other historically and culturally decisive intra-European differences (such as Judaism and Islam, not in the abstract, however, but with all their shades and forms), as well as to the many minor, or marginal, differences within Europe, this principal openness that the name Europe designates consists as well in the demand of unconditional receptiveness of the tradition of the non-European other. But the demand of such unconditional openness to other traditions and injunctions does not, therefore, exclude the opposite demand, one that is heterogeneous to the former, of conditional or determinate responsibility to oneself. One responsibility comes with the other; neither is possible without negotiation with its opposite. Responsibility as Europe — that is, Europe as responsibility — outlines a model of decision making that is respectful of mutually exclusive demands within the concept of responsibility itself and that endures the test of exigencies that, since they are equally valid, cannot be mediated except at the unacceptable price of rendering one exigency subservient to the other. If something like Europe exists and can be thought at all, it must be a conception that for reasons of structure or principle is open to responding to still more injunctions, including injunctions from other, or non-European, traditions. Responsibility as Europe coincides with a mode of being for which identity, or selfhood, is possible only in honoring conflicting, strictly speaking, aporetic injunctions. It means that Europe is the idea of an identity predicated on aporetic demands, hence of a mode of being that structurally is infinitely open — rather than being closed off — to what is other than oneself. Europe thus understood is a name for a project that Europe has still to live up to. But Europe, neither a figure nor a concept, neither an idea nor even an idea in the Kantian sense — all of which presuppose a formal unity of what they represent, or name — is something that can be realized only by way of approximation, something whose very conception remains open, still, perhaps forever, unfinished, hence something to come.

## Notes

1 Derrida, *The Other Heading*, 26.

2 Ibid., 28.

3 Derrida, *Specters of Marx*, 54. In "The Deconstruction of Actuality," Derrida writes:

> If to inherit is to reaffirm an injunction, not only a possession but also an assignation to be decoded, then we are only what we inherit. Our being is an inheritance, the language we speak is an inheritance. Hölderlin more or less says that language has been given us so that we may testify to what we inherit. Not the inheritance we have or receive, but the one that we are, through and through. What we are, we inherit. And we inherit the language that serves to testify to the fact that we are what we inherit. A paradoxical circle within which one must struggle and decide, by means of decisions that both inherit and invent — necessarily without any set norm or program — one's own norms. (*Negotiations*, 111)

4 Derrida's reference to heritage, and the responsibility to heritage, does not necessarily imply that he would dismiss the notion of "tradition." Let me only emphasize that, in contrast to Gadamer, Derrida does not hold tradition to be homogeneous. Indeed, within the tradition one finds "dominant structures, discourses which silence others, by covering or destroying the archive" (*Politics of Friendship*, 233). Even though he notes repeatedly that "it is no longer possible to *use* seriously the words of tradition" ("Some Statements and Truisms," 74) and that in the end all concepts of the tradition have to be put aside, he also "reaffirms the necessity of making recourse to them, at least, by in a crossed out fashion" (*Psyché*, 390, my translation). Responsibility to the tradition and its deconstruction go hand in hand.

5 Derrida, *The Other Heading*, 29.

6 Ibid., 26.

7 Derrida and Roudinesco, *For What Tomorrow*, 5.

8 Derrida, *The Gift of Death*, 29. Hereafter *GD*.

9 Moreover, Derrida does not seem to have been familiar with the basic tenets of Patočka's later phenomenology, in particular his reinterpretation of the Husserlian conception of the lifeworld. According to Patočka, the natural world is constituted by three movements which are fundamental for understanding his reference to the exceptional (the orgiastic, demonic, or sacred), the inauthenticity of everydayness, and, above all, the motif of the care of the soul. Nonetheless, Derrida's reading of the essay in question is a very fine account of Patočka's thought.

10 This genealogy also raises the question of whether it is not also modeled in accordance with the tripartite movement that, according to Patočka, makes up the natural world of the human being.

11 Plato, *The Dialogues of Plato*, 1: 667 (130d).

12 Plato, *The Collected Dialogues*, 66 (83a).

13 Patočka, *Plato and Europe*, 139.

14 Patočka, *Heretical Essays in the Philosophy of History*, 106.

15 In spite of the decidedly emphatic and crucial role of the conception of person for his thought, Patočka provides almost no information about how this concept is to be understood. However, from the contexts in which Patočka speaks of the person, it is clear that this notion serves to name the individual human being's absolute singularity. To my knowledge, Patočka never explains the philosophical sources for this concept. Undoubtedly, Saint Augustine and Duns Scotus, according to whom the human being is a singular being created in His image by a Creator-God who Himself is a Person, could have acted as models for Patočka's understanding of person. But it seems to me that the more likely, and more immediate, source is Max Scheler's phenomenological, sociological, and metaphysical idea of person, as well as his person-based ethics. Distinct from the human being qua human being, the Ego ("Ich"), the subject, and, in particular, the subject of reason (the moral person, according to Kant), Scheler understands person as the radically individualized and concrete center of all acts (and hence as a spiritual unity, or totality), that is, as the *absolute* individual. (God, in this sense, is "the person of all persons.") As the individualized center of all the performed acts, the person exists and lives only in the performance of intentional acts, experiencing himself or herself in the reflection upon these acts as being responsible for them, and hence as a "value-essence [*Wertwesen*]" that is both personal and individual in nature, "essence" here having nothing to do with universality, since it is "given only in one particular individual." All lived experiences of personal obligations are grounded in the prior experience of one's individual value-essence. Scheler writes, "It is this value-essence of a personal *and* individual nature that I also designate 'personal salvation.'" The link of Scheler's idea of person to that of Patočka becomes tangible especially when Scheler ties such personal salvation to an evidential insight into a good in which I experience a "reference [*Hinweis*] to me which is contained (descriptively put) in the special non-formal content of this good-in-itself, something that comes from this *content*

and points to 'me,' something that whispers, 'For you.'" "This, therefore, is to catch sight of the value-essence of my person — in religious terms, of the value-picture, so to speak, which God's love draws and bears before me insofar as this love is directed to *me*. This peculiar individual value-content is the basis on which a consciousness of an individual ought is built, that is, the evidential knowledge of a 'good-in-itself' but precisely in the sense of a 'good-in-itself-for-*me*'" (Scheler, *Formalism in Ethics*, 498–90). In more general terms, the question to be posed would have to concern the extent to which Patočka's heretically Christian conception of ethics is indebted to what Scheler, in *Wesen und Formen der Sympathie*, calls *acosmistic* ethics, an ethics based on love for the person, which originates in historical-occidental Christendom with the gospel of Jesus. Acosmistic ethics is "this synthesis of, on the one hand, Jewish and Roman thought of sovereignty over nature which is foreign to *Einsfuhlung*, and even hostile to it, and on the other hand, the Greek-Hellenistic-Romantic view of world and God." Breaking both with the orphic movements of Einsfuhlung with the cosmos, whose ultimate root is Eros, the acosmistic ethics "puts forth a wholly new floor of purely spiritual relations of men toward things, of men toward one another, and of man towards God," that is, as far as man and God are concerned, relations of genuine sympathy and spontaneous love, as well as a faith (*Glauben an*) in the person as master, by whose essential figure one becomes moved, seized, and overpowered (Scheler, *Wesen und Formen der Sympathie*, 92, 95–96).

16 Ricoeur, "Preface to the French Edition of Jan Patočka's Heretical Essays," ix.

17 Indeed, as Arendt has pointed out, "Goodness in an absolute sense, as distinguished from the 'good-for' or the 'excellent' in Greek Roman antiquity, became known in our civilization only with the rise of Christianity." The analysis of Goodness provided in *The Human Condition*, and in which Arendt highlights the constitutive secrecy of good works, which must remain hidden even to the one who performs them — a good deed being good only on condition that it is forgotten at the moment it is done — as well as Goodness's intrinsic hostility toward the public realm, converges in many respects with what Patočka, a reader of Arendt, says about this notion, as well as with all the implications that Derrida draws in systematic fashion from this conception in *The Gift of Death*. See Arendt, *The Human Condition*, 73–77.

18 Patočka, *Heretical Essays*, 106.

19 Ibid., 106–7.

20 Patočka, *Plato and Europe*, 35.

21 Patočka, *Heretical Essays*, 108.

22 Derrida asks, "Is the reference to this abyssal dissymmetry that occurs when one is exposed to the gaze of the other a motif that derives firstly and uniquely from Christianity, even if it be from an inadequately thematized Christianity? Let us leave aside the question of whether one finds something that at least represents its equivalent 'before' or 'after' the Gospels, in Judaism or in Islam" (*GD*, 28).

23 Derrida, *The Other Heading*, 79. See also Derrida, *Passions*.

# "Call me Ishmael"

ANNE NORTON

"Day and night," Derrida writes, in one of the most beautiful and revelatory passages in his work, "at every instant, on all the Mount Moriahs of this world, I am doing that, raising my knife over what I love."[1] In this passage, Derrida bears witness to the sacrifices (perhaps we should say, more harshly but no less accurately, the betrayals) that politics, religion, and philosophy demand.

On Mount Moriah Derrida stands at the site where politics and religion meet. This is the site of a great covenant, perhaps the greatest of covenants. Abraham is the father of a tradition, the man named by God, whose body, whose phallus bears the word. Word and flesh, divine command and political power, meet in his body. Abraham is the father of Isaac and Ishmael, of two nations and three faiths. At this site we see those things we, we Westerners, insist on separating. Politics and religion, philosophy and theology, Isaac and Ishmael are bound together here.

The old question "Who is Abraham?" asked by Pharaoh, Hegel, and Kierkegaard is asked again by Derrida. Abraham, once Abram, is a man changed by a journey, by faith, and by a covenant.

Abraham, Hegel taught, was always a man apart. "He tore himself free altogether from his family . . . in order to be a wholly self-subsistent, independent man, to be an overlord himself." He was, Hegel observed, "a stranger on earth, a stranger to the soil and to men alike. Among men he always was and remained a foreigner."[2]

Abraham's exile, Hegel insists, was his own work. He was not exiled, he was not expelled. He cut himself off "without having been injured or disowned. . . . He steadily persisted in cutting himself off from others." He refused a bond to the land. "Abraham wandered hither and thither over a boundless territory without bringing parts of it any nearer to him by cultivating and improving them." The wells he dug, the land his cattle grazed, the groves in which he had his theophanies were used and abandoned. "He was a stranger on earth, a stranger to the soil and to men alike." Hegel's Abraham is separated from family and kinship, land and nature. He refuses bonds with those he meets in his travels, preferring the sterility of commercial relations to personal bonds. "What he needed, he bought; from the good-natured Ephron he absolutely refused to take Sarah's burial place as a gift."[3] Abraham appears to Hegel as a negation of the world, a refusal of the world in favor of God. This refusal reaches its highest point on Mount Moriah, when Abraham undertakes the sacrifice of Isaac.

One might, however, see Abraham as something other than the world's negation. Hegel's account gives Abraham to us as a man intent on being apart. But if Abraham is a man intent on being apart, he is also a man who longs to be a part. He is husband and father, torn by Sarah's longing and anger, loving the son who was to be the late gift of God. He travels, he changes. He becomes what he is. Hegel gives Abraham to us as an individual: apart from the world and a part of the world. He experiences the power of Pharaoh and acquires power of his own. He has property, he engages in commerce. He is a party to small contracts and great covenants. The promise of God is present in him and to him before it is made real in the world. He has a rich interior life. His fear of the danger of Sarai's beauty, his plans for his steward, his hopes for Ishmael are set before us. These fears and plans and hopes prompt Abraham's actions. They are not always realized, however. The world, and God, sometimes resist them. In all of these ways, Abraham appears as an individual. He is given to us as the initiation of the individual. His progeny are as numerous as the stars.

He is the father of phallologocentrism. The word is written on his phallus. His authority is through the phallus. His history is to be written twice, through the word and the flesh. His authority is realized, he is taken into history, in the dissemination of his seed, in his progeny, as numerous and uncountable as the stars. He is made the divine text, bearing the word on his body, writing it on the bodies of his people. He is author and text, writing and written. His body bears the text, is borne in it, born from it. In him, desire is the servant of the word. All the great desires—for power in the world, to live beyond one's time, to make the world in the image of one's desires—are fulfilled in and through the word. (The small desires—to be loved in a particular way, by a particular person—do not seem here to have much connection with the word or with the divine. Sarah, who doubts the word and sees in sex pleasure as well as progeny, is one of the sites that marks for us the space between abstract and intimate longing.) The word becomes the phallus, the site and instrument of desire. The phallus, generative, intimate, is overwritten with authority.

Abraham is the modern man. Derrida enables us to read Hegel's account more fully. Abraham is not simply on the way to something, a necessary negation of the power of the material world. Something is completed in him, something achieved, something begun.

There is an old understanding in political theory that sees the Jew as the father of the individual. Readers of Spinoza have seen that philosopher and his work as the realization of individuality.[4] Spinoza lives, in this understanding, as another Abraham of the individual: the progenitor of many like himself. The rootless cosmopolites of a world liberated from religion are fathered on him.

Carl Schmitt saw the emancipation of the Jews as central to the liberal project. It was not, for Schmitt, liberalism's concern with the rights of man that placed the Jew at the center. The figure of the Jew marked the radical possibility (as Spinoza had earlier) of thinking differently. The radical interiority endorsed in the emancipation of the Jews was, for Schmitt, the undoing of the state.[5] Schmitt writes that Spinoza, "a liberal Jew[,] noticed the barely visible crack in the theoretical justification of the sovereign state. In it he immediately recognized the telling inroad of modern liberalism which would allow Hobbes' postulation of the relation between external and internal, public and private, to be inverted into its converse."[6] The Enlightenment appropriated, depended upon, ratified freedom of thought and a radical interiority. The space that Hobbes reserved within the body, within the mind, was disseminated as simple individuality. The individual, fathered by the Jew, was to be the undoing of the state. The integrity of the body was preserved against the state. The space of dissent held in the silent mind walked out into the world.

Kierkegaard saw Abraham as the "knight of faith." He is pledged to God, like a vassal to a lord, like the lover to the beloved, like the knight to the quest. God had given Abraham wealth and a son; God had promised him power and descendants beyond measure, an existence spread in space and time. With the demand for Isaac, God placed all that in hazard one more time. In this reading, Abraham is called to prove that he loves God without hope of reward, that his commitment to God is absolute. There is more than shamanism at work here. Abraham is called to disavow not only the hope of reward but reason and morality.

We might say, we who speak English, we who read Derrida, that Abraham is the night of faith as well. Abraham is the place the eye cannot reach, the place where theory is blind. The night of faith is a dark place. Abraham does not see, and yet he believes — so profoundly, so unreservedly, that he will sacrifice his child, his virtue, and the promise of the future. This is faith over reason, faith in defiance of reason. This is a faith at odds with enlightenment. This is faith in defiance of virtue and morality, and the powers that govern it are the powers of darkness. Kierkegaard met this faith with "fear and trembling," knowing that it raised again the old question: What if the good for God is not the good for man?

Derrida takes up those questions in the shadow of another sacrifice, another holocaust. He sees the conflict between Abraham's faith and ethics. He sees Abraham as Kierkegaard saw him: opposed to ethics, to morality. He writes of Abraham's "hatred for the ethical," a hate that grows from the coupling of his love for his son and for the ethical with the love of God that demands their sacrifice. His sacrifice of his own, his own son, "his own family, friends, neighbors, nation, at the outside, humanity as a whole, his own kind," is made from a hate, a rejection, a disavowal, that must also "remain an absolute source of pain."[7]

The story of Isaac and Ishmael is not a single story for Derrida, even an emblematic, iconic story. The story of the sacrifice of Isaac is the story of a truth of politics altogether, confronted "in this land of Moriah that is our habitat every second of every day."[8] Nietzsche recognized that all contracts, all covenants, like the beginnings of everything great on earth, are "soaked in blood thoroughly, and for a long time."[9] Derrida reads this text as a commentary on the costs of covenant, on the betrayals that belong to belonging. Politics is maintained and renewed day by day in sacrifices and betrayals small and great. The imperatives that cannot be accomplished, the duties that have to be neglected, the small sacrifices, the small betrayals, the daily cruelties of politics are counted here. In his attention to the demands of the absolute, Derrida does not lose sight of the particular.

Nor, in his attention to the divine text, does Derrida lose sight of the secular world. He gives the timeless text on faith a commentary that lights this place, this history, this politics. As he turns from Mount Moriah he gestures toward al Aqsa, to the tanks and bulldozers of his own time: "It is therefore a holy place but also a place that is in dispute, radically and rabidly, fought over by all the monotheisms, by all the religions of the unique and transcendent God, of the absolute other. . . . They make war with fire and blood. . . . Isaac's sacrifice continues every day. Countless machines of death wage a war that has no front."[10] For Derrida, the "bloody, holocaustic sacrifice" is still Isaac's, and so a story of redemption.

The sparing of Isaac is an answer to another text on covenants, and on the exception, that surrounds the Holocaust. In Schmitt's writing on constitutionalism, the covenant is secured by and subordinate to an existential enmity. For Schmitt, the site of the exception is the site of the unlimited power of the sovereign: "Sovereign is he who decides on the exception."[11] Much is accomplished in this brief profession of faith. Sovereignty, Schmitt reminds us, is beyond the law, the site of law's origin and undoing. The sovereign, he affirms, is not bound by the law and may decide exceptions to it. Schmitt transforms sovereignty from an attribute into a person, makes an act of a decision, and moves authority from the mind to the hand. He reads the moment of the exception as the moment not of sovereign, but of executive power. Such a reading relies, as Schmitt knew well, on a theological underpinning, on a Christian, Catholic faith. Catholicism depended (as all Christianity does) on the incarnation. Sovereignty is made incarnate in the decision as it was made incarnate in the body of Christ: it takes human form, and in doing so elevates one human form above all others. The redemption of all depends on the act of one.[12] The formula "The word was made flesh and dwelt among us" informs Schmitt's reading of the exception. (All political concepts are, Schmitt argued, secularized theology.)[13] Schmitt's sovereign is not fully realized in the world until he has become flesh and dwelt among us. Schmitt follows Donoso Cortes (that "Catholic philosopher of the state") in the assertion that with the end of kings "legitimacy no longer exists in the traditional sense" and records that, in that event "there was thus only one solution: dictatorship." When in Rousseau, in America, "the people became sovereign . . . the decisionistic and personal element in the concept of sovereignty was thus lost."[14] Though Schmitt could refer to the belief of the Americans that the voice of the people was the voice of God as "reasonable and pragmatic," the transcendent immateriality of this moment of sovereignty lacked, like the holy ghost, the corporeal presence requisite to Schmitt's understanding of sovereignty. The sovereign, like the Christian deity, is fully realized only in incarnation.[15]

In Schmitt's work, the site of the exception is the site of death: in its origin, in its issue, in its effects. Death is required of the incarnate God. The sovereign, human and divine, who decides the exception, gives life and takes it away. The decisions, like the distinctions, that belong to sovereignty concern mortality. In making sovereignty mortal and in moving the decision from the mind to the hand, Schmitt reduced the sovereign to an executive and the executive to an executioner.

Derrida responds with an opposing reading of the exception. The exception is not the occasion for violence but the moment when violence is arrested. The exception is not the occasion for the exercise of executive power, but the moment when the executive is restrained (and this by the voice of God: *vox populi, vox dei*). The exception is not the moment when the covenant is sacrificed, but the moment when it is preserved. Derrida's answer to Schmitt is threefold: textual, for Isaac is spared; historical, for the Jews are spared (they continue, and their progeny may be as numerous as the stars); political, for the belief in the leader is answered by belief in the people.

If one looks at the story of covenant as the story of the Binding (and unbinding) of Isaac, one reads a text on authority, one that captures certain of the hazards and commitments in Derrida's work. In the name of Isaac, the laughter of Sarah triumphs over the demands of faith. In the body of Isaac, Sarah's skeptical laughter and Abraham's ruthless faith are made flesh in a single living body. This is the body made, quite literally, of the coupling of skepticism and faith, pleasure and ruthlessness, reason and revelation. This is the absence at the center of genesis. This is the exception that founds a sovereignty bound like Isaac, not to death but to life.

Derrida gives the story of the sacrifice of Isaac a happy ending, as the canonical text does. Isaac is not sacrificed. In this reading, the sacrifice that faith demands never has to be made. I continue to doubt this comforting story. I think there was a killing done, "out on Highway 61."[16] Like Yehuda Amichai, and Derrida gesturing toward al Aqsa, I see that something is always lost, something betrayed, blood is shed, someone is sacrificed. The covenant, "like all things great on earth, is soaked in blood thoroughly, and for a very long time."[17]

The political reading of the binding of Isaac obliges us to read a death into the text. The sparing of Isaac is not, however, merely a veil cast over those truths that one should not see naked. Nor is it simply an alternative that literary authority poses to political authority. This is an account of the genesis of the people of the covenant. The sacrifice of Isaac, the instant when Abraham raises his knife on Mount Moriah, the instant when he puts his hand to the fulfillment of the divine demand, is a gate into another moment, into one holocaust after another.

Yehuda Amichai writes:

The real hero of the Binding of Isaac was the ram,
who didn't know about the collusion between the others
He was volunteered to die instead of Isaac
I want to sing a memorial song about him—

about his curly wool and his human eyes,
about the horns that were so silent on his living head,
and how they made those horns into shofars when he was slaughtered
to sound their battle cries.[18]

He was a wild ass of a man. Call him Ishmael. The ram is sacrificed as Ishmael was sacrificed. He didn't know about the collusion among the others. He took Isaac's place and Isaac his. He was silent, and his silence was transformed into the calling of others. Call him Ishmael, the man who is transformed from man to animal in the eyes of another. Call him Ishmael, the man who dies for another's calling.

The people of the covenant held in, written on, the body of Isaac, are brought into being when he is spared. The promise of the future, as yet unfulfilled, is preserved as he is preserved. In the Shoah, the Holocaust of the time before our time, the people of the covenant were no longer the fortunate, favored son. They became *Muselmanner.*

Isaac and Ishmael are conjoined in the figure of the Muselmann. At Yad Vashem "Muselmann" is defined as "a German word used to refer to prisoners who were near death due to exhaustion, starvation or hopelessness. The word *Muselmann* literally means Muslim. Some scholars believe the term originated from the similarity between the near-death prone state of a concentration camp *Muselmann* and the image of a Muslim prostrating himself on the ground in prayer."[19] In approaching death through exhaustion, starvation, or hopelessness, the descendants of Isaac became Ishmael, abandoned. They were cast out like Ishmael, killed like the ram. Time and the promise of the future died with the dead. It is for us to consider the dark past, the dark future, carried in the knowledge that they died as Muslims.

If we read Genesis in the shadow of the Holocaust, the binding of Isaac ends in freedom, and Abraham's abject submission to the unworldly leads to power in the world. This is a reading of triumphant beauty. But time does not stop there, nor does the text. Our time demands that we bear witness to the sacrifice of Ishmael: to the exile of Ishmael in the writings of Derrida, to the lost Muslims of philosophy, to the phantom friend on whom democracy depends, and above all to the Muselmanner, the Muslims, of Guantánamo and Abu Ghraib.

———————

Derrida insists on his own interiority, on his own secrets.[20] Perhaps he is philosophy's Marrano, hiding in philosophy something that it has disowned and disavowed, something that nevertheless belongs to its own ancestry, that is, theology. Perhaps Derrida is philosophy's *Arab*, traveling.[21] Derrida insists that democracy also has a secret at its heart. Perhaps Derrida's secret is akin to the secret of democracy.

Derrida has spoken and written of his preoccupation with the figure of the Marrano, the secret Jew, the *converso*. The Marrano is the figure of the secret, the unknown, perhaps the unknowable, other. The converso and the secret Jew alike know and work, live and bear witness in the space within the letter. Their meaning is made out of difference. They bear witness. They sacrifice and they are sacrificed. Derrida, in his writing and work, belongs to them.

Derrida's ancestors, coming from Spain to North Africa, may have known the Marranos well, might even have been numbered among them. But for the Jews of Derrida's time and place, in French colonial Algeria Judaism was not to be hidden. Judaism granted French citizenship and more, an open gate into the French language, and into France. One might say "into French letters," for the way was opened into the world of literature and the literati. But there was still a certain thin membrane that set the Jew apart and constrained the dissemination of Judaism even as it protected the Jews. One made one's Judaism visible in the North African colonial order, for it was, as it was for Isaac, the sign of the fortunate son.

The ethical problem this privilege imposed was described with particular clarity and force by Albert Memmi. Those privileged by the colonial regime, Jewish and gentile, could not effectively disavow that privilege. They might wish, they might strive to do so, but the privilege (like the oppression it mirrored) was embedded in the structures of the regime. These structures would have to be dismantled. The "colonizer who refuses," who confronted the burden of privilege, was faced not simply with an ethical, but with a political problem.[22] The experience of the *Loi Cremieux*, of Vichy; of privilege granted, taken away, reinstalled; of a partiality that was always only partial is a profoundly Marrano experience.[23]

Once the disavowal of political theology was fixed on the figure of the Jew. In the coupling of Athens and Jerusalem, the Jew stood in the place of religion. In the emergence of the liberal individual, the emancipation of the Jews testified to the political acceptance of internal difference in belief. The hidden confession was permitted—but also forced—into the open. The Marrano disappeared into the desert.

Derrida works in an economy of displacement, time, and witness. But in this *oikos*, this home economy, the experience of exile, the weight of history and the imperative to bear witness, the demand "Record it!" come in the name of Isaac. In the writings of Derrida, as in the Bible and Tanakh, Ishmael is sent into exile. Ishmael is *sous rature*, the one who is erased, who remains as a marked absence, the sign of a disavowal. The angel of the Lord tells Hagar that she will bear a son.

> You shall call him Ishmael
> For the Lord paid heed to your suffering.
> He shall be a wild ass of a man;
> His hand against everyone
> And everyone's hand against him.[24]

When Abraham abandons Ishmael to Sarah's will, Ishmael goes into exile with his mother. He fathers a nation of wanderers, of Arabs. He and his people are sent out of history, out of time, out of the text. Ishmael, though he is marked with the sign of the covenant, remains outside it. Abraham pleads for him; God rejects him. Abraham said to God, "Oh Lord that Ishmael might live by your favor," and God replied, "As for Ishmael, I have heeded you, I hereby bless him . . . but my covenant I will maintain with Isaac."[25]

In our time, in Europe and the Americas, Judaism is no longer the site of secret faith or forced confession. In the speech of the Judeo-Christian street, as in the Judeo-Christian academy, it is the Arab who has become the sign of religion. It is the Arab who is sous rature, who stands for that which is disavowed. The Arab is the Marrano of philosophy. The writings of al Farabi, Ibn Rushd and Ibn Sina, Ibn Tufayl and Ibn Khaldun are placed outside the canon, exiled scholastically to the provinces of area studies, religious studies, and anthropology. Political theology stands to political theory as Ishmael to Isaac, sent out to wander in the desert.

Ishmael is the name of an absence: the name of the exiled, the name of the child who is not Sarah's, the child who is not the heir. Ishmael is the alien, the lost brother. His is the absent language. He is the phantom friend.

The exile of Ishmael is the silence of Arabic in the texts of Derrida. There are many languages in Derrida: Greek and Latin, French and German, Hebrew and English. Derrida marks French as his own language: "I have only one language. I don't know any other. So, I was raised in a monolingual milieu — absolutely monolingual." He goes on to say, "Around me, although not in my family, I naturally heard Arabic spoken, but I do not speak — except for a few words — Arabic. I tried to learn it later but I didn't get very far. Moreover, one could say in a general way, without exaggerating, that learning Arabic was something that was virtually forbidden at school. Not prohibited by law, but practically impossible. So, French is my only language."[26] Arabic, Derrida tells us, is the forbidden tongue, the speech of the other, not of his family. Arabic remains a silence, a desert.

Derrida's Abrahamic writings send us out into that desert, into that elsewhere. This is the place of "some *khora* (body without body, absent body but unique body and place [*lieu*] of everything, in the place of everything, interval, place [*place*], spacing. . . . *Khora* is over there but more here than any here." Khora is the place of the secret: "Everything secret is played out here."[27] Khora is the place of revelation. This place is kept secret. This is the place of Ishmael, the absent but unique body (for, as Derrida tells us, the sacrifice must be unique) who stands for, in lieu of, the other. Khora is Derrida's elsewhere, across the Mediterranean, in one sense, across a more fortified boundary, but also the elsewhere carried in the heart and mind, another time, another place, a time past. Between that place and this, between one sound and another, there is the interval, and that, Heidegger tells us, is where thought arises.

The interval is also the place of the echo, the partial repetition produced over an interval of space and time. In the echo, one calls to oneself, one is called by an earlier self. In khora one can hear echoes of the place of revelation, of Derrida's elsewhere. You will see, Derrida writes, "why it is that we left the name *khora* sheltered from any translation. A translation, admittedly, seems to be always at work, both *in* the Greek language, and from the Greek language into some other."[28] One can hear in the Greek the echoes of the Arabic, of the word *qara'a*, with which Islam begins.

"Qara'a" is commonly translated as "recite," for the words which come from the mouth of Muhammed are written before they are given utterance in speech. The spoken words of the Messenger carry the already written. One need not hear *qara'a* echoing in *khora* to see the Maghreb as the "over there" that, in France, is "more 'here' than any 'here.'"[29] One need not hear *qara'a* echoing in *khora* to see Ishmael as the absent body. Still, I would remind the reader of Lacan's observation that the ear is the only orifice that cannot be closed. "Everything," Derrida writes, "comes down to the ear you are able to hear me with."[30]

Derrida closes the preface to *Rogues* with another invocation of khora:

On what here receives the name *khora*, a call might thus be taken up and take hold: the call for a thinking of the event *to come*, of the democracy *to come*, of the reason, *to come*. This call bears every hope, to be sure, although it remains, in itself, without hope. Not hopeless, in despair, but foreign to the teleology, the hopefulness, and the *salut*, of salvation. Not foreign to the *salut* as the greeting or salutation of the other, not foreign to the *adieu*, not foreign to justice, but nonetheless heterogeneous and rebellious, irreducible to law, to power, and to the economy of redemption.[31]

If we hear with the ears of Ishmael, in the language of the traveler and exile, we may hear something hopeful. The *salut*, which in France is the greeting and salutation of the other, in Algeria is the object of the Islamist coalition, the Front Islamique du Salut, the winner of the democratic elections set aside in 1992. The *adieu* commends all to God. "I am God's, for and to God, yours, for and to you, for and to the infinite": so Derrida translated the adieu in "Hostipitality."[32] The same greetings in the language of Ishmael are still more hopeful. One might say *salaam aleikum*, wishing the other peace. One might say *marhaba*, a word that means "there is plenty of room for all who come." The root *r-h-b* gives us "*rahb:* wide, spacious, roomy"; "unconfined" and "open-minded, broad-minded, frank, liberal." This is the root of *rahaba*, the word for "public square."[33] One might say *ahlan wa sahlan*, a formula that welcomes the other, saying "You are among your people and your keep is easy."[34] One can read (one cannot fail to read) liberality and liberalism and the welcome of the other in these salutations.

In "Circumfession" Derrida gives an account of the act that constituted him at once as Jewish and European, cutting him off from Algeria.[35] In this act, Algeria becomes a place of loss for him. That which is excised, that which is lost, was Derrida's and is so no longer. Perhaps this is "what the sexed being loses in sexuality." Perhaps it is what the political being loses in belonging to a polity. Perhaps it is what the political being loses with the enemy. Derrida enters the covenant as he is separated from that which once belonged to him. The circumcision is the site at which the word and the flesh, writing and the body meet. In this place, at this site, bandages are stained, texts written. The mouth and the pen, the author of the body and the author of the text meet.

This circumcision is the site at which speech and silence, frankness and concealment meet. For all the revelations, Derrida shows us that something is hidden. The text layers one time upon another. The time of writing and recollection gives way to the time of circumcision, the instant when Abraham raises his knife over Isaac, once in sacrifice, once in circumcision. The account is out of place: improper, inappropriate: it does not belong where it is. The text is out of place: displaced, timeless, separated from the material world, outside Algeria. The wound binds one time to another: the time of the text to the time of circumcision, to all the times of all the circumcisions, and to that time when Abraham raised his knife over Isaac, not to mark but to annihilate him. This is a text of loss and belonging, a timeless time lost in the collapse of memory into forgetting: "As Montaigne said 'I constantly disavow myself.'"[36]

What is held in the mouth? What is concealed here? Another writing, another language, perhaps another phallus, another logos, another center are hidden here. Even as we are told that this is a story of the phallus, of Derrida's phallus, of the Jew and the Frenchman, the all too frank narratives gesture toward the silent and the hidden. The text purports to reveal the author, the phallus, that which is inscribed, but it shows us a phallus and an inscription concealed, a hidden male member. In his account of circumcision Derrida occupies the place of Isaac, but he gestures toward the sacrifice of Ishmael. He marks Ishmael as that which he has lost.

"If we greatly transform ourselves," Nietzsche writes, "those friends of ours who have not been transformed become ghosts of our past: their voice comes across to us like the voice of a shade [in a frightfully spectral manner (*schattenhaft-schauerlich*)] — as though we were hearing ourself, only younger, more severe, less mature." Derrida makes this passage the epigraph to "The Phantom Friend Returning (in the Name of Democracy)."[37] In this chapter of *Politics of Friendship*, Derrida marks the presence of the phantom friend, the absent enemy, within and without himself. "Circumfession" suggested that the loss of the other was great, perhaps disempowering. "Circumfession" marked the loss of the other, once part of oneself, as the price of entry into the covenant, an obligatory exclusion exacted with violence. In *Politics of Friendship* the loss of this other is like shedding a skin, done without violence, accomplished as an overcoming. The lost other lingers as a shadow of a self "more severe, less mature," present only as one dead. For Derrida, as for Schmitt, democracy belongs to the *abendland*, to a world of shadows.

Derrida departs from Schmitt in his history, his politics, his faith and in his reading of the story of Abraham. He departs from Schmitt in his reading of the sacrifice of Isaac, and this departure holds within it the memory of the Holocaust and the memory of the spared. The recollection of the Binding of Isaac bears double witness: to horror and salvation, shame and redemption. Derrida follows Schmitt in seeing the political as dependent upon the presence of enmity. Derrida remains with Schmitt in his understanding of Europe, the European, and that which is their own; in the centrality of the distinction of friend and enemy to politics, in the identification of the enemy and the affirmation of the absence of democracy. Schmitt disavows democracy; Derrida defers it. Democracy is, Derrida writes, *à venir*, to come. Perhaps it belongs in the abendland, in an aporetic future in the West. Perhaps it will come bearing its death within it, in the form of a "suicidal autoimmunity." Perhaps it is already dead and appears to us only as a shadow, a *revenant*, as something we once knew, returning.[38]

In *Politics of Friendship* Derrida links the return of the phantom friend to the possibility and impossibility of democracy. The phantom friend, the one who is at once alien and one's own, belongs to an unprecedented time, a time without friends and enemies. This is a time of the radically contemporary, a time without past or future. "One would then have a time," Derrida writes, "of a world without friends, the time of a world without enemies," a time without love or hate, "but absolutely without indifference." When Derrida follows Schmitt, seeing the refusal of the distinction between friend and enemy as the end of politics, he sees this as a time of death and madness.[39] But he allows us to see otherwise. This is the time when, in the words of the great democrat Thomas Paine, "the earth belongs to the living."

Democracy protests, as Derrida once did, against authority, against authoritarianism. Derrida's characterization of this democratic time repeats criticisms once leveled against his own anti-authoritarianism. "It would resemble nothing, nor would it gather itself up in anything, lending itself to any possible reflection." "The effects of this destructuration would be countless: the subject in question would be looking for new reconstitutive enmities." Meaning depends upon difference, but difference need not be enmity: "*It would therefore be a matter of thinking an alterity without hierarchical difference at the root of democracy.*"[40]

Politics requires the other, requires radical heterogeneity, but as the Greeks knew well, one finds the other in the friend as well as the enemy. Friendship, not war, provides the form of the political. In this understanding the friend is not, as Derrida writes in *Rogues*, the "compeer . . . the *semblable*,"[41] but the radically other (another body, another mind, another will) that one takes as one's own. Politics, as the Greeks knew well, is properly found not in war, where human beings return to the condition of barbarians and animals, without language, but to the contentious peace within the polis: to an agon, a struggle — that is to say, a jihad — in language.[42]

Democratic politics does indeed, as Derrida fears, hold "the imminence of self-destruction" within it. Democracy is aporetic, willing itself to go forward into an uncertain future. Democracy presents, always and everywhere, the possibility that things — that we — could be otherwise. Democracy requires that the democrat accept not only the other in the polity, but the possibility (I think it is a certainty) that the demos (and oneself within it) will become other than it is.

Islam appears in *Rogues* as "the other of democracy." Muslims are, like Ishmael, cast out of the Abrahamic inheritance that runs in Derrida's writing, as in Jewish and Christian texts, from Abraham to Isaac. They are cast out too from the inheritance of democracy. Muslims are alien to democracy, which belongs to a "Greco-Christian and globalatinizing tradition."[43] One can read a similar argument in "Faith and Knowledge." Derrida writes that the concepts of democracy and secularization, "even of the right to literature," are not "merely European, but Graeco-Christian, Graeco-Roman."[44] Mindful that the Greeks were read by the children of Ishmael as well as those of Isaac and that Rome had an Eastern as well as a Western Empire, we might (taking liberties with the text that it not take liberties from us) argue against restricting the heritage of democracy to the "merely European." These adjectives — Greco-Christian, Greco-Roman, globalatinizing — which would seem to send the descendants of Ishmael into the desert as exiles from democracy might serve instead to remind us that there is a "Greco-Muslim" world and that Constantinople became Istanbul. If democracy is an inheritance from the Greeks, then it, like the philosophic city of speech, is our al Andalus holding Jews, Christians, and Muslims. If globalatinization proceeds through invasion and conversion, from the pagan to the Christian (and back again) in the Western Empire, it is no less present in the invasions and conversions that led Rome's Eastern Empire from the pagan to the Christian to the Muslim. If globalatinization leads to the democracy to come, then its past and future heartland encircles the Bosphorus.

Derrida attempts to restrict Muslim claims to the Greek heritage, reporting the "troubling fact that Aristotle's *Politics* was absent in the Islamic importation, reception, translation, and mediation of Greek philosophy."[45] He claims that al Farabi took nothing from Plato but the idea of the philosopher king. But he also cautions us against this merely European reading. "The Other of Democracy" is riddled with caveats. The errant claims quoted above are preceded by "from the little I know," "unless I am mistaken," and other expressions of uncertainty.[46] He does well to caution us. Al Farabi's knowledge of Aristotle's *Politics* is evident throughout "The Political Regime," "Selected Aphorisms," and "The Harmonization of the Two Sages" (that is to say, Plato and Aristotle).[47] Rather than "importing only the theme of the philosopher king from Plato's *Republic*," al Farabi's rendering democratizes the Platonic text, both in its much more generous praise of democracy and by replacing the idea of the philosopher king with that of the *mulk al haqiqa*, "the righteous regime" or "correct rule."

Derrida addresses the democratic possibilities of Islam at another site in *Rogues*, that of the *banlieux*. The *voyou* roams the streets and sets cars on fire, like the disaffected *shebab*, but the voyou also belongs "to what is most common and thus most popular in the people. The *demos* is thus never far away when one speaks of the *voyou*."[48] The rioting shebab of the banlieux are close to the demos, close perhaps to democracy. So too were other voyous, other shebab, those of Algeria, whose participation in democratic elections voted the Front Islamique de Salut into power. They were close to democracy, only to have it snatched away. "The Algerian government and a large part, though not a majority of the Algerian people (as well as people outside Algeria) thought that the electoral process would lead democratically to the end of democracy. . . . They decided to suspend democracy . . . for its own good."[49] Derrida commends this action, accepting the view that this democracy, the democracy of Islamists, would have put an end to democracy. Yet he shows us a democracy ended not by Islam, but by the partisans of "laic subjectivity" and the Enlightenment. Perhaps we can see democracy otherwise.

If politics is founded not in enmity but in friendship, perhaps we can think "an alterity without hierarchical difference at the root of democracy."[50] If we read the Greeks as a common heritage (one that extends beyond their cultural offspring to all who might find themselves in a city of speech) we need not bind ourselves within the confines of the merely European. If we can make common cause with the rebellious voyous of the banlieux, perhaps we will find ourselves closer to democracy. If we can greet the other not only with the adieu and salut but with "Marhaba," we may find a more liberal public space, one that has plenty of room for others. Whether we do so or not, we are called now to a common duty.

Derrida's quotation of Joyce's "Hear, O Ishmael" collapses Isaac and Ishmael in the imperative of the *Shema*.[51] The warrants of heritage and genealogy fall before the imperative to bear witness. The echo of *qara'a* in *khora* calls us similarly. "Qara'a," the command "Recite," carries a constellation of commands within it. This is the command to prophecy. This is the command that Muhammed obeys in bringing the Koran to the people. This is the command Muslims obey in the *shahada*, the testimony that answers the command to bear witness. Five times a day the muezzin calls out to the city in the voice of the people, "I testify that there is no God but God. I testify that Muhammed is the messenger of God." Tariq Ramadan, in rejecting the distinction between the *dar al harb* and the *dar al Islam*, writes that Western Muslims belong not to either (or to both) of these but to another understanding of place and time, another understanding of their relation to politics and the divine. They are called, he writes, to be the people of the *dar ash-shahada*, the people who bear witness.[52]

The command to speak, to bear witness, echoes in a poem by Mahmoud Darwish that became an anthem for Palestine. "Record," Darwish writes, "I am an Arab."[53] When Darwish came to recite his poetry those who came to hear him would recite the poem he wrote back to him. The people practice what Derrida makes visible to us: that authority is at once political and literary, that the word disseminates, that the author does not possess the text, that authority moves like a current between reader and read. One need not hear *qara'a* echoing in *khora* to recognize an evocation of the core of Islam in Derrida's complex of concerns: responsibility, bearing witness, the carrying of the written in the spoken word. One need not hear *qara'a* echoing in *khora* to recognize that we are called to bear witness to the Muselmanner of our time.

Speaking in the silence Derrida leaves, mindful of the echoing space between one set of camps and another, I say "Ashadu," I bear witness to the Arab in the text. I bear witness to the Muslim in the camps.

## Notes

As I write this, my people sail on a mad quest under a maimed captain, and I find myself coupled with the other, friend to friend.

1 Derrida, *The Gift of Death*, 68–69.

2 Hegel, *Early Theological Writings*, 185, 186.

3 Ibid., 185–87; Genesis 23:10–16.

4 Schmitt, *The Leviathan in the State Theory of Thomas Hobbes*. Schmitt cites, with qualifications, the view of "the Jewish scholar Leo Strauss" that "Hobbes regarded the Jews as the originators of the revolutionary state-destroying distinction between religion and politics" (10). On the relation of Spinoza to the emergence of the liberal individual, see also Yovel, *Spinoza and Other Heretics*, and S. Smith, *Spinoza, Liberalism and the Question of Jewish Identity*.

5 Schmitt, *Leviathan*, 10, 57–58; Kennedy, *Constitutional Failure*, 178–83. I am

deeply indebted to Ellen Kennedy for her guidance in reading Schmitt, but she is not to be held responsible for my interpretations.

6   Schmitt, *Leviathan*, 57.

7   Derrida, *The Gift of Death*, 64, 72.

8   Ibid., 69. Frantz Fanon offers a still darker reading, I believe. See Norton, *Bloodrites of the Poststructuralists*, 129–37.

9   Nietzsche, *On the Genealogy of Morals*, Second Essay, 65.

10  Derrida, *The Gift of Death*, 69–70.

11  Schmitt, *Political Theology*, 5.

12  Ibid., 52. See also Kennedy, *Constitutional Failure*, 176.

13  "All significant concepts of the modern state are secularized theological concepts" (Schmitt, *Political Theology*, 36). Also see chapter 3.

14  Ibid., 51–52, 48.

15  See also Schmitt, *Roman Catholicism and Political Form*.

16  Bob Dylan, "Highway 61 Revisited," 1965.

17  Nietzsche, *On the Genealogy of Morals*, Second Essay, 65.

18  Amichai, "The Real Hero," 156.

19  Yad Vashem, Shoah Resource Center. The mention of prayer is unusual. Through it, Muslims are linked to the Jews of the Shoah at the site, as through the habitus, of their faith: the marking of faith on the body and the experience of being killed but not sacrificed. Gil Anidjar takes up the figure of the Muselmann, in all its revelatory ambivalence, in his superb book *The Jew, the Arab: A History of the Enemy*. Giorgio Agamben writes of the Muselmanner, "It is certain that, with a kind of ferocious irony, the Jews knew that they would not die at Auschwitz as Jews" (*Remnants of Auschwitz*, 45). See also *Homo Sacer: Sovereign Power and Bare Life* 184–85.

20  This insistence is evident throughout Derrida's work. One sees its Algerian context, albeit partially and allusively, in *Derrida's Elsewhere* (*D'ailleurs, Derrida*).

21  In the Arabic language, "Arab" refers to travel and those who travel. There is a complex pattern of linguistic connections knitting Arabic to theory, restoring the unity theory has denied to itself in my time. Roxanne Euben observes that the Greek *theoria* refers not only to sight but to travel. The word binds theory both to travel and to theology. *Theoros* "has multiple meanings, including a spectator, a state delegate to a festival in another city, someone who travels to consult an oracle" (Euben, *Journeys to the Other Shore*, 21).

22  Memmi, *The Colonizer and the Colonized*, 19–44. Memmi later departed from the nuanced and humane work of his youth to issue comprehensive condemnations of the Arab, the Muslim, and Islam.

23  Yirmiyahu Yovel describes the experience with a rare attention to the play of privilege and deprivation in his study of Spinoza, *Spinoza and Other Heretics: The Marrano of Reason*.

24  Genesis 16:11–12.

25  Genesis 17:18–21.

26 An interview broadcast on the program prepared by Didier Cahen over France-Culture, "Le bon plaisir de Jacques Derrida," on March 22, 1986, and published with the title "Entretien avec Jacques Derrida" in *Digraphe* 42 (December 1987). This translation appeared as "There Is No *One* Narcissism," 204. Derrida lived in Algeria for the first nineteen years of his life. There, as throughout the Muslim world, the call to prayer is made in Arabic five times a day.

27 Derrida, "Sauf le nom," 56. Derrida brackets this account of khora between references to prayer and the desert "as a figure of pure place" counterposed to the "Greek, Christian, or Jewish" references to God.

28 Derrida, "Khora," 93.

29 Derrida, *On the Name*, 93. See also 56, 76, 83 (the conflict between maintaining a specific secret and inclusion), and 104, where Derrida points to the importance of politics in this question.

30 Derrida, "Otobiographies," 4.

31 Derrida, *Rogues*, xv.

32 Derrida, "Hostipitality," 406. In this text Derrida undertook an exploration of Islam and an exploration of the homosexual, that is, of the relation with the other who is one's own. Here he explores not only French and German, Hebrew, Latin and Greek, but also Arabic, notably *dawa*, the invitation, the prayer, the call, above all *dawat al mazlum*, the prayer of the oppressed.

33 Wehr, *A Dictionary of Modern Standard Arabic*.

34 I am grateful to Deborah Harrold, who gave me this translation by the poet and scholar Farouk Mustafa.

35 Derrida, "Circumfession," in Bennington and Derrida, *Jacques Derrida*.

36 Ibid., 199/38.

37 Derrida, *Politics of Friendship*, 75.

38 On suicidal autoimmunity and democracy, see Derrida, *Rogues*, 33, 35, 45, and *Politics of Friendship*, 73. On the spectral phantom being of democracy, see *Politics of Friendship*, 73, 76, in which the lost enemy and unfound friend appear as "the shadow of an ageless ghost," and 94, in which the dead and the unborn meet in the place that is not a place, the originary abendland of the khora.

39 Derrida, *Politics of Friendship*, 76. Derrida makes it clear that the question of the political, as Schmitt construes it, is dependent not only on the relation of friend and enemy but (in this time as in others) on a particular enemy, Islam. "It was imperative not 'to deliver Europe over to Islam.' . . . The stakes would be saving the political as such, ensuring its survival in the face of another who would no longer even be a political enemy but an enemy of the political," one who "shares nothing of the juridical and the political called European" (89).

40 Ibid., 76, 77, 232, italics Derrida's.

41 Derrida, *Rogues*, 11–12. Here Derrida asks, "Must one live together only with one's like, with someone semblable?" and affirms that ipseity, as he conceives it, belongs to the single self and "designates oneself as master in the masculine."

42  "Jihad" translates as "struggle." The greatest jihad, so the tradition holds, is the struggle to govern oneself.

43  Derrida, *Rogues*, 28.

44  Derrida, "Faith and Knowledge," 46. The "right to literature" alluded to is connected by Derrida to Khomeini's fatwa against Salman Rushdie.

45  Derrida, *Rogues*, 31. The ancient Greeks again appear as the (sole) ancestors of (only) modern Europeans.

46  Ibid., 28, 31, 32. Derrida's apology for a "Greco-Judeo-Christian" tradition alien to Islam is more fully elaborated in "Faith and Knowledge," yet here too he points the way to the text's undoing.

47  Alfarabi, *Selected Aphorisms and Other Political Writings*.

48  Derrida, *Rogues*, 64, 65, 66.

49  Ibid., 33.

50  Derrida, *Politics of Friendship*, 232.

51  Gil Anidjar remarks on Derrida's fondness for this injunction in "Once More, Once More: Derrida, the Arab, the Jew," *Acts of Religion*, 9. Anidjar's brilliant reading of the Arab, the Jew, tends here to collapse the Arab in the Jew, concealing once again the presence of Ishmael, the presence of the Muslim.

52  Ramadan, *Western Muslims and the Future of Islam*, 65–78.

53  Darwish, "Identity Card."

# Algeria as an Archive

SORAYA TLATLI

> Death has touched me. . . . It had to be under an African sky.
> —Jacques Derrida, in Malabou and Derrida, *Counterpath*

There is one visual image from Derrida's Algerian childhood that particularly fascinated him, that of a loose tile in the floor of his home. When the filmmaker Safaa Fathi made a documentary on him in 1999, *D'ailleurs, Derrida*, it was this still image that remained in Derrida's memory.[1] He asked the filmmaker specifically to film the cracks around this tile, still visible in his former home in El Biar. It was again this central image that Edwy Plenel chose in his homage to the philosopher, shortly after his death, in an editorial in *Le Monde:* "It is an image taken from a film, of a simple cement-tiled floor filmed in a house in El Biar, near Algiers. It is the image of a flaw that interrupts the harmony, breaks the pattern and creates a gap: one of the tiles is poorly fitted, laid improperly, somehow out of place."[2] This crack has many resonances in Derrida's philosophy, elaborated in part around disjuncture, nonlinearity, and the flow of time, but also around the gap and the disconnection between the trace and its inscription. At a more personal level, it is the emblem of a torn identity, of an initial wound. Commenting on this image, Derrida also described this break as the emblem of memory: "Memory is constructed on the wound, the disjointed, the heterogeneous."[3]

In this paper I analyze the Derridean concept of the archive as presented in *Mal d'archive*, focusing specifically on the way the violence of the archive sutures the disjointed, the cracks of memory, by imposing its law, which is one of community membership based on the mechanical repetition of memory. I argue that *Mal d'archive* can shed new light on the historicity of Algeria, on how Algeria became an archive at two crucial historical moments, first for the French nation, and second through the creation by postcolonial Algeria of its own archival law. "Algeria as archive" must be understood in the double sense of an archive for France and something created by an independent Algeria. One can easily object that there are no apparent connections between *Mal d'archive* and Derrida's more autobiographical texts, such as "Circumfession," *Monolingualism of the Other*, and *Counterpath*, where Algeria is presented in an intimate, afflicted manner. It might, then, seem paradoxical or even incongruous to include an Algerian dimension in my reading of *Mal d'archive*. I would like to stress, however, that Algeria is indeed less a physical place than a construction; it is an object of memory for both Derrida and the French nation. How does Algeria become a memory object, a cause of amnesia and trauma for Derrida and for the French nation? It is this intersection of the ideological, the philosophical, and the personal that I explore. Do recurring memories inform Derrida's particular conception of the archive? In other words, to what extent do Derrida's own narrated recollections of his childhood in Algeria and his later conception of the archive mirror each other?

## The Archive as Repetition of the Origin

We speak of archives in the plural to refer to collections of historical documents as well as their places of storage. They are part of one's heritage and are thus associated with preservation, conservation, and the safeguarding of a shared past, a founding order, a duration, and the materiality of a memory recognized as national in character. It is precisely this instituting, preserving function that Derrida calls into question in *Mal d'archive*. With this movement to the singular form of "archive" our attention shifts from the objects that archives represent to the condition of possibility of archives: the "archive" still refers to a document or material trace, but, more important, it also refers to the process of archiving.[4] We are dealing, therefore, with a dynamic process, the archival construction whose singular course Derrida maps, showing that it is deadly rather than vital, that it can separate rather than assemble, that it can contribute to concealing and destroying the shared memory it is meant to preserve. This is the critical moment, the return to the word's unformed thought, what "the concept of the archive shelters in itself," namely, the Greek *arkhe*, referring to "the originary, the first, the principal, the primitive, in short to the commencement."[5] "Arkhe," therefore, means the origin, but, more fundamentally, it is an inaugural gesture in the form of commandment. "But even more, and *even earlier*," Derrida emphasizes, "'archive' refers to the *arkhe* in the *nomological* sense, to the *arkhe* of the commandment. . . . Its only meaning, comes from the Greek *arkheion*: initially a house, a domicile, an address, the residence of the superior magistrates, the *archons*, those who commanded."[6] Henceforth, archiving represents the unchecked exercise of political power, and the documents "recall the law and call on or impose the law" (*AF*, 2). The inaugural gesture of archiving is that of the commandment, of the power of the law, of singularity and of the privilege of political decision making. It is constituted around a totalizing imperative of unification: the "archontic" principle entails a unifying act that assembles by eliminating the heterogeneous according to "an ideal configuration" (*AF*, 3). The act of archiving thus involves a hermeneutic operation already at work and supposes implicit goals: totalizing, unifying political power, and eliminating the heterogeneous. It also implies an unconscious drive, or a compulsion to repeat.

It is through Freudian psychoanalysis that Derrida revisits the archive as a place of consignation (*arkheion*) and repression. The Freudian concept of the death drive is at the core of Derrida's conception of the archive. He stresses a decisive paradox:

> If there is no archive without consignation in an *external place* which assures the possibility of memorization, of repetition, of reproduction, or of reimpression, then we must also remember that repetition itself, the logic of repetition, indeed the repetition compulsion, remains, according to Freud, indissociable from the death drive. And thus, from destruction. Consequence: right on what permits and conditions archivization, we will never find anything other than what exposes to destruction, in truth what menaces with destruction introducing, *a priori*, forgetfulness . . . into the heart of the monument. . . . The archive always works, and *a priori*, against itself. (*AF*, 11–12)

With this understanding of the archive, Derrida returns to an earlier text, "Freud and the Scene of Writing," in which he analyzed Freud's unconscious memory. He gives it a new meaning by stressing the Freudian concept of the death drive. This layering of texts is significant: Derrida exhumes his own archive and reads it in such a way that the archive becomes the symbol of destruction through two main notions: the mechanical and repetition. In his earlier reading, Derrida argued that the mystic writing pad, which Freud uses to illustrate the functioning of unconscious memory, is presented "only through the solid metaphor . . . of a *supplementary* machine, *added to* the psychological organization to supplement its finitude." In this specific context, the meaning of "archives" (in the plural) was temporal; it was defined as "already transcriptions," in accordance with the thesis of the belatedness or supplementarity of the unconscious text.[7] In *Mal·d'archive*, Derrida returns to Freud and unconscious memory, but in a very different context. Repetition is now defined mainly in terms of automatic repetition and of the death drive. It is the threat of the death drive that comes to define the archive. What is highlighted is the difference between life and death, between the spontaneity of one's own memory and the automatic and destructive character of the archive. The passage he cites from "Freud and the Scene of Writing" foregrounds this new orientation: "Far from the machine being a pure absence of spontaneity, its resemblance to the psychic apparatus, its existence and its necessity bear witness to the finitude of the mnemic spontaneity which is thus supplemented. The machine, — and consequently, representation — is death and finitude within the psyche" (AF, 14). The archive, far from being a possible substitute for one's memory, "takes place at the place of the originary and structural breakdown of said memory" (AF, 11). It is precisely this exteriority of the archive as a technical support that makes it lethal, as it is caught in a circle of compulsive repetition. Freudian psychoanalysis can lead to a theory of the archive that explains how archiving can lead to the eradication of the archive, to "the annihilation of memory" (AF, 11). The archive enacts the movement of the death drive. The *trouble de l'archive* stems from a *mal d'archive*. To suffer from this mal d'archive is "to have a compulsive, repetitive, and nostalgic desire for the archive, an irrepressible desire to return to the origin, a homesickness, a nostalgia for the return to the most archaic place of absolute commencement" (AF, 91). At an institutional level, archiving puts into motion this unconscious drive. This means that political forms of censorship are not merely conscious forms of suppression.

## Control of the Archive and the Politics of Memory

We may assume that any government engaged in a twofold process of legitimizing its power and rereading the past exerts control over its archives. Consequently, concealment, secrecy, and rejection of the heterogeneous are principles favored by a politics of the archive as memory control. The issue of the political control of memory and history is germane to the selection and control of archives: "The question of a politics of the archive . . . runs through the whole field and in truth determines politics from top to bottom as *res publica*. There is no political power without control of the archive, if not of memory. Effective democratization can always be measured by this essential criterion: the participation in and the access to the archive, its constitution, and its interpretation" (*AF*, 4). This is not, however, the only dimension Derrida brings into question, since the issue is not the setting aside of previously formed archives. Rather, the very process of archiving, the construction of an archive is, by its nature, dominated by denial and repression.[8] In an archive — that is, in the process of archiving — the pro-scription dominated by the figure of denial is already at work. There is no construction of archives without a vast process of denial, connected simultaneously to the "denied archive," the "repression of the archive" and the "power of the state over the historian" (*AF*, 4 n. 1). The institutionalization of the archive is politics itself revealed in its historical essence.

## ALGERIA AS ARCHIVE

"There is no political power without control of the archive, if not of memory" (*AF*, 4). We might also add that a certain political theory emerges from the Derridean conception of the archive: it is based on a critique and refusal of the nation-state and of community membership and the logic of exemplarity it entails. "Deconstructions would be weak," states Derrida, "if they were negative, if they did not construct, but especially if they did not first and foremost challenge institutions at their points of greatest resistance."[9] To challenge the archive is precisely to confront the very center of the nation, its historical and memorial constitution. Through this Derridean understanding of the archive we can see how Algeria was instituted, for France, as the archive par excellence. If we consider the archive through its archontic principle, that of a synthetic assembly that unites and brings together by eliminating the heterogeneous according to "an ideal configuration," we might understand the *Lieux de mémoire* project as the archive par excellence. The volumes, directed by Pierre Nora, represent the writing of a new symbolic history of the French nation. Despite the monumental nature of the project, which enlisted 120 historians and produced seven volumes and several thousand pages, despite its sheer amplitude, which extended over a long historical period, only a single chapter is allotted to the colonial period. This is devoted to the colonial exposition of 1931.

The erasure of the empire at the very heart of the republic and the exclusion of Algeria from the nation to which it belonged for 130 years raised many questions.[10] Nora attempted to justify his choice in an interview, claiming that he had already written a study of Algeria. More interesting, he seems to think that the memory of the Algerian War contributes to what he calls a "loss of common ground," that it involves a sort of particularistic memory and belongs only to a specific group. In an interview given to France Culture he stated, "The memory work and memory movements today are very dangerous instruments. Private memory for a long time functioned within a liberationist dynamic. This is now over for the most part and it has since become a dynamic of self-enclosure, a lack of understanding of the other, alienation from one's own history as a means of legitimizing oneself, the loss of common ground and very often a powerfully aggressive ethnic nationalism that sometimes even results in murder."[11] Nora favors, in a Renanian manner, "a more unifying kind of history." Reading *Mal d'archive* reveals how closely the notion of the archive is connected with the constituted, unified body of the nation. But even more, it allows us to examine a point that Nora seems to take for granted and that is in fact the most difficult to determine: What exactly is "a more unifying history"? What factor renders it "more unifying," and at the expense of what memory? It has often correctly been stated that the official forgetting of the Algerian War, its nonrecognition, was due both to the enormous traumatic power it had on individual psyches and to the political destabilization of which it was a significant cause, up to the present day. This is Benjamin Stora's most well-known thesis in *La Gangrène et l'oubli*. I suggest that even if the name of Algeria is not present, one of the theoretical points of *Mal d'archive* is to point out that Algeria will remain within the French archive, simultaneously fragmentary, repeated, restated, but also repressed, as long as the terms of the equation (France, Algeria) are conceived on the basis of the nation-state. As soon as one adopts the conception of a unifying history, in the name of the unifying body of the nation-state, one is required to make cuts, to reject and destroy, and above all, to deny the very thing one presents in the very gesture of its presentation — to deny, therefore, the most important upheaval, the greatest internal wound in this unified body of the French nation: Algeria. In contemporary France, the history of the Algerian War continues to play a divisive role. According to Richard Derderian, "Official amnesia envelops the Algerian War, because it has undercut and destabilized both the Left and the Right, representing a double crisis of the republic."[12] This official amnesia and the politics of control of the archive are the object of Jean-Luc Einaudi's *La Bataille de Paris*, published in 1991.[13] Seven years after its publication, the author publicly accused the French government of concealing important archives regarding the slaughter of thousands of Algerian workers under the orders of Maurice Papon: "In October 1961, a slaughter actually took place in Paris, undertaken by the police forces under the orders of Maurice Papon."[14] Antagonistic experiences lived before and during the Algerian War still shape diverse writings of history that get increasingly close to struggles for group recognition. What expresses itself through these widely diverging narratives is what Gil Anidjar has called "the haunting of forgetting with and by remembering."[15] As Raphaëlle Branche noted in *La guerre d'Algérie: Une histoire apaisée?*, while written accounts and testimonies about the war abound, they still obey a community-based politics and are thus fragmented and disjointed: "Different memory groups elaborate narratives on the past, following imperatives dictated by the present time."[16] The remembering of Algeria in France often seems to fall under the Derridean logic of the archive.

To say "archive" instead of "archives," then, is to recognize, beyond the material nature of the documents, an essentially destructive act that organizes their uniformity. But to say "archive" in the singular is also to avoid saying "our archives" and to situate oneself in a position of exteriority in relation to what serves as the fabric of the national gesture, of the writing of history. It is also to question not so much the validity of the documents that represent sources for the writing of history as their predetermined nature: these archives already bear a certain historicity. The act of synthesis is an act of exclusion. In the archive, a series of wounds is perpetuated and repeated. The typically French opposition between a national memory, consensual and united, and the memories of smaller communities fraught with violence is not tenable if we accept the Derridean conception of the archive because a single gesture of assembling implies also an activity of discarding, in the very figure of sorting that it accomplishes. This filtration of the archive is based upon the same sacrificial gesture that Derrida analyzes in *The Gift of Death:* the act of choosing presupposes discarding and is, in itself, sacrificial. We must not think of this reexamination of an economy of foundation as a rejection of tradition in itself. Derrida often proclaimed and positioned himself as an inheritor, favoring the image of filiations and transmission, but he did so through a plurality that renders any identification impossible, especially the identification of a citizen with a nation.

Derrida often mentioned the arbitrary deprivation of his citizenship and his childhood despair in relation to the exclusion he experienced. In the following pages, I present his personal case and consider what *Mal d'archive* can teach us about the connection between destruction and the politics of memory in postcolonial Algeria. Derrida was stripped of his nationality in 1942, during the German occupation that took place on the other side of the Mediterranean, in France: "Along with others, I lost and then gained back

French citizenship. I lost it for years without having another. In essence, a citizenship does not sprout up just like that. It is not natural. . . . The withdrawal of French citizenship from the Jews of Algeria, with everything that followed, was the deed of the French alone. . . . They implemented it all by themselves."[17] I consider this connection to citizenship as such, a citizenship lived out during the period of colonial Algeria, the French Algeria that Derrida exposes in its falsity.

What becomes evident in this sudden withdrawal of the French passport is an often denounced injustice at the heart of French colonial politics, between French subject and French citizen. In *Of Hospitality* Derrida makes reference to this regime, unique in its kind: "In what had been, under French law, not a protectorate but a group of French departments, the history of the foreigner, so to speak, the history of citizenship, the future of borders separating complete citizens from second-zone or non-citizens, from 1830 until today, has a complexity, a mobility, an entanglement that are unparalleled, as far as I know, in the world and in the history of humanity."[18] Still, it is not only this profound difference of regime between two kinds of relationship to French nationality that Derrida exposes here; what is at stake is a reinterrogation of all community membership. The profound juridical hypocrisy, the double status, gave rise to a rejection of all identification in community. Expelled from his French school, Derrida became a young urchin, refusing for a year to attend the Jewish school out of fear of a collective fusion to his community: "So that thus, expelled, I became the outside, try as they might to come close to me, they'll never touch me again."[19]

## "I became the outside"

Not to experience the outside, but to become it, means to position oneself as foreign to any community, Jewish, Arab, French, or Algerian French. This position, which appears to be one of rupture and exodus, is also, however, one of unlimited welcome, in the sense that it is not limited by identification or belonging. I have so far argued that *Mal d'archive* poses, in an oblique way, the fundamental question of belonging or not belonging. My hypothesis was that by writing "archive" in the singular form Derrida also performs a gesture of radical dissociation: the refusal of "our archives" understood as a symbol of national belonging. This theoretical gesture could be understood against the background of the various estrangements he suffered as a child growing up in French Algeria. The question of belonging leads in turn to the question of identity. In "Circumfession," in *Counterpath*, as well as in *Monolingualism of the Other*, *The Postcard*, and *Glas*, Derrida makes intricate, sometimes cryptic connections between the narrative of his life and his philosophical writings. This occurs in connection with key concepts, such as the dispossession of language, circumcision, national identity, disidentification. These key notions all center on the problematic of belonging and what it brings about: the fragmentation and unity of the self in its double dimension, social and individual.

Derrida strongly asserts that when it comes to the archive the presumable act of synthesis, or gathering, is in fact the performance of exclusion, a sacrificial action. Archiving is not a passive gesture. It comes close to a Greek etymology of "critique," meaning an act of separating and ultimately of excluding. In this context, one notion in particular deserves further analysis, that of the "disorder of identity." "To be a Franco-Maghrebian, one 'like myself,'" Derrida writes, "is not, not particularly and particularly not, a surfeit or richness of identities, attributes, or names. In the first place, it would rather betray a *disorder of identity* [*trouble de l'identité*]."[20] What does this disorder mean in terms of the repressive and destructive nature of the archive? Is this disorder of identity ("trouble de l'identité") at the core of what Derrida defines as the archive par excellence, in other words, its repressive, destructive nature ("trouble de l'archive")? "It is undoubtedly during those years (1942–1943) in Algeria," argues Geoffrey Bennington, "that J. D. was stamped as 'belonging' in this curious manner to Judaism: a wound, certainly, a painful sensitivity schooled in anti-Semitism as in all forms of racism . . . but also an impatience with gregarious identification, with the militantism in general, even Jewish belonging. . . . This belonging sickness, one might almost say identification sickness, affects the entire corpus of J. D.'s work in which the deconstruction of one's own is, it seems to me, at the heart of his afflicted thought."[21]

In Derrida's body of work, the autobiographical dimension does not consist in recalling the events of one's life; it can be described in terms of reiterations of single past traumas, the reiteration and the reinscription of a wound in a written text that does not produce self-identity: "An identity is never given, received or attained, only the interminable and indefinitely phantasmatic process of identification endures."[22] To belong to a nation is also to be a victim (of an artificial nationality). To belong to Judaism, as a religious subject, is also to be the object of a symbolic and physical violence. These series of trauma are still at work in *Mal d'archive*.

"I became the outside." This is, I believe, Derrida's implicit point of departure in his critique of Yerushalmi's book *Freud's Moses: Judaism Terminable and Interminable*. Derrida's own memory informs his reading of, and his confrontation with, Yerushalmi, whose violence consists in imposing a community on the basis of Freud's name: "Therefore in speaking of the Jews I shall not say 'they.' I shall say 'we,'" asserts Yerushalmi (*AF*, 41). For Derrida, this gesture equals the violence of circumcision: "*Mutatis mutandis*, this is the situation of absolute dissymmetry and heteronomy in which a son finds himself on being circumcised after the seventh day and on being made to enter into a covenant at a moment when it is out of the question that he respond, sign, or counter sign" (*AF*, 41). *Mal d'archive* is for Derrida one of the arenas in which he confronts his cryptic Jewishness through a critical reading of Yerushalmi, who is, in turn, interpreting Freud's *Moses and Monotheism*.[23] The "yes" to the unforeseen event, to the opening surprise of alterity, to "the inaugural engagement of a promise" (*AF*, 74), will be opposed to the repetition of "yes" required by adherence to a community. His reading thus functions on the basis of an unavoidable notion, a conception of the self as multiplicity and interior division, as developed in other texts. In *De quoi demain* (*For What Tomorrow*), he affirms that "this division, this dehiscence (more than one, and more than two, and more than three, beyond all arithmetic and all calculability etc.) it is around this that I am working all the time, and always have been. This incalculable inner multiplicity is my torment, precisely, *my work and travail* . . . my passion and my labor. . . . *Finally*, and I would say *especially*, I vindicate this uprooting."[24] In this quote we perceive the full complexity of the question of self-identity as identification. By what object should identification take place if divisions are internal and multiplicity is inherent in the self? For ethical reasons, this multiplicity cannot be reduced by an injunction of memory. This is the main point on which Derrida takes issue with Yerushalmi.

The archive is a trace of the past that opens not only toward the interpretation of a future, but also toward a mode of being together, a shared future. The imperative of the archive is therefore twofold: the initial act of selection and repression, but also the injunction that opens and must open toward a being together. The ethical question of the archive is tied "to a very singular experience of the promise" (*AF*, 36). Yerushalmi, however, expresses in his interpretation of Freud an unconditional affirmation, a unique trait of Jewishness, according to Derrida: "The being-Jewish and the being-open-toward-the-future would be the same thing, the same unique thing, the same thing as uniqueness — and they would not be dissociable the one from the other. To be open toward the future would be to be Jewish. And vice versa. And in *exemplary* fashion" (*AF*, 74). What enables this identity between the uniqueness of community and the future is precisely "the anteriority of the archive" in this exact case, "a verse of the last of the prophets, as it is interpreted by the archivist" (*AF*, 75). The promise (future) and the injunction of memory (past) are thus indestructibly linked. Because there has been an archived event, because the injunction or the law has already presented and inscribed itself into historical memory as an injunction of memory, with or without a substrate, "the two absolute privileges are bound the one to the other" (*AF*, 76). Derrida "trembles" at the idea of an indissoluble union, a collective belonging in which one's openness to the future is regulated by the obligation of memory. But what he objects to in Yerushalmi's text is also what he has always refused in the experience of his own Jewishness, what he has unflaggingly rejected in his conception of politics, and what he painfully lived through in the experience of factional violence in Algeria. The law of the archive is, for Derrida, precisely the reduction of multiplicity into an exemplary unity: "The question of exemplarity . . . situates here the place of all the violences" (*AF*, 77). It constitutes a unique model that is figured as an absolute norm and eliminates the others as such. The first definition of the archive is of a classification effected not by chance, but in the form of a totalizing assembly. According to this interpretation, the archive is potentially the central principle of all violence:

> The words that make (me) tremble are only those that say the One, the difference of the One in the form of uniqueness . . . and the One in the figure of totalizing assemblage ("to an entire people"). The gathering into itself of the One is never without violence, nor is the self-affirmation of the Unique, the law of the archontic, the law of *consignation* which orders the archive. Consignation is never without that excessive pressure (impression, repression, suppression) of which repression (*Verdrängung* or *Urverdrängung*) . . . are at least figures. . . . As soon as there is One, there is murder, wounding, traumatism. *L'Un se garde de l'autre*. The One guards against/keeps some of the other. (*AF*, 77–78)

This movement must be understood as a movement of the self toward the outside, the unknown, but also as a movement of disavowal of its initial division, its self-rupture, and its own internal difference. This figure of denial of internal otherness, of forgetting one's division, is the basis for exterior violence. The archive injunction is, thus, a repetition of this repressed violence and takes the form of a compulsion of repetition: "It is necessary that this repeat itself" (*AF*, 79). If it must repeat itself entirely outside responsibility, we are in the domain of tragic necessity (*anankhe*), but also of Freudian psychoanalysis. Derrida's psychoanalytical reading of the archive undermines its preserving function. It ultimately demonstrates that what we are driven to repeat is what is ultimately going to destroy us as singularities. Because what we perpetuate in the form of the archive is simultaneously the death drive and the violence of repression, "what exposes to destruction, in truth what menaces with destruction" (*AF*, 12).

The means of passing from the archive to the future is a particular form of repetition, the repetition of a collective being. What is repeated mechanically in the archive injunction is the repetition, the affirmation, and the celebration of the community in the name of the archive, in the name of the indissoluble belonging to the past. This is one main source of violence. Death is already inscribed in the future as repetition of the past. Here, we understand better the initial questioning of the archive: in this gesture of assembling exemplarity is formed, a future read, a collective law drawn up, a program of exclusion based on unity established. For Derrida, "the gathering into itself of the One is never without violence" (*AF*, 77–78). This conception of the past as a death threat echoes Derrida's own living memory of Algeria as the locus of an initial wound: an "archive marked once in his body" (*AF*, 41).

Death is at the heart of Derrida's recollection of Algeria. It plays a significant role in his living memory, "anamnesis," as opposed to the mechanical death drive of the archive. As an object of conscious anamnesis and of hallucinatory memory, Algeria, from the beginning, is stained with blood. It is the blood of belonging and not belonging at the same time. This specific mode of belonging expresses itself through cuts in one's flesh, through the dispossession of language, and in voluntary and involuntary memory. As in negative theology, the locus of community, of belonging, allows a telling of what the experience of not belonging means. His community, Derrida writes, was "first of all, cut off from both Arabic or Berber (more properly Maghrebian) language and culture. It was also cut off from French and even European language and culture. . . . It was cut off, finally, or to begin with, from Jewish memory."[25] These various "cuts" affected him not as mere events in the thread of his life but in their destructive character, to the point of rendering reality and terror inseparable. Terror manifests itself through wounds inscribed in the body itself. One of these wounds — that of a recurring image of circumcision which is recalled in such a hallucinatory way that it keeps repeating itself in his conscious memory as both a phantasm of an event to come and a trauma of an event that happened — is evoked at the opening of "Circumfession." His voice is from the start enshrined in blood. He evokes what "blood will have been for me." He describes a vivid phantasm, that of a "continuous flowing of blood." In this scenario, the vein embodies life and death through a wished for indefinite, continuous bleeding. This imagined "glorious appeasement," the one obtained by Derrida looking at himself as a self-sacrificatory figure, host and hostage of this country, Algeria, is recurrent.[26] It is, one might say, finally reaching oneself as a self-contained individual, only One, but as a dead body. Finally, emptied of his blood, he can write, "It's me but I'm no longer there."[27] In the French version of "Circumfession" Derrida reformulates and changes the meaning of a common French saying by simply adding a comma and a temporal adverb. The usual "N'y être pour rien" or "Je n'y suis pour rien" in the sense of "I am not responsible for whatever happened" becomes "Je n'y suis plus, pour rien," thus creating two separate expressions: "Je n'y suis plus," followed by, and separated rhythmically from, "pour rien," so that "Je n'y suis plus" comes to the forefront. "I am no longer there, but this is me," or "It is me, but I am not there anymore." One can argue that, in Derrida's memory of Algeria, the "I" is glimpsed as a closed entity only through the experience of death, thus giving to the cohesion of the self a posthumous meaning witnessed by the writing subject.

## DERRIDA AS GRADIVA

In "Taking a Stand for Algeria" Derrida laid out a program to be followed in order to reach peace in a country torn apart by civil war (1992–99). He takes extreme care to state his profound solidarity but also to show the limits of his position of spokesman: "Our appeal should be made first *in their name*, and I believe that even before being addressed to them, it comes from these men, it comes from these women, whom we also have to hear. This is at least what I feel resonating, from the bottom of what remains Algerian in me, in my ears, in my head and my heart." To speak in the name of Algeria renders it impossible to dissociate the emotional and the political. Derrida concludes his remarks with this powerful confession: "All I will say is inspired above all and after all by a painful love for Algeria, an Algeria where I was born, which I left, literally for the first time at nineteen . . . an Algeria to which I have often come back and which in the end I know to have never really ceased inhabiting or bearing in my innermost."[28] What are the connections between the lasting memory of an Algeria Derrida bears in his "innermost" and his phantasms of death? It seems that many subsequent experiences, and particularly those of death, are measured against his memory of Algeria. In *Counterpath*, he evokes "an Algeria that I always knew as both wounded and murderous, I ask myself again today whether the taste of death that never left me didn't in fact come from there. . . . Sometimes that country seems to me to bear the death in its soul that has persecuted its body throughout time. For centuries."[29] Derrida has created a system of communicating vessels here. Death circulates from Algeria's spirit, to its body, and to the body and soul of Derrida himself. What is striking about this passage is the hyperbolic role of time, marked by the temporal adverbs "always," "never," "throughout time," and "for centuries." They convey at once a vast temporal expanse and an immobility of time, an almost mythical presence of the self to itself and to Algeria, "which in the end I know to have never really ceased inhabiting."

The perception of Algeria as an ever-present memory seems to represent an unusual fusion of the divisions we often associate with Derrida's philosophy, a philosophy of the caesura between the imprint and the trace, of the division that settles into the very heart of the present. Writing his postscript to *Mal d'archive* in Naples, Derrida describes this miraculous moment of suspension of "difference." He refers to Jensen's *Gradiva*. Its character, Hanold,

> recalls that he came to see if he could find her traces, the traces of Gradiva's footsteps. . . . He dreams of bringing back to life. He dreams rather of reliving. But of reliving the other. Of reliving the singular pressure, or impression which Gradiva's step . . . must have left in ashes. He dreams this irreplaceable place, the very ash, where the singular imprint . . . barely distinguishes itself from the impression. And this is the condition . . . for the uniqueness of the printer-printed, of the impression and the imprint, of the pressure and its trace in the unique *instant* where they are not yet distinguished the one from the other, forming in an *instant* a single body of Gradiva's step, of her gait, of her pace (*Gangart*), and of the ground which carries them. The trace no longer distinguishes itself from its substrate. (*AF*, 98–99)[30]

As I have argued, Derrida's own memory of Algeria—as the ever present memory of a fatal wound—bears a structural resemblance to this miraculous moment, when "the singular imprint . . . barely distinguishes itself from the impression." Turning to Freud's reading of *Gradiva*, Derrida interrogates the psychoanalyst's motivations: "We will always wonder what, in this *mal d'archive* [Freud], may have burned. We will always wonder, sharing with compassion in this archive fever, what may have burned of his secret passions, of his correspondence, or his 'life'" (*AF*, 99, 101). It is precisely the unquiet relationship between Derrida's buried archive, Algeria, and his understanding of the archive that I have been exploring.

## Postcolonial Algeria

Several modalities can be distinguished in the connections of the life and works of Derrida. First, his own position in the heart of what was called French Algeria can be seen as illustrative. He illustrates this moment in time when the juxtaposition of several cultures in a colonial space transformed itself in a series of losses. I have argued that Derrida's own archived past and memory contributed to his understanding of the archive in its destructive character by showing that his memory of Algeria, which is a memory of a "trouble d'identité," still resonates vividly in *Mal d'archive*, defined as a "trouble d'archive." The traumatic experience of a wound and the early refusal of any politics of identity he experienced after having been deprived of his citizenship shapes his comprehension of the archive as radical evil: first, as an endless, mechanical repetition of repressed violence; second, as the reaffirmation of community in the form of the One. This reduction to the One symbolizes precisely the experience of forced belonging that he still carries in his body and memory as a wound. Only these memories can help us understand why Derrida literally and not figuratively "trembles" when he hears in Yerushalmi's text the words "the One . . . and the One in the figure of totalizing assemblage ('to an entire people')."

Derrida's relation to Algeria does not stop here, however. It opens up to a critique of postcolonial Algeria. The Derridean concept of archive allows a new reading of postcolonial Algeria, in the sense that it renders possible a new understanding of the relationship between the writing of history and nationalist ideology in postcolonial Algeria. Since the nineteenth century, the profound effects of an abrupt historical transition struck Algeria twice, first during the 130 years of French colonization that, beyond the sheer violence of the conquest, accompanied an operation of identity dispossession, and thus a dispossession of a shared history. We observe the reinscription of this historical rupture in a different form, this time nationalistic, in independent Algeria. It is here that the radical nature of the Derridean critique of the archive as a repetition of an originary collective identity appears in its full scope. For the act of reappropriating the identity and the origins erased by colonization is typical of a nation constructing itself. At an autobiographical level, Derrida's personal, poignant quest can also be read as a collective question for postcolonial Maghreb: "With whom can one still identify in order to affirm our own identity and to tell ourselves our own history?"[31]

The origin can be perceived as a locus of vitality, the ground in which a national future takes root. But, as the entire corpus of the Algerian writer Kateb Yacine shows, these origins are muddled and multiple: Phoenician, Roman, Berber, Arab, Jewish, Christian, and Muslim. In political terms, historians of modern Algeria such as Mohammed Harbi in *Le FLN: mirages et réalité* and Lahouari Addi in *l'Algérie et la démocratie* have certainly criticized the total institutional power of the ruling party from 1962 to the present under the FLN's iron rule. Along with this single political power comes a monolithic notion of culture, embracing in the present an old slogan from Ben Badis in the 1930s: "Algeria is my homeland, Arabic is my language, Islam is my religion." A series of exclusions and dualities are set up in the name of assuming the unity of a nation, whence the mutual exclusions of the Arab and Berber, Francophiles and Arabophiles, and the masculine and feminine worlds. In this competition between genealogies, we must recognize the movement toward a fantasized origin, a transfer to a phantasmatic place of origin as the location of absolute purity, through which the impurity of the Other is revealed. It is in this sense that the archontic law is violent: "The gathering into itself of the One is never without violence, nor is the self-affirmation of the Unique, the law of the archontic" (*AF*, 77–78).

The vitality of the creation of a new state, postcolonial Algeria, derives from a profoundly sacrificial gesture. It is this negativity in action that we recognize in certain forms of nationalism and, more specifically, Algerian nationalism. It is this dimension of the argument, observable in postcolonial Algeria, which gave Derrida such a strong resonance with Maghrebian authors such as Abdelkebir Khatibi and Fethi Benslama,[32] haunted by the deadly nature of all origin-oriented foundation. As Benslama emphasizes in "Identity as a Cause," "Movements of identity, at a collective level, are not forces that are affirming, active, and inventive; they do not offer any true alternative to the Western model. They are reactive, vengeful, and separated from their potentials by their imaginary withdrawal into themselves. Their awareness of the world seems to have fallen victim to reminiscence, as if their memory has submerged their current perception of the world, thereby disallowing any of their attempts at anticipating the future."[33] As we have seen, Derrida's position is more extreme in that he shows that it is less reminiscence, as Benslama indicates, than the archive injunction — a memory injunction — that imposes its violence on any future, thus indicating the mortal danger implicated in reconstruction of the national community on the basis of a unified origin. To have archive fever, *le mal d'archive*, is to conceive of community identity as agony of the self and potentially of the other.

## Notes

1 *D'ailleurs, Derrida*, released in English as *Derrida's Elsewhere* (1999).
2 Edwy Plenel, "Au vif: En souvenir d'Algérie avec Derrida," *Le Monde*, October 27, 2004.
3 Jacques Derrida quoted ibid.
4 This notion has inspired historians with a certain outrage. See Steedman, "Something She Called a Fever": "The puzzling etymological prolegomenon may be seen as one more example of the textual techniques exercised in Derrida's philosophy. The binary oppositions that underpin Western Metaphysics can be made to shift, by inflating a concept so that it joins up with its supposed opposite, thereby demonstrating that — there is no opposition at all. 'Archive' is thus inflated to mean — if not quite Everything — then at least the ways and means of state power: Power itself, perhaps, rather than those quietly folded and filed documents that provide the mere and incomplete records of its inaugural moments" (1161–62).
5 Derrida, *Archive Fever*, 2.
6 Derrida, *Archive Fever*, 2. Subsequent references are to this English translation and are cited parenthetically in the text as *AF*.
7 Derrida, "Freud and the Scene of Writing," 228.
8 Derrida points to this fundamental slippage in a footnote referring to the title of a recent work by Sonia Combe, *Archives interdites (Les peurs françaises: Face à l'histoire contemporaine)* (4 n.1): "under this title which we may cite as a metonymy of all that is important here" (*AF*, 4 n.1).
9 Derrida, *Psyché*, 101, my translation.
10 See Derderian, "Algeria as a Lieu de mémoire"; Valensi, "Histoire nationale, histoire monumentale."
11 Quoted in Derderian, "Algeria as a Lieu de mémoire," 40.
12 Ibid., 32.
13 A second, revised edition was published in 2001.
14 "En octobre 1961, il y eut à Paris un massacre perpétré par des forces de police agissant sous les ordres de Maurice Papon." *Le Monde*, May 20, 1998. For a full

understanding of this concealment of the archives in contemporary France, see Jim House and Neil Macmaster, *Paris 1961: Algerians, State Terror and Memory*.

15 Anidjar, "Once More, Once More," 14.

16 Branche, *La guerre d'Algérie*, 13, my translation.

17 Malabou and Derrida, *Counterpath*, 85. From this experience Derrida retained above all the complexity of his links to the language that marks his nonbelonging: French. "I do not doubt that exclusion for example, from the school reserved for young French citizens could have a relationship to the disorder of identity. . . . Such exclusions come to leave their mark upon this belonging or non belonging of language. . . . 'Never was I able to call French, this language I am speaking to you, my mother tongue'" (86). The last sentence is a quote from Derrida's *Monolingualism*.

18 Derrida, *Of Hospitality*, 141–43.

19 Malabou and Derrida, *Counterpath*, 82.

20 Derrida, *Monolingualism*, 14.

21 Bennington and Derrida, *Jacques Derrida* (1991), 300–301. In *Marrano as Metaphor* Elaine Marks reflects upon Bennington's statement. She insists on the assimilation of the others in oneself, and thus on the open-ended multiplicity of selves that Derrida's Jewishness, like hers, implies: "This 'belonging sickness' which I and others seem to share with Jacques Derrida as diagnosed by Geoffrey Bennington and Jacques Derrida is the refusal of identity politics and ultimately of stereotypes. It is the acceptance of being Jewish and being assimilated, of being Jewish and being others at the same time" (151). In "Once More, Once More" Anidjar considers this scrutiny of Derrida's identity as "the persistence of a referential moment the—'autobiographical'—that as such testifies to its unreadability. . . . I remain, if anything at all, to follow, to be followed—and (to be) read—there where it is unreadable, impossible" (35). For a reading of Derrida's experience of Judaism through circumcision, see Jill Robinson's review of "Circumfession" in "Circumcising Confession."

22 Derrida, *Monolingualism*, 28.

23 In her *Portrait de Derrida en jeune saint juif*, Hélène Cixous describes Derrida as "a true Marrano," which she characterizes as "the sublime figure of oblivion in which memory keeps watch" (81, my translation).

24 Derrida and Roudinesco, *For What Tomorrow*, 112–13.

25 Derrida, *Monolingualism*, 55.

26 Derrida, "Circumfession," 6, 7, 6. In "Hospitality" Derrida analyzes the concept of sacred hospitality in Louis Massignon's work (*L'hospitalité sacrée*). He shows the complementary nature of the figures of host and hostage in the Muslim tradition (*Acts of Religion*, 358–420).

27 Derrida, "Circumfession," 12.

28 Derrida, "Taking a Stand for Algeria," 306–7, 303. This text was read during a meeting organized by the International Committee in Support of Algerian intellec-

tuals and the League of Human Rights on February 7, 1994. It is translated by Anidjar in Derrida, *Acts of Religion*.

29 Malabou and Derrida, *Counterpath*, 32 n. 8.

30 Here, Derrida refers to a specific passage from Jensen, where the narrator explains his trip to Pompeii by his need to find Gradiva's trace. See Jensen, *Gradiva Fantaisie pompéienne*, 90.

31 Derrida, *Monolingualism*, 55.

32 Khatibi, *Love in Two Languages*. For an interesting example of a dialogue with Derrida, see Benslama, *Idiomes, Nationalités, Déconstructions*, 13.

33 Benslama, "Identity as a Cause," 38.

# Fine Risks, or, The Spirit of
# a Pacifism and Its Destiny

SATOSHI UKAI · *Translated by Suzanne Guerlac*

What is the time of a promise? How does this time dislocate the "vulgar representation of time" and "the metaphysics of presence"? Why and how does a coherent reflection on the promise invite, even incite us to radically rethink any concept of politics, law, religion, ethics, history, economy, language, literature, art, friendship, and love? These questions remain at the heart of Jacques Derrida's work throughout his entire career. The interesting meditations on the gift, hospitality, pardon, secret, lying, and perjury that he engaged in after the mid-1970s are also inseparably linked to this permanent concern with the promise.

Far from being abstract thinking, there is nothing more concrete than the way he dealt with these questions for an attempt at determining philosophically the historical situation of postwar Japan, which began precisely with a promise. It is well known that Article 9 of the Constitution of Japan (1946) stipulates the renunciation of war. "The Japanese people" promise this to what the Constitution's preface calls "peace-loving peoples of the world." Here, perhaps, is an unprecedented event in the history of political sovereignty. While a sovereign people according to the classical political theory of the modern Occident is supposed to pledge, to swear to, to promise only itself in its very act of self-constitution, the "Japanese people" here promise not only themselves, but also, at the same time, other peoples to "renounce war as a sovereign right of the nation." This decision can be considered deconstructive in a determined sense, and without taking into account this aspect of the event one cannot accurately see what is at stake in the current crisis of this Constitution for Japan as well as for the world.

Today more than ever, wherever we may live, wherever we may happen to be—at home or in exile—we should know how to distinguish peace from security. Not that these terms are in mutual opposition to one another point for point, but they should never be identified with one another without remainder. If they were considered identical, if there were no difference at all between them, we would have no future. Absolute security, pure immunity from any danger, would not constitute peace. On the contrary. It is not necessary to refer to the tragically ongoing situation in the Middle East, in spite of, or rather because of the events of September 11, 2001, and its aftermath, we all know this.

Yet beyond this general knowledge, is it possible to distinguish between peace and security? Is there a knowledge that would make this possible, before and beyond any historical experience? Or does this difference between peace and security appear only through an experience that is singularly painful each time? Is it possible to have only an empirical knowledge of it, and never an a priori knowledge?

Perhaps there can be no knowledge that would authorize us to distinguish, a priori and *completely safely (en toute sécurité)*, peace from security. If such knowledge were available, if we could formulate an absolute difference between peace and security, always and everywhere, there would be no more difference between the two, because a kind of peace that would be perfectly determined thanks to this knowledge would simply be anther form of security. So we find ourselves before an aporia, and it is necessary that this be so for something like peace to finally become "possible."

What is required, to be sure, is another thinking of risk, a different thinking of risk, as the only possible approach toward this *différance* (we note that this is henceforth to be written with an "a") between peace and security, to the extent that, whereas the latter entails, by definition, a negation, an elimination, even a destruction of all possible risks, the former would consist, in its very indeterminability, in knowing how to live with certain risks, in living *together* with *certain risks*.

My opening sentence should now be reformulated as follows: We ought to know how to distinguish *these* risks from all possible risks, on the basis of a criterion other than the calculable or quantifiable degree. These risks that peace would require us to experience together would not actually be lesser risks than others, but risks to *run* in the strong sense of the term. There would thus be, according to this différance between peace and security, certain risks to run and others to avoid, assuming that "to run" and "to avoid" are, in this case, two mutually exclusive gestures.

Now it happens that Emmanuel Levinas has qualified the risk to run as "fine [*beau*]." He speaks of the "fine risk" "to be run in philosophy." We find this expression at the very beginning of *Otherwise Than Being or Beyond Essence*. Having sketched the "itinerary" of his book, he writes, "Is the itinerary whose stages we have just indicated sufficiently reliable? Is its beginning indeed accessible? Will the reproach not be made that this provided itself with means to ward them off? No doubt it is not completely disengaged from pre-philosophical experiences, and many of its byways will appear well-worn, many of its thrusts imprudent. But a fine risk [*un beau risque*] is always something to be run [*à courir*] in philosophy."[1]

By means of this interpretive quotation of Plato of the famous utterance attributed to Socrates just before he drank the hemlock in the *Phaedo*, Levinas, in supporting Husserl and Heidegger against Hegel, tries both to defend a certain naïveté of experience, which, without belonging to it, makes philosophy possible, and to underline the necessity of taking into account, within philosophy, the always risky passage from the prephilosophical to the philosophical.[2]

In a second step, however, this time abandoning the operation of Husserl —which amounts, according to Levinas, to claiming that "if philosophy consists of assuring an absolute origin, then philosophy has to erase the trace of its own steps and, continually, the traces of the effacement of these traces, in an endless methodological treading in place"—he appeals to "the critique exercised by the *other* philosopher" (*OTB*, 39/20). Here we find the real "fine risk" "to run in philosophy," for this dimension of the other, reducible neither to the dialogue of the "teamworkers in science [*équipiers en science*]" nor to the Platonic dialogue, denies the philosopher any chance of "assuring oneself of an absolute origin," that is to say the solid and primary security of a ground on which the world would found itself. On the contrary, it forces the philosopher to become open to another, affirmative experience of the trace. Affirmative because now the trace, in its very resistance to reduction to the form of an intuition, lets into this "drama between philosophers" not only "new interlocutors to find fault with" but "the ancients" who "take the floor to answer." The "fine risk" of which Levinas speaks proves to be a hospitality with respect both to those who are still to come and to those who are already dead and, as such, will return.

But why does Levinas qualify this risk as "fine"? Where does the beauty of this risk lie? To put the question another way: Why, by what necessity, does Levinas take precisely this risk that consists, not exactly in speaking about it, but at least in suggesting the beauty of this risk? For this expression, which has its own undeniable beauty, does it not risk connoting a certain warlike risk, in spite of the essential critique of virile courage before death that Levinas presented earlier in *Totality and Infinity*?[3]

The second occurrence of the same expression in the same book seems to me to indicate a way to better orient our questioning. It is toward the end of chapter 3, entitled "Sensibility and Proximity":

> The approach (which in the last analysis will show itself to be a substitution) cannot be surpassed speculatively; it is the infinition or glory of the infinite. A face as a trace, trace of itself, trace expelled in a trace, does not signify an indeterminate phenomenon; its ambiguity is not an indetermination of a noema, but an invitation to the *fine risk* [*beau risque*] or approach qua approach, to the exposure of one to the other, to the exposure of this exposedness, the expression of exposure, saying. (*OTB*, 150/94, emphasis added)

In this important paragraph, Levinas has just energetically refused the temptation of the ontological argument about the existence of God by way of the transformation of the trace into sign. He says, "A face does not function here [in proximity] as the sign of a hidden God that my fellow man [*le prochain*] would impose on me." Conjointly, he marks a difference from the Kantian *ought* (*Sollen*) as "an asymptotic approach to its 'end' [*terme*]." The approach, according to Levinas — what he calls the "approach as approach" — is, in effect, nothing less than "the infinition of the infinite" in virtue of which "the more I respond the more I am responsible," or again, "the more I approach my fellow man [*le prochain*] for whom I bear responsibility, the more I am distant" (*OTB*, 149/93).

The "beauty" of the risk refers to this movement of the infinite that also is its "glory." If any attempt to discover the being or the transcendental signified by reduction of the trace is destined to failure from the start, it is because it is the trace of the *third* whose exteriority is not a matter of ontology. The risk of this approach is "fine [*beau*]," it shines with another light than that of the logos. Here, however, it is not "fine" unless the third, that is, the "illeity," presides through its very exteriority to this approach of the one to the other, thereby introducing a universalizing outside element in the pure face-to-face encounter of the two. This passage from the "exposure of one to the other exposure of this exposedness," indeed, the "expression of exposure" that ends up revealing itself as the "Saying [*Dire*]," describes the structure of a strange witnessing that seems to me essential to Levinasian thinking about peace.

If, now, brutally interrupting this dialogue with Levinas, we put this risk into the plural while retaining this adjective to speak here of *fine risks* instead of *the* fine risk, do we run a supplementary risk or avoid the single major risk? We know that Derrida often cites Freud and his essay "The Head of Medusa," first in "Hors Livre" ("Outwork") and subsequently in *Glas*, to remind us that, for the founder of psychoanalysis, the multiplication of the penis in the male phantasm signifies a defense against castration.[4] He also makes this remark, which inspires deep reflection on our part, concerning pluralizing not the word "risk" but "resistance": "To put into the plural is always to give oneself an escape, up to the point where it is the plural that kills you."[5]

To put in the plural is thus to avoid the risk, the foreseeable risk that accompanies all presupposition of conceptual unity, but at the same time it is to run, to await or let come an unanticipated risk. The expression "unanticipated risk" can be understood either as a pleonasm or as an oxymoron. For if, on the one hand, a certain unpredictability is analytically deducible from any concept of risk, on the other hand, when one waits for something without having any knowledge of it, that is, waits for it without waiting, one cannot even claim that to know what will come is, for certain, a risk. "The worst is not always sure," as Claudel would say, and Derrida, aware of this paradox, never risks speaking of risk when it is not predictable, without evoking at the same time the "possibility" of its reversal into chance.

We are tempted to see in this very gesture a certain movement of deconstruction that would have started by putting itself into the plural even before its "origin." By pluralizing itself, it "globalizes" itself, without passively following what we call today the "globalization" of market capitalism. A little like Zarathustra, it advances by dove-like steps (and this is not just any animal) as a "shadow of what is to come." It disseminates itself in this way, and it is this dissemination that brings us together today and tells us to run a risk, to take a risk in taking an example.

For almost twenty years there has been a word for risk in the work of Derrida, or rather two words, brought together in a movement of translation. It is indeed a question of the word *translation*, translation as experience, understood as a voyage that crosses borders. Is it not one of the effects of this translation experience, triggered, accelerated, deepened, and invented at the same time as discovered, signaled, named, and rendered visible by deconstruction, that today we are more and more sensitive to the singularity of the risk that, everywhere in the world, each in our own historical, cultural, geopolitical, or religious contexts, our friends run, who recognize themselves, in one way or another, in this general movement of deconstruction? More precisely, we can no longer ignore that the writings of Derrida, which reassure no one, can themselves represent singular risks in each of these cases, depending on whether their reader is French or German, English or American, a North American or a South American, an Italian or a Finn, an Arab or a Jew, a Palestinian or an Israeli, an African or an Asian, an Indian or a Chinese, a Korean or a Japanese, without speaking of these major differences that would exist depending on whether the texts are read by a male or a female reader. And these singularities that are already worked through in their proper constitution, by a movement of translation, are in their turn immediately put into translation by the others. In so doing, deconstruction simply registers a certain state of the world. Derrida says nothing different, it seems, when, speaking of the concept of the political in Carl Schmitt, of its spirit and its destiny, he has this to say:

> To be ready to listen to this screaming chaos of "voiceless," one has only to lend an ear to any "news item." At the very instant when I am rereading this manuscript, *all* points in the world, all the places of the *human* world, and not only *on the earth*, and not only in Rwanda and in Italy, in ex-Yugoslavia and in Iran, in Israel and in Palestine, Cambodia and Ireland, Tahiti and Bangladesh, Algeria and France, Ukraine and the Basque Country, etc., are — and will always have been — just so many forms of the abyss for Schmitt's "clear-cut distinctions" and his nostalgia. Still to give them country names is to speak a language without an assured foundation.[6]

I ask you to excuse me, then, for speaking for a moment this "language without assured foundation," that is, for running a risk in order to give you another example of this "chaos." It is a question of the endless debate that has been going on for half a century, but that has become more urgent than ever today, concerning the constitutional pacifism of Japan. I remind you, first of all, that the present Constitution of Japan, the promulgation of which goes back to 1946, involves a very particular kind of translation. In the context of the defeat of Japan at the end of the Second World War and the occupation that followed, the Americans began by letting the Japanese leaders compose a new charter based on the principles declared by the Allies at the Potsdam Conference and accepted by Japan. But the Japanese were too imbued with the ideology of the old regime to successfully carry out this task. When he realized this, Douglas MacArthur organized a team composed of twenty-four Americans from various backgrounds, but none of whom were constitutional specialists, to draft the democratic Constitution of Japan. They were given one week to do this. One can only imagine the amazement and dismay of the Japanese leaders when MacArthur handed them the result of this effort that presented an idea of constitution that bore no relation to the

Constitution of the Empire of Japan of 1890. A few days later, the Japanese returned to general headquarters with a so-called Japanese version of this draft. Thus began the "translation marathon," as John Dower, the author of the latest panoramic historiography of this period for an English-reading public, *Embracing Defeat*, put it.[7] Indeed, the Americans spent no less than thirty hours straight trying to verify the faithfulness of the Japanese version, translating it word for word back into English. It goes without saying that they discovered many omissions, deformations, in a word, traces of a desperate attempt to neutralize the revolutionary character of this draft and to approximate the old Constitution. The final argument, which succeeded in convincing the Japanese to give up this effort at recuperation, was to explain that the United States was, among the Allies, the most indulgent power both toward the imperial system and toward Emperor Hirohito himself, whom the Japanese wanted to protect at all costs, and that the acceptance of this draft of the Constitution was the only way to spare the emperor from being held accountable for his wartime responsibilities. It was thus in order to save the sovereign that Japan agreed to abandon part of its sovereignty. I do not know if there are other examples in the history of sovereignty of this kind of bargaining.

But do not think that this Constitution was received by the Japanese people as if it fell from the sky when the draft was presented to Parliament, debated, modified to the extent possible, and voted on, even if everyone suspected the kind of secret negotiation that I have just described. I must make clear that a certain public opinion, which the Japanese leaders of the time really did not represent, emerged just a few months after the capitulation of the military regime and was all the more powerful for being repressed for some time. The proof is that there were no fewer than twelve drafts of the Constitution published on the initiative of political parties and civilian groups that the American team could have taken, at least partially, into consideration.

Thus at the end of this process full of paradoxes, of which I have noted only a few, a new Constitution was born. This Constitution is organized according to three major principles. The first is popular sovereignty, with the important restriction that reserves the status of "symbol" for the emperor. The first article stipulates (I cite the English version), "The Emperor shall be the symbol of the State and of the unity of the people, deriving its position from the will of the people with whom resides sovereign power." Among the multitude of problems raised by the interpretation of this article, I will limit myself to the problem of the translation into Japanese of the word " people,"

which I will return to later. The second principle is the constitutional pacifism that is my subject here, the famous Article 9, in which the Japanese state
denies itself the right not only to have recourse to war as a means of resolving
an international conflict, but also to possess any military arms. The third
principle is the guarantee of fundamental liberties, very limited under the old
regime, such as freedom of expression and opinion, of property, of association and assembly. Note that sexual equality was given significant emphasis,
thanks to the efforts of a twenty-two-year-old journalist of Austrian Jewish
origin, Beate Sirota, the only member of the American team who was bi-
lingual in English and Japanese. These three pillars together constituted the
whole of the program of the democratization of Japan and to this extent
provided a kind of negative silhouette of the defunct empire.

A reading of the Constitution of Japan invites this preliminary remark. In
his *Theory of the Constitution* Schmitt tries to distinguish clearly and rigorously between (a) constituent power (*Verfassungsgewalt*), (b) the Constitution (*Verfassung*), and (c) constitutional law (*Verfassungsgesetz*). He is careful to privilege the relation between a and b at the expense of c because he
believed that a constitution, in its very essence, should not be divided into a
number of relative laws but should form a "unique totality" corresponding to
the absolute oneness of the voluntary decision of the power that founded it.[8]

In the case of the Constitution of Japan, it is undeniable that the military
power of the victors represents a founding violence (*die rechtsetzende Gewalt*)
in Benjamin's sense, and it is therefore not surprising that the partisans of its
revision, in particular of the abolition of Article 9, take this as a pretext for
calling its legitimacy into question. One could nevertheless maintain that,
just as Schmitt tried to argue for the legitimacy of the Constitution of Weimar in 1928 by pointing to the permanence of a constituent power, in this
case, the German people, so too the Constitution of Japan, once it had been
voted on by the Imperial Parliament before being promulgated in the name
of the emperor as an amendment to the Constitution of the Empire of Japan,
would have as constituent power the Japanese people. Nevertheless, the
fragility of this distinction between the two powers (*Gewalten*) haunts the
foundation of this new regime, and here we see the topicality in our own
context of the problematic that Derrida derives (in "Force of Law" in particular) from the exchange between Schmitt and Benjamin during the 1920s
and beyond.[9]

But the place of this Constitution in the political life of contemporary
Japan will soon become overdetermined thanks to a change in U.S. policy
which began to demand of it, no later than during the 1940s, things that

openly contradicted the spirit of the Constitution. The victory of communism in China and the outbreak of war in the Korean peninsula, in short, the exacerbation of a war that could hardly be called "cold" in this region of the world, led the Americans to reconsider the strategic value of Japan and to desire its rearmament. Under these conditions we could speak of a double death of the "father" of the Constitution of Japan, and of a double bastardization that it has not ceased to undergo since that date. That is perhaps the secret of its paradoxical surviving (*survivance*) through all these vicissitudes that provoked as many passions as political, juridical, and philosophical reflections. In speaking of the spirit of this constitutional pacifism, I thus evoke at the same time a certain inheritance of Western pacifism of which, by the intervention of these Americans, we are the beneficiaries today and all the interpretations spoken or unspoken, rational or affective, that the postwar Japanese give to it and through which they try to animate the letter in their effort at reappropriation. Here is Article 9 of the Constitution, still in the English version, preceded by a few paragraphs of the preamble of the Constitution, indispensable if one is to have an idea of the spirit that inspired it:

> We, the Japanese people, desire peace for all time and are deeply conscious of the high ideals controlling human relationship, and we have determined to preserve our security and existence, trusting in the justice and faith of the peace-loving peoples of the world. We desire to occupy an honored place in an international society striving for the preservation of peace, and the banishment of tyranny and slavery, oppression and intolerance for all time from earth. We recognize that all peoples of the world have the right to live in peace, free from fear and want.
>
> We believe that no nation is responsible to itself alone, but that laws of political morality are universal; and that obedience to such laws is incumbent upon all nations who would sustain their own sovereignty and justify their sovereign relationship with other nations.
>
> We, the Japanese people, pledge our national honor to accomplish these high ideals and purposes with all our resources.

And Article 9:

> Aspiring sincerely to an international peace based on justice and order, the Japanese people forever renounce war as a sovereign right of the nation and the threat or use of force as means of settling international disputes.

In order to accomplish the aim of the preceding paragraph, land, sea, and air forces, as well as other war potential, will never be maintained. The right of belligerency of the state will not be recognized.

I would like to draw your attention first to the use of the present perfect tense in the sentence of the preamble that begins with the phrase "We have determined." The past is not usually the tense of the law, which is usually stated in the present or future. One might consider that the function of this preamble is to attach the body of law to a date, on the threshold of the Constitution, and, in so doing, to confer on it the value of a promise or "pledge." But which date? The date of its promulgation? Yes, to the extent that the preamble is nonetheless part of the Constitution and that this "we" would never have existed without this performative utterance. Not entirely, however, because by its very place it invites us to inscribe this date in a larger context, thereby establishing, or rather, producing a certain contemporaneity. In fact, it inscribes this Constitution within the framework of international law that has just been redefined through the establishment of the United Nations. The expression "the peace-loving peoples of the world" explicitly refers to member countries of United Nations, from which Japan has been excluded. It is thus the charter of the United Nations, in its letter and in its spirit, that inspires this preamble, in the light of which Article 9 can be interpreted as a decision on Japan's part to confer on this newly created international entity total responsibility for its national security.

However, the Constitution of Japan cannot be contemporaneous with the U.N. Charter, whose birth in San Francisco dates from June 26, 1945. *The time is out of joint*, for between the two dates of the creation of the U.N. and the promulgation of the Constitution of Japan, an event has occurred, the unique and double event that radically challenged any concept of international law as it operated at the time. Of course, I am thinking of the dropping of atomic bombs on Hiroshima and Nagasaki, of the destruction, within a three-day interval, of two Japanese cities. Does the universality of "laws of political morality," of which the preamble speaks, remain the same before and after August 6 and 9, 1945? Is it not possible, or even necessary, to give new meaning to Article 9 from the date of this unprecedented catastrophe and in its name? Can one not remove from it the character of a punishment that one inflicts on the conquered and allow oneself to accept it with a certain national pride? None of this was ever clearly or publicly expressed. But a certain national consensus was created, which developed to the point that, throughout the 1950s, expressions such as "Japan, the only nation to have been the victim of atomic bombs" became commonplaces in the rhetoric of the political discourse on both the Right and the Left.

Constitutional pacifism in postwar Japan, its singular character, thus finds its origin in the hiatus of these two references, one being the U.N. Charter, the other the historical rupture inflicted on the planet by the appearance of nuclear arms. At the same time universalizing and nationalizing, this pacifism, which never stops appropriating itself, is thus not foreign to that exceptional exemplarity that Derrida reveals to be a constant, citing other examples of national affirmation, for instance, in "Interpretations at War."[10] The sentence engraved on the monument to the dead in Hiroshima summarizes all these ambiguities. In Japanese it says "過ちは二度と繰り返しません." One could offer several possible translations: "Never again"; "The same error will not be repeated"; "We shall not commit a new crime." But since this sentence that surely expresses a certain remorse or repentance does not have a grammatical subject, one cannot know who utters it, and this structural deficiency clearly affects its whole signification. Who promises what to whom, in fact? Are we really dealing with a promise? First, we must ask ourselves: Is it possible to imagine that the Japanese people promise the American people to never make war again, admitting that the atomic bomb was a punishment they deserved? Before and in the name of the dead of Hiroshima? Or, according to another hypothesis, just as improbable as the previous one, that of a maximal universalization, is it a question of a sort of forced hand (*carte forcée*), and is all of humanity, of which the Americans make up a part, invited by and in this sentence to sign it and make it their own, taking the place of the missing subject? The promise would then be to all of those men and women dead in this place and, at the same time, to each human being, indeed to all living beings in the future, here and elsewhere. At the other extreme, finally, the worst hypothesis, which unfortunately is not to be excluded, is that through this sentence in Japanese, the Japanese speak only to the Japanese, the survivors, promising their dead never to make the same mistake — not the crime or the sin (*faute*), but the error in the sense of a political, diplomatic, military, or strategic or tactical mistake. The polysemia of the word "過ち" (*ayamachi*), especially given its proximity to another word, close but different, "誤り" (*ayamari*), would allow this slippage. As if the Japanese wanted to finally find themselves on the side of the winners in an eventual next war, believing that it would be the only way to grant themselves, after the fact, an honorable meaning to the sacrifice of their compatriots. It is easy to see that this interpretation is no longer compatible with the letter of the Constitution. However, what is disturbing here is that this hypothesis is not incompatible with the first, according to which this pledge would be addressed to the Americans.

This brings us to the most essential question: What specific place, not drowned in the generality of all of humanity, is reserved for the victims of the Japanese war from other Asian countries, as virtual addressees of this promise? For the constitutional pacifism of postwar Japan is anything but a hospitable pacifism. How is it that a country proud of being given the most pacifist Constitution in the world has let so many years go by before, in the 1990s, making even a first timid gesture to apologize for the damage it caused in China, the Philippines, Singapore, Malaysia, Indochina, Thailand, Burma, Indonesia, East Timor, New Zealand, and Australia? Knowing that among the dead of Hiroshima and Nagasaki were hundreds of thousands of Koreans who had been mobilized or brought by force to these cities from their country, at the time a Japanese colony, the enormity of the injustice leaps out at you that, until a few years ago, it was not even permitted to erect a monument dedicated to them in the Peace Park of Hiroshima. And this incredible exclusion is written into the body of the Constitution of Japan, if not in its English version, at least in its Japanese version.

The English word "people" was in fact translated as "国民" (*kokumin*), a term that signifies both the collectivity and the individual, the nation and the citizen, or rather, the "national." It is true that this was a small step forward compared to the old Constitution, in which each Japanese was designated as "臣民" (*shinmin*), that is to say, "subject." But "kokumin" remains a word too loaded with nationalist connotations not to conjure up a closed and exclusive community with the emperor at its center. The idea that dictated this choice was soon revealed by the imperial decree, on the eve of the day the Constitution was to take effect, to suspend the citizenship of all people who came from the old colonies and happened to find themselves in Japanese territory. When Japan recovered its independence in 1952, these people summarily lost their civil rights, without ever having been consulted.

Such is the "internal," constitutive threat, if I can put it this way, that lies in wait for this constitutional pacifism that, because it does not go beyond national limits, does not succeed in attaining, following the Kantian tradition, a federalist perspective. Since those "peace-loving peoples of the world," to whom it manifests its trust, do not share the same idea of peace, the phrase attributed to Aristotle, "Oh, my friends, there is no friend," would be its sigh from birth.

But there is also an "external' menace, no less constitutive for that, that apparently calls into question its survival *from the outside*. The founding violence that any constitution presupposes is in this case the military force of a foreign conqueror at the end of an international war. The Constitution of Japan implicitly recognizes that the Allies' war was a "just war." However, the letter of Article 9 appears to deny the justification of all war. Is this not a typical example of what is called a performative contradiction?

In reality, it must be admitted that postwar Japan still remains an accomplice, more or less avowed, of the military adventures of the United States, whether in Korea or Vietnam or elsewhere. The Japanese-American Security Treaty, concluded in 1951 independently of the U.N. Charter, consolidates and aggravates this de facto military alliance. The largest U.S. military base outside the United States is located indefinitely on Okinawa, the country of a people colonized and annexed to the Japanese islands in the nineteenth century. The force of Japanese self-defense only grows larger, becoming, in terms of equipment, the third largest army in the world, with its warships now participating in the operation in Afghanistan. It is true that the army does not have legitimate status in the eyes of the Constitution (it is "anti-constitutional but legal," according to the well-known fanciful formula of the U.S. Supreme Court), and this is not insignificant. In the name of the "normalization" of Japan as a sovereign nation-state (the formula is "a State like the others"), political pressure is increasingly being brought to bear to approach not the reality of the law, but the law of reality.

But this is not to say that partisans of the revision of the Constitution have all the cards in their hand; they can no longer designate an enemy as easily they could during the cold war. There is now a peace treaty with China. Peace with the Chinese, security with the Americans — such is the geopolitical posture of Japan today. This is why I emphasized the contrast of these two terms at the beginning. It is significant that in the course of a recent parliamentary debate about a law of emergency, the government obstinately refused to state the name of a country as a potential enemy, claiming that since the state of emergency is a concept that refers to a virtuality that is always exceptional, it is not appropriate to give an example. "Oh, enemy, there is no enemy," this Nietzschean "cat'apostrophe" seems to answer to the sigh of the pacifists.[11] But this virtualization of the enemy doesn't necessarily make the task of the pacifists any easier, for, as Derrida shows in *Politics of Friendship*, it can lead to a hyperpoliticization, in the form, for example, of a "war on terror."

In any case, these two threats, internal and external, the one residing in the inability of the Japanese pacifists to grasp the essential link between peace and hospitality, and the other coming from the reappearance of the idea of a "just war" on the horizon of international relations since the Gulf War, to which the U.N. gave a legal guarantee, today form in their crossing something like the destiny of this constitutional pacifism. That pacifism, however, is the only legal barrier that prevents Japan from being led indefinitely into the increasingly bellicose logic of U.S. hegemony. How is it possible to resist this destiny, not in a negative manner, but lucidly, affirmatively, by trying to deconstruct the very notion of destiny and to think peace differently?

In "A Word of Welcome," Derrida sets up a confrontation between the two great traditions of reflection on peace, that of Kant and that of Levinas, in order to mark what he calls "a typological destiny" for a "structural complication of the political." What is at stake in this expression? In spite of Levinas's desire to situate peace beyond the political, Derrida shows that the latter nevertheless undermines the purity of the former. Conversely, we could think that for the Japanese constitutional pacifism, everything begins with the State, which is to say with the political (the pacifism that it inherits from the West, is, in this respect, of Kantian descent). But when a State gives up its right to war and denies itself the right to have an army, not as the result of a "peace process" but through a solitary and unilateral decision (this gesture seems to me rather Levinasian), something radically heterogeneous to the political lodges itself in the heart of its politics. Except it is not enough to be pacifist to have access to this something. Listen to Derrida:

> What is peace? What are we saying when we say "peace"? What does it mean "to be at peace with" — to be at peace with someone else, a group, a State, a nation, oneself as another? In each of these cases, one can be at peace only with some other. . . . With the same, one is never at peace.
>
> Even if this axiom appears impoverished and abstract, it is not so easy to think through. What is the semantic kernel, if there is one and if it has a unity, of this little word *paix* [peace]? Is there such a semantic kernel? In other words, is there a concept of peace? One that would be *one*, indestructible in its identity? Or must we invent another relation to this concept, as perhaps to any concept, to the non-dialectical enclosure of its own transcendence, its "beyond-in"?[12]

The necessity of this invention, its urgency, is perhaps felt more intensely in Japan today than anywhere in the world because of the place "this little word" occupies in the historical situation I have just presented. But this also means that because this invention to come does not leave intact the classical opposition between peace and war upon which pacifist discourse still relies, this invention of "another relation" to the concept of peace "as perhaps to all concepts" evidently entails a significant risk. But will this invention take place, precisely, at the discursive level? The "fine risk," for Levinas, is a risk "to run" in and through language, and it is this thesis that Derrida has questioned since "Violence and Metaphysics." "Peace is made only in *a certain silence*," he said in 1963, "which is determined and protected by the violence of speech. Since speech says nothing other than the horizon of this silent peace by which it has itself summoned and that it is its mission to protect and prepare, speech *indefinitely* keeps silent and guards the silence [*garder le silence*]. One never escapes the *economy of war*."[13]

I would like to end with a citation that perhaps is the kind of speech that holds such a silence, and that gives peace. It would have emerged almost on the fringes of this constitutional pacifism, as far as possible from the State and the nation. It is said that one day an old woman of Nagasaki, who survived the 9th of August, said, "It is a good thing that it happened here. Others would not have been able to bear it." To understand these words, one must know that in Nagasaki there is a Christian community whose origins go back to the sixteenth century and that a church was located at ground zero of the atomic explosion. But this knowledge is not enough to identify the presumed subject of this speech. She is Christian and Japanese, no doubt, but who knows what she meant by "others"? Other Japanese, who were not Christian, or other Christians who were not Japanese? Or perhaps these words bear witness not only to the recent catastrophe, but also to the ancestral suffering of this community of crypto-Christians and their long-standing persecution in this country so exceptionally and forcefully closed to the Christian religion. In virtue of this secret meaning that lives at the heart of the word, one will never know whether the prayer that one might hear there is thoroughly Christian, or if, in crossing or moving back through what Derrida calls "mondialatinization (globalatinization)," it is not come, perhaps, already, from another shore: "Let this misfortune be spared the rest of humanity, for the substitution already took place."[14]

## Notes

The first version of this essay was written for the colloquium "La démocratie à venir: Autour de Jacques Derrida," held at Cerisy-la-Salle in France, July 8–18, 2002. It was delivered in the presence of Derrida, who actively participated in a discussion after the lecture. He then accepted an invitation to make his fourth visit to Japan in spring 2003. But this visit was postponed and then canceled because of his illness. He also agreed to devote one of his conferences to Kant's essay on "Perpetual Peace." Readers are kindly requested to keep in mind that the theme, the style, and the economy of arguments of this paper are largely dictated by this context.

1  Levinas, *Autrement qu'être ou au-delà de l'essence*, 38; *Otherwise Than Being*, 20, translation slightly modified, and with emphasis. Hereafter *OTB*, cited parenthetically in the text with page references from the French text followed by those of the translation.

2  Plato, *Plato's Phaedo*, 114d6. The original expression in Greek is *kalos kindunos*. According to *A Greek-English Lexicon*, *kalos* is used to describe outward form, parts of the body, clothes, but also moral sense or action, and means "beautiful," "good," "fine," "noble," and "honorable." *Kindunos* means "hazard," "venture," "risk" or "peril," but also "uncertainty," even "chance."

   In the French version of this essay, "De beaux risques, ou l'esprit d'un pacifisme et son destin," in *La démocratie à venir: Autour de Jacques Derrida*, I could not take into account this reference to Plato. After my presentation, Derrida pointed out this reference to me privately, and I have tried to integrate this point with minimal modification in this version. My intellectual debt to Derrida is without limit, and I would like to express a special thanks to him for this remark.

3  Levinas, *Totalité et Infini*, 284; *Totality and Infinity*, 306–7.

4  Derrida, *La Dissémination*, 47–48; *Dissemination*, 40–41; Derrida, *Glas*, 55–57; *Glas* (in English), 45–47.

5  Derrida, *Résistances*, 39; *Resistances of Psychoanalysis*, 25.

6  Derrida, *Politiques de l'amitié*, 165; *Politics of Friendship*, 143–44, translation, slightly modified.

7  Dower, *Embracing Defeat*, 379.

8  Schmitt, *Théorie de la Constitution*, 151–52.

9  Derrida, *Force de loi*, 77–78; "Force of Law," 29–31.

10  Derrida, *Psyché, Invention de l'autre II*, 299; "Interpretations at War," 183.

11  Cf. Derrida, *Politiques de l'amitié* and *Politics of Friendship*, especially chapters 2, 3, and 5.

12  Derrida, *Adieu à Emmanuel Lévinas*, 152; *Adieu to Emmnuel Levinas*, 85.

13  Derrida, *L'écriture et la Différence*, 220; *Writing and Difference*, 148, translation slightly modified.

14  Derrida, "Foi et savoir," 42; "Faith and Knowledge," 67.

# PART IV

---

Between Ethics and Politics

# The Aporia of Pure

## Giving and the Aim of Reciprocity:

## On Derrida's *Given Time*

MARCEL HÉNAFF · *Translated by Jean-Louis Morhange*

> For there to be a gift, there must be no reciprocity.
> — Jacques Derrida, *Given Time*

> Do unto others as you would have done unto yourself.
> This is the entire Law. Everything else is commentary.
> — Talmud of Babylon

> Human history is the long succession of the synonyms
> of a single word. Contradicting it is a duty.
> — René Char

In *Given Time* Derrida presented a seminal aporia of giving, which generated a large number of commentaries, some in the form of refutations. However, all these reactions — the most notable of which is Jean-Luc Marion's in *Being Given* — accepted the terms and language in which Derrida chose to raise the question, even when they proposed divergent conclusions. In fact, it seems to me that the question needs to be reexamined at the very level of the presuppositions it involves. The aporia of giving, according to Derrida, can be summarized as follows: giving is always understood as a relationship between a giver and a recipient and as an exchange that generates a debt, which amounts to saying that it remains within the boundaries of economic reciprocity. Derrida claimed that in order to escape this logic and in order for giving to be true giving, the giver should be unaware that he or she is giving and the recipient should not know who is doing the giving (which is possible only, under certain conditions, when what is given is time). Starting from this requirement, Derrida presented a critical reading of Marcel Mauss's *The Gift*, a work in which the *obligation to reciprocate a gift* found in ethnographic data was understood as being at the core of the gift relationship. Derrida's purpose was of course not to reject these data but to challenge

the legitimacy of calling "gift" a gesture that presupposed a reciprocity requirement. It is this criticism I find highly questionable, for a number of
reasons. The most significant one has to do with the way Derrida used
certain concepts, following a long-established tradition, inconsiderately applying them to "the gift" without discussing their origins or relevance and
above all without wondering if it was even possible to speak of gift in
general. These are the questions that I propose to reexamine with all the
necessary rigor. My assessment will seem severe and will indeed be so from a
particular perspective. On the other hand, in the end it will make it possible
for Derrida's approach to be accepted and fully appreciated from a more
limited perspective and from that perspective alone.

## Questioning Derrida's Rereading of Mauss's The Gift

From the outset, Derrida's approach to giving was situated in aporia and
wished for aporia. But what kind of aporia?

### GIVING AS *the* IMPOSSIBLE

Contrary to what has often been said, Derrida did not claim "Giving is
impossible"; this would be absurd in view of the factual evidence that things
are indeed given and other things are often given in return. What Derrida
stated was the following: "Not impossible but *the* impossible. The very figure of the impossible. [The gift] announces itself, gives itself to be thought
as the impossible."[1] This statement remains enigmatic for two reasons. First,
the logical difference introduced between adjective (impossible) and noun
(the impossible) is not made clear from the outset; it seems that the adjective would designate one attribute among others within the logical square of
modalities (possible/impossible, necessary/contingent), whereas the noun
would be the equivalent of a definition and, if this were the case, would be
identified with the *thinkable*. However, the adjective constitutes a statement
of existence (something either takes place or does not); the noun concerns
the statement of what is logically acceptable (and therefore thinkable), but
in this case gift-giving "gives itself to be thought" as what would be contradictory par excellence, according to the inconceivable equation A = not A.

Second, if gift-giving is "the very figure of the impossible," then as a concept it constitutes aporia par excellence: not just any aporia but *the aporia*, its
"very figure" and therefore absolute aporia. This exceptional status may
seem strange, since it amounts to claiming that the action designated by the

verb "to give" has the unique property of never occurring. This action would be conceivable without being actually realized. Yet we know (according to the first point) that it does occur. In this case only one reasonable conclusion remains: this action is not what we believe it to be. This is indeed the explanation put forth by Derrida: anyone believing he or she is giving is in fact performing an *exchange* and thus remains subjected to the economic order. Giving therefore takes place — is possible — but only as empirical gesture; it is never *giving*, since it is never what we claim it to be, "never" in the very moment when it takes place: in this it is *the* impossible. This would be the first aspect of the aporia, in a temporal perspective. But where does gift-giving's privilege of excellence in aporia originate? Precisely from the fact that the gift-giving relationship involves time and does so in a unique way. Not only does it make irreconcilable things — giving and exchange — simultaneous, but it can take place only within and in the form of a gift that came before it: time itself. The aporia of gift-giving is therefore not just one case among others but involves the ontological structure of every aporetic statement. We are within time and time is given to us. Husserl understood this *a priori intuition* — to use Kant's oxymoron — as first givenness of perceptive experience, whereas Heidegger understood it in a more essential way as the founding experience of *Dasein*, "the being for which in its being what is at stake is being"; *Dasein* is time as being's internal distance to itself. Hence the implicit syllogism *given time* opens the possibility of every relationship; every relationship brings into play *the gift of time;* the *gift relationship* is the expression par excellence of this gift of time. This helps us understand why Derrida claimed that to give was always to give time.

One can only admire the subtle logic according to which Derrida refined and developed the aporia that was his starting point: "Giving is *the* impossible." But we cannot fail to notice that several of the terms in his argument were put forth without taking into account their semantic plurality. This is not merely a formal plurality but one that relates back to a plurality of data. This makes its logical articulation fragile, if not shaky, since it presupposes the assigning of a certain conventional sense — and only one sense — to certain concepts, without prior definition or discussion; the entire reasoning runs the risk of collapsing if certain presumably self-evident equivalences are shown to be unfounded or to have only partial relevance. Let me briefly point out these question marks before returning to the main points of Derrida's analysis and presenting a more substantial analysis of a different, or even, on certain points, contrary argument.

The first question concerns the very concept of *gift*. We must ask from the outset whether it is possible to speak of "gift" without running a considerable risk. The answer is probably no. Anyone who has taken the trouble to study practices of (festive, reciprocal, and prodigal) ceremonial exchange between partners in traditional societies will find it difficult to place them in the same category as (utilitarian and unilateral) gifts of assistance given to those in need or distress; in the same way, no comparison is possible between these two social practices and the (nontangible and unconditional) gift of oneself that lovers give to each other and mystics to their god. I could go on. As for the "gift of being," it is neither a social practice nor the gesture of an agent but the statement of a philosophical perspective on the experience of the world. The same could be said of the "gift" as it is discussed within the phenomenological tradition. A concept that refers to radically divergent practices in terms of their fields of relevance, required procedures, and goals cannot be used *in general* without running a constant risk of confusion. This use makes it tempting to play one meaning against another without realizing that the entire field has shifted. The progress of objections then risks becoming a sophistic game of substitutions; the general term becomes a single mask under which different and discordant voices alternate and hide each other. As a result, these voices end up being assessed by reference to the only voice recognizable and recognized by our entire religious and moral tradition: purely generous gift-giving. From this point of view, I would claim in Derrida's manner — but based on a critical and non-aporetic requirement — that "the gift" does not exist; what does exist is various gift-giving practices belonging to different categories that must be defined based on epistemologically convincing criteria.

The same type of question applies to the concept of *exchange*. Dealing with it in general, as if it kept the same meaning whether it designates ritual exchange of presents, contractual exchange of goods, functional exchange of messages, and exchange of blows in combat or play, among other examples, once again amounts to playing on meanings that belong to different semantic fields as if they were situated on an isotropic plane. Not only is this not the case, but in fact meanings often get reversed from one field to another. It then becomes permissible to create aporias aplenty. Moreover, the indetermination of the concept of *gift* combined with that of *exchange* leads to this most trivial and arbitrary presupposition: gift-giving practices, whether ritual or not, are above all exchanges and ultimately have an economic purpose. It was because Derrida implicitly and firmly shared this presupposition that he viewed all reciprocity as indicative of an *interest* sought by the giver and that he put forth a model of gift-giving that required an absolutely *oblatory* character. This constituted an unacceptable reduction and even confusion. It is self-evident that every gift-giving *practice* constitutes a relationship, since there is no giver without a recipient; yet this relationship does not necessarily constitute an exchange, if we accept the fact that every exchange entails a dual movement and therefore reciprocity. As for reciprocity itself, it can indeed be symmetrical and equivalent (as in contracts), but it can also be agonistic (as in games or fighting) and have no profit element. In fact, Derrida prejudged that all reciprocity was "selfish," involving a return to oneself and thus a canceling of time, if time is understood as what tore us away from any acquired or closed position; this amounted to understanding reciprocity as mere circular movement closed upon itself and reducing it to its weakest representation as symmetry or back-and-forth movement. Reducing reciprocity to this "circle" amounts to ignoring its agonistic form, in which it becomes *alternating dissymmetry*, as observed in ceremonial gift exchange, the sparring of love, and generous rivalry. In other words, the reply — the counter-gift — does not amount to erasing the gesture of giving or to extinguishing a debt but to opening the time of the relationship.

For Derrida this suspicion regarding exchange merged with another suspicion concerning the very idea of economy. *Ekonomia*, he said, is the movement of return toward the *oikos* (house); it was the journey of Ulysses, who traveled far away only in order to come back, "repatriate" himself, and find himself at home after his adventures in the space of the nonself. According to Derrida, this movement was a metaphor for the Hegelian movement of the Idea, the movement of *Aufhebung* through which the Idea recovered and reintegrated what had first been left behind or lost during its journey through otherness. This would define economy in its limited sense, already described in an earlier writing.[2] For Derrida, every exchange amounted to this overly cautious return and overly calculating economy; hence the following claims:

> The gift, *if there is any*, would no doubt be related to economy. One cannot treat the gift, this goes without saying, without treating this relation to economy, even to the money economy. But is not the gift, if there is any, also that which interrupts economy? That which, in suspending economic calculation, no longer gives rise to exchange? That which opens the circle so as to defy reciprocity or symmetry, the common measure, and so as to turn aside the return in view of the non-return? If there is gift, the *given* of the gift (*that which* one gives, the gift as given thing or as act

of donation) must not come back to the giving (let us not already say to the subject, to the donor). It must not circulate, it must not be exchanged, it must not in any case be exhausted, as a gift, by the process of exchange, by the movement of circulation of the circle in the form of return to the point of departure. (*GT*, 7)

Derrida's equations were clearly formulated: as soon as gift-giving could be observed by empirical means deemed problematic — "if there is any" — it is said to come under the realm of economy since it would merely amount to exchange, and as such to mere reciprocity, return to the giver, and thus circular movement. But did these equations have a foundation? Perhaps not, since nothing allows us to identify exchange or reciprocity to economy, either at the level of concepts or at that of observed practices. Nor to any kind of circularity. If this were the case, the entire demonstration would end there; at best it would be acceptable for one of the possible meanings of the concept of gift: pure generosity. Thus the aporia supposedly brought to light is not an aporia; or it is so only if these uncertain equations are accepted as truth. This is anyway the serious problem that Derrida's writing raises for us, in a preliminary approach.

## THE FOUR SIDES OF THE APORIA

"The gift is *the* impossible," Derrida claimed. Before determining whether this claim is acceptable, it is important to examine more closely the different steps of his argument. It dealt with the four major aspects involved in the empirical procedure of giving: (1) the gesture itself, (2) the beneficiary of the gift or recipient, (3) the author of the gift or giver, and (4) the thing given.[3] Let us consider each of these.

### 1. The Gesture of Giving

From the outset, Derrida disqualified Mauss's approach (the subtitle of Mauss's *The Gift* is *Forms and Functions of* Exchange *in Archaic Societies*) by claiming the existence of complicity between the concepts of exchange, economy, and circularity:

If the gift is annulled in the economic odyssey of the circle as soon as it appears *as* gift or as soon as it signifies *itself as* gift, there is no longer any "logic of the gift," and one may safely say that a consistent discourse on the gift becomes impossible: It misses its object and always speaks, finally, of something else. One could go so far as to say that a work as monumental[4] as Marcel Mauss's *The Gift* speaks of everything but the gift: It deals with economy, exchange, contract (*do ut des*), it speaks of raising the stakes, sacrifice, gift *and* counter-gift, — in short, everything that in the thing itself impels the gift *and* the annulment of the gift. (*GT*, 24).

These claims are unacceptable for any observer of the societies of the type studied by Mauss; what is at stake is not economy but sumptuary offering. As for the so-called synallagmatic *do ut des* contract,[5] it is the legal form of a reciprocity meant to be symmetrical and thus the opposite of potlatch, which requires giving more than one received; in addition, this raising of stakes does not involve the market but challenge in generosity. As for sacrifice, which Mauss mentioned in a note, it belongs to the complex gift relationship with the deities, yet by including it in the list above, Derrida acted as if it were an obvious aspect of economic logic, which is to say self-interested exchange. In fact, this amounted to a trivial and reductive thesis; Derrida did not seem to be aware that he shared it with the strictest and most consistent of functionalists. In short, whereas throughout *The Gift* Mauss was at pains to demonstrate that these offerings were inseparable from public expressions of generosity, prestige, honor, the granting of trust, promises of fidelity, and the creating and reinforcing of bonds, Derrida interpreted the entire language of the gift as a language of trade and profit. That Derrida reduced exchange in general to trade is clearly shown by the following claim: "Mauss does not worry enough about this incompatibility between gift and exchange or about the fact that an exchanged gift is only a tit for tat" (*GT*, 37). This is precisely what an exchanged gift is not: it never consists of a loan; instead, it consists of risking oneself toward the other through the thing given and prompting a reply. To what aim? In order to understand it, we will have to present a different reading of ceremonial gift-giving.

Based on this accumulation of distortions or even misinterpretations, Derrida was able to claim, "The truth of the gift is equivalent to the non-gift or to the non-truth of the gift" (*GT*, 27). The gift Derrida referred to in this passage was indeed the one discussed by Mauss, but it may be that the nontruth in question was above all that of his interpretation, which mistook ceremonial gift exchange for commercial exchange and, based on this arbitrarily set equivalence, judged it by the yardstick of an entirely different type of gift: generous and unilateral giving, which happened to be the type valued by every moral and religious tradition in the West. This type of gift is certainly laudable; it involves the entire realm of grace (*gratia, kharis*); it has a rich and complex philosophical and theological history, yet nothing authorizes us to implicitly constitute it as the exclusive norm and reference for other modalities of giving, especially ritual gift exchange, which must precisely be reciprocal in order to be sensible. Why? This is what we will have to demonstrate.

### 2. The Recipient

How can we understand the attitude of the recipient of a gift? Once again, it depends on the type of gift being discussed. Derrida wrote, "For there to be a gift, it is necessary that the donee not give back, amortize, reimburse, acquit himself, enter into a contract, and that he never have contracted a debt" (GT, 13). Here again, attributes pertaining to trade and contractual exchange in general are assigned to ceremonial gift exchange. It then becomes possible for Derrida to discuss debt in the financial sense of the term while assigning it the metaphorical status of symbolic debt, or conversely. There is a shift from one semantic field to another, and Derrida wrote as if this shift did not affect the relevance of these concepts. It is easy to show that this is not tenable. For instance, the word "reimbursing" can be used in a broad sense, but there is no measure common to both reimbursing a bank loan and "reimbursing" (or "acquitting oneself of") a gesture of assistance. This view of ritual gift-giving as mere generator of debt amounts to reducing it to an alienating gesture, a relationship of dependence toward the giver. It generates inequality, it is said. It may be that what distorts giving and generates debt is in fact economic inequality. As stated by Derrida, this implicit dilemma takes the form of a double deadlock: if the recipient reciprocates the gift, he turns it into commercial exchange; if he does not, he remains in debt. But it may well be that this is one more false dilemma based on misunderstanding of ritual gift-giving.

### 3. The Giver

In the same way that the recipient should not "return" the gift, the giver should not claim he or she is giving, Derrida explained, invoking the category of forgetting in the sense that "forgetting is another name of being" (GT, 23). Only by forgetting that a gift occurs can the possibility of giving be opened: "As the condition for a gift to be given [se donne, literally 'gives itself'], this forgetting must be radical not only on the part of the donee but first of all, if one can say here first of all, on the part of the donor. It is also on the part of the donor 'subject' that the gift not only must not be repaid but must not be kept in memory, retained as symbol of a sacrifice, as symbolic in general. For the symbol immediately engages one in restitution" (GT, 23).

From the outset all sorts of questions are prompted by this statement. What does it mean to say that a gift *gives itself*? This reflexive form of the very gesture or of the thing given seems to presuppose a process without a subject, which would be the result of an erasure of the partners involved in giving. To legitimize this exclusion, what Derrida once again suspected in the gesture of giving was self-interested exchange — *repayment*, he wrote — but in a more essential way this suspicion affected the *memory* of the relationship between the agents involved in giving (even though this memory indeed plays an essential part in constituting an enduring social bond). In short, memory *retains;* it records what is owed. But beyond it what Derrida also suspected was symbolism understood as mere conventional order in which positions are exchanged; he tended to reduce this order — which can be understood in a very different way as *alliance* between partners — to a strictly contractual engagement calling for *restitution*. Finally, he incriminated *sacrifice*, which he reduced to the figure of *renouncement* alone (the importance of which appears late in history). It is not surprising that, based on these various presuppositions, Derrida would have claimed, "To tell the truth, the gift must not even appear or signify, consciously or unconsciously, *as* gift for the donors, whether individual or collective subjects. From the moment the gift would appear as gift, as such, as what it is, in its phenomenon, its sense and its essence, it would be engaged in a symbolic, sacrificial, or economic structure that would annul the gift in the ritual circle of the debt" (*GT*, 23).

This statement clinched the aporia since it amounted to saying that, from the moment of its appearance (*appearing* being understood here in its phenomenological rigor), giving (presupposed to be a gesture of pure offering) *disappeared* since it appeared only through the figures of calculating reciprocity — this symbolic, sacrificial, and economic regime — which were assumed by Derrida and which negated giving, according to him. In this, giving was indeed "*the* impossible." However, this statement applied only either to the gesture of giving or to the thing given; it had to be placed at the very core of the giving subject; this was the aim of the next step in Derrida's argument, summed up by the following proposition: "A subject as such never gives or receives a gift" (*GT*, 24). Why not? Because that would mean that the subject would be reduced to being the correlate of an object, in short, still according to Derrida, to being nothing more than one of the two poles in a relationship of exchange of goods. Interpreting reciprocal gift exchange in this manner, Derrida could then add, "The subject and the object are arrested effects of the gift, arrests of the gift. At the zero or infinite speed of the circle.[6] — If the gift is annulled in the economic odyssey of the circle as soon as it appears *as* gift or as soon as it signifies *itself* as gift, there is no longer any 'logic of the gift,' and one may safely say that a consistent discourse on the gift becomes impossible: It misses its object and always speaks, finally, of something else" (*GT*, 24). Once again these statements assume it to be self-evident that the ceremonial exchanges discussed by Mauss about traditional societies somehow amount to barter and return on investment; if this were indeed the case, then it would be true that Mauss "speaks of everything but the gift" (*GT*, 24). Unless it was Derrida that spoke of everything but the gift Mauss talked about. Having reached this extreme degree of suspicion regarding reciprocity, Derrida went as far as to question not only the actual practice of the gift (assumed to negate giving by amounting to exchange) but the very fact of *intending to give*, which would amount to carrying over the model of exchange within oneself: "The simple intention to give, insofar as it carries the intentional meaning of the gift, suffices to make a return payment to oneself. The simple consciousness of the gift right away sends itself back the gratifying image of goodness or generosity, of the giving-being who, knowing himself to be such, recognizes itself in a circular, specular fashion, in a sort of auto-recognition, self-approval, and narcissistic gratitude" (*GT*, 23). In his or her intention to give, the subject would be at the same time giver and recipient, thus performing a somehow incestuous exchange with him- or herself. Hence this question: "What would be a gift that fulfills the condition of the gift, namely, that it not appear as gift, that it not be, exist, signify, want-to-say as gift? A gift without wanting, without wanting-to-say, an insignificant gift, a gift without intention to give? Why would we still call that a gift?" (*GT*, 27). Why indeed? Our own doubt is no less steadfast than Derrida's, but for inverse reasons, namely, that the problem he raised exists only because of a complete misunderstanding of the very concept of ceremonial gift-giving.

### 4. *The Thing Given*

It seems obvious that if gift-giving — as it appears in its observable phenomenality — is understood to be self-interested exchange, then the thing given cannot be *given;* it is merely an external thing, the objective *res* defined by contract in Roman law. If the ceremonial gift-exchange relationship consisted of transferring a good from one partner to another, then speaking of gift-giving would indeed become a contradiction in terms. But Mauss precisely said something entirely different of the thing given; he said that it had value only because the giver invested himself or herself in it: "Yet it is also because by giving one is giving *oneself*, and if one gives *oneself*, it is because one 'owes' *oneself*—one's person and one's goods—to others."[7] The purpose of the gift is therefore to engage oneself. Let us go further: the thing given is not valued as such, as a good, but as a *pledge* and *substitute* of the giver. It is the means to an alliance or a pact; it is a sign of the value of the group engaged in giving; it carries prestige and testifies to the bond that has been established. Its highest expression is the wife who is transferred to the allied group, according to the exogamic rule; exogamy is "the supreme rule of the gift," Lévi-Strauss wrote.[8]

It must therefore be acknowledged and clearly stated that Derrida's reading of Mauss's work missed its object. Derrida's reference was obviously a form of giving that is no doubt admirable: unconditional oblatory giving. But is it legitimate to constitute this particular form as a norm of reference for gift-giving practices that belong to a profoundly different type and have precise social purposes that need to be assessed? This is what we must now clarify in order to rigorously support this critical reading.

### Rethinking Ceremonial Gift-Giving: Alliance and Reciprocity

We must reexamine the anthropological question of the gift as discussed by Mauss, since his book *The Gift* was the primary target of the aporia that lies at the core of the argument developed in Derrida's *Given Time*. This reexamination requires that the most simple questions be raised anew. Thus when we ask ourselves what it means to give, we believe that we can agree on a broad definition that applies to every case and can be stated as follows: giving is providing a good or service in a non-self-interested manner, which means that no reciprocation is guaranteed or expected. This definition seems perfectly reasonable, yet applying it to every form of gift-giving can lead to the most serious confusions *since ritual gift-giving precisely includes the strict obligation to reciprocate the gift.* We must therefore acknowledge that the character of oblation that is at the core of this definition is not relevant in this case. The solution generally chosen to confront this problem has been to dismiss ritual gift-giving from the scope of this definition by calling it "archaic" and suspecting that the reciprocity requirement involves the expectation of an advantage (or interest) that would be the damning evidence for this archaic character. This approach already performs a discrimination between "true" gift-giving (which is supposed to have a character of oblation and be unconditional) and its impure instantiations that can be identified by their deviation from the definition. In contrast to this approach, one could resort to casuistic considerations on the amphibology of the word "interest" in order to associate it in a paradoxical way with the word "gift," so as to preserve this "old-fashioned" notion of gift-giving. Recognizing that several models of gift-giving exist and that they are significantly different from each other provides a more promising approach than claiming to force a single mold onto overly diverse practices.

## THE THREE CATEGORIES OF GIFT-GIVING

Clarification is required, so I will start with a few convincing examples. It is hard to see how the following could be placed under the same label: (a) the festivals and gifts that chiefs offer each other in turn in traditional societies; (b) the celebrations and presents that parents give to their children on the occasion of their birthdays or that anyone offers to loved ones in order to give them joy; (c) the donations given to populations in distress on the occasion of catastrophes. These examples are significant: they exemplify three main types of gift-giving. (a) The first is generally called "archaic," a concept heavily loaded with presuppositions; I prefer to keep to descriptive criteria and call it *ceremonial* gift-giving. It is always described as *public* and *reciprocal*. (b) The second could be called *gracious* or oblatory gift-giving, which may or may not be private but is primarily *unilateral*. (c) The third is *giving aid*, pertaining to either social *solidarity* or so-called philanthropic activity; it is viewed by some as constituting the modern form of traditional gift-giving.

When a concept — such as that of gift-giving — applies to such different practices and is open to such divergent arguments, there is reason to believe that its definition is imprecise or even confused and that the practices involved have not been sufficiently described and categorized. It is thus likely that these three examples do not constitute a homogeneous class of objects. Whereas forms of gift-giving pertaining to cases b and c are still common practice to this day, it is clear that ceremonial gift-giving as a public form of exchange of presents between groups is not predominant in modern societies. From this point of view gift-giving is mostly a phenomenon of the past that barely survives in the form of official gifts. This seems to legitimize the use of the term "archaic" and to explain the temptation to identify traces of ceremonial gift exchange in the two other forms of gift-giving that are still occurring. I had the opportunity to show in another work that an entirely different approach of ceremonial exchanges is possible, and perhaps required; it amounts to understanding them above all as exchanges not of goods but of symbols, more precisely as *public procedure of reciprocal recognition between human groups*.[9] This reading (the central elements of which I will now sum up) provides a starting point making it possible to show that in any society that endows itself with a central organizing authority — such as a city-state and a kingdom, in short every entity that we now call a state — this *public recognition* is ensured by *law* and the whole of civic institutions.

## GIFT-GIVING RITUALS: MARCEL MAUSS'S LESSONS

We must seriously reexamine the question of ceremonial gift-giving and — like Derrida, but with a different aim — reread Mauss's seminal book, *The Gift*, Mauss was not the first to show interest in this type of social phenomenon, which he too called "archaic," but he was the first who epistemologically *articulated* this *question*. Without dwelling on this book, which is probably familiar to most readers, I would like to briefly mention his main conclusions, along with a few questions.

1.  Mauss defined gift exchange procedures as "total social phenomena," which means that they encompass every dimension of collective life, such as religion, politics, economics, ethics, and aesthetics, and above all that they constitute the central fact around which everything else is organized. Hence this question: What has become of such central facts in modern societies?

2.  Mauss showed that gift-giving procedures consist of three inseparable and mandatory steps: giving, accepting, and reciprocating. To him this *mandatory* character appeared as the most enigmatic; he documented it but did not explain it. Is it possible to present a convincing interpretation of this obligation?

3.  Mauss was clearly aware that this exchange in no way amounted to trade; he even noted that the well-known *kula* circuit of exchange of the Trobriand Islanders, in which precious goods are offered by both partners, coexists with a profitable exchange called *gimwali*, which is regarded as the opposite of kula and conducted *with entirely different partners*. Gift exchanges and commercial exchanges coexist and belong to two very different realms. How can we understand that the mandatory response to the gift that was received is not motivated by self-interest?

4.  The last important character Mauss emphasized was the fact that what

is given through this exchange of precious goods is always *oneself*: what is literally handed over to the other through the good that is offered is the Self of the giver; hence the magic that protects it. What does the presence of the giver in the thing that is given imply?

It is clear that ceremonial gift-giving raises a set of questions that are specific to it and radically distinguish it from the two other forms of gift-giving.

Note that the two other types of gift-giving (type b, which I call *gracious*, and type c, which I call *solidarity-based*) share only one or two of these variables with ceremonial gift-giving. *It is therefore clear that discussing "gift-giving" in general entails a serious epistemological risk*. Gift-giving cannot be discussed without qualifying it with the adjective that specifies the realm in which it is practiced. This clearly forces us to acknowledge that there are at least three paradigms rather than a single one. They can be described as different *orders* in Pascal's sense: each of them has its own procedure of justification. Thus reciprocity, which is essential to ceremonial gift-giving, is not relevant to gracious gift-giving but may or may not be valued within solidarity-based gift-giving. Similarly, discretion—self-effacement of the giver—which is often expected (and sometimes indispensable) in gracious gift-giving would make no sense *in ceremonial gift-giving*, which is public by definition.

## CEREMONIAL GIFT EXCHANGE AS
## A PACT OF RECIPROCAL RECOGNITION

We must then present an entirely different interpretation of ceremonial gift-giving, one that breaks even with Mauss's. I already mentioned the central argument of my hypothesis: ceremonial gift-giving is primarily a procedure of public and reciprocal recognition between groups in traditional societies. It still remains to determine what this *recognition* means and why it occurs through such a procedure. I will indicate this only briefly in order to avoid repeating a demonstration that I have presented elsewhere.[10]

A central lesson is provided by investigations concerning *first encounters*. Numerous testimonies have taught us that these encounters primarily take the form of reciprocal exchanges of presents: the *opening gifts*. This may seem sensible and courteous to us. Our surprise arises once these exchanges are presented as *mandatory*—the alternative being conflict[11]—whereas we realize that polite phrases and friendly attitudes nowadays seem sufficient for us. The whole question lies in these two observations. Nothing can better help us understand what is at stake than a short narrative that was reported by a

British anthropologist who had heard it from his New Guinean informant. During the 1920s, the latter had witnessed the arrival of the first white man to his village. It so happens that, according to local legends, the dead could return as light-skinned cannibalistic ghosts. It was decided that a test would be performed to determine whether or not this potentially dangerous stranger was a human being. The villagers offered him some pigs, and the white man, who was a well-informed Australian administrator, offered them precious shells in return. The informant concluded, "We decided that he was a human like us."[12]

It seems to me that this story can be viewed as an exemplary parable that can help us understand the most general meaning of reciprocal, public, and ceremonial gift-giving, as well as its essential relationship with the phenomenon of *recognition*. The opening gifts ritual is a *procedure of reciprocal recognition* in the triple sense of *identifying*, *accepting*, and finally *honoring* others. A major question must be raised at this point: Why does this recognition have to occur through exchanged *goods*? Other questions arise: What is it that is recognized in the other? What is made possible by this recognition?

## RECIPROCITY, TRIADIC RELATIONSHIP, AND CONVENTION

To answer these questions it seems to me that we have to move to an entirely different field and wonder whether or not other animal societies, starting with those closest to us (apes), exhibit behaviors comparable to these. The most advanced research on this, especially regarding chimpanzees,[13] shows us two things. First, mutual recognition as *identification* occurs through vocal messages, smells, and above all coordinated sets of gestures and attitudes. Second, recognition as *acceptance* takes place through postures and procedures of reciprocity (such as attitudes of appeasement, mutual grooming, and sharing of space), but never through *objects given as tokens and kept in exchange for others that are given either immediately or later* (which has nothing to do with the sharing of food among various mammals or with the mating rituals of certain birds, reptiles, and insects).[14] Adam Smith sensed this quite well: "Nobody ever saw a dog make a fair and deliberate exchange of one bone for another with another dog."[15] It seems that humans alone resort to the procedure consisting of committing oneself by giving something of oneself as a *token* and *substitute of oneself*. The fact that an agent *vouches for himself* in front of other agents *for the duration of a time period* can be provisionally considered as defining him as a Self. It is remarkable that this would occur through the mediation of a *thing*, a third element that constitutes a *token* of oneself. This recalls the classical Greek and Roman procedure of the *pact* performed through a *sym-bolon* (derived from *ballein*, "to put," and *syn*, "together"), a piece of pottery broken in two, of which each partner would keep one half that could fit the other as witness *for the future* that an agreement had been made. According to this model, reciprocal gift-giving is nothing else than the originating gesture of *reciprocal recognition* between humans, a gesture found in no other living beings in that it is mediated by a *thing*, but a thing that comes from oneself, stands for oneself, and bears witness to the commitment that was made. To form an alliance, a pact, means to bring together one's own self and the strangeness of the other through a thing that comes from oneself and is desirable by the other. This third party brings the two sides together: there is no alliance without an Ark of the Covenant. The thing given binds the two parties primarily by bearing witness that the bond has been accepted. This reciprocal recognition through the exchange of something that specifically belongs to the group (or its representative) and is offered to the other is at the core of the exogamic relationship and illuminates the prohibition of incest, which is above all a positive imperative of reciprocity: one is a human being to the extent that one moves outside of the "natural" group based on consanguinity by recognizing and forming an alliance with the *other*. In order to be oneself, one must recognize what one is not.

This is in short the new anthropological interpretation of ceremonial gift-giving that I am presenting; obviously, it does not apply to the other two models of gift-giving, namely, unilateral gracious gift-giving and gift-giving out of solidarity.[16] To say that there is an *alliance* — and in particular an exogamic alliance — means that there is a *pact* and therefore an *intentional* recognition between "us" and "you" beyond a mere social self-regulation among groups. To say that this alliance brings together what is not together — performs a *sym-ballein* — and belongs to the realm of intentionality means that the encounter between two autonomous beings involves a decision to give rules to oneself. Establishing a convention amounts to committing to these rules (which is one of the primary purposes of rituals) and involving oneself: giving oneself through the thing that guarantees the pact. What has been concluded through the *opening gifts* is extended through time by relationships that rituals aim at stabilizing; this is accomplished above all through the exogamic alliance, which indexes the agreement between groups on the reproduction of life itself and connects it to the succession of generations (this is particularly obvious in so-called generalized exchange, in which the response occurs over the long term and through extended networks). From the moment the exchange of gifts as a gesture of alliance occurs, it generates human groups that are regulated by a *convention*.

What is involved is necessarily a *gesture of reciprocity under a law*. This law is the *obligation* to reciprocate the gift implied in the triadic relation as such. This obligation was what Mauss found surprising; he reported and documented it but admitted he had no way to explain it. What is the meaning of the *obligation* to respond in ceremonial gift-giving? It is neither a physical necessity to react (as in the case of living organisms responding to external stimuli), nor a truly legal obligation (which would provide for sanctions, as when contracts are not abided by), nor a moral requirement (in the sense that it would be immoral not to respond). What we are dealing with is the *structure of a game* and an *alternation principle* analogous to that found in any game between two partners and even more precisely in a duel. Entering the game entails having to reply (as is the case in any exchange of salutations).[17] Not responding amounts to taking oneself out of the game. The obligation to respond lies in this. One does not throw the ball back in order to be generous or courteous or out of contractual obligation but because the response is part of the game, or rather of the system of accepted rules. The inseparable character of the three terms of the triad concerns not only the relationship between the partners but also their reciprocal action. The interplay of gift and counter-gift is a gesture of reply that precisely matches the alternation of blows (in fact, the same partners involved in the exchange of gifts are also responsible for vindicatory justice in case an offense was committed). The relationship is agonistic from the start. But there is more to this: the "game" is more than a game; it is a pact of trust offered and accepted through the goods exchanged.

### As a Conclusion: Reciprocity, Pure Generosity, and Hospitality

Let us return to Derrida. Or rather, let us try to: we seem to have moved so far away from his writing that returning to it may prove difficult. We might as well acknowledge that the aporia he presented as a radical objection to ritual gift exchange as described by Mauss was based on a serious misunderstanding; this misunderstanding was associated with a constant suspicion regarding the very idea of reciprocity, always reduced to a self-interested movement of return to the self, whereas reciprocity in ceremonial gift exchange actually belongs to a logic of glorious and generous reply. It must be noted that this suspicion regarding the idea of reciprocity was not specific to Derrida. It is also found in Lévinas, who stated, "The Work [as] relation with the Other . . . demands, consequently, *ingratitude* from the Other."[18] The recipient's indifference releases me from the claim that I have provided a gift. Should we consider this attitude an echo of a long tradition of religious abnegation? Perhaps, but remember that this was already the lesson Seneca expressed in *De Beneficiis:* "He who gave in order to receive in his turn did not give a gift."[19] We must give without expecting anything in return, as the gods do, Seneca said. Paul's, and Augustine's, message was more radical: God alone can give, since he alone knows how to give unconditionally. This is the order of Grace, whereas in the order of Nature (if we follow the contrast drawn by Pascal) the selfishness of egocentrism dominates. Yet a different tradition placed reciprocity highest of all in religious thought, proclaiming it as the Golden Rule: "Do unto others as you would have done unto yourself," the Talmud of Babylon states; the Gospel took up this statement, adding, "This is the law and the Prophets" (Matthew 7:12).

What the Golden Rule tells us and ceremonial gift exchange shows us is that every relationship is a call for a *response;* this is true on both sides of the relationship, but in a nonsymmetrical manner. It can be said along with Lévinas that we are infinitely and entirely responsible before the other, but it can also be said that to receive a response from the other amounts to recognizing his or her absolute right to remain other; this right is inseparable from his or her dignity. The relationship between call and response is necessarily articulated in time as a lapse between the one and the other. In this the relationship involves contingence: the uncertainty of the event. For the other, this lapse is not the time of debt but the time of response; in the same way, for us this lapse is not the expectation of an advantage but the recognition of this right to respond. The reciprocal relationship operates through alternating asymmetry. It is different from the unilateral oblatory relationship; it does not exclude it, but the oblatory relationship cannot be viewed as a standard by which the reciprocal relationship is to be judged, because these two forms belong to different orders.

Therefore the pure generosity requirement in no way obliterates the reciprocity requirement.[20] In the most generous, unconditional, humble, and secret gesture, the other is present and cannot but be so. *Given Time*, which affirmed a radical conception of the gesture of unilateral giving, deserves to be freed from the awkward and irrelevant contrast it drew with Mauss's book. It is possible to accept the aporia of pure giving without associating it with this false dilemma. It may be that Derrida understood this and was able to go beyond the terms of this debate in the intense meditation he developed in 1995 in *The Gift of Death*, starting from writings by Patočka, Lévinas, Heidegger, and Kierkegaard. His aim was then to rethink the most risky, exposed, and "mad" move forward in the will for nakedness required by the face of the other, or the name of the Other, or that which gives itself to me and gives me my own death in the death of the other. This presence of the other is no less obvious in the necessarily visible modality of giving constituted by *hospitality*, which Derrida, in another radical statement, proposed to regard as "absolute hospitality" beyond any right and any compensation, beyond even any possibility to name the stranger whom we are welcoming among us.[21]

## Notes

1  Derrida, *Given Time — I*, 7. Hereafter *GT*.

2  Derrida, *Writing and Difference*, chapter 9.

3  These are also the four aspects that Jean-Luc Marion considered in his presentation of Derrida's approach in *Being Given*. I will not pursue this comparison any further, since Marion's purpose was to assess Derrida's analyses, which questioned ritual gift exchange, in relation to the phenomenological question of "givenness" (*donation*). This does not seem possible, for the reason stated earlier: ritual giving is a social practice, whereas givenness in the phenomenological sense is said of the relationship to the world and to being within a particular philosophical tradition. These are two rigorously different types of questions.

4  This is an odd phrase for a work first published as a long article and published as a separate book only in translation.

5  In this type of contract, the Latin verb *do* (to give) does not mean to give a gift but to bring forward a good, as in barter.

6  This is a rather mysterious statement, and probably best kept so. Derrida remarked that Mauss (who was merely reusing Malinowski's terminology) discussed the *kula ring* of the cycles of ceremonial exchanges in the Trobriand Islands of Melanesia as the figure of this *circle* Derrida questioned in *GT* (6, 24, 30). In fact the kula ring is remarkable in that it is dual and never closed. It involves two different kinds of movements of exchanges of precious goods, one from East to West and the other from West to East; in one direction the exchange involves bracelets, which are female and worn by men; in the other it involves necklaces, which are male and worn by women. The two seek and meet each other as male and female; this dual movement is therefore agonistic. But what matters most is that these cycles are never closed; there is always a discrepancy that must forever be

dealt with, not because these exchanges would generate debt, but merely because the *challenges* associated with the precious goods given or received must be met.

7 Mauss, *The Gift*, 46.

8 Lévi-Strauss, *The Elementary Structures of Kinship*, 481.

9 See Hénaff, *Le Prix de la vérité*.

10 Hénaff, "Gift Exchange, Play and Deception."

11 Mauss clearly stated this: "Over a considerable period of time and in a considerable number of societies, men approached one another in a curious frame of mind, one of fear and exaggerated hostility, and of generosity that was likewise exaggerated, but such traits only appear insane to our eyes. . . . There is no middle way: one trusts completely, or one mistrusts completely; one lays down one's arms and gives up magic, or one gives everything" (*The Gift* [1990], 81).

12 Strathern, *The Rope of Moka*, xii.

13 Goodall, *The Chimpanzees of Gombe;* Waal, *Peacemaking among Primates*. McGrew, Marchant, and Nishida, *Great Apes Societies;* McGrew, *Chimpanzee Material Culture*.

14 Cf. Stanford, "The Ape's Gift."

15 Adam Smith, *An Inquiry into the Nature and Causes of the Wealth of Nations*, 21.

16 It also completely leaves aside another form of gift-giving *that is not a social practice*. See Derrida, *Writing and Difference*, chapter 9.

17 Cf. Goffman, *Encounters*.

18 Lévinas, *Humanism of the Other*, 27.

19 Seneca, *On Benefits*, I, I, 12.

20 The phrase "pure generosity" was chosen in agreement with the author to translate the French word *gratuité*. [Translator's note]

21 Derrida, *Of Hospitality*.

# Pseudology:

# Derrida on Arendt and Lying in Politics

MARTIN JAY

In 1993, Jacques Derrida was invited to participate in a lecture series at the New School dedicated to the memory of Hannah Arendt, who was closely associated with the school during much of her American exile. Although both can in some sense be called Heidegger's children (if perhaps by different intellectual mothers),[1] the result was his first sustained engagement with her legacy. Entitled "History of the Lie: Prolegomena," it was published in several places, most recently in the collection edited by Peggy Kamuf called *Without Alibi*.[2] The texts he discusses at length are Arendt's essays of 1967 and 1971, "Truth in Politics" and "Lying in Politics: Reflections on the Pentagon Papers."[3] Derrida masterfully situates Arendt's reflections in a long tradition of philosophical ruminations on lying, which he calls "pseudology."[4] Plato's *Hippias Minor*, Augustine's *De mendacio* and *Contra mendacium*, Montaigne's "On Liars," Rousseau's *Reveries of the Solitary Walker*, Kant's "On the Supposed Right to Lie Because of Philanthropic Concerns," even Alexandre Koyré's "The Political Function of the Modern Lie" are all brought to bear on the crucial questions raised by Arendt: What is the role of lying in politics, and does that role have a history?

As his title suggests, Derrida claims that his remarks were nothing but prolegomena to a more sustained treatment, which, alas, he never attempted to complete. He admits with his characteristic coyness, "I will not say everything, nor even the essential part of what I may think about a history of the lie. . . . I will not say the whole truth of what I think."[5] One of the other essays in *Without Alibi*, " 'Le Parjure,' Perhaps: Storytelling and Lying," returns, however, to the question of lying and perjury, this time stimulated by Henri Thomas's novel-play *Le Parjure*, which contains in it a novel called *Hölderlin in America*. The latter, Paul de Man confessed to Derrida, was a roman à clef paralleling his own checkered personal past, about which he had publicly lied. In yet another attempt to defend his friend against accusations of disingenuously denying his dubious political past, Derrida draws on J. Hillis Miller's essay "The Anacoluthonic Lie," which explores the implications of an internal narrative doubling, a resistance to following a single syntactic track, in Proust (the rhetorical trope of anacoluthon means a sudden change of syntax in a sentence, as often in stream-of-conscious writing). No straightforward confession, Derrida implies, can avoid the ambivalence of the anacoluthonic lie.

The plausibility of this defense of de Man is not at issue here, although it would be hard to find it entirely satisfactory. What is important to note for our purposes is that the second essay in *Without Alibi* adds little to the core arguments of "History of the Lie" and touches only fleetingly on politics in a final observation about Bill Clinton's perjury and his own private scandal. It does not work through in a sustained fashion the issues raised in the earlier essay about lying in politics. And although Derrida returned to the related question of secrecy in *A Taste for the Secret*,[6] here too not much was added to his earlier tentative ruminations on Arendt's questions.

If underdeveloped, "The History of the Lie" is still a rich text, far more than a mere prolegomenon, and opens up a number of important new lines of inquiry into the issues it treats. I ask your indulgence as I rehearse at some length its complicated and often convoluted reasoning. Whether or not it is fully fair to Arendt's own argument is a question I address at the end of this paper.

The essay opens with what Derrida calls two confessions or concessions — for some unexplained reason, he can't seem to decide between these terms — which he claims with no apparent irony are "sincere," even if they deal with fable, phantasm, and specters. He thus cloaks himself in the mantle of a truth-teller, what the Greeks would call a *parrhesiast*, to borrow the term Foucault adopted for himself near the end of his life.[7] The first confession or concession is that his title is a play on Nietzsche's "History of an Error" from *Twilight of the Idols*. Contrary to Nietzsche, however, Derrida claims he wants to maintain a strict distinction between the concept of error and that of lie. Whereas errors are mistakes about the truth of what actually is, including the ontological claim to know that such a truth exists, lies are deliberate, subjective attempts to mislead. They therefore have what Derrida calls an "irreducibly ethical dimension . . . where the *phenomenon* of the lie as such is intrinsically foreign to the problem of knowledge, truth, the true and the false. . . . One can be in error or mistaken without trying to deceive and therefore without lying."[8] Lying, as Aristotle pointed out in his critique of the overly capacious and vague treatment of the idea of *pseudos* in Plato's *Hippias Minor*, is understandable only as an intentional act, not one that merely gets the truth wrong. And it is an act with profound ethical implications, as Augustine understood. "The lie is not a fact or a state, it is an *intentional* act, a lying. There is not the lie, but rather this saying or this meaning-to-say that is called lying."⁹ Thus Nietzsche's attempt to look at truth and lying in an entirely "extramoral sense" was doomed to fail.

But having seemingly established a radical distinction between a constative statement, which is true or false, and the performative act of lying with all its ethical implications, Derrida, as might be expected, then proceeds to undo the distinction. "The lie," he writes, "includes a manifestation of the performative type, since it implies a promise of truth where it betrays it, and since it also aims to create an event, to produce an effect of belief where there is nothing to state or at least where nothing is exhausted in a statement. But, simultaneously, this performativity implies references to values of reality, truth, and falsity that are presumed not to depend on performative decision."¹⁰ Thus, unlike purely performative speech acts such as religious prayer, lying has some irreducible link with the truth, with what we may call "what is in fact the case." Truthfulness and the truth cannot be entirely disassociated, even if they cannot be equated either.

The strongest, most direct version of mendacity, based on the conscious intention of the speaker to deceive the listener about what the former truly believes, is what Derrida calls the "*frank concept* of the lie," which "delimits a *prevalent* concept in our culture . . . because no ethics, no law or right, no politics could long withstand, precisely in our culture, its pure and simple disappearance."¹¹ There are, to be sure, more indirect versions, such as silent dissimulation and nonverbal behavior designed to deceive—the example he gives is fake orgasmic ecstasy—but Derrida's focus is on the frank lie, a decision that will influence, as we will see, his critique of the concept of self-deception.

The history of the concept of lying, Derrida then adds, is tied up with the history of the actual practice of lying. Both are themselves dependent in turn on the possibility of our narrating a true history of their development. "How is one to dissociate or alternate these three tasks?" he wonders out loud, but doesn't pause to provide an answer, lamely saying only that "we must not ever overlook this difficulty."¹² But plunging on anyway without attempting to resolve it, he then makes his second confession or concession, to which I've already alluded: that he won't, after all, be telling us all he thinks about the question of lying, or certainly not the whole truth of what he thinks. "Does this mean that I have lied to you?" he asks teasingly. "I leave this question suspended, at least until the discussion period and doubtless be-yond that" (38). With the uncertainty of his own candor, his own status as a parrhesiast, now hanging tantalizingly in the air, Derrida then provides what he calls two epigraphs to his prolegomena: one touching on the historicity of lying, the other on the sacredness of truth. The first is from Arendt's essay "Truth and Lying" and establishes the intimate, perennial connection be-tween politics and lying; the second is from the philosopher Reiner Schür-mann's *Heidegger on Being and Anarchy* and links the concept of the sacred both to an originary moment, which is historical, and a contrary moment of presencing, which is outside of history. The duty one has to avoid lying, according to Augustine and Kant, is a "sacred imperative" in this dual sense. Precisely what constitutes its sacred quality Derrida does not really elabo-rate, however, nor does he tell us how much he shares this religious concep-tion of truth (if at all).

Derrida turns instead to Arendt's essays, which help him formulate a rough historical narrative based on what he calls a "mutation" in both the concept and practice of lying. That mutation involves the development in "our modernity" of the lie's attainment of its extreme limit, "a hyperbolic growth of the lie, its hypertrophy, its passage to the extreme, in short the absolute lie: not absolute knowledge as the end of history, but history as conversion to the absolute lie."[13] Derrida expresses some skepticism, how-ever, about how absolute the lie can ever be, insofar as the liar must know the truth in order to conceal it. As Socrates knew, there is a link between knowledge, self-consciousness, and the capacity to lie. "If it must operate in consciousness and in its concept," Derrida warns, "then the absolute lie of which Arendt speaks risks being once again the other face of absolute knowl-edge,"[14] which he clearly disdains as a philosophical fantasy. Still, he remains with Arendt's distinction between premodern and modern lying. Whereas the former is based on the hiding of a truth that is known, the latter involves the very destruction of the reality to which the lie refers. That is, the modern period is based on the substitution of simulacra "all the way down" for a belief in a reality that exists and can then be hidden (an argument perhaps most widely identified with Jean Baudrillard, although Derrida doesn't men-tion his name). "Because the image-substitute no longer refers to an origi-nal, not even to a flattering representation of an original, but replaces it advantageously, thereby trading its status of representative for that of re-placement, the process of the modern lie is no longer a dissimulation that comes along to veil the truth; rather it is the destruction of the reality or of the original archive."[15] Derrida then contrasts Arendt's historical account of the lie, as broad as it is, with Kant's very different, totally nonhistorical critique of it as an unconditional evil that must be opposed at all costs. Here the sacredness of the commandment always to tell the truth is evoked, with no considerations of consequences or allowance for mitigating factors. Derrida is clearly not on Kant's side on this issue, preferring the alternative position of his countryman Benjamin Constant, who argued that all social relations would cease if lies were utterly banished as immoral.[16]

But rather than dwelling on his reasons, he turns to two examples to hammer home his larger point about the performative dimension of lying. The first concerns the reluctance of several French presidents to apologize officially for the crimes against humanity committed by the collaborationist Vichy regime in World War II. Derrida claims that the concept of "crimes against humanity" was a performative invention not yet really in play when the acts were committed. But more important, he also argues that all states are themselves the product of performatives, which create their legitimacy, their boundaries, and their responsibility for acts committed in their name. Successful performatives — he ups the ante by calling them "acts of performative violence" — create the law. "For better or worse, this performative dimension *makes the truth*, as Augustine says. It therefore imprints its irreducibly historical dimension on both veracity and the lie. This original 'performative' dimension is not taken thematically into account, it seems to me, by either Kant or Hannah Arendt."[17]

In so arguing, Derrida may be passing too quickly from the insight that lies have a performative dimension to the conclusion that all performatives, such as creating a state, are like lies. But he does catch himself and acknowledges the dangerous implication that could easily be drawn from the claim that performative speech acts, including lies, actually "make the truth," for it opens up the possibility of rewriting history by falsifying past facts. Eyewitness testimony, he concedes, may never be sufficient to prove what happened; bearing witness to truth is not enough when it can be just as easily fabricated by lies. But he steps back from the full implications of this logic, whose outcome would be to countenance such abominations as Holocaust "revisionism." Although he rejects the idea that states can themselves verify facts for all time or legislate the truth — thus providing a defense in advance for Holocaust deniers like David Irving against being jailed by the Austrians — he struggles to provide an alternative. "Will this perversion be resisted by establishing by law a truth of state? Or rather, on the contrary, by reinstating

—interminably if necessary, as I believe it will be—the discussion, the recalling of evidence and witnesses, the work and discipline of memory, the indisputable demonstration of an archive? An infinite task, no doubt, which must
begin over and over again; but isn't that the distinctive feature of a task,
whatever it may be?"[18]

The second case study Derrida provides also takes off from the scandal
over the French presidents' delay in condemning Vichy complicity, but takes
the argument a step further. It involves an article in the June 19, 1995, *New
York Times* by the NYU historian Tony Judt, which lambasted French intellectuals, Derrida included, for failing to condemn the lack of presidential
condemnation. Settling scores with Judt, he notes that in fact in 1992, a
petition by more than two hundred primarily Leftist intellectuals, including
Derrida himself, did in fact call on President Mitterand to acknowledge and
apologize for Vichy responsibility for persecuting Jews. Judt, Derrida concedes, did not tell a deliberate lie, but rather committed an error, which he
would not have committed had he known the truth. But the reason he didn't
pause to find it out, Derrida then charges, is that Judt was in a hurry to
confirm his general thesis about the irresponsibility of French intellectuals,
developed in his book *Past Imperfect*, which meant he was anxious to produce an "effect of truth." "What I want to underscore here," Derrida tells us,
"is that this counter-truth does not belong to the category of either lie or
ignorance or error, doubtless not even to the category of self-deception that
Hannah Arendt talks about. It belongs to another order and is not reducible
to any of the categories bequeathed to us by traditional thinking about
the lie."[19]

But precisely what that different order might be Derrida does not pause
to spell out, despite having spent so much time venting his spleen against
Judt's transgression against the truth (and Derrida's own honor). Is it more
than simply a tendentious inclination to believe what one wants to believe
without regard to contrary evidence? Giving us no help in resolving the
problem, he turns instead to the vexed question of self-deception, which,
as I have noted, he thinks is problematic, at least from the perspective of
lying as deliberate trickery. It is not precisely "bad faith" in Sartre's well-
known sense, but like the countertruth uttered by Judt it too requires its own
unique logic, even another name: "It requires that one take into account
both some mediatic, techno-performativity and a logic of the *phantasma*
(which is to say, of the spectral) or of a symptomatology of the unconscious
towards which the work of Hannah Arendt signals but which it never de-

ploys, it seems to me, as such."[20] That is, in the first case, it would require an exploration of modern technical media informed by an appreciation of the "hauntology," the logic of ghostly traces that Derrida himself was developing around this time in *Specters of Marx*. In the second case, it would necessitate a more extensive application of psychoanalytic theory than Arendt felt comfortable attempting. Whatever it might be, it was not to be confused with frank, intentional lying. Making sense of the question of self-deception is nonetheless important, he avers, because Arendt thought it was intricately tied up with the modern practice of lying in mass democracies, which did so much to prepare the way for the totalitarian absolute lie.

To grasp its importance, Derrida turns in the final section of his essay to the work of another émigré, Alexander Koyré, whose "Réflexions sur le mensonge," published in 1943 and translated two years later as "The Political Function of the Modern Lie," anticipated all the major Arendtian themes. Written at a time when the modern version of the lie seemed equivalent to totalitarian total lying, Koyré's essay raises the question of whether a condemnation of lying necessitates a recognition of a categorical distinction between truth and falsehood, which an overly eager deconstruction of binary oppositions threatens. "How can one conduct the deconstructive history of the opposition of veracity and lie," Derrida ponders, "without discrediting this opposition, without threatening the 'frankness' of a concept that must remain decidable, and without opening the door to all the perversions against which Koyré and Arendt will always have been right to warn us?"[21] But having acknowledged the danger, Derrida then backtracks and wonders if Koyré's categorical distinction may itself have a cost, which is to deny the very "possibility of institutive and performative speech (be it only *testimony*, which is always an act that implies a performative promise or oath and that constitutes the element, the medium of all language, including constative language)." Veracity and lying, it must be understood, are "homogeneous with a testimonial problematic, and not at all with an epistemological one of true/false or proof."[22] Koyré himself, however, helps us to get beyond this dilemma when he notes that totalitarian leaders do not themselves challenge the traditional view, based on a stable metaphysics, that lying should be understood in the context of truth and falsehood (or error). Rather, they maintain the traditional view, refusing to acknowledge the performative dimension of truth telling, and simply reverse the hierarchy, believing in the "primacy of the lie"[23] or what is false or an error (not what is intended to be a deliberate act of lying). They accomplish this end in part by the perverse tactic of saying the truth while knowing that no one would take them seriously, what Arendt called a kind of conspiracy "in broad daylight."

The idea of conspiracy introduces yet another important issue, which Koyré develops in a way Derrida finds questionable. That is, Koyré argues in a proto-Habermasian manner that secrecy of any kind is anathema to an open, transparent democratic polity, in which the public sphere is an arena for open discussion. "I wonder," Derrida responds, "if we do not see here signs of the inverse perversion of politicism, of an absolute hegemony of political reason, of a limitless extension of the political. By refusing any right to secrecy, the political agency, most often in the figure of state sovereignty or even of reason of state, summons everyone to behave first of all and in every regard as a responsible citizen before the law of the *polis*. Is there not here, in the name of a certain kind of phenomenal truth, another germ of totalitarianism with a democratic face?"[24] That something might be amiss with this Rousseauist paean to perfect transparency is indicated to Derrida by Koyré's example of a problematic training in lying, that practiced by the Marrano, whom he lists along with the Jesuit and the young Spartan as emblematic dissemblers. For the Marrano, refusing to admit his still Jewish identity to forces of Catholic oppression, shows that secrecy can at times function as a justifiable resistance to power, a kind of clandestine civil disobedience.[25]

With these ruminations behind him, Derrida moves to his conclusion by returning to Arendt, asking what the positive implications of her work might be for writing a history of the lie. He first notes that, like Nietzsche, she clearly tries to distance any understanding of the role of lying in politics from moral judgments (which is puzzling for him now to account a virtue, for earlier in the essay he had contended it was a mistake). Second, he argues that unlike Koyré, she understood the new simulacral character of the public realm in which the very distinction between knowing the truth and intentionally lying no longer make any sense. The resulting artifactuality of images, which are appearances all the way down, is "at once less and more serious than the lie. Less serious because no one has, in bad faith, sought to deceive anyone else. More serious because the absence of any transcendent referent, or even of any meta-normative norm, makes the effect of the operation not only difficult to measure and to analyze, but fundamentally irreparable."[26] Third, he acknowledges Arendt's strong intention to delimit the boundaries of the political, a realm of plurality distinguished from the isolation of the solitary philosopher concerned with the truth. This realm is also different from that of the judiciary and the university, where the responsibility to seek the truth is also paramount (he might have added a free press as well, at least in its ideal form). And fourth and finally, Arendt understands, if perhaps with insufficient depth, the performative function of the lie, its links with imaginative action to change the world. "Between lying and acting, acting in politics, manifesting one's own freedom through action, transforming facts, anticipating the future, there is something like an essential affinity. . . . The lie is the future, one might venture to say, beyond the letter of her text but without betraying Arendt's intention in this context. To tell the truth is, on the contrary, to say what is or what will have been and it would instead prefer the past."[27] As a result there may be no history in general, and certainly none of the lie, without the freedom and action, the ability to imagine a different future, which is ensured by at least the possibility of counterfactual mendacity.

Having established these four positive reasons why Arendt helps us envisage a plausible history of lying, Derrida concludes his essay by pointing to four negative reasons preventing her argument from being fully satisfactory. The first problem is her inability to distinguish sufficiently between testimony and bearing witness, on the one hand, and the proof of textual evidence in an archive, on the other; the distinction she does draw between factual and rational truth, he claims, does not adequately register this important difference. Because she fails to acknowledge it, Arendt blithely assumes the self-evidence of the concept of lying. Second, she employs a confused psychology in invoking the idea of "lying to oneself" in her analysis of the modern totalitarian lie, which, as he argued earlier, is "logically incompatible with the rigor of the classical concept of the lie and with the 'frank' problematic of the lie," which will "always mean to deceive the other *intentionally* and *consciously*, while *knowing* what it is that one is *deliberately* hiding, therefore while not lying to oneself."[28] For all its problems, the Marxist concept of ideology, informed by a certain application of psychoanalysis, might have served her purposes better than the idea of self-deception. A third problem in her account is the latent optimism Derrida detects underlying her argument, an optimism based on the dubious assumption that ultimately the truth will win out. "By excluding the indefinite survival of mystification," he charges, "Arendt makes of history, as history of the lie, the epidermic and epiphenomenal accident of a parousia of truth."[29] Fourth and finally, her "certainty of a final victory and a certain survival of the truth (and not merely of veracity)," even as a regulating idea in politics or history, produces a diminished estimation of the history of the lie as such, a kind of comforting banalization that fails to confront the possibility of its infinite survival. Although such a future history cannot be proven or even become the object of secure knowledge, it must be entertained at least as a serious possibility. "One can only say, beyond knowledge, what could or should be the history of the lie — if there is any."[30]

With this ambiguous and cryptic final sentence, Derrida ends his prolegomena to a full history of the lie, which he never lived to complete (or abandoned as unworkable). It has been necessary to follow the twists and turns of his complicated argument in some detail in order to do justice to the dexterity of his mind and the indirectness of his approach, which characteristically involves ambivalently critical encounters with the texts of predecessors. But how close or persuasive a reader of these particular texts was Derrida? And how plausible are the conclusions he drew from his interpretations? In the case of Arendt he did derive many compelling conclusions from her two essays on lying, but in several instances he seems to have gone astray. In what follows, I highlight what I think are dubious readings of Arendt's texts and raise questions about the uses to which Derrida put them.

Perhaps the first thing to notice about Derrida's ruminations on lying is that although he pays lip service to the idea of writing its history, and even adopts for a moment Arendt's distinction between premodern and modern lying — the former based on the distinction between truth and falsehood, the latter premised on a Baudrillard-like claim that it is simulacra all the way down — he ultimately displays little confidence in carrying it out. As he admits in the aside mentioned earlier about the paradox of narrating a true history of lying, a difficulty which "we must not ever overlook," he has no practical way to resolve it. Insofar as statements about history refer to the past, while lying often points toward a future that may or may not ever be realized, it is hard to reconcile the two. Moreover, in his consideration of the arguments about the total or absolute lie in the modern era, a limit approached by totalitarian states at their most mendacious, Derrida stops short of agreeing that such an endpoint can ever be attained. For the very act of lying, in particular that of the frank, intentional lying he is most concerned to treat, assumes that the liar can know what is true, if not about the state of the world then at least about the state of his or her intentions. That is, there must always be a gap between internal belief and external statement to make the concept of lying plausible.[31] Otherwise we are on a slippery slope toward the idea of self-deception, which we have seen him deny. The absolute lie is as problematic as the ideal of absolute knowledge of the truth. But if it is incoherent to believe in a state of affairs in which the ability to distinguish between truthfulness and deceit is lost — an illusory world of simulacra all the way down — then the historical distinction between premodern and modern is hard, perhaps even impossible, to maintain. Without it, however, Derrida cannot pretend that he is giving us an even grossly periodized historical account of lying.

If there is a limit to what might be called the subjective side of lying — its dependence on the ability of the liar to distinguish between her real intentions and her public statements to others — Derrida holds on to an objective or external side as well. For in responding to the threat of complete historical revisionism, the making up of facts out of thin air, he appeals to what he surprisingly calls "the indisputable demonstration of an archive," which supplements that of the sometimes unreliable testimony of witnesses.[32] In other words, in texts in historical archives there is hard evidence that resists the ambiguity and undecidability that in other contexts Derrida seems to have attributed to all texts. Although he argues that veracity and lying are closer to the problematic of testifying than the epistemological problematic of knowing what is true or false, he nonetheless concedes that the latter can — indeed, must — intersect with the former in the way that the constative dimension of speech acts mingles with the performative dimension (except in the limited case of prayer).[33] Thus he is able to mobilize the record of his signing the petition urging the French president to deal with Vichy as an archival fact that refutes Judt's "counter-truth" about the alleged cowardice of the French intelligentsia. Here the cartoon version of deconstruction as a simple foe of truth and truthfulness breaks down.[34]

Lying in politics, both Arendt and Derrida emphasize, doesn't always involve making up false evidence about the past, but may point toward a promised future. Politicians who promise something if elected, but do so with their fingers crossed, cannot be contradicted by the "indisputable testimony of the archive," for there is no archive of things to come. It is for this reason that Derrida follows Arendt, indeed even intensifies her claim that lying and action, lying and imagination, and lying and even creating history are all closely related (although not, of course, identical).[35] He follows her in stressing the link between the ability to lie, to say what is not the case, and the freedom to change the world. One can lie also about one's plans for the future and produce action as a result, which changes the status quo.[36]

Derrida seems to go beyond Arendt, however, in calling the founding acts of politics a kind of "performative violence," for although Arendt did argue that the political arena, the space for political action, was founded according to no principles and by an act of ungrounded assertion, she did not identify it so readily with violence. In *On Revolution* she lavishly praised the American example for defying "the age-old and still current notions of the dictating violence, necessary for all foundations and hence supposedly unavoidable in all revolutions. . . . This revolution did not break out but was made by men in common deliberation and on the strength of mutual pledges."[37] She did, to be sure, acknowledge that at least the organized lies of governments "harbor an element of violence: organized lying always tends to destroy whatever it has decided to negate, although only totalitarian governments have consciously adopted lying as the first step to murder."[38] But in general she was careful to distinguish political action that involves acting in concert based on persuasion and judgment from the isolated exercise of violence, mute and speechless, to bring about an end.[39] That is, not all governments take the second step to outright murder that distinguishes totalitarianism from alternative modes of governing.

Arendt was, of course, an eloquent defender of the glories of political action, and she concludes "Truth in Politics" by reminding her readers that despite the ubiquity of mendacity in politics, it has a "greatness and dignity" and provides the "joy and gratification that arise out of being in company with our peers, out of acting together and appearing in public, out of inserting ourselves into the world by word and deed, thus acquiring and sustaining our personal identity and beginning something entirely new."[40] This paean is meaningful only if there is a fundamental distinction between political action and violence, genuine democracy and totalitarianism, no matter how performative both might be in disrupting the status quo. Not all performatives, she seemed to understand, are the same; acting together to change the world can involve sharing common intentions in a truthful way.

In stressing the distinction, Arendt fell back on the possibility of self-deception, which she indeed worried might well engulf those who spin the "big lies" of totalitarian politics. Undeterred by the logical qualm later introduced by Derrida — that "frank" lying necessitates a capacity to tell truth from falsehood absent from lying to oneself — she argued that "self-deception still presupposes a distinction between truth and falsehood, between fact and fantasy, and therefore a conflict between the real world and the self-deceived deceiver that disappears in an entirely de-factualized world."[41] But she was also convinced that "our apprehension of reality is dependent on our sharing the world with our fellow-men," which means it takes an unusual character to resist what others believe is true, especially because "the more successful the liar is, the more likely it is that he will fall prey to his own fabrications."[42] The modern lie, the lie that destroys more than it hides, she agreed with conservative critics of mass democracy, is especially dangerous today because of "the undeniable fact that under fully democratic conditions deception without self-deception is well-nigh impossible."[43]

The quarrel between Derrida and Arendt on this issue was an old one; curiously, her position was closer than his to that of Nietzsche, who famously said that "the most common sort of lie is the one uttered to one's self; to lie to others is relatively exceptional."[44] And their quarrel continues to exercise students of the problem.[45] Clearly, the outcome depends on what kind of self is understood to underlie the act of self-deception, with a split or incoherent self capable of an "internal" lie more easily than an integral and fully aware self. Derrida was certainly no champion of a fully integrated and entirely conscious self, so his evocation of what he calls the "classical rigor" of the frank concept of lying is not likely to be a straightforward endorsement of it. What he seems to be challenging is Arendt's failure to think through the contradictions entailed by calling whatever the self may be doing to occlude the truth a lie or act of deception. His alternatives to self-deception, however, are only suggested in the lapidary formula cited above — "some mediatic techno-performativity and a logic of the *phantasma* (which is to say, of the spectral) or of a symptomatology of the unconsciousness" — and are never fully fleshed out, at least in this essay. He is gesturing here toward a more developed theory that would incorporate elements of Freud's insights into the ways the conscious mind can know only a portion of what the unconscious really desires and Marx's analysis of the lures of ideology, neither of which Arendt fully exploited.[46] But he never elaborated beyond this gesture.

Be that as it may, a closer look at Arendt's argument about self-deception and the loss of the distinction between truth and falsehood shows that it is virtually as qualified in practice as Derrida's. For she also introduces limits to its full realization on a politywide level. One reason is the existence of a global information network that defeats attempts to create a seamless "big lie" in one country: "Under our present system of world-wide communication, covering a large number of independent nations, no existing power is anywhere near great enough to make its 'image' foolproof. Therefore, images have a relatively short life expectancy."[47] Another reason is that the political realm itself is surrounded by other institutions—the judiciary, the academy, and the press—that have a more principled devotion to truth, even if not always realized in practice. These often intersect with the political realm and prevent a wholesale triumph of even a "big lie" that destroys rather than hides the truth.

But even beyond these checks to the full realization of absolute political mendacity, there is a stubborn residue of truth within the political realm itself, no matter how much it resists being absorbed into other realms outside it. That Arendt acknowledged this residue is perhaps the reason for Derrida's final—and I think unsubstantiated—claim about her optimism that truth will ultimately win out, what he calls faith in the "parousia of truth" and "certainty of a final victory and certain survival of the truth (and not merely veracity)."[48] The issue is the vexed question of how truth intersects with politics.

Arendt clearly opposed the subordination of politics to the one truth of the rational tradition of philosophy derived from Plato. Favoring the Sophists in their confrontation with Socrates, she preferred the plural opinions, the messy unregulated doxa and rhetorical argumentation of public life, to the singular orthodoxy of the monologic philosopher's ivory tower. Or rather, she did so in the specific realm of politics to the extent that it can be set apart from other modes of human behavior. "To look upon politics from the perspective of truth," she writes, "means to take one's stand outside the political realm. This standpoint is the standpoint of the truthteller, who forfeits his position—and, with it, the validity of what he has to say—if he tries to interfere directly in human affairs and to speak the language of persuasion or of violence."[49] From within the political realm, the imposition of a singular truth is an act of domination and coercion, which stills the ongoing struggle among competing opinions and values that is the lifeblood of politics rightly understood. When truth therefore means the singular, monologic, contemplative, rational unity sought by philosophers, there can never be, pace Derrida, a parousia that will signal a triumphant overcoming of agonistic difference. Politics, by definition, is a space of human interaction unmastered by the tyranny of universal, univocal, unequivocal truth. For Arendt, in its precincts there is no "sacred imperative" to tell the truth.[50]

What about the second kind of truth Arendt postulates in her essays, that of the facts? Does she believe in the "certainty of a final victory and a certain survival of truth" in this acceptation of the term? Here the question grows decidedly murkier. In her consideration of the Pentagon Papers in "Lying in

Politics," it is clear that she faults the policymakers who got us into the quagmire of Vietnam for their blithe defactualization and lack of political judgment in the name of technocratic calculation. Accordingly, "Truth in Politics" begins with an attempt to incorporate factual truth into the political realm rather than place it outside, like philosophical truth: factual truth, she writes, is "always related to other people: it concerns events and circumstances in which many are involved; it is established by witnesses and depends on testimony; it exists only to the extent that it is spoken about, even if it occurs in the domain of privacy. It is political by nature. Facts and opinions, though they must be kept apart, are not antagonistic to each other: they belong to the same realm."[51] The solidity of facts about the past cannot be denied, as exemplified by Clemenceau's famous reply to a question about future historians' judgment about the origins of World War I: "This I don't know. But I know for certain that they will not say Belgium invaded Germany."[52]

But then Arendt expresses second thoughts and backs away from the full consequences of her claim: "When I stated that factual, as opposed to rational truth, is not antagonistic to opinion, I stated a half-truth. All truths — not only the various kinds of rational truth but also factual truth — are opposed to opinion in their *mode of asserting validity*. Truth carries with it an element of coercion. . . . Seen from the viewpoint of politics, truth has a despotic character. . . . Factual truth, like all other truth, peremptorily claims to be acknowledged and precludes debate, and debate constitutes the very essence of political life."[53] Thus, for all of her respect for the importance of factual truth as it intersects with political action, for all her understanding of the importance of the judiciary, the academy, and the free press in introducing uncomfortable facts to resist the imaginative excesses of political fantasizing, for all her faith that power cannot entirely erase the factual record, she never envisaged — and, a fortiori, never desired — a wholesale invasion of politics by truth telling, either philosophical or factual in nature. Thus her peroration to the joys and gratifications of the political life, cited earlier, concludes by saying, "It is only by respecting its own borders that this realm, where we are free to act and to change, can remain intact, preserving its integrity and keeping its promises. Conceptually, we may call truth what we cannot change; metaphorically, it is the ground on which we stand and the sky that stretches above us."[54] There is, in short, no parousia of truth for Arendt, factual or philosophical.

What can we say in conclusion about Derrida's ambivalent and sometimes tendentious reading of Arendt on lying in politics? Derrida perhaps needs to construct an overly optimistic Arendt, one who believes in the sacred imperative to tell the truth (thus his evocation of the religious concept of parousia, which as far as I can tell appears nowhere in her own discourse) to contrast with his own seemingly more skeptical alternative. Thus he asks about seemingly indisputable "facts" of the type Clemenceau cited about the German invasion of Belgium, "How can one still subscribe to them when the 'facts' in question are already phenomena of performative-mediatic discourse, structured by the simulacrum and the virtual, and incorporating their own interpretive moment?"[55] No contextual explanation, he argues against Arendt, will suffice to fix factual truth, which is always already a function of linguistic performance.

Moreover, Derrida clearly wants to place more weight than Arendt did on the image as opposed to linguistic discourse in describing modern politics. For all his stress on the importance of speech act theory, which Arendt never explicitly used in understanding lies, he went so far as to claim that "in the 'modern' simulacrum ('live television' for example) the substitute takes the place of what it replaces and destroys even reference to the alterity of what it replaces, by means of its selective and interpretive performativity, and by means of the absolute and indubitable 'truth effect' that it produces. Here, then, is doubtless the space of an absolute lie that *can always* survive indefinitely without anyone ever knowing anything about it or without anyone being there any longer to know it or remember it."[56] The destruction of the modern lie, as opposed to the hiding of its premodern predecessor, can be complete. The result is more than mere self-deception; it is a new ontological condition.

But then, catching himself in a contradiction — as we have seen, he stresses the logical necessity of being able to tell the truth in the frank concept of lying, absolute or not — he backtracks by returning essentially to Arendt's position: "It *can always do so, perhaps*, but we must maintain this regime of the *perhaps* and this clause of possibility if we want to avoid effacing once again the history of the lie into a history of the truth, into a theoretical knowledge that comes under the authority of determinant judgments."[57] Like Arendt in her ruminations on the importance of Kant's *Critique of Judgment* for politics, he resists the subsumptive, algorithmic logic of theoretical reason, although his weak "perhaps" does not match Arendt's vigorous endorsement of Kant's alternative idea of reflective judgments.[58] Both lying and politics, they agree, cannot be understood by subordinating them to determinant judgments, and one might add normative as well as epistemological. Neither can be judged from the point of view of abstract, universal rules or categorical imperatives (which is why the Kant of the first two critiques is not helpful in dealing with them).

If this is so, then the general claim that we live in a world entirely dominated by simulacral images and absolute lies can itself be challenged as an inappropriately determinant judgment that has no place in politics, an attempt to tell a universal truth that should not be allowed to dominate the messier realm of counterfactual political action. If we take seriously the "perhaps" that Derrida himself wants to emphasize, then we are no longer fully dominated by the ideological image machine that he sees as more prevalent than self-deception. Instead, we are in a more Arendtian world of agonistic political discourse in which opinions, rhetoric, and, yes, the ability to lie are signs of a freedom that is — perhaps — inextinguishable so long as politics resists the domination of sacred imperatives of whatever kind.

## Notes

1 R. Wolin, *Heidegger's Children*. Although Derrida is not included in this volume, Wolin has made extensive efforts elsewhere to link deconstruction to Heidegger's legacy, in particular its political dimensions. Derrida was not pleased by the results.

2 Citations in this paper to Derrida, "History of the Lie," are to the version of the essay reprinted in *Without Alibi*. Earlier versions appeared in *Graduate Faculty Philosophy Journal* (1997) and Rand, *Futures of Jacques Derrida*.

3 Arendt, "Truth in Politics" (the citation in *Without Alibi* misdates it in the 1961 collection, before the essay was added to the expanded 1968 edition) and *The Portable Hannah Arendt*, from which the following quotations are taken, and "Lying in Politics." For my own assessment of Arendt's thoughts on these issues, see "The Ambivalent Virtues of Mendacity." Here I spell out in somewhat greater detail the arguments she makes against truth-telling in politics.

4 Derrida, *Without Alibi*, 32. The term "pseudology" was used as early as John Arbuthnot's *Pseudologia Politika* (1712).

5 Derrida, *Without Alibi*, 38.

6 Here he confesses, "I have a taste for the secret, it clearly has to do with not-belonging; I have an impulse of fear or terror in the face of a political space, for example, a public space that makes no room for the secret. For me, the demand that everything be paraded in the public square and that there be no internal forum is a glaring sign of the totalitarianization of democracy" (Derrida and Ferraris, *A Taste for the Secret*, 59). He also developed an argument about Kant's discussion of secrets in *Politics of Friendship*, and criticized Lacan's distinction between animal deception and human lying in "And Say the Animal Responded?"

7 Foucault, *Fearless Speech*. The metaphor of being cloaked in a mantle suggests the

covering over of something beneath, some more basic truth about a person. For a consideration of this issue, see Smyth, *The Habit of Lying*.

8 Derrida, *Without Alibi*, 29.

9 Ibid., 34.

10 Ibid., 37. He repeats this point in "'Le Parjure,' Perhaps," where he approvingly cites J. Hillis Miller's essay "The Anacoluthonic Lie": "Contrary to what seems common sense, a lie is a performative, not a constative, form of language. Or, rather, it mixes inextricably constative and performative language" (169).

11 Derrida, *Without Alibi*, 37.

12 Ibid., 38.

13 Ibid., 40.

14 Ibid., 41.

15 Ibid., 42. In "Truth in Politics," Arendt puts it this way: "The difference between the traditional lie and the modern lie will more often than not amount to the difference between hiding and destroying" (565).

16 For a discussion of their debate, see Benton, "Political Expediency and Lying," which has all the relevant citations to the original texts.

17 Derrida, *Without Alibi*, 51.

18 Ibid., 52. For a similar argument, albeit from a Habermasian perspective, see my response to Hayden White and Carlo Ginzburg, "Of Plots, Witnesses and Judgments."

19 Derrida, *Without Alibi*, 57.

20 Ibid.

21 Derrida, *Without Alibi*, 59.

22 Ibid., 60, 61.

23 The phrase, cited ibid., 62, is from Koyré's essay.

24 Derrida, *Without Alibi*, 63.

25 This function is also explicit in the "Nicodemist" crypto-Protestant resisters to Catholicism and Catholic resisters to Anglican coercion during the Reformation. See the discussion in Zagorin, *Ways of Lying*. Whether or not civil disobedience can ever be fully clandestine is another matter. If it seeks to change laws rather than merely evade them, it has to have a public resonance.

26 Derrida, Derrida, *Without Alibi*, 65.

27 Ibid., 66.

28 Ibid., 67.

29 Ibid., 69.

30 Ibid., 70.

31 In places, Arendt agrees with this conclusion, for example in "Lying in Politics," where she writes, "The trouble with lying and deceiving is that their efficiency depends entirely upon a clear notion of the truth that the liar and deceiver wishes to hide. In this sense, truth, even if it does not prevail in public, possesses an ineradicable primacy over all falsehoods" (p. 31).

32  This is not the first time that Derrida considered the question of archives. See his *Archive Fever*, where the question of what is kept in an archive and what is not — secrets, for example — is raised.

33  There are many permutations of the relationship between the performative and the constative in lying. For example, one may intend to tell a lie but inadvertently reveal the truth.

34  See, for example, Campbell, *The Liar's Tale*, chapter 18. It also seems to me that this double-barreled quality of the lie as in part dependent on the ability to know what is true undercuts the claim made by Peggy Kamuf in her introduction to *Without Alibi*, that Derrida is focused entirely on truth as made rather than told, as entirely performative, despite his fondness for Augustine's formula about "making the truth" (11). For only if there is some external standard does it make sense to argue for the mixed quality — at once performative and constative — of the frank lie.

35  See, for example, Arendt, "Truth in Politics," where she asserts that the liar "is an actor by nature; he says what is not so because he wants things to be different from what they are — that is, he wants to change the world" (563).

36  To be sure, Arendt does admit that under certain circumstances, truth-telling can also lead to change: "Where everybody lies about everything of importance, the truthteller, whether he knows it or not, has begun to act; he, too, has engaged himself in political business, for, in the unlikely event that he survives, he has made a start toward changing the world" (ibid., 564).

37  Arendt, *On Revolution*, 215. In other cases, she stressed how often revolutions justified themselves as restorations rather than as absolute and violent breaks with the status quo.

38  Arendt, "Truth in Politics," 565.

39  Arendt, "On Violence."

40  Arendt, "Truth in Politics," 573–74.

41  Arendt, "Lying in Politics," 36.

42  Arendt, "Truth in Politics," 566.

43  Ibid., 567. Derrida notes this claim, but wonders what Arendt meant by "fully democratic conditions" ("History of the Lie," 58).

44  Nietzsche, *The Twilight of the Idols*, 212.

45  For a recent overview of the debate, see Barnes, *A Pack of Lies*, chapter 7. For a defense of the evolutionary value of self-deception by a sociobiologist — it serves the function of preventing us from providing our enemies with somatic clues to what we really think — see D. L. Smith, *Why We Lie*.

46  Such a theory might also draw on the extensive ideology critique of later Western Marxists, such as the members of the Frankfurt School. Although the relationship is uneasy between deconstruction and the tradition of ideology critique, based on a tacit belief that nonideological truth might be known, Derrida shared with the tradition an evident desire to unmask illusion that pretended to be truth, especially when it serves to legitimate and maintain social injustice.

47 Arendt, "Truth in Politics," 568.

48 Derrida, *Without Alibi*, 69.

49 Arendt, "Truth in Politics," 570.

50 There is, to be sure, no reason that telling the truth about one's intentions should be taken to imply a belief in a singular ontological truth about the world. Arendt sometimes seems to forget the distinction.

51 Arendt, "Truth in Politics," 553.

52 Referring back to this statement later in her essay, Arendt added, "A factual statement—Germany invaded Belgium in August 1914—acquires political implications only by being put in an interpretive context. But the opposite proposition, which Clemenceau, still unacquainted with the arts of rewriting history, thought absurd, needs no context to be of political significance. It is clearly an attempt to change the record, and as such, it is a form of *action*" (ibid., 562).

53 Ibid., 556. Strictly speaking, "truth" doesn't assert anything; only speakers can do that. Arendt was clearly less sensitive than Derrida to the linguistic dimensions of speech act theory.

54 Ibid., 574.

55 Derrida, *Without Alibi*, 293.

56 Ibid.

57 Ibid.

58 Arendt, *Lectures on Kant's Political Philosophy*.

# The Fragility of the Pardon
# (Derrida and Ricoeur)

SUZANNE GUERLAC

Une fragilité plus formidable que toute futilité.
— Hannah Arendt (cited by Ricoeur)

"There has never been, in the 1980s or '90s, a political turn or an ethical turn of 'deconstruction,'" Derrida affirms in *Voyous* (*Rogues*), "not at least as I have experienced it. . . . The thinking of the political has always been a thinking of difference and the thinking of difference [*différance*] has always been a thinking *of* the political."[1] Deconstruction, then, a matter of *espacement*, of différance, has always been political and the political deconstructive. Différance, for Derrida, was from the start "that which threatens the authority of the as is [*du comme tel*] in general."[2]

In simplest terms, deconstruction could be said to be political in that it confronts us with the ideological force of language, most specifically, of philosophical language, which constrains the concepts we use and hence the thoughts we can have. "Words bear the stamp of the metaphysics that imposed itself through, precisely, this language. . . . Deconstructive writing always attacks the body of this language and . . . the philosophical tradition that supplies us with the reservoir of concepts I definitely have to use."[3] Deconstruction also reveals that philosophical language does not operate in isolation, sealed off from everyday discourse. There is, Derrida maintains, "an irreducible complicity between everyday language and philosophical language."[4]

The parallel between the deconstruction of metaphysics and the deconstruction of what I call cultural performances—friendship, testimony, the gift, the oath (*le serment*), belief (*crédit, croyance*), and forgiveness—is that both share an aporetic logic. If there were a change in the two registers (that is, between what some refer to as Derrida's early and late work), it would have to do with the value given to aporia. In the deconstruction of metaphysics, aporia functioned as a weapon turned against the language of philosophy, "attack[ing]" its body and undermining its epistemological authority. In the more recent work, aporia takes on productive force, assuming an affirmative value. It "makes possible a kind of thinking," "constitutes the field of that which comes into being in the sense of the Kantian regulatory idea" (*V*, 122). To the extent that there might be a "passage by/through aporia" (*V*, 121) we could even say that it pressures historical events.

## The Pardon

Derrida devoted a number of his last seminars and lectures to the question of the pardon (sometimes linked to issues of perjury, responsibility, or cosmopolitanism); he published short essays on the subject, most notably "Pardonner: L'impardonnable et l'imprescriptible," and addressed the question in important interviews.[5] Paul Ricoeur responds directly to Derrida's analysis of the pardon in his epilogue to *La mémoire, l'histoire, l'oubli*. Whereas Derrida holds that the pardon is "im-possible," Ricoeur affirms that it is "very difficult." The fragile difference at play in this distinction illuminates specific tensions in Derrida's deconstruction — and reconstruction — of the political field.

A theme that pervades Western culture (its religious traditions, its philosophy, and its literature), forgiveness goes by many names — love, redemption, clemency, grace, or amnesty — depending on the discourses and institutions that are brought into play. If clemency (specifically in relation to the death sentence) and amnesty (in relation to acts of political violence or rebellion) have a very long history, more recent political events of pardon refer us to a new juridical category: crimes against humanity. This concept, Derrida writes, "remains at the horizon of the whole geopolitics of the pardon . . . furnishing it with a discourse and legitimating it."[6]

The concept of "crimes against humanity" was first formulated in 1907 at The Hague Court in its determinations of customary laws of armed conflict; it was subsequently invoked in the Nuremberg trials. The U.N. Charter and the 1948 Universal Declaration of Human rights paved the way for the juridical institutionalization of crimes against humanity, characterized as crimes that "shock the conscience of mankind" and "whose very execution diminishes the human race as a whole." The World Court of Justice in The Hague, which established that these crimes would be subject to no statute of limitations, wrote them into international law. In the early 1960s France incorporated this feature of international law into its national legal code, thereby enabling the prosecution of Nazi figures such as Klaus Barbie. Subsequently, the system of apartheid in South Africa was formally identified as a crime against humanity, a category now extended to include crimes that target race or gender.

I review these points because, as Derrida emphasizes, the question of the pardon is inscribed in concrete historical events from the start. As he puts it, "All reflection concerning an unconditional requirement [*une exigence inconditionnelle*] engages, from the start, with concrete history. It can induce endless processes of political and juridical transformation."[7] In the case of Ricoeur on the one hand and Derrida on the other, the question of the pardon is framed by two quite different horizons, events so disproportional to our experience and even our imagination that they seem to have occurred at the edges of history. For Ricoeur, in the register of the horrible, it is a question of the utter inhumanity of the Shoah. For Derrida, in the register of admiration, it is a question of the successful struggle against apartheid exemplified by the figure of Nelson Mandela. It is a question, then, of two quite different horizons of the sublime.

## Derrida

As the title of his essay "Pardonner: L'impardonnable et l'imprescriptible" suggests, Derrida frames his discussion of the pardon in reference to a polemical essay by the philosopher Vladimir Jankélévitch, initially published in 1971 and reprinted in a small book titled *L'Imprescriptible (Pardonner?)* in 1987. In this polemical essay Jankélévitch, who had published a philosophical study of forgiveness a few years earlier, vigorously defends the removal of all statutes of limitations for crimes against humanity, arguing passionately (even, as Derrida notes, violently) that in the case of Nazi war crimes, any form of amnesty or pardon is unthinkable.[8] The pardon, for Jankélévitch, must remain, as Derrida put it, "on a human scale [*à la mesure de l'humain*]."[9] It can be envisaged only when there exists a punishment that adequately corresponds to the crime. It implies a derogation of this commensurate punishment and is to be granted only by the victim to the perpetrator of the crime, once repentance has occurred. This is impossible in the case of the Shoah, since the crimes themselves were horrible beyond all human measure in their radical evil, and to this extent unredeemable. Furthermore, the victims of these crimes cannot speak for themselves, and there has been no convincing display of repentance. Crimes against humanity are essentially unpardonable. The pardon, Jankélévitch declares, "died in the death camps."[10]

In his essay "Pardonner: L'impardonnable et l'imprescriptible," Derrida works Jankélévitch's notion of the unpardonable crime into a definition of the pardon that precisely denies forgiveness the character of being on a human scale. When forgiveness is weighed and placed in relation to considerations of commensurate punishment, degree of repentance, and other criteria, it becomes instrumental, contaminated by political agendas. It engages us in acts of calculation. Against what he calls the geopolitics of the pardon — its banalization through a proliferation of theatrical scenes played out on the stage of international politics — Derrida returns to a rigorously ethical notion of forgiveness. The pardon, he writes, "only finds its possibility as pardon when it is called upon to do the impossible, to forgive the unforgivable [*pardonner l'impardonnable*]" (*P*, 31). This is the first aporia of the pardon: to forgive the unforgivable. To prevent forgiveness from becoming an empty ritual, a tic of international relations, Derrida brings us back to the Kantian realm of practical reason and to the notion of the dignity of man upon which the notion of crimes against humanity is founded. This dignity is unconditioned; it exceeds all measure or calculation. Derrida reconstitutes the pardon in relation to the aporia he presents in the following unanswerable question: "How to articulate this just incalculability of dignity with the indispensable calculation of law [*droit*]?" (*V*, 186). The pardon, he concludes, is *im-possible* (*V*, 198). We recognize here the structure of transaction between the conditional and the unconditional that characterizes Derrida's deconstruction of the political and draws him to consideration of the cultural performances that include both ethical and political dimensions.

To say that Derrida turns the discourse of Jankélévitch inside out only begins to characterize the situation. For the earlier, philosophical study of Jankélévitch, *Le Pardon* (1971; *Forgiveness*, 2005), which Derrida mentions but does not discuss, had anticipated a certain number of Derrida's conclusions. It had already carefully distinguished between what Jankélévitch called "the pure pardon" and various versions of pseudo-forgiveness analyzed in detail. The pure pardon, Jankélévitch maintained, is beyond any instrumental calculation. It is unconditioned, like an act of grace. And because it is unconditioned, nothing is intrinsically unpardonable. Jankélévitch, then, before Derrida, speaks of the *folie*, the madness, of the pardon to underscore the ethical character of the pardon in a discourse of hyperbolic ethics: "The inexcusable itself is material only for forgiveness, precisely because it is inexcusable. For if we can excuse it, then the *unjust* hyperbole of forgiveness would not be so necessary; forgiveness would be reduced to a formality and an empty protocol. . . . Reasons for forgiveness abolish the raison d'être of forgiveness."[11] We seem to hear the voice of Derrida, who evokes a "hyperbolic ethics" of the pardon (*P*, 29) and holds up the standard of the pure pardon.

Jankélévitch, however, appears to have reversed himself completely on the subject of the pardon within the space of a few years. Forgiveness, which in the earlier essay is unconditioned but not impossible, becomes both conditioned and impossible in the second essay, published a few years later. As Peter Kemp has pointed out, however, Jankélévitch had made an important distinction that subsequently got lost sight of, perhaps because of the violent rhetoric of his polemical essay. The first analysis concerned forgiveness only in relation to a personal affront; when the pardon is requested of and granted directly by the affronted party, nothing is intrinsically unforgivable. In the later essay it is a question of the pardon as a political, that is to say collective act, and this is where the pardon becomes impossible.[12]

Kemp suggests that Derrida overlooked this philosophical distinction between the personal and the political, since he appears to apply to the *political* domain — to collective or impersonal crimes — the unconditionality of the pardon Jankélévitch had reserved for the personal sphere only.[13] I doubt very much that Derrida would have been such a careless reader. It is more likely to say that he specifically deconstructs the opposition between the personal and the political.

In a passing observation that alludes to the same geopolitics of the pardon that Derrida complains of, Ricoeur remarks that, since the Shoah, the issue of political acts of forgiveness has arisen principally in relation to colonial and postcolonial conflicts. What is specific to these contexts, he points out, is the impossibility of separating the personal from the political. Ricoeur's observation calls our attention to the way Jankélévitch contrasted the crimes against humanity of the Shoah with colonial violence in his polemical essay "L'Imprescriptible (Pardonner)?," where he argues that it was the utter gratuitousness of the Holocaust that rendered it a crime against humanity. The Jew became the victim of Nazi atrocity simply by virtue of existing, he maintains: "A Jew does not have the right to be; his sin is to exist [*un Juif n'a pas le droit d'être; son péché est d'exister*]." It is in this sense that the Holocaust was a "metaphysical crime" (*I*, 25), indeed "a metaphysical abomination" (*I*, 40), and, as such, a crime against humanity. Jankélévitch contrasts this with colonial violence, which he presents as instrumental and, to this extent, rational. Since it was a matter of obtaining cheap labor to enhance profit there was nothing *essential* about colonial violence; the colonized, he argues, could in principle even one day move up in the world to become the oppressor in turn. Although Jankélévitch identifies anti-Semitism as racism, referring to a "Germanic racism" (*I*, 42), his analysis is shocking in its blindness to the essential articulation between colonialism and racism that writers such as Fanon, Sartre, Césaire, and Memmi have so clearly articulated.

Jankélévitch, then, retains a firm distinction between the personal and the political in analyses of the pardon that ignore the fact of racism, except in the case of anti-Semitism. Derrida, on the other hand, writes on the pardon not only in the wake of the Shoah (and the texts of Jankélévitch) but also in the context of Mandela and the South African Truth and Reconciliation Commission. Crimes against humanity now explicitly include state racism, where, as Ricoeur's comment suggests, the distinction between the personal and the political effectively breaks down.

I am suggesting, in other words, that Derrida does not *miss* the distinction between the personal and the political in Jankélévitch, but strategically unravels this distinction, intertwining (and deconstructing) the two intertextual strands of Jankélévitch's discourse. Derrida carries over key elements of Jankélévitch's philosophical consideration of the pardon (where it was a question of personal forgiveness) into an account of forgiveness in general that makes no distinction between the personal and the political. In so doing, he exacerbates the aporetic potential of Jankélévitch's two affirmations, namely, that nothing (in the personal sphere) is unpardonable since the pure pardon is unconditional, and that crimes against humanity are unpardonable. Taken together, we get the maximally aporetic structure in which the pardon "only finds its possibility as pardon when it is called upon to do the impossible, to forgive the unforgivable" (*P*, 31). Derrida, in other words, strategically links the philosophical horizon (the unconditioned) to the political field, the field of democracy that he evokes elsewhere through the differential temporal structure of the *à-venir* and also characterizes as impossible.

### Admiring Nelson Mandela

In *Voyous*, Derrida writes that the pardon "would be an example of the unconditioned" to the extent that it "exceeds the calculation of conditions" (*V*, 205). This is a surprising formulation, given that the unconditioned resists representation and exemplarity. If the pardon is an example of the unconditioned, however, it is so because it occurs in history and operates therefore according to what Derrida calls the logic of another exemplarity. The pardon provides an instance of "the exemplarity of the re-mark," (*M*, 26), that is, exemplarity in the special sense of that which "allows one to read, in a more dazzling, intense or even traumatic manner, the truth of a universal necessity" (*M*, 59). Derrida designates a specific order of experience — "the experience of injury, of offense, vengeance," and so on (*M*, 26) — for this mode of exemplarity which implies a reinscription of the structure of a universal law upon the body of a singularity. Such experiences — and much of Derrida's work during the last years of his career concerns these — are aporetic in that they provide what he calls "a fold which imprints itself upon the enigmatic articulation between a universal structure and its idiomatic testimony" (*M*, 59). In somewhat more technical language, they exemplify the fold of the empirico-transcendental that he elaborates in terms of the structure of the remark: "the re-application of the quasi-transcendental or quasi ontological within the phenomenal, ontological, empirical example" (*M*, 26).

I would like to turn now from the register of the horrible to the register of admiration and to consider Derrida's essay "L'Admiration de Nelson Mandela," a text that not only singles out Mandela as an exemplary historical figure, and as an example of the reflective structure of admiration, but also gives us an example of the mode of exemplarity of the re-mark as reinscription of the structure of a universal law upon the body of a singularity. In other words, if the pardon is "an example of the unconditioned," as I cited above, "L'Admiration de Nelson Mandela" shows us what this might mean. To this extent it not only informs our reading of the pardon, which shares this structure, it also tells us something about Derrida's gesture of engaging deconstruction with history, or the scene of unfolding events.

In this essay it is a question both of admiration *for* Mandela (the essay appears in the volume *Pour Nelson Mandela* edited by Derrida among others in honor of the South African leader) and of the admiration *of* Mandela, his admiration for the Law. And here the personal and the political are inseparable. Mandela has become identified with his people. "He reasons and signs in the name of 'us,'" writes Derrida. "He always says 'my people,' especially when he poses the question of the subject responsible before the law."[14] Any distinction between individual and collective identity collapses here.

Derrida writes Mandela through a logic of reflection, of the fold of reflection that he attaches to the notion of admiration etymologically. *Admirare* directs us to the mirror and to the sense of wonder or astonishment identified, from the start, with philosophy or theory in the Greek context. Mandela exists in admiration of the Law; this respect for the Law yields acts of transgression with respect to the laws established by the racist state constitution of South Africa.

When, for example, Mandela refuses to recognize the legality of the Constitution of South Africa and establishes instead a Charter of Freedom, his action reflects back "against the white minority the principles that supposedly inspire it and that it does not cease to betray" (A, 23). Through this act of reflection, Derrida affirms, Mandela revealed something not visible before, "something that was no longer visible in the political phenomenality dominated by the whites" (A, 25). Derrida clarifies that this act of reflection "would oblige us to see what was no longer, or not yet, visible. It tries to open the eyes of the whites. It does not reproduce the visible, it produces it" (A, 25). Reflection, then, is not mimetic, it does not just provide a copy, or return, of what is already apparent; adopting a Kantian terminology, Derrida writes that it "lets us discern [*donne à entendre*] what surpasses the understanding [*ce qui passe l'entendement*] and is only in accord with reason" (A, 25). This reflection is sublime.

In refusing to conform to the apartheid laws concerning the practice of law — laws that would restrict his activities because of the color of his skin — and in doing so for reasons of conscience (which is to say out of consciousness of the law, for this is what we mean by conscience), Mandela "acts *against the law according to the law* [*se conduit contre le code dans le code*] by reflecting the law . . . by making visible what the operative law [*le code en vigueur*] rendered unreadable" (A, 36, original emphasis). I doubt we can find a clearer account of deconstruction anywhere in Derrida's writings. Mandela performs deconstruction on the scene of history, not only *in* history but also as a mode of making history; he performs the event of the coming of history. With Mandela — and this is where admiration comes in — it is not only a question of the codes of philosophy or its language, it is not only a question of "attacking the body of a certain language" (M, 59) and the authority of the reservoir of concepts it imposes. It is also a question of codes of conduct and of the acts of reflection that deconstruct them; it is a question of différance, as precisely (as I cited earlier) "that which threatens the authority of the as is [*du comme tel*] in general." In "L'Admiration de Nelson Mandela," Mandela becomes exemplary on another level, allegorizing the translation of deconstruction into history.

Mandela's reflection reveals the difference between the unconditionality of the Law and the distortions of it that occur in the phenomenal appearance of the law, its institutionalization within history, specifically, in this case, by the apartheid government. To this extent it is a philosophical reflection. It further reveals that phenomenal instantiation, far from being the unveiling of something — of the Law, for example — dissimulates: Mandela's reflection "reveals that phenomenality still dissimulates [*exhibe que la phénoménalité dissimulait encore*]" (A, 36). Here Derrida further nuances — ontologically, this time — the philosophical structure of the reflection Mandela performs in this essay.

The crucial moment, however, comes in the next sentence of the text, where Derrida affirms that this philosophical difference (which combines critical difference in Kant with ontological difference in Heidegger), this difference between the unconditionality of the Law and institutions of law in history (its phenomenalization), is not neutral: "Phenomenal dissimulation should not be confused with some natural process. . . . There is nothing neutral about it. . . . It translates, here, the violence of the whites" (A, 36). In this concrete situation philosophical difference (a difference Derrida insists on writing back into his account of the pardon, as we have seen) reveals political violence for what it is, even when, as racial violence, it was invisible to the extent that the law supported it. Mandela's transgressions of the law, conducted in the name of the Law, make visible "the hatred of the whites for their own law" (A, 34); they do so by revealing palpably that "the white people do not feel obliged to answer to, do not feel themselves to be responsible before the black people" (A, 34). What is strange here is that the exposition of this invisible violence, which ostensibly occurs through an appeal to the unconditioned — admiration of the Law — nevertheless depends on an empirical mark, the visual difference Derrida evokes here by opposing the terms "white people " and "black people."

The example of Mandela "bears witness to the past . . . and confers the responsibility of a future on others . . . re-institutes the law for the future [*ré-institue . . . la loi pour l'avenir*]" (A, 39). We might also say that the reading and writing of Mandela proposes to us a reading of Derrida's writing on forgiveness, to the extent that it performs the exemplarity of the remark, folding the structure of a universal Law upon the body of a singularity. This, precisely, is where the notion of the im-possibility of the pardon comes in and the temporality of the *to-come* — the à-venir.

I would like to stress three points here before moving on to Ricoeur's response to Derrida:

1. For Derrida, the aporias of the pardon are activated by a separation between *savoir* and *non savoir*, between idealism and empiricism, or, as

he more regularly puts it, between the unconditioned and the conditioned (the concretely historical, the calculable, etc.). To this extent, the discourse of the pardon performs, as aporia, precisely the terms of the question I have addressed to the work of Derrida, that is, the question of the relation between — or passages across — the register of philosophy on the one hand and of history (or politics) on the other. This is the issue that guides our encounters with both Derrida and Ricoeur.

2. Mandela, as written by Derrida, performs the aporetic structure of the pardon in history.

3. Derrida's text on Mandela reveals precisely that the aporia carries a specifically political force, suggesting that the philosophical insistence in the discourse of the pardon (the insistence on the horizon of the unconditioned) can be read not as a way of staying clear of history (a retreat into ethics) but as a strategy that enables political intervention.

## Ricoeur

The encounter between Ricoeur and Derrida on the question of the pardon occurs in the epilogue to Ricoeur's impressive study *La mémoire, l'histoire, l'oubli*. In implicit response to Derrida, Ricoeur titles his epilogue "The Difficult Pardon" ("Le pardon difficile"). To Derrida's claim concerning the im-possibility of the pardon, Ricoeur replies that the pardon is not impossible; it is difficult, very difficult. In his homage to Ricoeur after the ninety-one-year-old philosopher's death, Derrida noted this corrective nuance lightheartedly and characterized, with undeniable generosity, the "singular" dialogue that took place between the two philosophers over the years as an exchange "without agreement or opposition"; the two, he said, *se côtoyaient* — they dialogued, in other words, along each other's edges.[15]

If the difference here appears thin, even fragile, when it comes to the conclusions reached concerning the pardon (as we shall see, Ricoeur agrees with Derrida on all major points), this difference that hinges on the fine distinction between the *very difficult* and the *im-possible* nevertheless marks a significant divergence in the way the two thinkers frame the question of the pardon and engage with the political.

In various interviews, Ricoeur has taken pains to isolate his epilogue to *La mémoire, l'histoire, l'oubli*. The study, he insists, is self-sufficient; it does not require the epilogue on the pardon that follows. One has the sense that he protests too much, however, given that, in the epilogue itself, he concedes that the pardon "constitutes the common horizon of memory, history and forgetting" — in other words, the subject of his book.[16] Indeed, he concedes that "what remains to be undertaken is a recapitulation of the whole undertaking [*l'ensemble du parcours*] of *La mémoire, L'histoire, l'oubli* in light of the pardon" (*MHO*, 595).

The question of the pardon is indeed marginal to the stated objective of the book — a study of the representation of the past "on the level of memory and history and at the risk of forgetting [*au risque de l'oubli*]" — marginal, that is, to the explicit tasks of a phenomenology of memory, an analysis of the epistemological issues associated with writing history, and an investigation of the ontology of historical time. Yet the question of the pardon is clearly central to an *implicit* focus of the book. This involves an investigation of the task of writing the history of singular events of historical violence and, more specifically, a reflection on the very possibility of writing the history of the Shoah, as well as a critical reflection on the "obligation to remember" that governs this project. The issues of forgetting and of the pardon go together and lie at the heart of Ricoeur's study, as he acknowledges.

Ricoeur opens the third section of his book, the section on the ontology of the past which will elaborate a theory of forgetting, with a citation from Nietzsche to the effect that "too much history kills man [*trop d'histoire tue l'homme*]" and that only a force of forgetting "will enable man of memory and of history to heal his wounds, redeem his losses and to reconstitute the broken forms through his own resources [*reconstituer sur son propre fonds les formes brisées*]" (*MHO*, 379). How surprising to hear Nietzsche sound like Desmond Tutu!

It is a risky venture to invoke forgetting, even in the most philosophical terms, in a discourse that engages with the history (or historiography) of the Holocaust. For unless, like Jankélévitch, one separates the personal from the political (and Ricoeur, as we have seen, recognizes that it is not meaningful to do so in the case of the pardon), the issue of amnesty invariably attaches to the question of forgiveness, which then becomes burdened by an inevitable polemical charge, freighted with politics. This would explain why Ricoeur cordons off his discussion of the pardon in an epilogue that he characterizes as entirely separate from the self-sufficient analysis of his book. He wants his analysis of the structure of forgetting to be heard without polemical noise. He needs to be able to introduce his analysis of structures of forgetting independently of the question of guilt (or amnesty) in order to let this analysis inform his conception of the pardon, to which questions of guilt and punishment attach. It is the theory of forgetting, and the stakes of this theory, that inform what we could call his *rhetoric* of the pardon — for the difference between "very difficult" and "impossible" is perhaps, in the end, a rhetorical difference, one that, in its very fragility, might be intended to counteract the bluntness of polemical language which tends to grind thinking to a halt.

Whereas Derrida writes difference — critical difference, ontological difference, and différance — as espacement, Ricoeur speaks from the perspective of *la condition historique indépassable de l'être*, an expression difficult to translate that we could render as "the impassable historical condition of being," but that also suggests "the historical condition that cannot cross the limit(s) of being." What is clear is that Ricoeur writes from a certain ontological position. But which one? Situating his investigation in relation to Heidegger's *Being and Time*, Ricoeur declares his interest in moving away from a Heideggerian ontology (which, perhaps mistakenly, he considers an ontology of substance) to an ontology of action that he locates in Aristotle, Leibniz, Spinoza, Bergson, and Arendt (*MHO*, 452). In privileging the future through the notion of being toward death, he maintains, Heidegger binds us to the past.

This shift in ontological perspective is fundamentally a strategic or political choice for Ricoeur, as he reveals in an essay titled "The Fragility of Political Language." There he distinguishes between two currents of political thought, one that considers individuals as intrinsic bearers of certain rights, and another, the one he prefers, that proposes that individuals become human (and bearers of rights) only through collective being, through social institutions "which mediate the actualization of capacities immediately worthy of respect."[17] For Ricoeur, in other words, there is no free agent apart from some sort of association (here he is close to the African notion of *ubuntu* that both Tutu and Mandela invoked in connection with the Truth and Reconciliation Commission).[18] With the switch to the second paradigm, the political issue shifts from being one of legitimation (which concerns power in relation to individuals as bearers of rights) to one of allegiance, which concerns the question Do I recognize myself in this form of society?

In *La mémoire, l'histoire, l'oubli*, Ricoeur patiently builds up to the question of forgetting ("emblem of the vulnerability of the historical condition") which comes at the end of the section devoted to the ontology of historical time. It is here, in line with his move away from Heidegger to an Aristotelian ontology of action, that Ricoeur turns to Bergson to ground an analysis of memory that is, at the same time, a mode of forgetting.

Bergson's conception of Pure Memory, ontologically real but not actual, which needs to be activated through the synthetic operation of attentive recognition (that is, through an interaction between perception and memory) in order to yield actual memory images, enables Ricoeur to articulate memory with forgetting and to give ontological value to the past: *ce qui n'agit plus*, as Bergson puts it, that which no longer acts.[19] It also enables Ricoeur to elaborate an affirmative mode of forgetting, one that in turn leads to a *mémoire paisible*, or calm memory. For to the extent that Pure Memory is virtual (that is, an unconscious reserve of memory) Ricoeur presents it as also being a reserve of forgetting (*oubli de réserve*) that is at the same time unforgettable, since for Bergson, the virtual implies a survival of the past. Bergson thus enables Ricoeur to make his most important claim, namely, that forgetting, in the affirmative sense Ricoeur wants to invent, is a mode of unconscious memory that gives an ontological value to the past: "Forgetting thus designates the unnoticed character of the perseverance of memory, its escape [*soustraction*] from the vigilance of consciousness" (*MHO*, 570). Through Bergson, Ricoeur is able to make a distinction between two types of forgetting. On the one hand there is a destructive forgetting, forgetting in the mode of repression or denial that attempts to wipe out the past, as if it had never occurred, thereby threatening a return of the repressed as repetition. This mode of forgetting gives urgency to the injunction concerning an obligation to remember. On the other hand Ricoeur elaborates an affirmative notion of forgetting, a "forgetting that preserves" (*MHO*, 572), a positive forgetting (*un oubli heureux; MHO*, 536), that makes possible calm memory. It is in these extremely nuanced (and rather difficult) terms that Ricoeur would like to envisage the pardon.

## The Difficult Pardon

For Ricoeur, forgiveness does not mean amnesty, which he characterizes as a kind of amnesia on demand. Indeed, the difficulty of the pardon has to do with the fine line that separates the pardon from amnesty and amnesia, a distinction he makes not, as Jankélévitch did, on the basis of an opposition between the personal and the political but rather in terms of the two types of forgetting he has identified.

The pardon raises questions of guilt and reconciliation with the past (*MHO*, 536). To this extent it belongs with the question of forgetting, which pertains to memory and to fidelity to the past. The two come together at the horizon of "calm memory" and "positive forgetting" (*MHO*, 536). For Ricoeur, the pardon belongs to the larger question of forgetting to the extent that it has to do with reconciliation understood as a calming of memory, an *apaisement de la mémoire*. The difficulty of the pardon refers us to the new territory of forgetting that Ricoeur has uncovered: a "force of forgetting" that would not be "an obligation to silence evil but to say it with calmness, without rage" (*MHO*, 589). In this sense the pardon becomes a figure for the attitude the historian must take to the violence of history so that history might not get stuck in this violence.

"Jacques Derrida," Ricoeur affirms in this epilogue, "whose path I cross here, is right: the pardon addresses the unpardonable if it is to exist at all [*s'adresse à l'impardonnable ou n'est pas*]. It is unconditional. . . . It does not presuppose a request for pardon: '. . . there is a pardon, if such a thing exists, only where there is the unpardonable' [*'il n'y a de pardon, s'il y en a, que là où il y a de l'impardonnable'*]" (*MHO*, 605–6). Indeed, "the whole problematic follows from this [*toute la suite de la problématique sort de là*]" (*MHO*, 606). There is thus no fundamental disagreement between Ricoeur and Derrida concerning the nature of the pardon. What Ricoeur wants to challenge is Derrida's conclusion concerning the *impossibility* of the pardon. The pardon is not impossible, Ricoeur maintains; it is difficult: difficult to ask for, difficult to offer, and difficult to think.

This apparently very thin difference between the impossible and the very difficult opens onto significant philosophical differences, however, concerning issues of agency and temporality. If the pardon is impossible, according to Derrida it is not only because of a certain logical impossibility — that of pardoning the unpardonable — or even because of the unconditionality of the pure pardon. There is also this problem: Who is being pardoned? The person one pardons becomes someone else through the performative of the pardon; therefore, one is not pardoning the same person who has committed the fault. And, finally, there is the question Who pardons?

In his homage to Ricoeur, Derrida comments upon the difference between his own discourse of the pardon and that of Ricoeur in the following terms:

What difference is there, and where does this difference pass, between the (non-negative) "im-possible" and the "difficult," the "very difficult," the "as difficult as possible [*le plus difficile possible*]. . . . It amounts perhaps, to put it telegraphically, to that of the ipseity of the "I can." The ipse is always the power or the possibility of an I (I want, I can, I decide). The impossibility of which I speak signifies perhaps that I *can and must never* claim that it is in *my* power to say, seriously, in a responsible manner, "I forgive" (or "I want or I decide"). It is only the other, myself as another, who in me wants, desires, decides or pardons, without exonerating any responsibility, or myself on the contrary.[20]

If to forgive is unconditional, exceptional, beyond calculation, then who might be the subject of such an act? Derrida's concern is with agency. Does the "I" have the right (or the obligation or the power) to forgive, that is, to say, performatively, "I forgive you"? Who pardons? What is the power of this one who pardons? The im-possibility of the pardon refers us to Derrida's critique of ipseity, of the unified subject of action. It is a critique based both on psychoanalytic grounds — the subject is always divided by repression (a structure Derrida formulates in *Voyous* and other writings in terms of auto-immunity) — and on time, as the subject is also divided within himself or herself through the giving of time: the self is never fully present to itself.

Ricoeur's concern is also primarily with agency, or, more precisely, with the capacity for action in history. Indeed, the analysis of forgetting, and of the pardon, is undertaken in the name of action — historical action — and by this I take Ricoeur to mean not only action in history but also action that makes history. Toward the end of his epilogue Ricoeur turns to Arendt's treatment of the pardon in *The Human Condition*. Arendt considers the pardon and the promise as a dialectical pair of actions that, together, over-come the vulnerabilities that attach to the historical condition, "the fragility of human affairs" (*MHO*, 632), which is to say, to the fact of existing in time. Together they make possible a renewed continuity of human action. The pardon disentangles the present from the past to the extent that it detaches the agent from his or her past action, freeing that agent to act anew in the present. The pardon is thus a temporal intervention that slices be-tween the agent who moves forward in time and the act that is left behind. It is dynamically and dialectically related to the promise, which intervenes in the discontinuity of time (its contingency) by binding the future to the present so that action remains possible. In other words, the pardon unbinds the agent from its action and in so doing unbinds the present from the past; the promise binds the present to the future, making it possible to act anew. For Arendt, these two speech acts — I forgive, I promise — compensate for the fragility of human action associated with the historical condition.

The crucial point in Ricoeur's analysis is that, through this reference to Arendt, he is able to envisage the pardon as a separation between agent and action that lets the action survive. The separation of the agent from its action does not result in impunity because it does not require a separation of memory from forgetting; it does not efface the act or deny its reality. The act survives and remains condemned, but it survives *in the past*. This affirmation of the *reality* of the past is the Bergsonian contribution. Memory is not separated from forgetting when the agent is detached from the act which survives precisely through a synthesis of memory and forgetting that Ricoeur alternately characterizes in terms of a positive forgetting and a calm remembering, both of which give reality to what has been and yet prevent this reality of the past from dictating our action in the present or present-future. The ontology of action, which gives being to the past as that which no longer acts (*ce qui n'agit plus*), provides a counterpoint to the ontology of Heidegger that is directed to the future: the à-venir.

The very thin difference, then, between Ricoeur's and Derrida's discourses concerning the pardon — the impossibility of the pardon or its extreme difficulty — carries implications on the level of ontology. It is a question of the difference between an ontology of the future, of what is absent as on its way or to come, à venir, and an ontology of *ce qui n'agit plus*, of what is absent through having been. Fundamental to this choice (and Ricoeur presents it in pragmatic terms, not as a matter of truth) is the shift in Ricoeur's own work to what he calls a discourse of human capability. It would be a mistake to read this as a return to an old humanism and to oppose Derrida to Ricoeur on this point.

Derrida's objection to Ricoeur concerning the possibility of the pardon would, it seems, be directed at the figure of the capable man, a notion Derrida's critique of ipseity would implicitly challenge. For Ricoeur the possibility of the pardon is crucial to the capacity for action that defines human beings in terms of capability. Derrida's reservations concerning the ipseity of the one who pardons calls agency into question and to this extent refers us to fundamental features of Heidegger's analysis in *Being and Time* where the structure of resoluteness involves *Dasein*'s coming back to itself futurally. One can only assume that Derrida would be extremely wary of a philosophy of the capable man, especially given that, as Ricoeur has demonstrated, this requires a rejection of fundamental features of Heideggerian ontology in order to be thought. And yet, was it not through a figure of the capable man par excellence that Derrida inscribed most convincingly the

translation of deconstruction into history in his exceptional text "L'Admiration de Nelson Mandela"? Was not Mandela's exemplary status linked to a
capacity for reflection that Derrida explicitly writes as political action?

There is one last step required in our consideration of the strange dialogue between Derrida and Ricoeur on the subject of the pardon. We should
perhaps ask, before closing: What does Derrida mean by "im-possible" (and
what might Ricoeur have understood by it?). Clearly, when Derrida writes
that the pardon, in its pure form, is im-possible, he does not mean this in the
sense Jankélévitch did, for whom the pardon became impossible historically:
it died in the camps. For Derrida the im-possibility of the pardon has quite
another value. The impossibility of the pardon belongs within a discourse of
what we might call the critique of the possible as "what can be achieved [*ce
qui peut se réaliser*]," that is, as something that is already there waiting to be
performed, which would imply repetition and conditionality. The critique of
the possible is linked to Derrida's critique of teleology in the name of a
temporality of invention, of contingency, of the unknown or the other. The
possible, as the Robert dictionary defines it, is "that which can exist, that
which one can do [*ce qu'on peut faire*]." But the pure pardon, in its unconditionality, cannot exist in this sense precisely because to exist implies conditionality (we can think this in a Kantian sense, as the difference between the
realm of the understanding — nature as representation conditioned by space
and time — and the realm of reason, which includes the ethical realm of
obligation). To admit to the possibility of the pardon in this sense would
precisely collapse the difference between the pure pardon and the banalized
pardon of geopolitics. One cannot think the pure pardon as something
there, waiting to be realized.

In a sense this is what our reading of the essay on Mandela revealed. To
consider the pure pardon as something we can just do would be to collapse
the distinction that is fundamental to the structure of admiration. Mandela's
admiration of the Law precisely revealed, or made visible, the gap between
the structure of the Law in its unconditioned universality, which is purely
formal, and the phenomenalization of the law in the apartheid regime. Put
another way, as "L'Admiration de Nelson Mandela" reveals, the difference
between the transcendental horizon and the phenomenal horizon is the
locus of political insight: here, *ici*, the power of the white regime was revealed. To speak too soon about the possibility of the pardon would be to
evacuate, in Derrida's discourse, the political meaningfulness of the difference between the Law (the unconditioned) and the political distortions of it

that occur in the phenomenological world. If the distinction can at times seem a bit precious, or appear to mark a privilege of the ethical over the political as the site of contestation, the essay on Mandela suggests that it is fundamentally political in the here and now. But the essay reveals this in what we might call, paradoxically, a certain blind spot: the indispensable moment of a visible distinction between black and white, and in a register of action — Mandela "*acts* against the law according to the law [*se conduit* contre le code dans le code]" (A, 36, emphasis added). Mandela, perhaps because he acts out of admiration for the Law — the unconditional Law, and to this extent, from the Other — escapes the censure of ipseity. And yet, it is rare indeed for individual agency to receive the kind of explicit and unequivocally affirmative treatment it does here. At the same time, Ricoeur's treatment of agency in the discourse of capability is not entirely susceptible to the critique of ipseity to the extent that the identity of the capable man depends upon a process of formation of social alliance, and to this extent, comes from the Other, though perhaps not in the sense of radical alterity that Derrida gives to this term.

Perhaps the proximity between Derrida and Ricoeur, the way they think at each other's borders (*se côtoient*), is the strategic force of the thinking of each one. Derrida chooses the path of im-possibility for strategic reasons, which are finally political. Ricoeur chooses to reject a Heideggerian ontology in favor of what he calls a pragmatic one, not in the name of truth, but in the name of the political, or the politics that a discourse of the capable man appeared to him to enable.

We could summarize this in terms of two meanings of the word "possible." There is one meaning that Derrida must reject when it comes to the pardon, namely, the possible of "ce qui peut se produire," that implies the absence of what we could call the critical difference between the transcendental and the phenomenal registers, or, in other terms, a fall into the illusions of pure presence and the mastery of ipseity. There is another definition of the possible that Ricoeur must embrace: possibility in the sense of a *capacité de faire*, a capacity for action that can move one beyond repetition, death, and melancholy. If we could find a region where Derrida and Ricoeur could approach one another's positions, *se côtoyer*, it might be phrased in the following terms: *le pardon — au possible*, in the double sense of "to the extent possible" for Ricoeur and "to the maximum" for Derrida, for whom the pardon "only finds its possibility as pardon when it is called upon to do the impossible, to forgive the unforgivable."

*Notes*

1  Derrida, *Voyous*, 64. All translations from this text are mine; subsequent references are cited in the text as *V*.

2  Derrida, *L'écriture et la différence*, 67. All translations from this work are mine.

3  Derrida, *Monolingualism of the Other*, 59. Hereafter *M*.

4  Derrida, "Violence et Métaphysique," 167.

5  Seminars on the pardon were given at the École des hautes études en sciences sociales over a period of years in the late 1990s under the rubric of "Perjury and Forgiveness [Le parjure et la pardon]" and under the general title "Questions of Responsibility"; they were also presented at the University of California at Irvine. Lectures on forgiveness were presented in Warsaw, Athens, Jerusalem, and Cape Town; the question is also treated in a number of Derrida's other works (*Given Time*, *The Gift of Death*, *Specters of Marx*, and *Rogues*). His interview on the subject, "Le siècle et le pardon," in *Le Monde des Débats* in December 1999 was subsequently published in English as *On Cosmopolitanism and Forgiveness*. On Derrida and the pardon, see also Thomson, "Derrida's Indecent Objection"; Krapp, "Amnesty."

6  Derrida, "Le Siècle et le Pardon."

7  Ibid.

8  The titles of the two works by Jankélévitch are *Le Pardon* (1967), now available in English as *Forgiveness*, and *L'Imprescriptible (Pardonner?)* (1986).

9  Derrida, *Pardonner: L'Impardonnable et l'imprescriptible*, 31. All translations from this work are mine; subsequent references to this work are cited in the text as *P*.

10  Jankélévitch, *L'Imprescriptible*, 50. Hereafter *I*.

11  Jankélévitch, *Forgiveness*, 106–7.

12  Peter Kemp, "Le Pardon," conference presented at the colloquium devoted to Jankélévitch at the Ecole Normale Supérieure in Paris, December 17, 2005, audio available at www.diffusion.ens.fr.

13  Ibid.

14  Derrida, "L'Admiration de Nelson Mandela," 28–29. All translations of this text are mine; subsequent references are cited in the text as A.

15  Derrida, "La parole: Donner, nommer, appeler," 20, my translation.

16  Ricoeur, *La mémoire, l'histoire, l'oubli*, 595. All translations from this work are mine; subsequent references to this work are cited in the text as *MHO*.

17  Ricoeur, "The Fragility of Political Language," 37.

18  See Tutu, *No Future without Forgiveness*.

19  Bergson, *Matter and Memory*, 68. For an explication of Pure Memory, see Guerlac, *Thinking in Time*, 139–42.

20  Derrida, "La parole," 20, my translation.

# Should Democracy Come?
# Ethics and Politics in Derrida

JACQUES RANCIÈRE

What is the place of politics in Derrida's thinking? We know that he was among the French philosophers most constantly involved in political issues: the reform of the university, the dissidence in communist Czechoslovakia, the apartheid in South Africa, the situation in Algeria, the new international order — or disorder. He supported a lot of causes with generosity and discretion, and, unlike many French intellectuals, it would be hard to charge him with having supported bad or dubious causes. We also know that, from the beginning of the 1990s he wrote several books devoted to political issues and notions.

The question was often raised: Are those engagements and reflections of the 1990s consistent with the apparently apolitical discourse of *Writing and Difference* or *Of Grammatology*? Derrida contended against the skeptics that his political commitments were the straight consequence of the seemingly apolitical concepts of difference and deconstruction. Whether the contention is right or wrong might not be the right question. What is worth examining is whether the link between the concepts of deconstruction and his commitments defines a political thinking, a thinking of the specificity of politics. There are two ways of dealing with the issue. The first one consists in reexamining the concepts that define the kernel of deconstructive thought and in discussing whether and how they entail a specific understanding of politics and account for the specificity of his political engagement. I am thoroughly unable to do that. This is why I must try another way, which is more modest and more presumptuous, more cautious and more risky. What I can do is focus on the texts where Derrida openly tackled political issues in order to examine what issues he considered to be strong political problems, what concepts he set to work or avoided in his way of addressing them, and what theoretical frame he built up to form his judgments. From this point on, it must be possible to determine whether his categories frame a specific rationality of politics or subsume political matters under another form of rationality. Therefore, I pick up some signifiers which seem to define his understanding of politics, confront them with what I understand to be the intelligibility of politics, and, on this basis, propose some hypotheses concerning the place or the nonplace of political thinking in Derrida's philosophy. It should come as no surprise that I concentrate on the notion of the "democracy to come," which is obviously the key notion in his approach to politics.

"Democracy to come": this means democracy with something more, on condition of that "something more." It is clear that this supplement is not something that should be added to democracy from the outside. It is also clear that the "to come" does not refer to the future. It does not mean "the democracy that we expect." It means "democracy *as* democracy to come." From then on, several questions must be raised: Why a supplement, and more precisely, why a supplement that cannot be separated from the thing itself? What is the exact nature of that supplement to democracy? Is it a supplement *of* politics or a supplement *to* politics?

It seems easy to give an answer to the first question. The supplement is necessary because the relationship between the word "democracy" and the thing designated by this word has always been problematic. The chief of the Athenian democracy, Pericles, stated, in order to praise it, that it was a democracy by name that was in reality a government of the elite. If we consider the present time, the situation looks even more puzzling. Our governments are called democracies and purport to enact the government of the people, by the people. But, on the one hand, they send armies to bring to other people by force that democracy which is supposed to mean the self-government of the people; on the other hand, they unrelentingly complain that democracy is ungovernable, that the democratic government is threatened by a mortal danger which is the excess of democratic life. There are two ways of understanding that duplicity. You can attribute it to the duplicity of the ruling elites and draw the conclusion either that politics itself means duplicity and lies or that such a democracy is a false one and call for a true democracy — a democracy that would be true to its name, which means the power of the people. Alternatively, you can take a different view of that duplicity and think that it points to something more fundamental, that it points to a difference inherent in the concept of democracy itself, a difference that prevents democracy from ever being achieved as a form of government. In that case, you have to assume that democracy is something more than one form of government among others, that it is an excess with respect to any form of government.

The question then takes on a new shape: How should we understand this excess or this supplement? I believe that there are two main answers. Either you understand it as the political excess itself; this means that democracy is the supplement which sets up politics as something which is irreducible to the practice of government. Or you understand it as the excess of something that exceeds the rationality of politics and makes it dependent upon another law, which is generally conceived of as the ethical law — no matter, at this stage, how you understand ethics. This alternative ties in with another one: either you make sense of the literal meaning of the word "democracy," the power of a subject named the people, which is the political way, or you make no sense of it, which is the ethical way.

In the first case, you assume that the "power of the people" is the excess or supplement which constitutes politics as such. You seek the principle of politics and of its supplementary nature in the conjunction, or disjunction, of the two terms "people" and "power." Such is the way I followed in my attempt to rethink politics. I tried to understand how the concept of the demos was implied in the very attempt to define politics as the act of a specific subject. The political subject, or the *polites*, was defined by Aristotle as the one who "takes part in the fact of ruling and the fact of being ruled." I argued that we should pay closer attention to that strange capacity to occupy two opposite places and play two opposite roles. I assumed that such a capacity for the opposites amounted to the dismissal of the "natural" legitimization of power — I mean the legitimization based on a dissymmetry. That "natural" principle of legitimacy has it that power is the exercise of a qualification by those who possess it over those who don't possess it: those who exercise the power are entitled to do so because they are the priests of God, the descendants of the founders, the elders, the best-born, the wiser, the more virtuous, and so on. This is the logic of the *arkhe*, the logic according to which the exercise of power is anticipated in the capacity to exercise it, and the capacity in turn verified by the exercise.

I contended that if we took seriously the definition of the citizen, or the polites, it canceled the logic of the arkhe. That definition set at the basis of politics the dismissal of any dissymmetry of positions. Now this is exactly what the notion of a demos means. The demos does not mean the population. Nor does it mean the majority or the lower classes. It means those who have no peculiar qualification, no reason for ruling rather than being ruled, for being ruled rather than ruling. Democracy means this astounding principle: those who rule do it on the grounds that there is no reason why some persons should rule over the others, except the fact that there is no reason. This is the anarchical principle of democracy, which is the disjunctive junction of power and demos. The paradox is that this anarchical principle of democracy turns out to be the only ground for the existence of something like a political community and a political power. This is what the democratic supplement or excess means: there is a variety of powers that work at the social level, in families, tribes, schools, workshops, and so on, the parents over the children, the elder over the younger, the rich over the poor, the teachers over the students. But as long as the community is made up of the conjunction of those powers and as long as it is ruled, as a whole, according to one or a combination of those powers, it is not yet political. In order for any community to be a political community, there must be one more principle, one more entitlement which serves as the basis for all the others. But there is only one principle left in addition to all the others: the democratic principle or entitlement, the qualification of those who have no qualification.

Such is the meaning of the democratic supplement as I understand it: the demos is a supplement to the collection of social differentiations. It is the supplementary part made of those who have no qualification, who are not counted as units in its calculations. I called it the part of those without part, which does not mean the underdogs but anyone, no matter whom. The power of the demos is the power of whomever. It means the principle of infinite substitutability, or indifference to difference, the denial of any principle of dissymmetry at the ground of the community. The demos is the subject of politics inasmuch as it is heterogeneous to the calculation of the parts or shares of a society. It is a *heteron*, but a heteron of a specific kind, since its heterogeneity is tantamount to substitutability. Its specific difference is the indifference to difference, the indifference to the multiplicity of "differences" — which means inequalities — that make up a social order. The democratic heterogeneity means the disjunctive junction of two logics. What is designated as "the political" is made of two antagonistic logics. On the one hand there are men who rule over others because they are — or they play the part of — the elder, the richer, the wiser, because they are entitled to rule over those who have not their status or competence. There are patterns and procedures of ruling predicated on this kind of distribution of places and competences. This is what I call the rule of police. But on the other hand, that power has to be supplemented by another one. To the extent that their power is a political power, the rulers rule on the ultimate ground that there is no reason why they should rule. Their power rests on its own absence of legitimacy. This is what the power of the people means. The democratic supplement is that which makes politics exist as such.

Let us draw some consequences from this regarding the mode of existence of the demos. On the one hand, the power of the demos is nothing but the inner difference that both legitimizes and delegitimizes any state institution or any practice of power. As such, it is a vanishing difference which tends to be unrelentingly annulled by the oligarchic functioning of the institutions. This is why, on the other hand, this power must be continuously reenacted by the action of political subjects. A political subject is a subject constituted through a process of enunciation and manifestation that plays the part of the demos. What does it mean to play the part of the demos? It means to challenge the distribution of the parts, places, and competences by linking a peculiar wrong done to a peculiar group with the wrong done to anyone by the police distribution — the police denial of the capacity of anyone. This is what I call a *dissensus*. A dissensus consists in putting two worlds, two heterogeneous logics on the same stage, in the same world. It is a form of commensurability of the incommensurables. This also means that the political subject acts in the mode of the *as if*. It acts as if it were the demos, that is, the whole made by those who are not countable as qualified parts of the community. This is what I see as the "aesthetical dimension" of politics: the staging of a dissensus — of a conflict of sensory worlds — by subjects who act as if they were the people made up of the uncountable count of the anyone.

Such is my way of understanding the democratic supplement as the principle of politics itself. I think that Derrida's interpretation is quite different. Indeed, he too emphasizes the idea that democracy can never be identified with a form of government. And he opposes the unconditional character of the democratic principle to the world of powers, laws, and rules where it is negotiated. But for him the democracy-to-come is not the supplement that makes politics possible. It is a supplement *to* politics. And it is so because his democracy actually is a democracy without demos. What is absent in his view of politics is the idea of the political subject, of the political capacity. As I view it, his reason for this is simple. There is something that Derrida cannot endorse, namely, the idea of substitutability, the indifference to difference or the equivalence of the same and the other. Consistently what he cannot accept is the democratic play of the *as if*.

Let me try to substantiate those affirmations. At first sight we can observe that Derrida rarely, if ever, addresses the concepts of *politics* and *the political* as such. Nor does he interrogate what a political subject might be. He does not lead his interrogation in that direction for a simple reason. He has the answer at hand, in the form of a widely accepted idea that he endorses without discussion: the essence of politics is sovereignty, which is a concept of theological descent. Sovereignty in fact reaches back to the almighty God. The almighty God gave it to the absolute kings, and the democratic people got it in turn as they beheaded the kings. Such is the answer that Derrida gave, in similar terms, to the journalist of *L'Humanité* and to the journalist of *Le Figaro*.[1] Sovereignty is a remainder of theology. Political concepts are theological concepts that have hardly been secularized. According to that view, the concept of the demos cannot have any specificity. It comes down to the concept of a sovereign, self-determined subject, which is homogeneous to the logic of sovereignty that sustains the power of the nation-states. Therefore, the force of the democracy to come cannot be that of the demos. That which comes under suspicion thus is not only a particular figure of the demos. It is the notion of the political subject itself and the idea of politics as the exercise of the capacity of anybody. Just as he identifies the concept of politics with the concept of sovereignty, Derrida equates the notion of the political subject with the notion of brotherhood. From his point of view there is no break between the familial power and the political power. Just as the nation-state is a sovereign father, the political subject is in fact a brother. Even the concept of citizen which has been abundantly used and misused in French political discourse for the past twenty years has no relevance in his conceptualization. *Citizen* is another name for brother.

It is worth paying attention to the role played by the notions of brotherhood and fraternity in Derrida's analysis. There is something strange about the way he dramatizes those issues. Why such a big trial against brotherhood and fraternity, notably in *Politics of Friendship*? Derrida once asked one of his interviewers to notice that he did not make much use of the concept of liberty. The same could be said about the concept of equality. However, these two notions still lie at the heart of political discussion. So why does he insist so strongly on the third term of the republican trilogy, which obviously is the whipping boy — or girl — of the family? Everybody agrees more or less with the idea that fraternity is a questionable notion that often goes hand in hand with terror. Why reopen the case? I cannot be satisfied with the answer that brotherhood is a phallocentric notion that rules out the sister, which means the women. I assume that phallocentrism is not what is at issue. The key point is that brotherhood means a certain equivalence, a certain substitutability. It is the issue of substitutability that is the main target of Derrida's polemics. Put in other terms, the polemic on fraternity might well be a way to put aside, without confronting it, the concept of equality, a concept with which Derrida cannot be much at ease, but that he would feel still less at ease ruling out. That point can be evinced by his discussion of the topic of parity. When he is interviewed on the issue of the parity of access to representation for men and women, he takes a significant stance. On the one hand, he says that if he is "obliged" to choose, he will choose the lesser evil and vote for parity. But once he has said that, he takes a very aggressive stand against parity. Parity, he says, entails "a fantasy of maternalist sovereignty."[2] An equal woman, a substitutable woman, a "calculable" woman still is a brother, a member of the sovereign family. A brother is whoever can be substituted for another, whoever bears a trait of substitutability with another. The democracy to come cannot be a community of substitutable persons, it cannot be a community of equals.

In other terms, what the democracy to come can oppose to the practice of the nation-states is not the action of political subjects playing the part of the "anyone." It is the commitment to an absolute other, an "other" who can never become the same as us, who cannot be substituted. We can add: an "other" who cannot stage his or her otherness, who cannot put on the stage the relationship between his or her inclusion and his or her exclusion. "Democracy to come" means a democracy without a demos, with no possibility that a subject perform the *kratos* of the *demos*. Such a democracy has to do with another status of the heteron. It has to do with what is outside, distant, asymmetric, nonsubstitutable. This first means that the field of action of democracy to come is that which exceeds the borders of the nation-states. It is what is called today the international order — or disorder. But this commitment to the outside is staged by Derrida in a very peculiar manner. Dealing with the outside means dealing with the "ten plagues" of the international order as he enumerates them in *Politics of Friendship*. Even if we leave aside the biblical reference, we are struck by the interpretation of the injustices of the international order in terms of plagues. Derrida's discourse is not the discourse of a humanitarian good soul, asking the international community to heal the wounds of the poor people. He does not call for charitable action; he calls for a new International. But this new International has nothing to do with the struggling and conquering International of the brother-workers. It is an immaterial link of distant people, a link of "affinity, suffering and hope."[3] That International "takes on to-day the figure of the suffering and the compassion for the ten plagues of the International order."⁴ Compassion indeed does not mean charity; it means "suffering with." But the "with" is a mark of distance at the same time. It precludes democratic reciprocity or substitutability. The international extension of the field of democratic action means its extension up to a point where there can be no reciprocity. It is only where reciprocity is impossible that we can find true otherness, an otherness than obliges us absolutely. At this point "suffering with" the other is the same as obeying the law of otherness.

This is what hospitality means. The *hospes* is the subject that comes in the place of the demos. As Derrida understands it, the hospes means more than the link of affinity which oversteps the borders of the nation-states. What he oversteps is above all the borders within which there can be reciprocity. The character of the hospes opens up an irreconcilable gap between the stage of the possible or the calculable and the stage of the unconditional, the impossible or the incalculable. Derrida emphasizes the difference between conditional and unconditional hospitality. For him there is a duty of unconditional hospitality toward any newcomer, no matter who. But that unconditional hospitality cannot be political. What can be political is conditional hospitality, which means the calculation of how many strangers — and notably, how many poor unqualified strangers — can be accepted by a national community. We cannot, Derrida says, impose the law of unconditional hospitality on our national communities. That would bring about "pernicious effects."⁵ The expression sounds strange in his mouth, because it usually belongs to the rhetoric of realistic Right-wing politicians: too much equality, too much freedom, too many strangers, this is dangerous, this has pernicious effects. In Derrida's view the most pernicious effect of the confusion is not to bring social disorder; it is to bridge the gap between the sphere of political compromise and the sphere of the unconditional, between the calculable of the law and the incalculable of justice. Among the most striking features in Derrida's approach to politics is the violence — and, I dare say, the simplism — of his opposition between the idea of the rule and the idea of justice. Very often, and mostly in the same terms, we meet in his political writings with the statement that, whenever there is a simple rule, there can be no justice. This is how he sets up the issue in "Force of Law": "Every time that something comes to pass or turns out well, every time that we placidly apply a good rule to a particular case, to a correctly subsumed example, we can be sure that Law may find itself accounted for, but certainly not Justice."⁶ There is an extraordinary overtone of contempt in the evocation of the "good" rule that requires only application, subsumption, and calculation. Whenever it comes to the rule and its enactment, the same image shows up in Derrida's argumentation: the image of the machine. If there is a rule, a knowledge which gives its ground to our decision, it is no decision, we don't decide. As he states it in *Rogues*, "The decision then no longer decides anything but it is made in advance and is thus in advance annulled. It is simply deployed without delay, presently, with the automatism attributed to machines."[7]

Some commonsense arguments could be easily opposed to such statements. The first would be that those who suffer from one or more of the "ten plagues" would, in most cases, be glad that there exists a "simple" rule "placidly" applicable to their case, rather than being subjected to the arbitrariness of unlimited state powers and corrupt administration. The second would be that, in many instances, neither the existence of the rule nor our knowledge of what has to be done so simply annuls the decision or makes things happen automatically. But those commonsense arguments would be irrelevant because what is targeted by Derrida's argumentation is precisely the idea of a common sense — not only common sense as vulgar wisdom but common sense as the anticipation of a possible agreement even at the cost of a dissensus or a disagreement. When a small group of protesters takes to the street under the banner "We are the people," as they did in Leipzig in 1989, they know that they are not "the people." But by doing so they help build another people in front of the people embodied in the "popular state." Or when they say "This is just" or "This is unjust," their "is" is not the deployment of a determinant concept subsuming its objects. It is the clash of two "justices," the clash of two worlds. This is what dissensus means. But Derrida substitutes the aporia for the dissensus. Aporia means that there can be no anticipation of agreement in the practice of a disagreement. It also means that there can be no substitution of the whole by the part, no subject performing the equivalence between sameness and otherness.

This is what the "to come" means. It means that democracy cannot be presented, even in the dissensual figure of the demos, of the subject that acts *as if* it were the demos. In the expression "democracy to come," the "to" in fact separates the two terms, *democracy* and *coming*. This means that, strictly speaking, it takes the place of the demos. The "to come" is the equivalent of a "not being here," "not being anticipated." The *kratos* of *democracy* thus turns out to be the *akratia* of the *demos*. The supplement of the "to come" is a supplement *to* politics. It falls under a rationality which is not the rationality of politics. Such is the real stake of the polemics against the rule. This is why, in the example I quoted earlier, Derrida restates the argument on the "calculating machine" in a context which apparently has nothing to do with any case of automatic application of the rule. In this passage he wants in fact to dismiss the identification of the democracy to come with a Kantian regulative idea. The first argument he presents is that it cannot be a regulative idea since it has to act here and now. But the real meaning of the argument is that it has to act here and now as the impossibility of any *here* and any *now*. This is why the second argument that comes immediately after is the argument of the calculating machine, though obviously the Kantian regulative idea does not entail the idea of a knowledge that would only have to be "placidly" applied in order to bring about an automatic effect. What Derrida wants to do is to clear the space in order to have a simple polarity between two terms: the determinant judgment that applies a rule to a particular case and the wholly heterogeneous decision of justice. There must be nothing between the "automatic" rule and the absolute decision. This is why Derrida lumps together not only the determinant judgment, but the regulative idea and also the self-determination of the ethical subject by the Imperative of Reason and eventually the aesthetic *as if*—I mean the anticipation of a new common sense by the *as if* of the aesthetic judgment. By the same token, he also lumps together with them the act of the political subject framing a new polemical common sense. In front of the rule of the determinant judgment he gives room only to the unconditionality of the "to-come" that can never come.

I am aware that Derrida always says that "incalculable justice urges us to calculate,"[8] and that politics is an unrelenting negotiation between calculation and the incalculable, the possible and the impossible, autonomy and heteronomy. But before urging us to negotiate, he has carefully cleared the space between the two terms in order to turn that negotiation into the impossible reconciliation of two irreconcilable laws. The justice that is inherent in the idea of democracy to come is the justice of the unforeseeable event or the unforeseeable coming of the other. In the same passage of *Rogues*, he emphasizes the principle of heteronomy which is at the heart of this relationship: "It is a question of a heteronomy, of a law come from the other, of a responsibility and decision of the other, of the other in me, an other greater and older than I."[9]

It would be difficult to spell out more clearly that democratic supplementarity or heterogeneity means heteronomy. The openness to the event of the other is tantamount to the decision of "an other greater and older than I." So the reconciliation of autonomy and heteronomy is predicated on the power of a heteronomy, of a law and decision of the other. It is predicated on the power of the injunction that "comes upon me from the high."[10] Justice thus means a radical dissymmetry, a radical unsubstitutability. It means sheer heteronomy. That affirmation of a radical heteronomy is what some of our contemporaries make the touchstone of ethics: ethics would properly mean the law of the heteron, a heteron that was constructed at the crossroads of the Levinasian Other and the Lacanian Thing. That conception of ethics substitutes the unconditional law of heteronomy for the Kantian unconditional law of the self-determination of the subject. The Derridean interpretation of democracy as democracy to come is undoubtedly predicated on that interpretation of ethics. That's why it may seem to belong to the logic of what I called the ethical turn, a turn that, for the past twenty years, has reframed political matters in ethical terms and brought back into question some key concepts of the modern Enlightenment and revolutionary tradition, such as autonomy, democracy, and emancipation. Indeed, many Derridean statements echo the statements made by Lyotard in his last texts, where he emphasized the law of the Other and the unredeemable debt of the human being to the Untamable (*l'Intraitable*) or the Inhuman of which it is the hostage or the slave. However, the common reference to a set of ethical concepts apparently leads to very different interpretations of the relationship between ethics and politics and to quite different political stances. In his texts of the 1980s and 1990s Lyotard openly overturned the modernist paradigm that tied artistic avant-gardism to political emancipation. He put modern art under the concept of the sublime, which he reinterpreted against Kant as the law of an irreducible heteronomy that makes us depend on the power of the law of the Other. From this point on, he overtly dismissed the European dream of emancipation that he aligned with the denial of that dependency. He interpreted the Holocaust as the criminal consequence of that denial, involved in the dream of autonomy. And he eventually reinterpreted human rights as the "Rights of the Other" in a way that contributed to framing a new intellectual adhesion to the military campaigns against the "axis of Evil."[11]

Out of a similar reference to the Levinasian concept of the Other, Derrida drew quite different consequences. He tied the rule of the Other to the promise of democracy to come and he substituted its messianic character for Obedience to the Law. What he performed can be described as a *second turn* in the conceptualization of otherness. If the first turn led from heterogeneity to heteronomy and from political *heterology* to an otherness that amounted to the otherness of God, the second one turned that radical otherness back into the otherness of an *any other one* so as to reset the heteron on the political stage by turning heteronomy back into mere heterogeneity. To understand this point, we must go back to the first turn and see in what particular way Derrida achieved the transformation of the political anyone into the ethical figure of the Other.

Not surprisingly, the switching point for the transformation was the dismissal of any similarity or brotherhood, which in my view means the dismissal of any substitutability. We can understand it from the interpretation of the anyone that is proposed in *Rogues:* "This anyone comes before any metaphysical determination as subject, human person or consciousness, before any juridical determination as compeer [*semblable*], compatriot, family member [*congénère*], brother, neighbour, fellow religious follower or fellow citizen. Paulhan says somewhere, and I am here paraphrasing, that to think democracy is to think the 'first to happen by.' "[12] Paulhan's "first-comer" is quite close to what is called in French *l'homme de la rue*, as opposed to the men of power. Derrida gives it a quite surprising new meaning: "anyone, no matter who, at the permeable limit in fact between *who* and *what*, the living being, the cadaver and the ghost."[13] Justice for him has to do with what exceeds any family of living "compeers." It must go beyond the limits of humanity and include animals. But above all, it has to annul the difference between the "who" and the "what," the living body and the "thing." The Derridean thing is not the Lacanian *Ding*; it is the corpse or the ghost. The corpse and the ghost in fact play a double role. On the one hand they are left to our guard, entrusted to our care. As they can no longer answer, we have to answer for them. And this is what deconstruction does, in fact: answering for Plato, Aristotle, Kant, Hegel, or any other, extricating the difference or the promise concealed or entangled in the text, reopening it. Far from any iconoclastic view, deconstruction is an act of piety toward the dead, a way of being faithful to the life of the dead, or the life of Death. This is what is summed up in a striking passage in *Specters of Marx:* "One must think the future, that is, life. That is, Death."[14] The idea and even the music of the sentence remind us of the great French poet of the "life of death" whom Derrida cites in *Politics of Friendship*, Jules Michelet. Derrida indeed remains faithful to a certain nineteenth-century French tradition that sees humanity as a great being made of more dead people than living people.

The other, in that sense, is whoever or whatever needs me to answer for him, her, or it. This is what responsibility means: the commitment to an other that is entrusted to me, for whom or which I have to answer. But, on the other hand, the other or the "thing" is whoever or whatever has a power over me without reciprocity. This is the demonstration that is epitomized in *Specters of Marx* by the analysis of the visor effect or helmet effect: the ghost or the thing looks at us in a way that rules out any symmetry; we cannot cross its gaze. Derrida adds that it is from that visor effect that we first receive the Law — not Justice, but the Law, a law the justice of which is tantamount to our ignorance, to our incapacity to check the truth of its words: "The one who says 'I am thy Father's spirit' can only be taken at his word. An essentially blind submission to his secret, to the secret of his origin: this is a first obedience to the injunction. It will condition all the others."[15] To understand what is at stake in that matter of "obedience" we must have in mind another scene between father and son for which the confrontation between Hamlet and the ghost has obviously been substituted. Hamlet is here in the place of Abraham and the ghost in the place of the God who orders him to kill his son.

At this point, it may seem that we are at the end of the ethical turn: the end of the trip that has led us from the "anyone" of democratic action to the foreigner, from the foreigner to the ghost, and from the ghost to the almighty God who demands the absolute sacrifice, the sacrifice of all family ties, and demands also the secret, the betrayal, and the sacrifice. However, it is precisely there that the second turn occurs, with the help of Kierkegaard. Instead of the law of God that demands the humiliation of the creature, there is this criminal God who is also a liar since it appears that he gives an order that has to be betrayed, that he says one thing to suggest its opposite. As Derrida puts it in *Donner la mort*, this God says, You have to obey me unconditionally. But what he wants us to understand is: You have to choose unconditionally between betraying your wife and son or betraying me, and you have no reason to choose me rather than Sarah and Isaac. Sacrifice only means choice: "As soon as I enter into a relation with the other, with the gaze, look, request, love, command or call of the other, I know that I can respond only by sacrificing ethics, that is, by sacrificing whatever obliges me to also respond in the same way, in the same instant, to all the others. . . . I don't need to raise my knife over my son on Mount Moriah for that. . . . I am responsible to any one (that is to say to any other) only by failing in my responsibility to all the others."[16]

It would be hard to imagine a quicker shift from the unconditionality of the commandment of God, urging Abraham to sacrifice his only son, to the commonsensical affirmation that, while you are caring for somebody, you are forced to neglect the rest of the world. But the apparent triviality of the affirmation must not hide what is at the core of the "second turn": the ethical commandment, the commandment of the absolute Other turns out to be a false commandment. There is no reason to choose God rather than Isaac, to choose the absolute Other rather than a member of the family. The shift from Mount Moriah to common sense is the affirmation of the equivalence of any other with any other, or the equivalence of the "any other" with the "anyone." If being faithful to the commandment of God is the same thing as betraying it, and if sacrifice means only the choice of any other instead of any other one, the formula of ethical heteronomy turns out to be identical to the formula of political equality. "Tout autre est tout autre": this is the formula of the identity of the contraries, the formula of the identity between absolute inequality and full equality. Anyone can play the part of the "any other" that is wholly other. Thanks to the God of Abraham, anyone can play the role of the God of Abraham. As Derrida puts it in "La littérature au secret," "At that moment, but only from that moment, autonomy and heteronomy are only one thing, yes only one thing."[17]

Did we really need that detour by Mount Moriah to get to this point? It can be answered that we needed it in order to tie the practice of political equality to the sense of absolute responsibility. Indeed, too many crimes have been accomplished and legitimized in the name of the laws of history, science, or the objective necessity. The detour through Abraham—and Kierkegaard—is necessary to break with the alignment of political action with any kind of necessity and with any justification of the means by the ends. That is the ultimate sense of the detour that led us through the Levinasian unconditionality of the Other to the Sartrean unconditionality of freedom and responsibility. The argument is clear, but it might prove undecidable. As is well known, the Sartrean insistence on the unconditionality of freedom and responsibility sometimes led Sartre to find a reason—hence a theoretical justification—to some forms of communist oppression that even the communist parties and intellectuals did not care to justify. But the main question remains: What does it mean to predicate politics on the act of an absolutely free decision? If political equality has to be predicated on the absolute difference of God, and if that absolute difference has to be negotiated through crime, complicity, and betrayal, we can say that it is predicated on what Derrida wanted it to be freed of, I mean sovereignty. Sovereignty, he said, is a theological concept which has been transferred from religion to the political community. But what the sacrifice on Mount Moriah presents is another idea of sovereignty. In my view, this means that politics is still predicated on theology, even if it is on some kind of heretic theology. Would it not thus be the case that Derrida, in order to oppose an alleged dependency of politics on theology, has to make it dependent on another theology? I think that the question must be left open.

*Notes*

1 See Derrida, *Paper Machine*, 105–6, 118; *Papier Machine*, 327–28, 345.

2 Derrida, *Paper Machine*, 106; *Papier Machine*, 328. See also Derrida and Roudinesco, *De quoi demain*, 46.

3 Derrida, *Specters of Marx*, 85; *Spectres de Marx*, 141.

4 Derrida, *Paper Machine*, 125; *Papier Machine*, 354.

5 See Derrida, *Paper Machine*, 131; *Papier Machine*, 361; Derrida and Roudinesco, *De quoi demain*, 102.

6 Derrida, "Force of Law," 16.

7 Derrida, *Rogues*, 84–85; *Voyous*, 123–24.

8 Derrida, "Force of Law," 28.

9 Derrida, *Rogues*, 84; *Voyous*, 123.

10 Derrida, *Rogues*, 84; *Voyous*, 123.

11 For the development of this point, see Rancière, *Malaise dans l'esthétique*, and "Who Is the Subject of the Rights of Man?"

12 Derrida, *Rogues*, 86; *Voyous*, 126. Derrida is referring to Paulhan, "La démocratie fait appel au premier venu," 5: 277/281. This text will be included in a collection of texts of Jean Paulhan edited by Jennifer Bajorek to be published by the University of Illinois Press. I thank Jennifer Bajorek, who gave me the exact reference to Paulhan's text and provided me with a copy of the text.

13 Derrida, *Rogues*, 86; *Voyous*, 126.

14 Derrida, *Specters of Marx*, 113; *Spectres de Marx*, 185.

15 Derrida, *Specters of Marx*, 7; *Spectres de Marx*, 28.

16 Derrida, *The Gift of Death*, 68, 70; *Donner la mort*, 98.

17 Derrida, "La littérature au secret," 209. This text was added when the essay "Donner la mort" was republished as a volume. This is why it is not included in the English translation, entitled *The Gift of Death*. The translation of the quotation in the text is mine.

# PART V

---

Afterword

# Finishing, Starting

JUDITH BUTLER

The conversations continued in this text are ones that, in some instances, have been going on a long time. The event of a conference brings those interlocutors together and then stages a new venue for these exchanges. The event emerges as a way of constellating the exchange, and the papers that finally emerge are less a record of the event than a response to its various incitements. One can discern in this volume the contours of an ongoing set of contestations and controversies that remain attached to the name of "Derrida" and which, for better or worse, animate the continuing life of his work. The resultant essays importantly postdate the conference, sever a certain relation to the event, even as the event postdates the life of the man Derrida, whose writing forms the continuing preoccupation of our work. So there is a certain problem of temporality that besets this volume from the start, since there can be no recovery of the event of the conference and, in some ways, no recovery of the life of Derrida. In the absence of his life, his name and his words continue to center the discussion, and the persisting question of these essays seems to me to be less a matter of understanding the life of the author than of understanding *the life of the work*, and in particular, the animating force of his words and of language more generally. If something "survives" here that takes place under the name of Derrida, it surely does not take the form of a consensus of views. Something more active, difficult, and dynamic is at work than singing in unison.

One way of arguing about Derrida reduces quite quickly to questions of property and fidelity. Of course, certain forms of mourning (or certain failures to mourn) can become litigious, righteous, can lay claim to "what he really meant," even to "what he surely intended," and even further to "what he told me." The desire in such invocations is to reattach the work to the person and doubtless to reanimate the person who is lost, to reassert the attachment to the person after the person is gone. But are we preparing the conditions for the life of the work, which, one might say, is the only possible mode of living on for the name, if we hue to orthodoxies that brook no criticism, that fear or condemn contestation, that seek to stabilize the text and its possible permutations? Is this, perhaps, even a way of refusing to let the writings "live on" in states of relative dissemination, and to let the words become truly and finally untethered from the intentions of the author? How difficult to have been attached to the person and yet to allow the work to become detached, in every sense, from the living person. But how crucial it must be for the life of the work, for the living on of the name, to insist upon that detachment, *to detach*. The practice of dissemination, one that takes place without one's will, against one's will, afflicts every practice of author-ship: Here, take my words, do with them what you will. This will happen in any case, and in spite of the author, and so dissemination establishes the incidentality of the person of the author, one that presupposes (all along) and prefigures that greater and more final incidentality, death. "What he must have meant" and "what he told me" are both efforts to retether the text to the person who is lost, to reanimate the lost one. And since we cannot be indifferent to this loss, or to that claim of proximity that binds some to him more closely than others, how do we resist that temptation to be the one who "knows" in his place what he "would have thought and said" and to conjecture time and again his presence and his speaking? What is left is the text. What was, from the outset, always left, always surviving, were the texts.

What I am suggesting is something other than a kind of textualism. Rather, precisely in the face of death, a death that is already in place, waiting, the text assumes not only another temporality, but another life. It is not a redemption or a new life, nor is it the continuation of the person in the trace; it is, rather, the animating of the name through and by the trace. This is, in my view, what is happening in this volume. One mode of animation is the quarrel, the difficulty, the unsettled question about what is meant, could be meant, might still be meant — all of which are distinct from "what he really meant." As a result, there must be a certain forgetting, if not a certain be-trayal, in order to let the work live, even to make good on a certain promise, if such a promise has been made, to let the work live.

In this collection, one sees both disagreement and divergent trajectories, and then there are moments of uncanny echoing, the repetition of a phrase that continues to compel a certain attention. One of these is the following citation from Derrida published in 2003 that appears in at least three dif-ferent essays: "There never was in the 1980s or 1990s, as has sometimes been claimed, a political turn or ethical turn in 'deconstruction,' at least not as I experience it. The thinking of the political has always been a thinking of *différance*."[1] What interests me here is the "always" that pertains to the political and the "never was" that pertains to the nonpolitical and the nonethical. If the political is to be thought in some way, then it will not be that which suddenly emerges or toward which anyone can make a turn at a given time, a situation that presumes sequence and teleology. It must be there, already, as the condition of possibility of thinking, and so essential to the structure of what is. Its temporality will not be that which comes into being (as a result of contract or covenant) nor as that toward which an individual can turn: In what crucible, through what matrix will that "individual" have been formed? If the political is implied by, or implicit in, the thinking of différance, it is already operative, whether or not it is explicitly named as such, recognized as part of the political, that is, whether or not the political has been rethought to include this thought. Derrida refuses the language of the "turn" yet asks us to consider that what he wrote late is already implied by what he wrote earlier, which is not to say that there is a seamless continuity between the past and the present; it means only that the same problem continued to make its demand upon him, and that he did not so much turn in another direction as return to a set of thoughts that preoccupied him from the start. Or, if we put this in a way that dislocates the centrality of the subject and any possible turning and returning, we could say: the thought of the political is there in the thought of différance, and there never was a thinking of différance that was not a thought of the political.

I am aware of the risks involved in taking a term such as "différance" as a technical term, as if its meaning were settled once upon a time and has now been readied for use. The term appears time and again, or it fails to appear, which does not mean that the thought that the term names is not operating in another way. My suggestion is that the "we" is centrally riven by this term, one that does not, as a consequence, produce a plural or internally heterogeneous subject. Something more and different is at stake. We can explain the term philosophically — which would mean making clear its difference from philosophical concepts more generally — or we can try to trace its operations in another way. There are the claims that Derrida makes about it; there are the different ways it appears or fails to appear in his text; there is a certain discord that emerges over the interpretation of the text and, more specifically, over the fundamental terms that we think must anchor the domain of the political. There is discord within the pages of this text on the question of whether and how to rethink the "we" of politics, and some strong claims are made. Let me suggest from the start that Derrida will mobilize certain kinds of discourse that impinge upon him, including liberalism and theology, and that this is different from "holding to the view that this or that discourse is correct." We have to ask how they are used, and for what rhetorical purpose, and it seems that we have to ask further: How do they fit in the wider constellation of his writing, especially the key concepts that have recurred throughout his oeuvre?

The arguments included here that are made in his name, or in his spirit, or, indeed, in his wake, may or may not be "Derridean" arguments per se. But they are, it seems, arguments that cannot take place without him and which, in this way, animate the life of the work, even if there is — or precisely by virtue of — a certain indifference to the person of the author, real or imaginary, although certainly *not* an indifference to the words.

Some argue that Derrida remains attached to a liberal individualism defined by personal choice; others claim that he resists modes of collectivization that are essential to democracy, such as equality, that apparently require the substitutability of one person by another. Some argue that he adheres to notions of sovereignty that are impossible; others claim that impossibility is a constitutive feature of the kind of sovereignty he describes. Others focus on exile, Algeria, on never having had a mother tongue, certainly not French. And yet others suggest that every invocation of the "we" is haunted by populations who are excluded or spectralized, especially in the case of French Algeria, where the question arises whether the "Muslim" is exterior to democracy. Some argue that freedom must be defended against every sacred dictate; others suggest that whatever future there is for freedom will be one that is thought, at least partially, through a religious lexicon. Some of these arguments are "about Derrida," but more often they are arguments that take hold on the occasion of reading Derrida during a time in which we are all arguing about sovereignty, secularism, democracy, and the future. What is perhaps less obvious is the way that notions introduced earlier in Derrida's career continue to circulate in and through these pressing, contemporary discourses: the gift, sovereignty, democracy, pardon, the archive, writing, monolingualism, to name a few. I would add: iterability. Can any of these notions be thought without différance, and if they are thought "as" différance, how are they rethought?

It should be clear that I do not seek to settle these questions, and that I do not think they should be easily settled. Derrida has unsettled something, left us a host of questions to try to settle, and this constitutes a certain inheritance, even a gift. The questions that are left for us sometimes take a less than useful form: "Can Derrida be political?" "Are there political uses of Derrida?" "Is there a distinctively Derridean political theory?" All of these questions presume to know in advance what the sphere of the political is, its proper predicates, and so they have not paused to consider how the political is circumscribed, and at what cost. They suffer as well from a certain impatience, perhaps even an unwillingness to read and, perhaps, an unwillingness to read Derrida. If politics requires, minimally, a problem of living together, of a form that is given to living together or, indeed, a form that those who live together give to themselves, we can see that we are already confronted with a set of questions: the "we" who is included by virtue of the form; the "we" who is able, with or without authorization, to give form to itself; the name for the "act" which authorizes such a form, whether it is the act of a subject, singular or plural, or is a form of self-constitution that is precisely not the act of a subject at all. Even "living together" cannot be easily imagined, since there are polities that are internally divided not only by walls but by revolutionary outcomes or brutal apartheid separations, so we cannot impute any easy topology to this claim. The "we" may not be bounded by borders and may well designate postnational forms of belonging. But even when borders are more or less firm, the "we" is clearly riven by its own self-difference, understood as a condition of its own possibility. It is constituted as well through those variable forms of delimitation that establish criteria of inclusion and exclusion. These produce the citizen, the noncitizen, the refugee, and they form the immigration *dispositif* within which legal personhood is variably distributed, qualified, and denied. The "we" begins in a certain coming together, one that requires an address, and so a scene of interlocution. It also means that the "we" is not unified from the start, but is constituted through a difference that ceaselessly differentiates those it binds. How does this differentiation condition and unsettle the formation of the "we"?

At stake is a shift from modes of thinking the "we" that lay claim to a nondifferentiated totality or, indeed, to the "we" as a contingent collection of radically particular individuals. We can falter precisely here in trying to think through this problem of the doubly differentiated "we." We can (and I invoke the "we" precisely on this occasion in which there is no agreement) worry that in refusing certain forms of collectivization, Derrida reverts to the radical particularism of individualism. Or we can claim that his apparent commitment to a Levinasian ethic, in which the "singularity" of the other seems primary, precludes the thought of those modes of collectivity, including notions of equality, that demand substitutability. But perhaps we must take on the demands of a polyvocal language and understand those textual and political occasions in which one set of discourses emerges without evincing the clear trace of another. I want to suggest that it is within the scene of politics that the ethical relation emerges, and that we cannot think the "we" of the political without that turn. It is not a turn that Derrida makes, strictly speaking, but a turn that is internal to the political, precisely in response to the demand to rethink the relevant collectivities of politics.

Of course, one concern that has been raised about the putative "ethical turn" is that it substitutes a dyadic relation for a political one; the former seems to presuppose a subject who must consider his or her relations to alterity generally, and its relations to others specifically; the latter, conceived democratically, seems to presuppose the "we" who constitutes a certain polity for itself. So under the rubric of "ethics" we are to understand the gift, hospitality, responsibility, and the pardon, to name a few central concerns of Derrida's later work. And under the sphere of politics, we are to understand sovereignty, law, force, and democracy. But are these actually separable in this way? Or are they separated only on the condition that we fail to rethink the "we" as a further thought of différance? Of course, to use the term is not yet to accomplish the thought (if the thought can be accomplished), but it does begin a line of questioning. And the first step along such a path would surely be to ask whether we can think a certain difference within or of the "we" that is not simple pluralistic heterogeneity (the "we" is composed of different parts) or intersectionality (the "we" is the site where different valences of power converge and diverge). Nor could it be the case that the "we" is in some absolute and definitive way established over and against a "they" in the way that contemporary Schmittians continue the reactionary romance with stark binarisms. If not heterogeneity and not pluralism, not intersectionality and not stark binary (and absolute) difference, then how do we begin again the thought of the "we"? This thought is one that has to begin again, is always beginning again, and this is surely part of its temporality, the temporality without which we cannot begin the thought. But let me here acknowledge some of what these various readings teach us, namely, that France is haunted by an Algeria that was and was not France; that the Jew is haunted by the Arab, who sometimes is the Arab Jew; that the sovereign, however forcefully defined, lacks the force that its definition would confer; that the "subject" presupposed as sovereign is always constituted in a heterogeneity that limits, if not undoes, its more radical claims to self-constitution.

As a result, the "we" is never a subject as such and even, I would suggest, displaces the subject as the certain ground of democratic self-constitution. The one who is empowered to constitute himself or herself is empowered from elsewhere, and never fully by virtue of his or her own autarchic operation or internal impetus. The thought of this self-propelling impetus is doubtless part of the fantasy of the sovereign that haunts the political theory of the sovereign, but it fails to explain that every self-constituting subject is, at the same time, constituted; that no self-constitution can take place without this prior constitution; and that no self-constitution can ever fully overcome that prior and continuing constitution. We would have to rethink activity and passivity and consider both in their simultaneous operation to see how the more phantasmatic claims of sovereignty blind us to its actual operations (indeed serve as a blinder to the theorization of sovereignty itself). We can hold out for an upsurge of sovereignty that is radically unconditioned, but that would be precisely to wish for that more radical idea of self-constitution that would be unbound from all enabling social and historical conditions of possibility. What politics could come from this, the one that idealizes a "break" and believes, contra Hegel, that a "break" is never conditioned by that from which it breaks? Could we even have a notion of "critique" at all if we were to hold to this romantic revolutionary ideal? Could we even start a revolution, if we wanted to, on such terms?

The "we" may not exist prior to the exercise through which it performs a certain self-constitution. But any such exercise will never take place ex nihilo, if for no other reason than that it takes place in language. The différance that rifts the "we" and proves its impossibility as a unity without difference is at once the différance by which the "we" is constituted, its very condition of possibility, and there is no way around this double bind. Further, the preliminary address by which a social bond is made — that is, the promise, understood as the precondition for entering into a covenant — always comes from somewhere, has its location, and does not emerge in the abstract or, indeed, in a state of nature. And the expression of freedom is invariably determinate, at which point the idea of freedom as radically undetermined is undone in the moment of its "realization." So however we might return to the original scenes of political liberalism — contract, covenant, personal liberty, or broader conceptions of political freedom — we will have to situate such notions within that structure of language in which the conditions of possibility for their exercise are, at the same time, the conditions of their impossibility — or final unrealizability. Whatever "we" is constituted through an exercise of self-declaration or self-institutionalization will be at once un-done by its own exercise, and there seems to be no way around this paradox. It is not, however, a contradiction that leads to the defeat of freedom. On the contrary, the paradox implies only that a set of constraints is essential to the rethinking of freedom. Even if freedom contains within it the thought of the unconditional, it will never *realize* that thought through historical means without becoming conditional and compromising its definition. It may well be that this "compromise" is precisely the invariable situation of freedom. And if freedom purports to come from nowhere, it can do so only by disavowing the sites from which it does emerge, only to have those sites reemerge as the haunted grounds of its own possibility. Specters, ghosts, traces—we are never quite free of them, and we cannot think freedom with-out them.

It seems true that Derrida, writing post-1968, feared certain coercive notions of collectivity, obligatory forms of political sociality that permit no dissent or that assume social unities that are falsifying, if not violent, in their insistence. If the putative ethical turn has any political meaning for this time, it surely has to do with trying to think through what noncoercive forms of solidarity might be. The point of politics is not to assemble a "we" who can speak or, indeed, sing in unison, a "we" who knows or expresses itself as a unified nation or, indeed, as the human as such. The idea of a common norm that would define us as human and differentiate us from animals he opposed as an instrument that afflicted cruelty on animals, including human animals. The question of politics resides instead in the encounter with what troubles the norm of sameness. It is a question that seems to be presumed by contem-porary models of multiculturalism but rarely ever probed: What encounter is possible with those with whom I do not immediately share a world, a com-mon set of norms, with whom I share, rather, a globe or, indeed, a planet, and the event of encounter itself? How do any of us forge a "we" in the context of countervailing moral and historical schemes? The "we" cannot be taken for granted. The "we" cannot be unilaterally produced through perfor-mative fiat. It does not include only those who are already recognized as citizens, and so there is no legal rule we might follow—or want to follow—to decide the question of who may speak as the "we." If those who "live together" are precisely those who are divided by legal status and entitlement (Arab/Jew, Algerian/French, to name two mentioned in this volume), then the question of hospitality is not only central to the question of how to conceive the "we" but implies more radically that the "I" and the "you" and the "we" and the "them" are constitutive of the field of the "we," which, in turn, calls to be thought as a heterogeneity irreducible to pluralism, neither fully "inside" nor fully "outside" the polity as such. To think the "we" — that crux of politics — is precisely to realize that it references a host of other pronominal problems, the "I" and the "you" among them. For if the "we" is constituted through its exercise (one performative dimension of democracy), then it is formed or, rather, forms itself only on the condition of a negotiation with alterity. No collectivity comes into being by suddenly exercising a speech act in common; rather, a covenant is presupposed by the act of address, a promise is implicitly made in the act of addressing another truthfully. The social bond has to be made good, and the promise is the means through which that happens time and again, articulating a temporal future for that bond.

The idea that the social bond is wrought through the means of address makes the "ethical" problematic central to the very possibility of politics. How are we, for instance, addressed by the dead? What obligations do we owe them? When the dead include those who die in unjust wars and from brutal means, performed in our name, how should we respond to that address from those who can no longer speak but who form part of who "we" are? What form does mourning take for those we do not know and who constitute a nameless, incorporated part of the "we," those who are as completely unmarked as they are fully human? What call can we hear from the animal? What form does pardon take for crimes that are unpardonable, and who is authorized to make that judgment and issue that declaration? Under what political conditions does the demand for pardon emerge, and is the demand ever fully thinkable outside the site of its enunciation? Is it an extrajudicial moment, or one that belongs to an order of law that allies with the ethical? Do politics and ethics become confounded in the act of the pardon?

How is it that every "we" is negotiated through a set of exchanges that requires that the "I" rethink itself on the basis of the "you," without whom it could not exist socially? And to what extent does the "we" form itself through an exclusion that casts a population outside its jurisdiction?

If sovereignty is understood to be the political form that the will of the people takes, then we are faced with having to rethink plurality in order to understand the "representative" function that the sovereign performs. If the "we" fails to be constituted finally or definitively through any such performative exercise (and is, in this sense, "impossible"), this suggests an internal limit to any and all sovereign claims (a limit without which sovereignty remains unthinkable). Moreover, it suggests that politics cannot be thought outside the problem of the time of action, one that is secured by a form that realizes, without ever fully realizing, freedom. This would involve a critique of those versions of teleology that assert a final end to history. We are then left with a "we" that achieves its unity only at the expense of its own internal complexity and through the effacement of its exclusions. We are left with problematics that are central to political thinking in this time: How do we find a representative political form for a heterogeneity that is irreducible to pluralism? In other words, how do we think politics in ways that are not preemptively constrained either by national border or teleological history?

Our time, which, of course, is not one time, is a time in which several forms of temporality converge or, indeed, prove incompatible, and in which political struggles emerge concerning how time is to be understood. Spurious claims are made about Islam never having achieved "modernity," and as a consequence it becomes more difficult to refer to a "progressive" sense of history.[2] We are left to find other ways of conceptualizing "moving forward." The very act of "self-constitution" that is central to the thinking of democracy presupposes a beginning, an action that takes place in time, that takes time, and a set of effects that follow from that performative exercise. The effects are not always known in advance, cannot be known in advance, if the exercise of self-constitution is freely performed. That freedom pertains less to the particular kind of will that is deployed than to the opening up of the space of the political itself. And this seems to follow from an activity of self-constitution that is renewable, iterable, and open-ended. The "open end" can be understood as a certain kind of teleology, but it would be decidedly post-Aristotelian in that case. Perhaps teleology undergoes a certain catachresis in the course of becoming the "open end" of democratic politics.

Whatever "democracy to come" might mean, it returns us to the problematic of différance as deferral. It would be a mistake, however, to understand the "to-come" as the simple affirmation of the unrealizability of certain democratic ideals or simply as the indefinite postponement of any and all realizations. The point is not simply to hold out for a future that will never come and avoid all interventions in the present. If the "to-come" seems to be outside of politics, it is a "constitutive outside," one without which politics itself could never have gotten off the ground. In this sense, the "democracy to come" is a presupposition of any existing democracy, and we err if we think that it belongs only to a future that is somehow dissociated from the past and present. The reverse would seem to be the case: the democracy "to come" is presupposed by any historical effort to find and establish democratic regimes, to use the name to describe and evaluate their working, and so it operates as part of the very act by which any and all democracies are delimited. And though it is always a struggle, a task, a difficulty to know how to move between a concept such as justice, which is not yet realized and which remains, to some extent, unrealizable, and the "ordinary" situations of political life, it is precisely the imperative of "intervention" to traverse that divide without set prescriptions and without established forms of mediation on hand.

This vexed question of what is "to come" raises the status of the messianic in Derrida's work, and some worry that he finally grounds his politics in a theology, while others suggest that religion has always informed ways of thinking about temporality on the Left. Still others maintain that a democratic politics has to remain distinct from any and all religion claims. Of course, claiming that our ideas of eschatology and teleology, including those that have informed Marxist and post-Marxist thought, are informed by religious notions of temporality is not the same as claiming that politics should be based on religious claims. In this case, however, it is probably important to consider that, for Derrida, the messianic is something that introduces another temporal trajectory into an established historiographical scheme; in other words, it introduces a different notion of the "future" than any which is already encoded within the historical present. The future of the future is a significant redoubling in this sense: Can there be a future that is not already imagined and anticipated by us, that breaks the mold currently containing and preempting the "future"? Can we introduce new forms of imagining and anticipating that are not constrained by the teleologies that inform the progress of capitalism or certain versions of historical determinism? If such historical schemes are exhausted, what, if anything, comes next? Textually, the question of what is "to come" introduces the situation of uncertainty that characterizes revolutionary situations, the multiple possible outcomes, as Balibar suggests, and a certain unknowingness concerning what comes next, and how. On the one hand, we can say that religion (actually, a very specific reading of the messianic) conditions this future; on the other hand, we can say that religion has become, in this instance, only another way of marking a future that exceeds what any and all religions have predicted or anticipated about what the future will hold. Either way, we are surely not in danger of dissolving politics into religion or finding in religion the final justification for politics.

Importantly, the idea of the "to-come" does not pertain only to the future, but to an entire rethinking of the problem of time. Derrida writes in "Faith and Knowledge" a set of notes that are meant to lead to an axiomatic formulation: "Of a discourse to come — on the to-come and repetition. Axiom: No to-come without heritage and the possibility of *repeating*. No to-come without some sort of *iterability*."[3] He cautions us against understanding the promise of the messianic, for instance, as a simple "return to religion." And he argues forcefully for a distinction between *messianism* and *messianicity*, in which the latter is understood to be "more originary" and "older than all religion." What is older than all religion is "the general structure of experience itself" and, specifically, "the act of faith or . . . the appeal to faith that inhabits every act of language and every address to the other." Implicit in every address is a certain trust, the possibility of forging a social bond, but also an implicit ideal of justice. Faith is, in these terms, opposed to dogma, but also to any particular institutionalization of religion: "It follows no determinate revelation, it belongs properly to no Abrahamic religion."[4] What Derrida means by entering into a covenant can be understood only through a general structure of experience that requires an address to another and an implicit or explicit promise that is made in the act of such an address. Further, the address has its own historicity, and this is what is meant by the *iterability* of the promise. The promise must repeat, even mechanically, in order to hold firm as a bond of any kind. The social is being theorized again, but this time through the speech act as a kind of gift, one that is enacted or, rather, given time and again. The bond must be temporally renewable to qualify as a bond at all.

How does faith enter here, and what can it possibly mean? A promise is made, but on what basis? Is there any ground for making the promise, or does the promise emerge precisely without ground, as an act of "faith" in this restricted sense? This seems to be what Derrida referred to as the "mystical foundations of law"[5] in his initial reading of Benjamin's *Critique of Violence*. And it constitutes, in the later work, a clear refinement and elaboration of the speech act that became, as it were, the signature of his theory with the publication of "Signature, Event, Context" in 1977. For this "faith" to be operative, it must be repeated (no promise can remain a promise without iterability). Moreover, there can be no promise that does not open up a future in which that promise will be kept. We know this already from Nietzsche's *On the Genealogy of Morals*, in which the "promise" opens up a future for the human animal. For Derrida, the promise, when given, becomes part of the structure of a covenant, and this social bond has no structural or necessary existence outside the memory that is reinvoked and the future that is opened up through its iteration; in other words, an open-ended temporality must be established (and reestablished) in order for the promise to exist at all. The promise, understood as covenant and gift, as social bond, is precisely a realization of what is unrealizable without destroying that unrealizability. Earlier I raised the question of what form could be given to freedom that would sustain freedom in its unrealizability. The promise is that specific speech act without which there is no social covenant and no social bond, and though it must take place in space and time, it also establishes space and time in new ways that make for the possibility of politics itself.

We might be tempted to conclude that difference carries a specific meaning as iterability, and that there is no politics without the performative and no performative that is not in some way bound up with an act of faith, of promising, and a covenant. But it is important to understand that the promise is bound up with the sense of "to come"; the future that is opened by the promise is not precisely "induced" by the promise. By definition, the future cannot be expected, which does not mean that we should throw all caution to the wind. What exceeds anticipation, what troubles the conceptual limits of expectation, is precisely the future. If a promise were fully realized it would vanquish the future, but if it is the kind of promise that must continue to be honored, then its viability depends fundamentally on its unrealizability. The man who waits for admission at the open gates in Kafka's famous parable "Before the Law" will not finally be greeted by any Messiah or any message that will explicitly bid him entry. This is a situation in which such finalities never arrive. If the future is "to come" it is precisely a future that will never arrive, and this distinguishes the messianic (or messianicity) essentially from messianism. It also helps us understand why the "to-come" does not substitute for social relations or for politics itself. The "to-come" is inaugurated by the fact of linguistic address, and this way of offering the future is essential to the renewability and, hence, the very possibility of a social bond. It is also why the "to-come" is part of a general structure of experience, of a linguistic offering without which there can be no sociality bound by promissory relations. This is the foundation not merely of law, but of politics, one that requires that the gift of speech makes possible the emergence and sustainability of the "we." There is a speaking to another that precedes and makes possible any sovereign act in which the "I" comes to represent the "we." The relation to the other, understood as the articulation of the ethical itself, thus makes possible that social bond that inaugurates, time and again, the political. Finally, we can see that the social bond at issue here requires a certain reconceptualization of time. Over and against the idea that the "to-come" evacuates the present of politics, and, indeed, its past, we might consider instead that the "to-come" is a way of rethinking the conditions of possibility for politics itself.

Perhaps to understand this problem of what it is to come and not to arrive we would be well advised to return to Kafka, whose invocations of the messianic clearly informed both Derrida and Benjamin (however divergent their views became). In his wonderfully ironic parable "The Coming of the Messiah" Kafka writes, "The Messiah will come [*kommen*] only when he is no longer necessary; he will come only on the day after his arrival [*Ankunft*]; he will come, not on the last day [*am letzten Tag*], but on the very last [*am allerletzten*]."6 Which Messiah could this be? He will be no longer needed (*nötig*), and his "coming" is clearly not the same as his "arrival" (in German, the latter, *Ankunft*, is a past participle of the former, *kommen*, though the preposition "an" suggests that there must be a place for a certain coming to land). We think of arriving as the endpoint of coming, but in this parable, we are asked to think the reverse: How can the Messiah arrive and *then* come? What difference are we asked to note between these two terms? His coming will land at no place, will not arrive, or rather it will be the kind of coming that comes after our concept of arrival. Does this mean that in whatever sense he comes, he does not arrive? And if he does not come on the last day, but on the very last, do we have any conceptual resources by which to think this difference? If the last belongs to a sequence, and the "very last" is different from the last, then perhaps the very last is the day that belongs to no sequence, that defies chronology itself. If we cannot rely on usual notions of sequence to understand the difference between *coming* and *arriving* or between the *last day* and the *very last*, then it seems that the Messiah is that which produces a certain upheaval in our usual modes of conceptualizing the possible time and meaning of an arrival. To come after arriving is to introduce an idea of "coming" that cannot be realized, since the realization would be arrival itself. Hence, we will not be able to say, probably never be able to say within the usual sequential schemes when and whether this Messiah *has come*, and this means that there will, finally, be no coming that we can mark as past; moreover, there will be no coming that will be "necessary" for us, that will prove useful, that we will require. Thus, something gratuitous is in the offing, if anything is. So if this idea of "coming" is a useless one, it seems to follow that a certain noninstrumental and equivocal future is opened up by this invocation of the Messiah. The Messiah seems to be the subject of or for a future speculation and so not someone or some event that *will have arrived*, not some person or event about which it will be possible to say that *an arrival has taken place*. The invocation of the Messiah seems to take place when the thought of progressive redemption in and through history is no longer possible, which means that one major way that religion has structured historical thinking has found its point of exhaustion. This Messiah will be, in that sense, postreligious, a figure for thinking about the event when established modes of thinking history have reached their limit. In other words, the Messiah is not a figure at all, and certainly not a person or an event, but precisely the resistance to realizability in either form, the resistance to realizability as such.

One could end there, but it would be to supply, I think, a false sense of an ending. The unrealizable is not just the permanent "to-come" that will never assume the form of a person or event. The unrealizable is also the condition of possibility (what Derrida might call the "impossible condition of possibility") for events and for persons, and in this sense what is "to come" is already there, even always, as the condition of possibility for what exists. If, with regard to politics, we were to restrict ourselves to what has been realized or what is currently conceived as realizable, we would ratify the status quo, offer legitimacy to forms of social and legal positivism, and undermine the critical capacity to differentiate what is from what might have been or is yet to be. The "we" that is never singular, that is constituted through a performative exercise, and whose heterogeneity is irreducible is precisely that mode of belonging that, from the start, supplied the "future" without which there can be no self-constitution. The future (in the sense of the "to come") is thus the presupposition and prerequisite of collective self-making. This is the principle of its final nondeterminability and unrealizability and so the condition of the open-ended self-making of the "we," even the insuperability of *différance* itself. This means that what is to come is there from the start, as the start, without which there could be no starting of what we call the political.

## Notes

1 Derrida, *Rogues*, 39.

2 See, for example, Thomas Friedman, "Foreign Affairs: The Real War," *New York Times*, November 27, 2001, Opinion Page, A19.

3  Derrida, "Faith and Knowledge: The Two Sources of 'Religion' at the Limits of Reason Alone," 83.

4  Ibid., 56.

5  Derrida, "Force of the Law: The 'Mystical Foundation of Authority.'"

6  Kafka, *Parables and Paradoxes*, 81.

# Bibliography

Addi, Lahouari, *L'Algérie et la démocratie*. Paris: La Découverte, 1994.

Agamben, Giorgio. *Homo Sacer: Sovereign Power and Bare Life*. Trans. Daniel Heller-Roazen. Stanford: Stanford University Press, 1998.

———. *Remnants of Auschwitz: The Witness and the Archive*. Trans. Daniel Heller-Roazen. New York: Zone Books, 2000.

———. *State of Exception*. Trans. Kevin Attell. Chicago: University of Chicago Press, 2005.

Alfarabi. *Alfarabi, The Political Writings: Selected Aphorisms and Other Texts*. Trans. Charles Butterworth. Ithaca, N.Y.: Cornell University Press, 2001.

Althusser, Louis. *Écrits philosophiques et politiques*. Vol. 1. Paris: Stock/Institut Mémoires de l'Edition Contemporaine, 1994.

———. *Lire le Capital*. Paris: Presses universitaires de France, 1996.

———. *The Specter of Hegel*. Trans. Geoff Goshgarian. London: Verso, 1997.

Amichai, Yehuda. "The Real Hero." In *The Selected Poetry of Yehuda Amichai*. Trans. Chana Bloch and Stephen Mitchell. Berkeley: University of California Press, 1996.

Amin, Samir. *Spectres of Capitalism: A Critique of Current Intellectual Fashions*. New York: Monthly Review Press, 1998.

Anidjar, Gil. *The Jew, the Arab: A History of the Enemy*. Stanford: Stanford University Press, 2003.

———. "Once More, Once More: Derrida, the Arab, the Jew." Introduction to *Acts of Religion*, by Jacques Derrida. Ed. Gil Anidjar. New York: Routledge, 2002.

Antelme, Robert. *L'Espèce Humaine*. Paris: Gallimard, 1957.

———. *The Human Race*. Trans. Jeffrey Haight and Annie Mawler. Marlboro, Vt.: Marlboro Press, 1998.

Arendt, Hannah. *The Human Condition*. Chicago: University of Chicago Press, 1958.

———. *Lectures on Kant's Political Philosophy*. Ed. Ronald Beiner. Chicago: University of Chicago Press, 1982.

———. "Lying in Politics." In *Crises of the Republic*. New York: Harcourt Brace Jovanovich, 1972.

———. *On Revolution*. New York: Viking Press, 1965.

———. "On Violence." In *Crises of the Republic*. New York: Harcourt Brace Jovanovich, 1972.

———. *The Portable Hannah Arendt*. Ed. Peter Baehr. New York: Penguin Books, 2000.

———. "Truth in Politics." In *The Portable Hannah Arendt*, ed. Peter Baehr. New York: Penguin Books, 2000.

Balibar, Étienne. *We, the People of Europe? Reflections on Transnational Citizenship*. Princeton, N.J.: Princeton University Press, 2004.

Barnes, J. A. *A Pack of Lies: Towards a Sociology of Lying*. Cambridge, England: Cambridge University Press, 1994.

Bataille, Georges. "L'expérience intérieure." Vol. 5 of *Oeuvres complètes*. 12 vols. Ed. Denis Hollier. Paris: Gallimard, 1970–88.

Beardsworth, Richard. *Derrida and the Political*. London: Routledge, 1996.

———. "In Memoriam Jacques Derrida: The Power of Reason." *Theory and Event* 8, no. 1 (2005).

Bennington, Geoffrey. "Demo." In *The Politics of Deconstruction*, ed. M. McQuillan. London: Pluto Press, 2007.

———. "La démocritie à venir." In *La démocratie à venir: Autour de Jacques Derrida*, ed. M-L. Mallet. Paris: Galilée, 2004.

———. *Dudding: Des noms de Rousseau*. Paris: Galilée, 1991.

———. "The Fall of Sovereignty." *Epochè* 10, no. 2 (2006): 395–406.

———. "For Better and Worse (There Again . . . )." Paper presented at the conference "Who or What? Jacques Derrida," Gainesville, Fla., 2006.

———. *Frontières kantiennes*. Paris: Galilée, 2000.

———. *Frontiers: Kant, Hegel, Frege, Wittgenstein*. ebook, 2003, www.bennington .zsoft.co.uk.

———. *Interrupting Derrida*. London: Routledge, 2000.

———. "Lecture: De Georges Bataille." In *Georges Bataille après tout*, ed. D. Hollier. Paris: Belin, 1995. Reprinted in *Open Book/Livre ouvert*, by G. Bennington. 2005, www.bennington.zsoft.co.uk.

———. *Legislations: The Politics of Deconstruction*. London: Verso, 1994.

———. "The Matter with Democracy." Unfinished manuscript.

———. *Sententiousness and the Novel: Laying Down the Law in Eighteenth-Century French Fiction*. Cambridge, England: Cambridge University Press, 1985. 2nd ed., www.bennington.zsoft.co.uk.

———. "La souveraineté défaillante." In *Derrida à Coimbra/Derrida em Coimbra*, ed. F. Bernado. Viseu, Portugal: Palimage Editores, 2005.

———. "Superanus." *Theory and Event* 8, no. 1 (2005). Online at http://muse.jhu .edu/journals/theory_and_event/v008/8.1bennington.html.

Bennington, Geoffrey, and Jacques Derrida. *Jacques Derrida*. Paris: Seuil, 1991.

Bennington, Geoffrey, and Jacques Derrida. *Jacques Derrida*. Trans. Geoffrey Bennington. Chicago: University of Chicago Press, 1993.

Benslama, Fethi. "Identity as a Cause." *Research in African Literatures* 30, no. 3 (1999): 36–50.

———, ed. *Idiomes, Nationalités, Déconstructions: Rencontre de Rabat avec Jacques*

*Derrida*. Cahiers Intersignes, no. 13. Paris and Casablanca: Editions Toubkal, 1998.

Benton, Robert J. "Political Expediency and Lying: Kant vs. Benjamin Constant." *Journal of the History of Ideas* 43, no. 1 (1982): 135–144.

Bergson, Henri. *Les Données immédiates de la conscience*. Paris: Presses universitaires de France, 1997.

———. *Matter and Memory*. Trans. N. M. Paul and W. S. Palmer. New York: Zone Books, 1988.

———. *Time and Free Will: An Essay on the Immediate Data of Consciousness*. Trans. F. L. Pogson. New York: Dover, 2001.

Blanchot, Maurice. *L'Amitié*. Paris: Gallimard, 1971.

———. *Celui qui ne m'accompagnait pas*. Paris: Gallimard, 1953.

———. *La Communauté Inavouable*. Paris: Minuit, 1983.

———. "Les trois paroles de Marx." In *L'Amitié*. Paris: Gallimard, 1971.

Branche, Raphaelle. *La guerre d'Algérie: Une histoire apaiseé?* Paris: Seuil, 2005.

Butler, Judith. *Gender Trouble: Feminism and the Subversion of Identity*. New York: Routledge, 1991.

Campbell, Jeremy. *The Liar's Tale: A History of Falsehood*. New York: Norton, 2001.

Cheah, Pheng. "Postnational Light." In *Inhuman Conditions: Cosmopolitanism and Human Rights in the Current Global Conjuncture*. Cambridge, Mass.: Harvard University Press, 2006.

———. *Spectral Nationality: Passages of Freedom from Kant to Postcolonial Literatures of Liberation*. New York: Columbia University Press, 2003.

Cixous, Hélène. *Portrait de Derrida en jeune saint juif*. Paris: Galilée, 2001.

Combe, Sonia. *Archives interdites (Les peurs françaises: Face à l'histoire contemporaine)*. Paris: Albin Michel, 1994.

Connolly, William. *Pluralism*. Durham, N.C.: Duke University Press, 2005.

Corlett, William. *Community without Unity: A Politics of Derridean Extravagance*. Durham, N.C.: Duke University Press, 1989.

Cornell, Drucilla. *Beyond Accommodation: Ethical Feminism, Deconstruction and the Law*. New York: Routledge, 1991.

———. *The Philosophy of the Limit*. New York: Routledge, 1992.

Critchley, Simon. *The Ethics of Deconstruction: Derrida and Levinas*. 2nd ed. West Lafayette, Ind.: Purdue University Press, 1999.

*D'ailleurs, Derrida*. Dir. Safaa Fathy. Arte-Gloria, 1999. Released in English as *Derrida's Elsewhere*, 1999.

Darwish, Mahmoud. "Identity Card." 1964. www.ipoet.com.

Derderian, Richard. "Algeria as a Lieu de mémoire: Ethnic Minority Memory and National Identity in Contemporary France." *Radical History Review* 83 (Spring 2002): 28–43.

Derrida, Jacques. *Acts of Religion*. Trans. M. Ron, S. Weber, M. Quaintance, and others. Ed. Gil Anidjar. New York: Routledge, 2002.

——. *Adieu à Emmanuel Lévinas*. Paris: Galilée, 1997.

——. *Adieu to Emmnuel Levinas*. Trans. P.-A. Brault and M. Naas. Stanford: Stanford University Press, 1999.

——. "L'Admiration de Nelson Mandela." In *Pour Nelson Mandela*, ed. Jacques Derrida. Paris: Gallimard, 1986.

——. "The Age of Hegel." In *Who's Afraid of Philosophy? Right to Philosophy I*. Trans. Jan Plug. Stanford: Stanford University Press, 2002.

——. "And Say the Animal Responded?" In *Zoontologies: The Question of the Animal*, ed. Cary Wolfe. Minneapolis: University of Minnesota Press, 2003.

——. *Aporias: Dying-Awaiting (One Another at) "the Limits of Truth."* Trans. Thomas Dutoit. Stanford: Stanford University Press, 1993.

——. *Archive Fever: A Freudian Impression*. Trans. Eric Prenowitz. Chicago: University of Chicago Press, 1996.

——. "As If It Were Possible, 'Within Such Limits.'" In *Paper Machine*. Trans. Rachel Bowlby. Stanford: Stanford University Press, 2005.

——. "Autoimmunity: Real and Symbolic Suicides: A Dialogue with Jacques Derrida." In *Philosophy in a Time of Terror: Dialogues with Jürgen Habermas and Jacques Derrida*, ed. Giovanna Borradori. Chicago: University of Chicago Press, 2003.

——. "Autrui est secret parce qu'il est autrui." Interview. *Le Monde de l'Education* 284 (September 2004), www.lemonde.fr.

——. "La bête et le souverain." In *La démocratie à venir: Autour de Jacques Derrida*, ed. M-L. Mallet. Paris: Galilée, 2004.

——. "Circumfession." In Geoffrey Bennington and Jacques Derrida, *Jacques Derrida*. Trans. Geoffrey Bennington. Chicago: University of Chicago Press, 1993.

——. "Différance." In *Margins of Philosophy*. Trans. Alan Bass. Chicago: University of Chicago Press, 1982.

——. *La Dissémination*. Paris: Seuil, 1972.

——. *Dissemination*. Trans. B. Johnson. Chicago: University of Chicago Press, 1981.

——. *Donner la mort*. Paris: Galilée, 1999.

——. "D'un ton apocalyptique adopté naguère en philosophie." In *Les fins de l'homme: À partir du travail de Jacques Derrida*, ed. Philippe Lacoue-Labarthe and Jean-Luc Nancy. Paris: Galilée, 1981.

——. *L'écriture et la différence*. Paris: Seuil, 1967.

——. "The Ends of Man." In *Margins of Philosophy*. Trans. Alan Bass. Chicago: University of Chicago Press, 1982.

——. "Enlightenment Past and to Come." *Le Monde Diplomatique*, English ed., November 2004. http://mondediplo.com/2004/11/06derrida.

——. "Entretien avec Jacques Derrida." Interview. *Digraphe* 42 (December 1987): 14–27.

——. *Etats d'âme de la psychanalyse*. Paris: Galilée, 2000.

——. "Une Europe de l'espoir." *Le Monde diplomatique*, November 2004, 3, www .monde-diplomatique.fr.

——. "Faith and Knowledge." Trans. Samuel Weber. In *Acts of Religion*. Trans. M. Ron, S. Weber, M. Quaintance, and others. Ed. Gil Anidjar. New York: Routledge, 2002.

——. "Faith and Knowledge: The Two Sources of 'Religion' at the Limits of Reason Alone." In *Religion*, ed. Jacques Derrida and Gianni Vattimo. Stanford: Stanford University Press, 1998.

——. "Les fins de l'homme." In *Marges de la philosophie*. Paris: Minuit, 1972.

——. "Foi et savoir: Les deux sources de la 'religion' aux limites de la simple raison." In *La Religion*, ed. Jacques Derrida and Gianni Vattimo. Paris: Seuil, 1996.

——. *Foi et savoir: Les deux sources de la "religion" aux limites de la simple raison.* Paris: Seuil, 2000.

——. *Force de loi: Le "Fondement mystique de l'autorite."* Paris: Galilée, 1994.

——. "Force of Law: The 'Mystical Foundation of Authority.'" In *Deconstruction and the Possibility of Justice*, ed. Drucilla Cornell, Michel Rosenfeld, and David Gray Carlson. New York: Routledge, 1992.

——. "Freud and the Scene of Writing." In *Writing and Difference*. Trans. Alan Bass. Chicago: University of Chicago Press, 1978.

——. *The Gift of Death*. Trans. D. Wills. Chicago: University of Chicago Press, 1995.

——. *Given Time — I. Counterfeit Money*. Trans. Peggy Kamuf. Chicago: University of Chicago Press, 1992.

——. *Glas*. Paris: Galilée, 1974.

——. *Glas*. Trans. J. P. Leavy Jr. and R. Rand. Lincoln: University of Nebraska Press, 1986.

——. "Globalization, Peace, and Cosmopolitanism." In *Negotiations: Interventions and Interviews 1971–2001*, ed. and trans. Elizabeth Rottenberg. Stanford: Stanford University Press, 2002.

——. "History of the Lie: Prolegomena." In *Futures of Jacques Derrida*, ed. Richard Rand. Stanford: Stanford University Press, 2001.

——. "History of the Lie: Prolegomena." In *Without Alibi*. Trans. Peggy Kamuf. Stanford: Stanford University Press, 2002.

——. "History of the Lie: Prolegomena." *Graduate Faculty Philosophy Journal* 19, no. 2 and 20, no. 1 (1997).

——. "Hostipitality." In *Acts of Religion*. Trans. M. Ron, S. Weber, M. Quaintance, and others. Ed. Gil Anidjar. New York: Routledge, 2002.

——. "Interpretations at War: Kant, the Jew, the German." In *Acts of Religion*. Trans. M. Ron, S. Weber, M. Quaintance, and others. Ed. Gil Anidjar. New York: Routledge, 2002.

——. "Khora." In *On the Name*. Trans. David Wood, John Leavey, and Ian McLeod. Ed. Thomas Dutoit. Stanford: Stanford University Press, 1995.

——. "The Law of Genre." Trans. Avital Ronell. *Glyph* 7 (1980): 202–29.

——. "La littérature au secret." In *Donner la mort*. Paris: Galilée, 1999.

——. "La loi du genre." In *Parages*. Paris: Galilée, 1986.

——. *Mal d'archive, une impression freudienne*. Paris: Galilée, 1995.

——. *Monolingualism of the Other, or The Prosthesis of Origin*. Trans. Patrick Mensah. Stanford: Stanford University Press, 1996.

——. *Negotiations: Interventions and Interviews 1971–2001*. Ed. and trans. Elizabeth Rottenberg. Stanford: Stanford University Press, 2002.

——. "Not Utopia, the Im-possible." In *Paper Machine*. Trans. Rachel Bowlby. Stanford: Stanford University Press, 2005.

——. "Of an Apocalyptic Tone Recently Adopted in Philosophy." *Oxford Literary Review* 6, no. 2 (1984): 3–37.

——. *Of Grammatology*. Trans. Gayatri Chakravorty Spivak. Baltimore: Johns Hopkins University Press, 1976.

——. *Of Hospitality: Anne Dufourmantelle Invites Jacques Derrida to Respond*. Trans. Rachel Bowlby. Stanford: Stanford University Press, 2000.

——. *On Cosmopolitanism and Forgiveness*. Trans. Mark Dooley and Michael Hughes. London: Routledge, 2001.

——. "On Reading Heidegger: An Outline of Remarks to the Essex Colloquium." *Research in Phenomenology* 17 (1987): 171–85.

——. *On the Name*. Trans. David Wood, John Leavey, and Ian McLeod. Ed. Thomas Dutoit. Stanford: Stanford University Press, 1995.

——. *The Other Heading: Reflections on Today's Europe*. Trans. Pascale-Anne Brault and Michael Naas. Bloomington: Indiana University Press, 1992.

——. "Otobiographies." In *The Ear of the Other*. Trans. Avital Ronell. Ed. Christie McDonald. Lincoln: University of Nebraska Press, 1985.

——. "*Ousia* and *Gramme:* Note on a Note from *Being and Time*." In *Margins of Philosophy*. Trans. Alan Bass. Chicago: University of Chicago Press, 1982.

——. *Paper Machine*. Trans. Rachel Bowlby. Stanford: Stanford University Press, 2005.

——. *Papier Machine*. Paris: Galilée, 2001.

——. *Pardonner: L'impardonnable et l'imprescriptible*. Paris: L'Herne, 2005.

——. "'Le Parjure,' Perhaps: Storytelling and Lying." In *Without Alibi*. Trans. Peggy Kamuf. Stanford: Stanford University Press, 2002.

——. "La parole: Donner, nommer, appeler." In *Paul Ricoeur*. Paris: L'Herne, 2004.

——. "Pas." *Gramma*, nos. 3–4 (1976). Reprinted in *Parages*. Paris: Galilée, 1986.

——. *Passions*. Paris: Galilée, 1993.

——. "Passions: An Oblique Offering." In *On the Name*. Trans. David Wood, John P. Leavey, and Ian McLeod. Stanford: Stanford University Press, 1995.

——. "Performative Powerlessness: A Response to Simon Critchley." *Constellations* 7, no. 4 (2000): 466–68.

——. *Points . . . : Interviews, 1974–1994.* Ed. Elisabeth Weber. Trans. Peggy Kamuf and others. Stanford: Stanford University Press, 1995.

——. "Politics and Friendship." In *Negotiations: Interventions and Interviews 1971–2001.* Ed. and trans. Elizabeth Rottenberg. Stanford: Stanford University Press, 2002.

——. "Politics and Friendship: A Discussion with Jacques Derrida." Centre for Modern French Thought, University of Sussex, December 1, 1997, www.sussex.ac.uk.

——. *Politics of Friendship.* Trans. George Collins. London: Verso, 1997.

——. *Politiques de l'amitié.* Paris: Galilée, 1994.

——. *Positions.* Trans. Alan Bass. Chicago: University of Chicago Press, 1981.

——. *Psyché: Inventions de l'autre.* Paris: Galilée, 1987.

——. *Psyché: Inventions de l'autre, II.* Paris: Galilée, 2003.

——. "Psychoanalysis Searches the States of Its Soul: The Impossible Beyond of a Sovereign Cruelty." In *Without Alibi.* Trans. Peggy Kamuf. Stanford: Stanford University Press, 2002.

——. *Résistances: De la psychanalyse.* Paris: Galilée, 1996.

——. *Resistances of Psychoanalysis.* Trans. P. Kamuf, P-A. Brault, and M. Naas. Stanford: Stanford University Press, 1998.

——. *Rogues: Two Essays on Reason.* Trans. Pascale-Anne Brault and Michael Naas. Stanford: Stanford University Press, 2005.

——. "Sauf le nom." In *On the Name.* Trans. David Wood, John Leavey, and Ian McLeod. Ed. Thomas Dutoit. Stanford: Stanford University Press, 1995.

——. "Schibboleth for Paul Celan." In *Readings of Paul Celan*, ed. Aris Fioretos. Baltimore: Johns Hopkins University Press, 1994.

——. "Le Siècle et le Pardon." www.hydra.umn.edu/derrida/siecle/html.

——. "Signature, Event, Context." In *Margins of Philosophy.* Trans. Alan Bass. Chicago: University of Chicago Press, 1982.

——. "Some Statements and Truisms about Neologisms, Newisms, Postisms, Parasitisms, and Other Small Seismisms." In *The States of Theory.* Trans. A. Tomiche. Ed. D. Caroll. New York: Columbia University Press, 1990.

——. *Specters of Marx: The State of the Debt, the Work of Mourning and the New International.* Trans. Peggy Kamuf. Introduction by Bernd Magnus and Stephen Cullenberg. New York: Routledge, 1994.

——. *Spectres de Marx.* Paris: Galilée, 1993.

——. *Spurs: Nietzsche's Styles.* Trans. Barbara Harlow. Chicago: University of Chicago Press, 1979.

——. "Taking a Stand for Algeria." In *Acts of Religion.* Trans. M. Ron, S. Weber, M. Quaintance, and others. Ed. Gil Anidjar. New York: Routledge, 2002.

———. "Taking Sides for Algeria." In *Negotiations: Interventions and Interviews 1971–2001*. Ed. and trans. Elizabeth Rottenberg. Stanford: Stanford University Press, 2002.

———. "'There is No *One* Narcissism' (Autobiophotographies)." In *Points . . . : Interviews, 1974–1994*. Ed. Elisabeth Weber. Trans. Peggy Kamuf and others. Stanford: Stanford University Press, 1995.

———. *Ulysse gramophone: Deux mots pour Joyce*. Paris: Galilée, 1987.

———. "The University without Condition." In *Without Alibi*. Trans. Peggy Kamuf. Stanford: Stanford University Press, 2002.

———. "Violence et Métaphysique." In *L'écriture et la différence*. Paris: Minuit, 1967.

———. *Voyous: Deux essais sur la raison*. Paris: Galilée, 2003.

———. *Without Alibi*. Trans. Peggy Kamuf. Stanford: Stanford University Press, 2002.

———. *Writing and Difference*. Trans. Alan Bass. Chicago: University of Chicago Press, 1978.

Derrida, Jacques, and Maurizio Ferraris. *A Taste for the Secret*. Ed. Giacomo Donis and David Webb. Trans. Giacomo Donis. Malden, Mass.: Blackwell, 2001.

Derrida, Jacques, and Elisabeth Roudinesco. *De quoi demain: Dialogue*. Paris: Flammarion, 2003.

———. *For What Tomorrow . . . : A Dialogue*. Trans. Jeff Fort. Stanford: Stanford University Press, 2004.

Descombes, Vincent, "Les essais sur le don." In *Les Institutions du sens*. Paris: Minuit, 1996.

Dower, John. *Embracing Defeat*. New York: Norton, 1999.

Einaudi, Jean-Paul. *La Bataille de Paris, 17 Octobre 1961*. 1991; Paris: Seuil, 2001.

Euben, Roxanne. *Journeys to the Other Shore: Muslim and Western Travelers in Search of Knowledge*. Princeton, N.J.: Princeton University Press, 2006.

Fanon, Frantz. *The Wretched of the Earth*. Trans. Richard Philcox. New York: Grove Press, 2004.

Foley, Barbara. "The Politics of Deconstruction." *Genre* 17 (Spring–Summer 1984): 113–34.

Foucault, Michel. *Fearless Speech*. Ed. Joseph Pearson. Los Angeles: Semiotext(e), 2001.

Fraser, Nancy. "The French Derrideans: Politicizing Deconstruction or Deconstructing the Political?" *New German Critique* 33 (Fall 1984): 127–54.

Fynsk, Christopher. "Intervention," "Séminaire 'politique.'" In *Les fins de l'homme: À partir du travail de Jacques Derrida*, ed. Philippe Lacoue-Labarthe and Jean-Luc Nancy. Paris: Galilée, 1981.

Fynsk, Christopher, and Philippe Lacoue-Labarthe. "'Political' Seminar." In Philippe Lacoue-Labarthe and Jean-Luc Nancy, *Retreating the Political*. Ed. Simon Sparks. London: Routledge, 1997.

Goffman, Erving. *Encounters: Two Studies in the Sociology of Interaction*. Indianapolis: Bobbs-Merrill, 1961.

Goodall, Jane. *The Chimpanzees of Gombe: Patterns of Behavior*. Cambridge, Mass.: Harvard University Press, 1986.

Guerlac, Suzanne. *Thinking in Time: An Introduction to Henri Bergson*. Ithaca, N.Y.: Cornell University Press, 2006.

Guyer, Paul. "Nature, Morality, and the Possibility of Peace." In *Kant on Freedom, Law, and Happiness*. Cambridge, England: Cambridge University Press, 2000.

Habermas, Jürgen. *The Inclusion of the Other: Studies in Political Theory*. Ed. Ciaran Cronin and Pablo De Greiff. Cambridge, Mass.: MIT Press, 1998.

——. "Die postnationale Konstellation und die Zukunft der Demokratie." In *Die postnationale Konstellation: Politische Essays*. Frankfurt am Main: Suhrkamp, 1998.

——. "The Postnational Constellation and the Future of Democracy." In *The Postnational Constellation: Political Essays*. Trans. and ed. Max Pensky. Cambridge, Mass.: MIT Press, 2001.

——. *The Postnational Constellation: Political Essays*. Trans. and ed. Max Pensky. Cambridge, Mass.: MIT Press, 2001.

Harbi, Mohammed. Le *FLN: mirages et réalité*. Paris: Jeune Afrique, 1980.

Hardt, Michael, and Antonio Negri. *Empire*. Cambridge, Mass.: Harvard University Press, 2000.

——. *Multitude: War and Democracy in the Age of Empire*. New York: Penguin, 2005.

Hegel, G.W. F. *Early Theological Writings*. Trans. T. M. Knox. Philadelphia: University of Pennsylvania Press, 1971.

——. *Phenomenology of Spirit*. Trans. A. V. Miller. Oxford: Oxford University Press, 1977.

Heidegger, Martin. "Letter on Humanism." In *Basic Writings*. Ed. David Farrell Krell. New York: Harper and Row, 1993.

Hénaff, Marcel. *Le Prix de la vérité: Le don, l'argent, la philosophie*. Paris: Seuil, 2002.

——. "Gift Exchange, Play and Deception." In *Deception in Markets: An Economic Analysis*, ed. Caroline Gerschlager. New York: Palgrave Macmillan, 2004.

Hillis Miller, J. "The Anacoluthonic Lie." In *Reading Narrative*. Norman: University of Oklahoma Press, 1998.

Hobbes, Thomas. *De Cive* (1642). *On the Citizen*. Ed. Richard Tuck and Michael Silverthoren. Cambridge: Cambridge University Press, 1999.

——. *The Elements of Law, Natural and Politic* (1640). Ed. J. C. A. Gaskin. Oxford: Oxford University Press, 1999.

——. *Leviathan*. 1651. Ed. Richard Tuck. Cambridge, England: Cambridge University Press, 1991.

Holland, Nancy J., ed. *Feminist Interpretations of Derrida*. University Park: Pennsylvania State University Press, 1997.

Honig, Bonnie. "Declarations of Independence: Arendt and Derrida on the Problem of Founding a Republic." *American Political Science Review* 85, no. 1 (1991): 97–113.

House, Jim, and Neil MacMaster. *Paris 1961: Algerians, State Terror, and Memory.* Oxford: Oxford University Press, 2006.

Jankélévitch, Vladimir. *Forgiveness.* Trans. Andrew Kelley. Chicago: University of Chicago Press, 2005.

———. *L'Imprescriptible (Pardonner?).* Paris: Seuil, 1986.

Jay, Martin. "The Ambivalent Virtues of Mendacity: How Europeans Taught (Some of) Us to Learn to Love the Lies of Politics." In *The Humanities and the Dynamics of Inclusion Since World War II,* ed. David A. Hollinger. Baltimore: Johns Hopkins University Press, 2006.

———. "Of Plots, Witnesses and Judgments." In *Probing the Limits of Representation: Nazism and the "Final Solution,"* ed. Saul Friedlander. Cambridge, Mass: Harvard University Press, 1992.

Jensen, W. "Gradiva Fantaisie pompéienne." In *Le Délire et les reves dans la Gradiva de Jensen,* Sigmund Freud. Paris: Gallimard, 1986.

Judt, Tony. *Past Imperfect: French Intellectuals, 1944–1956.* Berkeley: University of California Press, 1992.

Kafka, Franz. *Parables and Paradoxes / Parabeln und Paradoxe.* Ed. Nahum N. Glatzer. New York: Schocken, 1958.

Kant, Immanuel. *Critique of Pure Reason.* Trans. and ed. Paul Guyer and Allen Wood. Cambridge, England: Cambridge University Press, 1997.

———. "Idea of a Universal History with a Cosmopolitan Purpose." In *Political Writings.* Ed. Hans Reiss. Trans. H. B. Nisbet. Cambridge, England: Cambridge University Press, 1991.

———. *Idee zu einer allgemeinen Geschichte in weltbürgerlicher Absicht.* In *Schriften zur Anthropologie, Geschichtsphilosophie, Politik und Pädagogik I.* Ed. Wilhelm Weischedel. Frankfurt am Main: Suhrkamp, 1968.

———. *Kritik der reinen Vernunft.* Ed. Wilhelm Weischedel. Frankfurt am Main: Suhrkamp, 1968.

———. *Toward Perpetual Peace: A Philosophical Project.* In *Practical Philosophy.* Trans. Mary J. Gregor. Cambridge, England: Cambridge University Press, 1996.

———. *Zum ewigen Frieden: Ein philosophischer Entwurf.* In *Schriften zur Anthropologie, Geschichtsphilosophie, Politik und Pädagogik I.* Ed. Wilhelm Weischedel. Frankfurt am Main: Suhrkamp, 1968.

Kennedy, Ellen. *Constitutional Failure: Carl Schmitt in Weimar.* Durham, N.C.: Duke University Press, 2004.

Khatibi, Abdelkebir. *Love in Two Languages.* Trans. Richard Howard. Minneapolis: University of Minnesota Press, 1990.

Koyré, Alexander. "The Political Function of the Modern Lie." *Contemporary Jewish Record* 8, no. 3 (1945): 290–300.

Krapp, Peter. "Amnesty: Between an Ethics of Forgiveness and the Politics of Forgetting." *German Law Journal* 6, no.1 (2005): 185–95.

Kronick, Joseph, G. "Philosophy as Autobiography: The Confessions of Jacques Derrida." *MLN* 115 no. 5 (December 2000): 997–1018.

Laclau, Ernesto. "'The time is out of joint.'" *Diacritics* 25, no. 2 (1995): 86–96.

Laclau, Ernesto, and Chantal Mouffe. *Hegemony and Socialist Strategy: Towards a Radical Democratic Politics*. London: Verso, 1985.

Lacoue-Labarthe, Philippe. "Intervention," "Séminaire 'politique.'" In *Les fins de l'homme: À partir du travail de Jacques Derrida*, ed. Philippe Lacoue-Labarthe and Jean-Luc Nancy. Paris: Galilée, 1981.

Lacoue-Labarthe, Philippe, and Jean-Luc Nancy. "Opening Address to the Centre for Philosophical Research on the Political." In Philippe Lacoue-Labarthe and Jean-Luc Nancy, *Retreating the Political*. Ed. Simon Sparks. London: Routledge, 1997.

———. *Retreating the Political*. Ed. Simon Sparks. London: Routledge, 1997.

Lacoue-Labarthe, Philippe, and Jean-Luc Nancy, eds. *Les fins de l'homme: À partir du travail de Jacques Derrida*. Paris: Galilée, 1981.

Leitch, Vincent. "Late Derrida: The Politics of Sovereignty." *Critical Inquiry* 33, no. 2 (Winter 2007): 229–47.

Lévinas, Emmanuel. *Autrement qu'être ou au-delà de l'essence*. The Hague: Martinus Nijhoff, 1974.

———*Humanism of the Other*. Trans. Nidra Poller. Urbana: University of Illinois Press, 2003.

———. *Otherwise Than Being, or Beyond Essence*. Trans. Alphonso Lingis. Pittsburgh: Duquesne University Press, 1998.

———. *Totalité et infini: Essai sur l'extériorité*. The Hague: Martinus Nijhoff, 1961.

———. *Totality and Infinity: An Essay on Exteriority*. Trans. Alphonso Lingis. Pittsburgh: Duquesne University Press, 1969.

Lévi-Strauss, Claude. *The Elementary Structures of Kinship*. Boston: Beacon Press, 1969.

Löwy, Michael. *Rédemption et utopie: Le judaïsme libertaire en Europe centrale. Une étude d'affinité élective*. Paris: Presses Universitaires de France, 1988.

Malabou, Catherine, and Jacques Derrida. *Counterpath: Traveling with Jacques Derrida*. Trans. David Wills. Stanford: Stanford University Press, 2004.

Mallet, Marie-Louise, and Ginette Michaud, eds. *Jacques Derrida*. Paris: L'Herne, 2004.

Marion, Jean-Luc. *Being Given: Toward a Phenomenology of Givenness*. Trans. J. L. Kosky. Stanford: Stanford University Press, 2002.

Marks, Elaine. *Marrano as Metaphor: The Jewish Presence in French Writing*. New York: Columbia University Press, 1996.

Markus, György. "The Hope to Be Free: Freedom as Fact, Postulate and Regulative

Idea in Kant." In *From Liberal Values to Democratic Transition: Essays in Honor of János Kis*, ed. Ronald Dworkin. Budapest: Central European University Press, 2004.

Martin, Bill. *Humanism and Its Aftermath: The Shared Fate of Deconstruction and Politics*. Atlantic Highlands, N.J.: Humanities Press, 1995.

——. *Matrix and Line: Derrida and the Possibilities of Postmodern Social Theory*. Albany: State University of New York Press, 1992.

Mauss, Marcel. *The Gift: The Form and Reason for Exchange in Archaic Societies*. Trans. W. D. Halls. New York: Norton, 1990.

——. *The Gift: The Form and Reason for Exchange in Archaic Societies*. London: Routledge, 2006.

May, Herbert, and Bruce Metzger. *The New Oxford Annotated Bible*. Oxford: Oxford University Press, 1971.

McCormick, John P. "Derrida on Law; or, Poststructuralism Gets Serious." *Political Theory* 29, no. 3 (2001): 395–423.

McDouggal, James. "Myth and Counter Myth: The Berber as a National Signifier in Algerian Historiographies." *Radical History Review* 86 (Spring 2003): 66–88.

McGrew, W. C. *Chimpanzee Material Culture: Implication for Human Evolution*. Cambridge: Cambridge University Press, 1992.

McGrew, W. C., L. F. Marchant, and T. Nishida, eds. *Great Apes Societies*. Cambridge, England: Cambridge University Press, 1990.

Memmi, Albert. *The Colonizer and the Colonized*. Trans. Howard Greenfield. Boston: Beacon Press, 1991.

Mertes, Tom, ed. *A Movement of Movements: Is Another World Really Possible?* London: Verso, 2004.

Naas, Michael. "A Last Call for 'Europe.'" *Theory and Event* 8, no. 1 (2005).

Nancy, Jean-Luc. *La Communauté désœuvrée*. Paris: Christian Bourgois, 2004.

——. "*Ex nihilo summum* (de la souveraineté)." In *La création du monde ou la mondialisation*. Paris: Galilée, 2002.

——. *The Experience of Freedom*. Trans. Bridget McDonald. Stanford: Stanford University Press, 1993.

——. "The Free Voice of Man." In Philippe Lacoue-Labarthe and Jean-Luc Nancy, *Retreating the Political*. Ed. Simon Sparks. London: Routledge, 1997.

——. "La voix libre de l'homme." In *Les fins de l'homme: À partir du travail de Jacques Derrida*, ed. Philippe Lacoue-Labarthe and Jean-Luc Nancy. Paris: Galilée, 1981.

Nietzsche, Friedrich. *On the Genealogy of Morals*. Trans. Walter Kaufmann. New York: Random House, 1969.

——. *The Twilight of the Idols*. Vol. 16 of *Complete Works*. 18 Vols. Trans. Anthony M. Ludovici. Edinburgh: T. N. Foulis, 1911.

Nora, Pierre. "From *Lieux de Mémoire* to *Realms of Memory*." In *Realms of Memory:*

*Rethinking the French Past.* Ed. Lawrence D. Kritzman. Trans. Arthur Goldhammer. New York: Columbia University Press, 1996.

Norton, Anne. *Bloodrites of the Poststructuralists: Word, Flesh and Revolution.* New York: Routledge, 2002.

Ortigues, Edmond. *Le Discours et le symbole.* Paris: Aubier, 1962.

Parker, Andrew. " 'Taking Sides' (On History): Derrida Re-Marx." *Diacritics* 11, no. 3 (1981): 57–73.

Patočka, Jan. *Heretical Essays in the Philosophy of History.* Trans. E. Kohak. Chicago: Open Court, 1996.

———. *Plato and Europe.* Trans. P. Lom. Stanford: Stanford University Press, 2002.

Paulhan, Jean. "La démocratie fait appel au premier venu." In vol. 5 of *Œuvres complètes.* 5 Vols. Paris: Cercle du Livre Précieux, 1966.

Peirce, Charles S. *Collected Papers.* Cambridge, Mass.: Harvard University Press, 1931–1958.

Plato. *The Collected Dialogues.* Ed. E. Hamilton and H. Cairns. Princeton, N.J.: Princeton University Press, 1980.

———. *The Dialogues of Plato.* Vol. 1. Trans. B. Jowett. Oxford: Clarendon Press, 1953.

———. *Plato's Phaedo.* Trans. R. Hackforth. Cambridge, England: Cambridge University Press, 1955.

Ramadan, Tariq. *Western Muslims and the Future of Islam.* New York: Oxford University Press, 2003.

Rancière, Jacques. *Dis-agreement.* Trans. J. Rose. Minneapolis: University of Minnesota Press, 1999.

———. *Malaise dans l'esthétique.* Paris: Galilée, 2004.

———. "Who Is the Subject of the Rights of Man?" *South Atlantic Quarterly* 103, nos. 2–3 (2004): 297–310.

Ricoeur, Paul. "The Fragility of Political Language." *Philosophy Today* 31, no. 1 (1987): 35–44.

———. *La mémoire, l'histoire, l'oubli.* Paris: Seuil, 2000.

———. "Preface to the French Edition of Jan Patočka's Heretical Essays." In *Heretical Essays in the Philosophy of History*, by Jan Patočka. Trans. E. Kohak. Chicago: Open Court, 1996.

Robinson, Jill. "Circumcising Confession: Derrida, Autobiography, Judaism." *Diacritics* 25, no. 4 (1995): 20–38.

Rousseau, Jean-Jacques. *Œuvres complètes.* 5 vols. Ed. Bernard Gagnebin and Marcel Raymond. Paris, 1959–85.

Ryan, Michael. *Marxism and Deconstruction: A Critical Articulation.* Baltimore: Johns Hopkins University Press, 1982.

Said, Edward. "The Problem of Textuality: Two Exemplary Positions." *Critical Inquiry* 4, no. 4 (1978): 673–714.

Scheler, Max. *Formalism in Ethics and Non-Formal Ethics of Values*. Trans. M. S. Frings and R. L. Funk. Evanston, Ill.: Northwestern University Press, 1973.

———. *Wesen und Formen der Sympathie*. Frankfurt am Main: Verlag G. Schulte-Blumke, 1948.

Schmitt, Carl. *The Leviathan in the State Theory of Thomas Hobbes: Meaning and Failure of a Political Symbol*. Trans. George Schwab and Erna Hilfstein. Westport, Conn.: Greenwood Press, 1996.

———. *Political Theology*. Trans. George Schwab. Cambridge, Mass.: MIT Press, 1985.

———. *Roman Catholicism and Political Form*. Trans G. L. Ulmen. Westport, Conn.: Greenwood Press, 1996.

———. *Théorie de la Constitution*. Trans. Lilyane Deroche. Paris: Presses Universitaires de France, 1993.

———. *Verfassungslehre*. Berlin: Duncker and Humblot, 1993.

Seneca. *On Benefits. Addressed to Aebutius Liberalis*. Trans. Aubrey Stewart. London: George Bell and Sons, 1900.

Smith, Adam. *An Inquiry into the Nature and Causes of the Wealth of Nations*. Ed. Kathryn Sutherland. Oxford: Oxford University Press, 1993.

Smith, David Livingstone. *Why We Lie: The Evolutionary Roots of Deception and the Unconscious Mind*. New York: St. Martin's Press, 2004.

Smith, Steven. *Spinoza, Liberalism and the Question of Jewish Identity*. New Haven: Yale University Press, 1997.

Smyth, John Vignaux. *The Habit of Lying: Sacrificial Studies in Literature, Philosophy, and Fashion Theory*. Durham, N.C.: Duke University Press, 2002.

Spinoza, Baruch. *Tractatus Theologico-Politicus*. Trans. H. M. Elwes. New York: Dover, 1951.

Spivak, Gayatri Chakravorty. "Can the Subaltern Speak?" In *Marxism and the Interpretation of Culture*, ed. Cary Nelson and Lawrence Grossberg. Urbana: University of Illinois Press, 1988.

———. "Feminism and Deconstruction, Again: Negotiations." In *Outside in the Teaching Machine*. New York: Routledge, 1993.

———. "Scattered Speculations on the Question of Value." In *In Other Worlds: Essays on Cultural Politics*. New York: Routledge, 1987.

———. "The Setting to Work of Deconstruction." Appendix. In *A Critique of Postcolonial Reason*. Cambridge, Mass.: Harvard University Press, 1999.

———. "Speculations on Reading Marx: After Reading Derrida." In *Post-Structuralism and the Question of History*, ed. Derek Attridge, Robert Young, and Geoff Bennington. Cambridge, England: Cambridge University Press, 1987.

Sprinker, Michael, ed. *Ghostly Demarcations: A Symposium on Derrida's* Specters of Marx. London: Verso, 1999.

———. "Textual Politics: Foucault and Derrida." *Boundary 2* 8, no. 3 (1980): 75–98.

Stanford, C. "The Ape's Gift." In *Tree of Origin: What Primate Behavior Can Tell Us about Human Social Evolution*, ed. Frans de Waal. Cambridge, Mass.: Harvard University Press, 2001.

Stedile, Joao Pedro. "Brazil's Landless Battalions: The Sem Terra Movement." In *A Movement of Movements: Is Another World Really Possible?*, ed. Tom Mertes. London: Verso, 2004.

Steedman, Carolyn. "Something She Called a Fever: Michelet, Derrida and Dust." *American Historical Review* 106, no. 4 (2001): 1159–80.

Stora, Benjamin. *La Gangrène et l'oubli: la mémoire de la guerre d'Algéric*. Paris: La Découverte, 1991.

Strathern, *The Rope of Moka: Big Men and Ceremonial Exchange in Mount Hagen, New Guinea*. Cambridge: Cambridge University Press, 1971.

Thomson, Alexander John Peter. *Deconstruction and Democracy: Derrida's Politics of Friendship*. London: Continuum, 2005.

——. "Derrida's Indecent Objection." *Journal for Cultural Research* 10, no. 4 (2006): 295–308.

——. "What's to Become of 'Democracy to Come.'" *Postmodern Culture* 15, no. 3 (2005). http://muse.jhu.edu.

Tutu, Desmond. *No Future without Forgiveness*. New York: Doubleday, 1999.

Valensi, Lucette. "Histoire nationale, histoire monumentale: Les lieux de mémoire." *Annales HSS* November 1995: 1271–77.

Waal, Frans de. *Peacemaking among Primates*. Cambridge, Mass.: Harvard University Press, 1989.

Weed, Elizabeth, and Ellen Rooney, eds. *Derrida's Gifts*. Special issue of *differences: A Journal of Feminist Cultural Studies* 16, no. 3 (2005).

Wehr, Hans. *A Dictionary of Modern Standard Arabic*. Ed. J. Milton Cowan. Beirut: Librairie du Liban, 1980.

Wolin, Richard. *Heidegger's Children: Hannah Arendt, Karl Löwith, Hans Jonas and Herbert Marcuse*. Princeton, N.J.: Princeton University Press, 2001.

Wolin, Sheldon S. *Politics and Vision*. Expanded ed. Princeton, N.J.: Princeton University Press, 2004.

"Yad Vashem." Shoah Resource Center, www.yadvashem.org.

Yerushalmi, Yosef Hahim. *Freud's Moses: Judaism Terminable and Interminable*. New Haven: Yale University Press, 1991.

Yovel, Yirmiyahu. *Spinoza and Other Heretics: The Marrano of Reason*. Princeton, N.J.: Princeton University Press, 1989.

Zagorin, Perez. *Ways of Lying: Dissimulation, Persecution, and Conformity in Early Modern Europe*. Cambridge, Mass.: Harvard University Press, 1990.

Zarka, Yves Charles, ed. *Derrida politique: La deconstruction de la souveraineté (puissance et droit)*. Special issue of *Cités: Philosophie, Politique, Histoire* 30, no. 2 (2007).

# Contributors

ÉTIENNE BALIBAR is Emeritus Professor of Moral and Political Philosophy at the University of Paris X, Nanterre, and Distinguished Professor of Humanities at the University of California, Irvine. His numerous books include *Reading Capital* (with Louis Althusser, 1965), *On the Dictatorship of the Proletariat* (1976), *Race, Nation, Class: Ambiguous Identities* (with Immanuel Wallerstein, 1991), *Masses, Classes, Ideas* (1994), *The Philosophy of Marx* (1995), *Spinoza and Politics* (1998), *Politics and the Other Scene* (2002), *We, the People of Europe? Reflections on Transnational Citizenship* (2004), *Extreme Violence and the Problem of Civility* (forthcoming), and *Citoyen Sujet: Essais d'anthropologie philosophique* (forthcoming).

GEOFFREY BENNINGTON is Asa G. Candler Professor of Modern French Thought at Emory University. He is the author of a dozen books, including *Sententiousness and the Novel in Eighteenth-Century France* (1985), *Legislations* (1995), *Frontières kantiennes* (2000), and more recently a number of electronic volumes, including *Other Analyses: Reading Philosophy* (2005). He is currently working on a book of political philosophy and is a member of the group of scholars preparing Jacques Derrida's seminars for publication in French and English.

WENDY BROWN is a Professor of political science at the University of California, Berkeley. Her books include *Manhood and Politics* (1989), *States of Inquiry* (1995), *Politics Out of History* (2001), *Left Legalism / Left Critique* (2002, coedited), *Edgework* (2005), and *Regarding Aversion* (2006). She is currently working on a book on the several formulations of critique in Marx, and another on contemporary nation-state walling considered through the lens of sovereignty.

JUDITH BUTLER is Maxine Elliot Professor in the Departments of Rhetoric and Comparative Literature at the University of California, Berkeley. She is the author of numerous books, including *Gender Trouble* (1990), *Bodies that Matter* (1993), *Excitable Speech* (1997), *The Psychic Life of Power* (1997), *Antigone's Claim* (2000), *Precarious Life* (2004), *Undoing Gender* (2004), *Giving an Account of Oneself* (2005), and most recently, *Who Sings the Nation-Sate?* (with Gayatri Chakravorty Spivak, 2007). Her current work focuses on contemporary politics and Jewish philosophy, in particular post-Zionist critiques of state violence.

PHENG CHEAH is a Professor in the Department of Rhetoric at the University of California, Berkeley. He is the author of *Spectral Nationality: Passages of Freedom from Kant to Postcolonial Literatures of Liberation* (2003) and *Inhuman Conditions:*

*On Cosmopolitanism and Human Rights* (2006). He coedited *Cosmopolitics: Thinking and Feeling beyond the Nation* (1998) and *Grounds of Comparison: Around the Work of Benedict Anderson* (2003). He is currently working on a book on world literature and another book on the concept of instrumentality.

HÉLÈNE CIXOUS is a French writer, playwright, critic, and activist who continues to influence writers, scholars, and feminists around the world. She is a Professor at the Centre de Recherches en Etudes Féminines, University of Paris VIII, Vincennes. Her recent works in English include *The Third Body* (1999), *Veils* (2001, with Jacques Derrida), *Portrait of Jacques Derrida as a Young Jewish Saint* (2004), *The Writing Notebooks* (2004), *Dream I Tell You* (2006), and *Reveries of the Wild Woman* (2006).

RODOLPHE GASCHÉ is SUNY Distinguished Professor and Eugenio Donato Professor of Comparative Literature at the State University of New York at Buffalo. His books include *Die hybride Wissenschaft* (1973), *System und Metaphorik in der Philosophie von Georges Bataille* (1978), *The Tain of the Mirror: Derrida and the Philosophy of Reflection* (1986), *Inventions of Difference: On Jacques Derrida* (1994), *The Wild Card of Reading: On Paul de Man* (1998), *Of Minimal Things: Studies on the Notion of Relation* (1999), *The Idea of Form: Rethinking Kant's Aesthetic* (2003), *Views and Interviews: On "Deconstruction" in America* (2006), and *The Honor of Thinking: Critique, Theory, Philosophy* (2007). His new book, *Europe, or the Infinite Task. A Study of a Philosophical Concept*, will be forthcoming soon.

SUZANNE GUERLAC is a Professor of Modern French Thought and Nineteenth- and Twentieth-Century French Literature at the University of California, Berkeley. She is the author of *The Impersonal Sublime: Hugo, Baudelaire, Lautréamont and the Esthetics of the Sublime* (1990), *Literary Polemics: Bataille, Sartre, Valéry, Breton* (1999), and *Thinking in Time: An Introduction to Henri Bergson* (2006). Her most recent publication is "The Useless Image: Bataille, Magritte, Bergson" (2007). She is currently working on Proust.

MARCEL HÉNAFF is a philosopher and anthropologist and Professor in the Departments of Literature and Political Science at the University of California, San Diego. He is the author of *Sade: The Invention of the Libertine Body* (English translation 1999), *Lévi-Strauss and the Making of Structural Anthropology* (English translation 1998), *Public Space and Democracy* (with Tracy Strong, 2001), *Le Prix de la Vérité: Le don, l'argent, la philosophie* (2002), *La Ville qui vient* (2008), and *Le Don des Philosophes* (2008).

MARTIN JAY is Sidney Hellman Ehrman Professor of History at the University of California, Berkeley, where he has been teaching modern European intellectual history since 1971. Among his works are *The Dialectical Imagination* (1996), *Marxism and Totality* (1984), *Adorno* (1984), *Permanent Exiles* (1985), *Fin-de-Siecle*

*Socialism* (1989), *Force Fields* (1993), *Downcast Eyes* (1993), *Cultural Semantics* (1998), *Refractions of Violence* (2003), and *Songs of Experience* (2004). He is currently working on a book on lying in politics.

ANNE NORTON is Edmund and Louise Kahn Professor of Political Science and Comparative Literature at the University of Pennsylvania. Her most recent books are *95 Theses on Politics, Culture and Method* (2004) and *Leo Strauss and the Politics of American Empire* (2004). She is studying the figure of the Muslim in contemporary Western politics, rhetoric, and philosophy.

JACQUES RANCIÈRE is Emeritus Professor of Philosophy at the University of Paris, St. Denis. Among his works that have appeared in English are *The Nights of Labor: The Worker's Dream in Nineteenth Century France* (1989), *The Ignorant Schoolmaster: Five Lessons in Intellectual Emancipation* (1991), *On the Shores of Politics* (1995), *The Names of History—On the Poetics of Knowledge* (1996), *Disagreement: Politics and Philosophy* (1999), *The Politics of Aesthetics: The Distribution of the Sensible* (2004), *The Hatred of Democracy* (2006), *The Philosopher and His Poor* (2006), and *The Future of the Image* (2007).

SORAYA TLATLI is an Associate Professor of French at the University of California, Berkeley. Her research interests are francophone literature, particularly from North Africa, and colonial and postcolonial historiography. She has also researched and written on twentieth-century French psychoanalysis, philosophy, and intellectual history. Her publications include *Le psychiatre et ses poètes: Essai sur le jeune Lacan* (2000) and *La Folie lyrique: Essai sur le surréalisme et la psychiatrie* (2004). She is currently writing a book on the writing of history in Algerian literary depictions of the nation.

SATOSHI UKAI is a Professor of French Literature and Postcolonial Studies at Hitotsubashi University in Japan. His most recent book is *Responsibilities* (2003). Other recent publications in English are "The Future of an Affect: About the Historicity of Shame" (2001), "The Road to Hell Is Paved with Good Intentions—For a 'Critique of Terrorism' to Come" (2005), and "Reflections beyond the Flag: Why Is the Hinomaru Flag 'Auspicious/Foolish'?" (2005). He is currently studying the idea of hospitality in Louis Massignon, Jean Genet, and Jacques Derrida.

# Index

abendland (world of shadows), 169–70

Abraham: circumcision and, 168–69; Hegel on, 158–60; obedience and, 286–88. *See also* Ishmael, Isaac, and Abraham

acosmistic ethics, 157n15

action, ontology of and capacity for, 270

"L'Admiration de Nelson Mandela" (Derrida), 261–64, 271–72

admiration of the Law, 261–62, 271–72

affirmative deconstruction, 6–8

Agamben, Giorgio, 113n27, 174n19

agency and pardon, 269–72

Ages, 35n19

Algeria: as archive, 181–84; death and, 188; disorder of identity in, 185–89; Marrano figure and problem of privilege, 165–66; nationalism and, 93–94; as place of loss, 168; postcolonial, 191–93; suspension of democracy in, 172; "Taking a Stand for Algeria," 189, 194n28; "*voyous*" reference to, 47

Algerian War, 181–83

alliance and giving, 223, 225–31

alterity. *See* otherness (alterity) and the other

*altermondialisation* (worldwide-ization), 90–91, 94. *See also* mondialatinization

Althusser, Louis, 57, 69–70

Althusser-Derrida virtual dialogue: aleatory materialism of the encounter and, 58–59; Derrida on Althusser in *Specters*, 62–63; humanism-antihumanism debate and, 57–58; Marxist critique and, 59–61, 71–72; phenomenology and the teleology-eschatology distinction in Derrida, 65–68; presence of consciousness and conjuncture, 69; *Reading Capital* and presence, 68–71; suspended dialogue, 58; teleology and the eschatological problem, 63–65

America, deconstruction as, 46–47

Amichai, Yehuda, 163–64

amnesia, 178, 182, 267

amnesty, 265, 267

anamnesis, 188

anarchical principle, 276–77

Anidjar, Gil, 176n51, 183, 194n21

animal and human, opposition between, 43

animal societies, 229

"the animal-that-therefore-I-am (following)", 51–52

"anyone," 46, 277, 285, 287

apartheid, 262–63

Arab as the Marrano of philosophy, 166

Arabic language, 166–68, 174n21

archidemocratic moment, 106

archive: Algeria as, 181–84; archives, archiving, and, 178, 181, 183, 185, 193n4; control of, 180–81; disorder of identity and Jewish belonging and, 184–89; floor tile image, 177; memory of Algeria, 189–91; overview of, 177–78; postcolonial Algeria, critique of, 191–93; as repetition of origin, 178–80; truth and, 245; unifying history and, 181–82

PHENG CHEAH is a professor of rhetoric at the
University of California, Berkeley. He is the author
of *Inhuman Conditions: On Cosmopolitanism and
Human Rights* (2006) and *Spectral Nationality:
Passages of Freedom from Kant to Postcolonial
Literatures of Liberation* (2003).

SUZANNE GUERLAC is a professor of French at
the University of California, Berkeley. She is the
author of *Thinking in Time: An Introduction to Henri
Bergson* (2006), *Literary Polemics: Bataille, Sartre,
Valéry, Breton* (1999), and *The Impersonal Sublime:
Hugo, Baudelaire, Lautréamont and the Esthetics of the
Sublime* (1990).

---

Library of Congress Cataloging-in-Publication Data
Derrida and the time of the political / edited by
Pheng Cheah and Suzanne Guerlac.
p. cm.
Includes bibliographical references and index.
ISBN 978-0-8223-4350-9 (cloth : alk. paper)
ISBN 978-0-8223-4372-1 (pbk. : alk. paper)
1. Derrida, Jacques — Political and social views.
2. Deconstruction.  I. Cheah, Pheng.  II. Guerlac,
Suzanne.
JC261.D44D47 2009
320.092 — dc22    2008040670